OXFORD

KT-485-138

DISCARDED
Northamptonshire Libraries

Professor John Cannon held the chair of Modern History at the University of Newcastle upon Tyne until 1992. He has edited several titles, including *The Letters of Junius* (1978), *The Oxford Companion to British History* (1997), and *The Blackwell Dictionary of Historians* (1988), which was awarded a Library Association prize for reference works. His other publications include *The Fox–North Coalition* (1969), *Parliamentary Reform* (1973), *Aristocratic Century* (1984), *The Oxford Illustrated History of the British Monarchy* (1986, 1998), and *Samuel Johnson and the Politics of Hanoverian England* (1994).

Dr Anne Hargreaves was formerly a clinical academic at the Welsh National School of Medicine, and at the Universities of Liverpool and Newcastle. She was co-editor of *Medicine in Northumbria* (1993) and author of *White as Whales Bone* (1998), a study of dental ...... in England. She ...... was a major ...... British History.

80 002 409 375

Oxford Paperback Reference

The most authoritative and up-to-date reference books for both students and the general reader.

*forthcoming

The Kings & Queens of Britain

JOHN CANNON &
ANNE HARGREAVES

OXFORD
UNIVERSITY PRESS

OXFORD
UNIVERSITY PRESS

Great Clarendon Street, Oxford OX2 6DP
Oxford University Press is a department of the University of Oxford.
It furthers the University's objective of excellence in research, scholarship,
and education by publishing worldwide in

Oxford New York

Auckland Bangkok Buenos Aires Cape Town
Chennai Dar es Salaam Delhi Hong Kong Istanbul Karachi
Kolkata Kuala Lumpur Madrid Melbourne Mexico City Mumbai Nairobi
São Paulo Shanghai Singapore Taipei Tokyo Toronto

Oxford is a registered trade mark of Oxford University Press
in the UK and certain other countries

Published in the United States
by Oxford University Press Inc., New York

© Oxford University Press 2001, 2004

The moral rights of the authors have been asserted
Database right Oxford University Press (maker)

First published 2001
Reissued with new covers 2004

All rights reserved. No part of this publication may be reproduced,
stored in a retrieval system, or transmitted, in any form or by any means, without
the prior permission in writing of Oxford University Press,
or as expressly permitted by law, or under terms agreed with the appropriate
reprographics rights organizations. Enquiries concerning reproduction
outside the scope of the above should be sent to the Rights Department,
Oxford University Press, at the address above

You must not circulate this book in any other binding or cover
and you must impose the same condition on any acquirer

British Library Cataloguing in Publication Data
Data available

Library of Congress Cataloging in Publication Data
Data available

ISBN 0-19-860956-6

1

Typeset in Sv   ndia
Printed in Gr

NORTHAMPTONSHIRE LIBRARIES	
802409375	
Cypher	12.10.04
941.0099	£8.99
189519	NW

Contents

List of Maps

List of Genealogies

Preface

Over the last twenty years, there has been agitated controversy over all aspects of national identity, in Britain and in many other countries. The progress of devolution has been welcomed as a means of retaining the unity of Britain, and denounced as a slippery slope which would bring disintegration. The remorseless advance of 'Europe' raised the question of whose image and endorsement should be on coins and passports, and where sovereignty resided between European and national courts and parliaments. At a less dignified level, there is the question whether England should have a Swedish football coach.

Nations themselves were, to a great extent, created by their monarchs. Century after century, rulers tried to standardize coinage, impose laws, promote one religion, and, above all, to persuade their subjects, often of different races, to live together in peace. The Magonsaete were told not to fight with the Hwicces, nor Saxons with Danes, Normans with English, or English with Welsh. Often these appeals were ignored. But kings remained the driving force behind the development of national identity and when, in 1649, Charles I stood in the Banqueting Room in Whitehall, accused of treason by the English people, it was as though the nation had turned on its creator.

By the mid-twentieth century, it seemed that monarchy everywhere was on the way out, and crowned heads an endangered species. After the First World War, the monarchs of Germany, Russia, Austria, and Turkey tumbled, preceded by those of France (1870) and followed by Spain (1931) and Italy (1946). But the late twentieth century saw signs of a comeback. Spain voted to restore its monarchy; after the break-up of Communism, the Russians recovered the bones of the Romanovs from the cellar at Ekaterinburg and gave them decent burial in the renamed St Petersburg; the royal families of Austria and Yugoslavia were allowed home. It may be only a whimper, and in other countries the forces of republicanism make progress. But one explanation may be the widespread disillusion with party politicians, the corridors of 'ex-power' littered with disgraced presidents and corrupt prime ministers. Monarchs, in their reduced role of constitutional umpire, may seem less divisive and more widely acceptable as heads of state.

History casts a long shadow. Our lives are influenced by men and women long-forgotten by most of us—by Vortigern who, if Gildas is to be believed, invited in the Saxons to protect the Britons from the Picts; by Offa, who pushed the Welsh back into their mountain fastnesses; by

Tostig, whose bitter quarrel with his brother Harold may have let in the Normans; by Dermot MacMurrough, king of Leinster, who called the Anglo-Normans into Ireland; by Edward II, whose ineptitude may have done as much to preserve Scottish independence as the valour of Robert Bruce; by William III, summoned to rescue England and Scotland from popery and autocracy, and derided as soon as he had accomplished his mission. They helped to shape the language we speak, the loyalties we profess, and the attitudes we adopt.

We have included short biographies of a number of people who were not themselves monarchs—Godwin, Simon de Montfort, Cromwell, Albert, and others—but who were so close to the throne that their influence cannot be disregarded. Many readers will, of course, disagree with our choices and our opinions, but we would welcome comment and correction.

JC and AH
2001

Abbreviations

abdic.	abdicated	incl.	include(d)
acc.	acceded	kinsw.	kinswoman
b.	born	leg.	legitimate
bur.	buried	m.	married
c.	circa	nr.	near
cr.	created	rebur.	reburied
d.	died	rest.	restored
da(s).	daughter(s)	s.	son(s)
dep.	deposed	succ.	succeeded
illeg.	illegitimate	wid.	widow

The Kings & Queens of Britain

Myths

Most nations have their own founding myth, intended to give them dignity and importance, and sometimes to comfort them in bad times. Christian Europe derived many of its myths from the Bible, and dynasties traced their descent from Noah or Adam. The pagan Anglo-Saxons claimed ancestry from the heathen gods, Odin and Thor. The classical world was also a fertile source, with myths of descent from the Greeks or Trojans. Most myths accumulated detail and embellishment as they developed. When they moved into literature, painting, or music, they acquired a fresh vitality. Wagner's *Tristan und Isolde* or Tennyson's 'Idylls of the King' are no less beautiful for being based on shaky historical foundations. At the least, myths tell us how nations would like to see themselves and promote concepts of bravery, chivalry, loyalty, and fortitude.

Brutus. The legend that Britain was founded by Brutus, a descendant of Aeneas, who escaped from the fall of Troy, was started by Nennius in the ninth century. Geoffrey of Monmouth, a prolific myth-maker of the early twelfth century, elaborated by explaining that Brutus landed at Totnes, overcame the giant Gogmagog, and founded London under the name of Trinovantum or New Troy. The story held credence until Tudor times, with John Leland protesting its authenticity as late as 1544.

Scota. Scotland's reply to England's claim of descent from Brutus was Scota, a daughter of Pharaoh of Egypt. According to Nennius's account, written in the ninth century, Scota was married to a Scythian nobleman living in Egypt at the time of the escape of the Hebrews from captivity. His offspring, after many vicissitudes, reached Dalriada (modern Kintyre and mid-Argyll) via Spain. The myth was popularized by John Fordun in his *Scotichronicon* written in the fourteenth century.

Bladud is said by Geoffrey of Monmouth to have succeeded Hudibras as king of the Britons, to have founded the city of Bath, and to have killed himself while attempting to fly, 'dashed into countless pieces'.

Lud is said by Geoffrey of Monmouth to have been the elder brother of Cassivellaunus, to have founded (or re-founded) London, and to be buried there. There is, at present, no evidence that London existed before the Roman occupation of AD 43. Ludgate was said to have been named after him, but its earliest mention is as Lutgata *c*.1100–35.

Leir (Lear). The earliest accounts of king Leir and his three daughters is in Geoffrey of Monmouth's *History of the Kings of Britain*, written in the twelfth century. Though it probably draws on previous sources, they have not been securely identified. Geoffrey described Leir as the son of Bladud. The basic story of his three named daughters and the love test is outlined, and Leir is credited with founding Leicester. In Geoffrey's version, Leir was buried at Leicester in a tomb under the river Soar. He offered a happy ending, with Leir restored to his kingdom by Cordelia's aid, thus providing some excuse for the ending which Nahum Tate made in 1681 for Shakespeare's play.

Cole. The nursery rhyme which gave fame to Old King Cole and his fiddlers three was extant in the seventeenth century. In the account given by Geoffrey of Monmouth in the twelfth century, Cole founded Colchester and submitted to the Roman, Constantius, who subsequently married Cole's daughter, Helen. Their son was the emperor Constantine. The name Colchester derives in fact from the river Colne on which the town stands.

Arthur. The story of king Arthur and the Knights of the Round Table is one of the most enduring of all legends, popular with poets and dramatists, composers, and film-makers. The usual setting is the thirteenth and fourteenth centuries, when the cult of chivalry was developing. Edward I and his queen visited Glastonbury in 1278 to see what were said to be the bones of Arthur and Guinevere, and his grandson Edward III had a round table made (still at Winchester), held a great tournament there in 1344, and based the Order of the Garter in part on the story.

The first writer to popularize Arthur's deeds was Geoffrey of Monmouth, whose Arthur was an heroic leader of the Welsh (Britons) in their struggles against the Saxons. Having dealt with them, Arthur proceeded to crush the Scots, Picts, and Irish, and occupy Iceland and Gotland, before tackling Rome itself, which he would certainly have overcome had he not been called home by news of Mordred's treachery. Geoffrey placed these events in the immediate post-Roman period (late fifth century), and quoted from Gildas and from Nennius, writing in the

King Arthur's Round Table was first mentioned in Arthurian literature in 1115 by Wace, a Norman poet, who explained that it was designed to avoid disputes among the knights about precedence. The round table now in Winchester castle has been dated to the late 13th cent.

late sixth and the ninth centuries. Gildas has no mention of Arthur, and his hero in the struggle against the Saxons was Ambrosius Aurelianus, a noble Roman, though he did mention a later British victory at Mons Badonis. Nennius retained Ambrosius but added an Arthur, who took over his task. The tenth-century *Annales Cambriae* recorded that Arthur defeated the Saxons in 516 at the battle of Badon and was killed in 537.

The Welsh poem *Gododdin*, written about 600, referred parenthetically to a hero called Arthur.

With this, the hunt was on to identify 'Badon' and 'Camlann', where Arthur was said by the *Annales* to have died. The first is usually identified as Badbury near Swindon or Baydon near Lambourn, either of which would fit a Saxon/British encounter in the late fifth century; the second has been identified with the river Camel in Cornwall. However, Arthur has also been claimed for many other regions, including Cumbria and Scotland.

Romano-British Rulers

Although the occupation of Britain did not take place until after AD 43, contacts with the Roman world had been increasing since the Roman seizure of Gaul in the first century BC, particularly in southern England. Trade developed, and British kings in the later first century BC issued coins based upon Roman models. For a time after the Claudian conquest, Rome ruled through client kings, but the revolt of Boudicca in AD 60 caused the abandonment of that policy. Kingdoms did not reappear until Roman Britain began to break up, after Honorius in 410 had warned it to expect no more help from Rome.

Cassivellaunus is well known through the prominence given to him in Caesar's account of his second expedition in 54 BC. Caesar described his territory as north of the Thames and some eighty miles from the Kentish ports, which places it in Hertfordshire, and commented that 'our arrival moved the Britons to appoint him commander-in-chief for the whole campaign'. His resistance showed him to be a man of skill and some authority, capable of giving orders for a diversionary attack upon the Roman base-camp back in Kent, but after Caesar had overrun his headquarters at Wheathampstead, near St Albans, he was forced to submit and promised not to molest his neighbours to the east, the Trinovantes. Nothing more is heard of Cassivellaunus, and though coins circulated, he did not inscribe his name. It has recently been suggested that he was not necessarily ruler of the Catuvellauni and that Caesar may have magnified his importance. Geoffrey of Monmouth, writing in the twelfth century, devoted much space to his exploits.

Mandubracius, young son of Imanventius, king of the Trinovantes, fled to Gaul when his father was killed by Cassivellaunus, and sought Caesar's protection. He was reinstated when Caesar invaded Britain in 54 BC. He is identified in Caesar's *De Bello Gallico*, but it has been suggested that Celtic sources give his name as Avarwy, the Roman version being a nickname meaning 'the black traitor'.

Commius, a Belgic Gaul, served with Caesar and was made king of the Atrebates after their defeat at the battle of the river Sambre. The continental Atrebates had close links with Belgic tribes in southern England, and in 55 BC Commius was sent by Caesar to negotiate a friendly welcome. He was taken captive but released when Caesar landed. The following year he accompanied Caesar on the second expedition and negotiated Cassivellaunus's capitulation, but two years later he joined Vercingetorix's rebellion in Gaul and for some time maintained resistance to the Romans. Surviving a plot to assassinate him, he surrendered, with the proviso that he should never have to look upon a Roman again. He moved to Britain, becoming king of the Atrebates in the Hampshire region, issuing his own coins. His territories were divided between his sons or grandsons Tincommius, Verica, and Eppillus.

Addedomarus is known only through his coins, found over a wide area between Oxfordshire and Essex, suggesting that he ruled the Catuvellauni and Trinovantes, probably *c*.30 BC.

Andoco is another ruler known only by his coinage, and the name is presumably an abbreviation of Andocomius. His coins, which are not plentiful, are found almost exclusively in the Catuvellauni heartland between west Essex and Oxfordshire. His dates are not certain, but 10 BC to AD 10 have been suggested.

Tincommius, one of the three sons or grandsons of Commius, took the kingship of the Regni in Sussex and issued coins. He was forced out of his kingdom and journeyed to Rome *c*.AD 7 with Dubnovellaunus, king of Kent, to ask Augustus to protect them. There is no evidence that help was forthcoming.

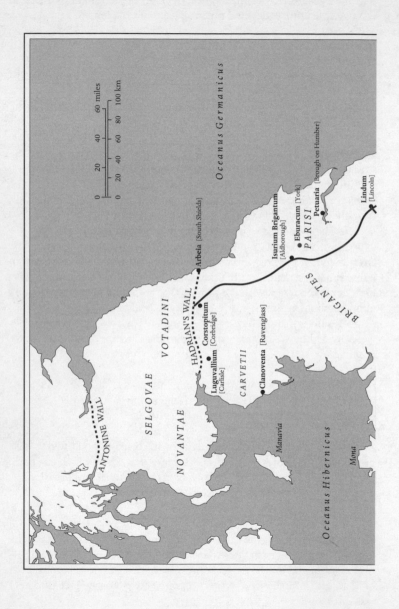

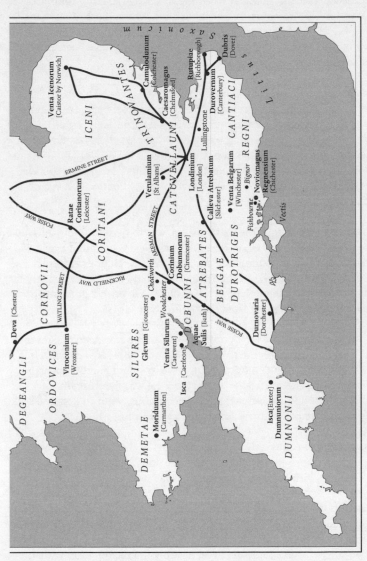

Roman Britain

Eppillus was a son or grandson of Commius and seems to have succeeded Tincommius as ruler of the Atrebates, striking coins at Silchester. He subsequently moved to Kent, where most of his coins have been found. He was overthrown in Kent by Dubnovellaunus, who was in turn overthrown by Cunobelinus. His coins have been dated 10 BC to AD 10.

Verica poses problems. On his coins he claimed to be a son of Commius, king of the Atrebates *c.*50 BC, but these were struck in the early first century AD. Moreover, Dio Cassius reports 'a certain Berikos' seeking help from the emperor Claudius *c.*AD 42, and thus facilitating the Roman invasion. Unless there are two Vericas, it seems more likely that he was a grandson of Commius. He appears to have been pushed out of his Atrebatian territories by Epaticcus, a son of Tasciovanus.

Tasciovanus, king of the Catuvellauni, was father of Cunobelinus and the first of his dynasty to strike coins. They have been found over a wide area from Essex to Oxfordshire and south of the Thames in Surrey. He appears to have taken over the Trinovantes to the east, since some of his coins were minted in Colchester. He could have been a grandson of Cassivellaunus, reigning from *c.*20 BC to about AD 10.

Dubnovellaunus was ruler of Kent, where he struck coins. Another ruler with the same name struck coins in the Essex area *c.*10 BC. It is possible that the first Dubnovellaunus was a son of Mandubracius, reinstated by Caesar in 54 BC. After AD 7 he was overthrown by Cunobelinus and, accompanied by Tincommius, went to Rome to seek the assistance of Augustus. It was not forthcoming.

Dumnocoveros is only recorded in coins of the Coritani, whose territory comprised modern Lincolnshire and Leicestershire, in association with Volisius. They have been dated *c.*AD 20–45.

Epaticcus was a son of Tasciovanus and probably a brother of Cunobelinus. His coins, of good quality, are not plentiful, but have been found in southern England, mainly south of the Thames. He may have ruled the Atrebates for some time, possibly in collaboration with Cunobelinus. If, as has been suggested, he pushed Verica out of Atrebates territory, he would appear to be coining *c.*AD 35–40.

Volisius was king of the Coritani, whose territories were in Leicestershire and Lincolnshire, though his coinage has also been found in Yorkshire. He appears to have been ruling in the early days after the Roman occupation of AD 43.

Cunobelinus is probably the most famous British king before the Roman occupation. He was a son of Tasciovanus, and succeeded his father in the early first century, reigning until c.AD 40. His first capital was Verulamium (St Albans) but he subsequently moved it to Colchester. Though his power base was the Catuvellauni and the Trinovantes, his influence extended over a wide area, and his coins, of high quality, are found in north-east Kent, north Berkshire, Bedfordshire, and Cambridgeshire. Most of them carry on the obverse an ear of corn. Geoffrey of Monmouth, not the most reliable of sources, claimed that he was brought up by Augustus Caesar, and Suetonius called him 'rex Brittonorum'. He seems to have been assertive in Britain but took care not to antagonize the Romans. A quarrel with his son Adminius, however, may have given the emperor Claudius the pretext for an expedition, which arrived in AD 43 after Cunobelinus's death. In Shakespeare's *Cymbeline* the historical background, borrowed mainly from Holinshed, is sketched in lightly. It has been suggested that the great tumulus at Lexden, near Colchester, might be his burial-place.

Adminius, or **Amminus**, a son of Cunobelinus, ruled the Cantiaci in Kent, presumably as a sub-king. In AD 40 he lost control or was expelled and fled to Gaul, where he begged the emperor Caligula for help. Caligula treated this as a surrender of the whole country, but his assassination removed any chance of intervention, and it was left to his successor Claudius to set in train the successful expedition of AD 43.

Togodumnus was a son of Cunobelinus and brother, or close relative, of Caratacus. On the death of his father c.AD 41, he took control north of the Thames, with Colchester as his capital. When the Roman army invaded in AD 43, he joined forces with his brother and gave battle on the line of the Medway. After heavy fighting, Togodumnus was killed and Caratacus fled westwards to continue the struggle.

Caratacus, son of Cunobelinus, with his brother Togodumnus led British resistance to the Roman invasion of AD 43. After a defeat on the Medway, in which Togodumnus was killed, Caratacus fled to Wales to

seek support from the Silures, and then the Ordovices. When Ostorius
Scapula advanced in AD 50 to complete the work of Aulus Plautius,
Caratacus gave battle on a fortified hill. Newtown or Caersws are the
most likely of many places in Wales which have been suggested. After a
bitter struggle, Caratacus's wife, daughter, and brothers were captured,
but he escaped and appealed to Cartimandua, queen of the Brigantes in
Yorkshire. She handed him over to the Romans and he was taken to
Rome where he ended his days. His demeanour at Claudius's victory
parade is said to have won admiration, and Tacitus provided him with a
heroic speech. More moving is the remark attributed to him by Dio
Cassius, when he beheld the splendour of Rome: 'when you have all
this, why do you begrudge us our poor hovels?'

Prasutagus, king of the Iceni, was the husband of Boudicca. His
territories were ruled from his capital at Venta Icenorum, near Norwich.
He seems to have been a client king of Rome, possibly installed after
some discontent among the Iceni in the late 40s. At his death in AD 60,
he made the emperor Nero coheir with his own daughters, but the
brutal conduct of the Roman officials led to Boudicca's great revolt.

Hadrian, Roman
Emperor AD117–38 and
builder of the wall from
Carlisle to Newcastle.
This fine head was
found in the Thames
near London Bridge in
1834.

Boudicca, or **Boadicea**, was wife of Prasutagus, king of the Iceni, whose territories were modern Norfolk. At his death, the local Roman officials treated the Iceni with contempt, flogging Boudicca and raping her daughters. Her response was to raise a terrifying insurrection, probably the greatest in British history, which came close to sweeping Roman rule out of Britain. Colchester, the Roman capital, was taken and burned, and its inhabitants put to the sword. Paulinus, the Roman governor, was campaigning in Anglesey but, in a desperate cavalry dash, tried to hold London. He reached it before the rebels but was obliged to withdraw to wait for reinforcements. Both London and Verulamium (St Albans) were sacked. In all three cities, ashes from the devastation survive below the surface, and 70,000 are reported to have been slain. Paulinus succeeded in gathering forces and, advancing to join his infantry from North Wales, gave battle at Atherstone, near Watling Street. Against all odds, he won a decisive victory, and Boudicca took poison to avoid capture.

Dio Cassius, writing more than one hundred years after the event, described Boudicca as 'very tall, in appearance most terrifying...the glance of her eye most fierce, her voice harsh...a great mass of the tawniest hair fell to her hips'. For centuries, this vivid portrait, real or imaginary, seems to have unnerved male historians and their attitude to Boudicca was cautious. Gildas in the sixth century referred to her as 'a treacherous lioness', and Holinshed in the sixteenth century dwelt mainly on her atrocities. The emergence of Boudicca as a national heroine was largely Victorian. Thomas Thornycroft offered a large statue of her at the Great Exhibition of 1851, and his sculpture, after some vicissitudes, was placed on the Victoria Embankment opposite the Houses of Parliament in 1902.

Cogidubnus was placed or confirmed by the Romans as ruler of the Regni soon after the invasion of AD 43. He took the name Tiberius Claudius Cogidubnus and claimed to be 'rex magnus Britanniae'. His capital was Noviomagus (Chichester), and the great palace at Fishbourne is believed to have been built for him. As a client king of Rome, he seems to have had a comfortable, dignified and lengthy reign. The main authority is Tacitus (*Agricola*), augmented by a remarkable stone found at Chichester in 1723.

Cartimandua was queen of the Brigantes, a very powerful northern tribe or confederation, which had come to terms with the Romans after

the invasion of A D 43. Their main capital was probably at Stanwick, near
Richmond in Yorkshire. In 51 Caratacus fled to her after his defeat at the
hands of Ostorius Scapula to seek assistance; instead, she handed him
back to the Romans. At that time she was ruling jointly with Venutius,
with whom she was on bad terms. It was of critical importance to the
Romans that the Brigantes did not join in Boudicca's revolt of 61. During
the 50s she was protected by the Romans, but *c.*69 she took Vellocatus,
standard-bearer to Venutius, as her consort. Civil war followed, and
Cartimandua was rescued by the Romans, with the kingdom remaining
in the hands of Venutius. Tacitus, our chief source for these events,
describes her as 'lustful and of savage temper'.

Venutius, consort of the redoubtable Cartimandua, queen of the
Brigantes, seems at first to have concurred with her pro-Roman policy,
but by A D 69 had abandoned it. The breakdown of the royal marriage
was accompanied by civil war, in which his queen had to be rescued by
the Romans. Venutius remained in control of the Brigantes. In 72
Petillius Cerialis led an expedition against him; Venutius seems to have
fallen back on his capital at Stanwick and heavy fighting took place. He
may have retreated further into the Cumbrian hills and certainly lost his
grip on his former territories. Tacitus praised his military skill.

Calgacus. In his account of Agricola's advance into Scotland in 84,
Tacitus recorded that his adversaries were led by Calgacus, 'pre-eminent
by character and birth'. 'Calgacus' is a Celtic name meaning 'swordsman'.
He was defeated at the battle of Mons Graupius in north-east Scotland.
In accordance with Roman rhetoric, Tacitus credited Calgacus with a
long speech to his men, accusing the Romans of being 'the robbers of
the world', and observing 'atque ubi solitudinem faciunt, pacem
appellant' ('they make a desolation and call it peace'). These sentiments,
sophisticated for a first-century chieftain, are one of the great and bitter
maxims of world history.

Vortigern was first reported by Gildas, writing *c.*540, as a 'proud
tyrant' who, soon after the departure of the Romans in the fifth century,
devised the plan to combat the depredations of the Picts and Scots by
calling in the Saxons. 'How desperate and crass the stupidity',
commented Gildas mournfully. Bede identified him as UUertigern.
Nennius, about 800, called him Guorthigirnus, adding a story that
Vortigern handed over Kent to the Saxon king Hengist in exchange for

his daughter in marriage. Geoffrey of Monmouth elaborated greatly on the story, bringing in St Germanus and Merlin. It has been suggested that Vortigern was a real person, perhaps originally a Roman governor or general, and that he may have been responsible for the move of Cunedda from Scotland into north Wales (Gwynedd, *see* p. 99).

Ambrosius Aurelianus is another of the shadowy figures credited with defending the Britons in the years after the withdrawal of Roman protection. According to Gildas, he gained an important victory over the Saxons at Mons Badonis after decades of British defeats and won a respite of forty years from attack. The date of the siege, usually presumed to have taken place in Wiltshire, was about 500. Ambrosius is described as 'a gentleman who, perhaps alone among the Romans, had survived the shock of this notable storm; certainly his parents, who had worn the purple [i.e. were of royal birth] perished in it'. Welsh sources give the name as Emrys. Geoffrey of Monmouth provided him with a pedigree as a son of king Constantine, a long list of heroic deeds, and death from poison at Winchester.

Kent

Kent began life as the territory of the Cantiaci. It developed as a kingdom in the fifth century after substantial immigration, particularly of the Jutes. There was a long-running division between east and west Kent, reflected in the establishment of two dioceses, one at Canterbury, the other at Rochester. For many years most of Surrey was also under Kentish control. The conversion to Christianity under Aethelberht I and the recognition of Canterbury as an archbishopric gave the kingdom much prestige, but it remained small and had increasing difficulty in protecting itself against larger predators. Its failure to establish control over London deprived it of valuable resources. During the eighth and ninth centuries it was balanced precariously between Wessex and Mercia, sometimes falling under total domination, until after *c*.825 it was incorporated into Wessex, while retaining many regional characteristics.

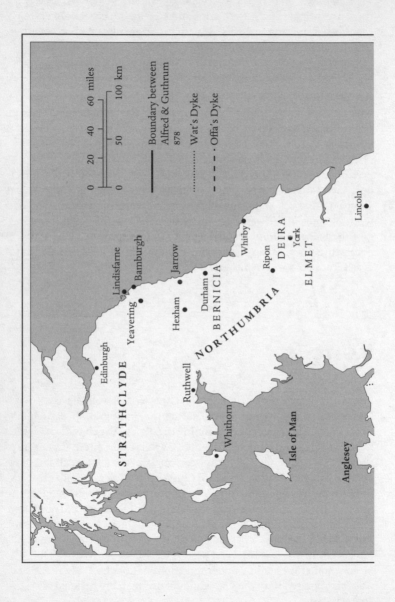

Boundary between
Alfred & Guthrum
878
.... Wat's Dyke
– – – Offa's Dyke

0   20   40   60 miles
0   50   100 km

STRATHCLYDE

Edinburgh

Lindisfarne
Yeavering   Bamburgh
Hexham   Jarrow
Ruthwell   Durham
Whithorn

NORTHUMBRIA

BERNICIA

Whitby
Ripon   DEIRA
York
ELMET

Lincoln

Isle of Man

Anglesey

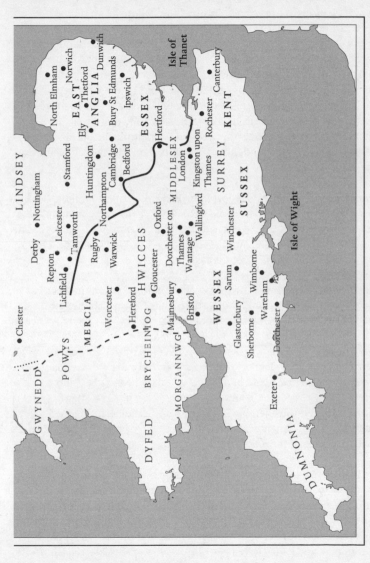

Anglo-Saxon England

Hengist and Horsa. The identity of Hengist and his brother Horsa was first suggested by Bede, writing in 731. They were described as leaders of the Jutes, brought over to help protect the Britons from the ravages of the Picts. Bede named 449 as the date of Vortigern's invitation. Nennius, in the early ninth century, provided Hengist with a pedigree back to Woden, adding that he was granted Kent in exchange for his daughter's marriage to Vortigern. When the Saxons turned on the British, Vortigern's son, Vortimer, is said to have slain Horsa. Geoffrey of Monmouth stated that Hengist was at length defeated and beheaded by Ambrosius Aurelianus. His death is given by the *Anglo-Saxon Chronicle* under 488. The events have been severely scrutinized, and since the names mean 'stallion' and 'horse' it seems more likely that they were legendary heroes.

Oeric, surnamed **Oisc**, is reported by Bede as a son of Hengist, but by Nennius as a grandson. He is said to have succeeded as a king of Kent in 488 and ruled until 512. Welsh sources, calling him Aesc, claim that he was killed by Ambrosius Aurelianus ('Emrys') at Mons Badonis. The dynasty took the name of Oiscingas.

Octa. Bede gives him as the grandson of Hengist. Nennius describes him as a son, brought from the north to fight Arthur and the Britons, i.e. the Welsh. The historical basis of events is shaky.

Eormenric was king while Kent was in comparative eclipse. He is described as son of Octa or Oeric, and was therefore a descendant of Hengist. Eormenric's date of death is given by Bede as 560, but a reference by Gregory of Tours to 'a certain king in Kent' suggests that it may have been considerably later. His son, Aethelberht, reigned for many years; his daughter, Ricula, is said to have been the mother of Saeberht, king of the East Saxons.

Aethelberht I. With Aethelberht, the first Anglo-Saxon king to be baptized, we are on more secure historical ground, though chronological difficulties remain. The son of Eormenric, he turned Kent briefly into a dominant English power, with some claim to overlordship as bretwalda. The date of his accession implied by Bede (560) has been questioned, and it may have been one or two decades later. His first wife, Bertha, was daughter of Charibert, one of the Merovingian kings of Paris; on her death, he married again, and his eventual widow then married his son Eadbald (i.e. her stepson). His daughter, Aethelburga, married Edwin, king of Northumbria, in 625.

The great event of Aethelberht's reign was the arrival of St Augustine in 597 on his evangelical mission. Bede reported that Bertha was already a Christian, that the king allowed Augustine a dwelling in Canterbury, and that he himself was subsequently baptized. By the end of his reign, the framework of a Christian hierarchy was apparent, with the archbishopric of Canterbury supported by bishoprics at Rochester and London, and plans for a second archbishopric at York.

Further evidence of a more settled society was Aethelberht's promulgation, after his conversion, of a list of ninety laws. They were concerned largely with compensation for injury: three shillings for a thumb-nail, fifty shillings for the loss of a foot. Bede reported, very precisely, that Aethelberht died on 24 February, 'twenty-one years after accepting the faith'. This implies 617 or 618, though the *Anglo-Saxon Chronicle* enters it under 616. He was buried at Canterbury.

Eadbald succeeded his father Aethelberht *c*.617 and reigned until 640. His first action was to marry his father's widow (i.e. his stepmother), which was not uncommon under pagan conventions. This form of marriage was the subject of the fifth question put by Augustine to pope Gregory, and received the answer that it was a grave sin. When the king converted to Christianity, the marriage was annulled, and he married Emma, the daughter of a Frankish king. Bede commented that Eadbald had 'less royal power' than his father and found himself unable to restore Christian worship throughout his kingdom. But when his sister Aethelburga married Edwin of Northumbria, Eadbald insisted that she should be free to practise Christianity and sent Paulinus with her as chaplain and evangelist.

Earconberht, son of Eadbald, ruled from 640 until 14 July 664, and was married to Seaxburh, daughter of Anna, king of the East Angles. Bede credited him with the continued promotion of Christian worship and praised him as a ruler of distinction. Meanwhile, political and military power was passing to Mercia and Northumbria. His daughter Eormenhild was married to Wulfhere, king of the Mercians, presumably as an insurance policy.

Ecgberht I succeeded his father Earconberht in 664, ruling until July 673. He is reported by a late source to have murdered his two cousins,

Aethelred and Aethelberht. His wife's name is unknown and he was succeeded by his brother Hlothere, though his sons Eadric and Wihtred later became kings.

Hlothere took over the kingdom of Kent when his brother Ecgberht died in 673, possibly because his nephews were still young. He must have profited from the unexpected defeat of the Mercians by the Northumbrians *c*.674 since the latter had little interest in Kent, while Mercia was a constant danger. His sixteen-point code was published jointly with his nephew Eadric. The oldest extant Anglo-Saxon charter is a grant of land by Hlothere to the abbey of Reculver in 679. It is not easy to tell whether Hlothere, who seems to have been a capable ruler, usurped his nephew's throne or whether he fell victim to an impatient young man, but Bede reported that on 6 February 685 Hlothere was mortally wounded in battle with the South Saxons, whom Eadric had called to his assistance.

Eadric, son of Ecgberht, recovered the kingdom in 685 from his uncle Hlothere with the help of the South Saxons, but he died on 31 August 687 after a reign of only eighteen months. Henry of Huntingdon, writing in the twelfth century, commented that Eadric reigned 'sine amore et reverentia Centensium'—without the love or respect of the Kentish people.

Mul, brother of Caedwalla of Wessex, joined him in a conquest of the Isle of Wight in 686 and then laid waste to Kent. Placed in Kent as a sub-king by Caedwalla, Mul fell victim to a rising and was burned to death. Later, in 694, the Kentishmen were reported to have come to terms with Ine, Caedwalla's successor, paying 30,000 sceattas in compensation.

Oswine seems to have ruled Kent during the disputed succession between Hlothere and Wihtred. He is known only by charters issued in 690. Bede commented that after the death of Hlothere 'various usurpers and foreign kings plundered Kent'. Though from the Kentish royal family, Oswine clearly represented Mercian interests.

Swaefheard, son of Sebbi, king of the East Saxons, seems to have ruled Kent jointly, first with Hlothere, then with Wihtred. He is referred to in a charter which has been dated 690. Since the confirmation was by

Aethelred, king of the Mercians, it is probable that Swaefheard was only a sub-king.

Wihtred, second son of Ecgberht, became king *c.*690, ruling at first with Swaefheard, a Mercian sub-king, whom he seems to have dispossessed. Bede recorded that he ruled for thirty-four and a half years, dying on 23 April 725. One of his earliest decisions was to pay Wessex compensation for the murder of Mul, presumably in order to enlist support for an alliance against Mercia. His earliest known charter is dated 694 and the following year he issued a law code, dealing mainly with ecclesiastical questions and reflecting the close relations in Kent between church and state. His three wives, mentioned in charters, were Cynegyth, Aethelburh, and Werburh, the first of whom has been queried.

Aethelberht II, son of Wihtred, succeeded to the throne in 725, probably sharing power with his brother Eadberht. His last charter is dated 762 and he died later that year. A letter to St Boniface is extant, sending gifts and asking for a pair of falcons who would fearlessly attack cranes. He seems to have acknowledged Aethelbald of Mercia as overlord.

Eadberht I was a son of Wihtred and reigned jointly with Aethelberht II. Though the *Anglo-Saxon Chronicle* recorded his death under 748, there are charters extant for 761. His son was Eardwulf.

Alric, a third son of Wihtred, is named by Bede (whose sources for Kentish history were good) as sharing the succession to the throne with his brothers Aethelberht and Eadberht. However there is no charter evidence, nor any details of his reign. The possibility is that he was a sub-king who died young.

Eardwulf, son of Eadberht, is known from charters granting lands to the church, the second dated 767. By then the power of Kent was in sharp decline.

Sigered, whose ancestry is unknown, described himself as king of half Kent in a charter which has been dated between 761 and 765. He is not referred to by chroniclers and is unlikely to be the same man as the last king of the East Saxons, who died as late as *c*.827. It has been suggested that he was a Wessex prince, brought in to resist Mercian pressure.

Eanmund is known only by confirmation of a charter of Sigered. The probability is that he was, in fact, Ealhmund (*below*).

Headberht is named as king of Kent in a charter by Offa of Mercia, dated 764. The following year he confirmed a grant by Ecgberht II, king of Kent. By this time, Kent was firmly under Mercian control. He introduced a new silver penny, presumably with Offa's permission.

Ecgberht II was reigning in 765 when he granted a charter giving land to the bishop of Rochester. The grant was confirmed by Headberht, another king in Kent, and by Offa, indicating that the kingdom was under Mercian control. The latest charter which can be dated was granted in 779. Offa's suzerainty was very much a reality, since on one occasion he countermanded a charter which Ecgberht had authorized.

Ealhmund is identified in the *Anglo-Saxon Chronicle* as the son of Eafa, of the Wessex dynasty, ruling in Kent in 784. The date is confirmed by a charter granting land to the abbey of Reculver. It has been suggested that Ealhmund represented a resistance to Mercian authority after the battle of Otford in 776; if so, it did not last long, since Offa of Mercia resumed granting charters in Kent in 785. However, Ealhmund's son Ecgberht succeeded as king of Wessex in 802.

Eadberht II succeeded as king of Kent, according to the *Anglo-Saxon Chronicle*, in 796, as the leader of a revolt against Mercian control. His nickname 'Praen' meant priest, and, at the request of archbishop Aethelheard (acting for the Mercians), he was anathematized by pope Leo III. He survived long enough to strike a number of coins, but in 798 Cenwulf of Mercia laid waste the kingdom as far as Romney Marsh, captured Eadberht, and mutilated and deposed him. Cenwulf himself then took the kingship, issuing charters. Eadberht's date of death is unknown, and some sources credit him with a lengthy survival in a monastery.

Cuthred was established as king of Kent by his brother Cenwulf, king of the Mercians, after the deposition of Eadberht in 798. They issued charters jointly 801–5, and Cuthred died in 807.

Baldred is identified as a king of Kent by the *Anglo-Saxon Chronicle*, which described how he was driven out *c.*825 by Ecgberht, king of Wessex. No charters survive, but a considerable number of his coins are extant. He was presumably a ruler supported by Mercia, whose kings continued to grant lands in Kent 808–23, until Wessex gained supremacy.

Sussex

Sussex, the land of the South Saxons, was one of the earliest Anglo-Saxon kingdoms to be established, but the heavily forested weald to the north made expansion difficult. It also offered some measure of protection and the kingdom survived until taken over, first by Offa of Mercia in 771, then by Ecgberht in 825 on behalf of Wessex. Throughout its history there were significant divisions between east and west Sussex, and an eastern portion of the kingdom, near Hastings, which looked towards Canterbury and Kent.

Aelle, the reputed founder of the Sussex kingdom, is described in the *Anglo-Saxon Chronicle* in suspicious detail as landing at Selsey in 477 with three ships and three sons, Cymen, Wlencing, and Cissa. He is said to have won a decisive victory over the Britons at Andredesweald soon after landing, and another in 491 at Anderida, near Pevensey. His son, Cissa, is credited with refounding Chichester. Bede named Aelle as the first bretwalda of southern Britain, which magnifies his importance; nevertheless Sussex was, for a time, a power of some consequence. Henry of Huntingdon gave his date of death as 514, which seems late if he had sons of fighting age in 477. No names of sixth-century Sussex kings have survived, though some sources suggest that Cissa inherited.

Aethelwald. There is a gap of 150 years between the legendary founder of Sussex, Aelle, and Aethelwald, whose ancestry is not established. With Aethelwald we are on more secure ground. Bede reported that he married Eafa, a niece of Eanhere, king of the Hwicces, and that he was baptized in the presence of Wulfhere, king of the

Mercians, who acted as sponsor. Wulfhere is said to have given him c.661 the Isle of Wight and the valley of the Meon. Bede's further story that bishop Wilfrid taught the Sussex men how to fish is less easy to believe, but Aethelwald certainly gave him land near Selsey for a monastery. Aethelwald was killed when Caedwalla, future king of Wessex, raided Sussex c.680.

Berthun and **Andhun** are said to have taken over the defence of Sussex when Aethelwald was slain c.680 and to have driven out Caedwalla of Wessex. He returned and c.685 killed Berthun, bringing the kingdom under Wessex control. It is not clear what the status of the two men was, but it has been suggested that Berthun represented west Sussex and Andhun the eastern part.

Nothhelm or **Nunna** granted a number of charters between c.688 and c.725, including a grant to his sister, Nothgyth, for a monastery at Aldingbourne. His existence is separately confirmed by the *Anglo-Saxon Chronicle*, which records that in 710 Ine, king of Wessex, and Nunna 'his kinsman' attacked Geraint, king of Dumnonia (Cornwall).

Watt is known only as a witness to a number of charters by Nothhelm which have been dated c.692–c.725. There were several kings and sub-kings at this period, possibly corresponding to east and west Sussex.

Aethelstan and his wife queen Aethelfryth witnessed a charter granted by Nothhelm, dated 714, giving land to the monastery at Selsey. He was presumably a sub-king for east Sussex.

Aethelberht made a grant of land for a monastery at Wittering, dated between 733 and 754, with a subsequent confirmation by Offa of Mercia. It has been suggested that he was a son of Aethelstan.

Ealdwulf granted a charter c.765 as king, giving land for a monastery at Stanmer, with a confirmation by Offa of Mercia. In two subsequent charters he is described as *dux* (leader).

Osmund granted lands by charter in 765 and 770, the second being confirmed by Offa of Mercia. In 772 Osmund was witness to a grant by Offa himself of land in Sussex for the bishopric of Selsey.

Aelwald witnessed a charter of Ealdwulf *c*.765 as king, and a charter of Offa of Mercia in 772 as *dux*. He was presumably a sub-king.

Oslac granted a charter at Selsey in 780 as *dux*, with a later confirmation by Offa of Mercia at Irthlingborough. No more Sussex kings or sub-kings have been identified.

Essex

Essex, the kingdom of the East Saxons, was settled in the fifth century, the dynasty tracing its pedigree back to Seaxnet, a Saxon deity. There were a number of sub-groups, such as the Brahhingas (people of Braughing) or the Rodingas (people of the river Roding). Overshadowed by its northern neighbour, East Anglia, its future depended mainly on the possession of London. At times the kingdom stretched into Middlesex and Surrey, and the diocese of London, founded in 604, was specifically for the people of Essex. But the rulers of Kent wielded much power in the early seventh century, and when their power waned Northumbria, Mercia, and, finally, Wessex took over. The critical moment was probably when Aethelbald of Mercia took possession of London and Middlesex *c*.730. After Ecgberht of Wessex gained control *c*.825, there were no more Essex kings.

Saeberht, the son of Sledd, is the first East Saxon king who can be securely identified. His mother was said to be Ricula, sister of Aethelberht I of Kent, and Kentish influence was predominant. The Kentish kings having been converted to Christianity, Mellitus was ordained bishop of London to evangelize the people of Essex. Saeberht was baptized, but when he died *c*.616 the kingdom reverted to paganism.

Seaxred and **Saeweard** were the eldest of the three sons of Saeberht and succeeded jointly *c*.616. They at once renounced Christianity, jeering at Mellitus, the recently ordained bishop of London, who fled the kingdom. Bede reported, with satisfaction, that the brothers at once went to war with the men of Wessex, by whom they were killed.

Sigeberht I 'Parvus' ('Little'), son of Saeweard, succeeded *c*.617 on the death in battle of his father and uncle. Though his immediate predecessors had not been fortunate, Sigeberht remained a pagan. The reconversion of the East Saxons, which resulted from the death in battle of Penda, pagan king of Mercia, in 655, suggests a long reign for Sigeberht, ending, perhaps, *c*.650.

Sigeberht II, son of a certain Sigebald, succeeded *c*.650. Bede described him as a friend of Oswiu, king of Bernicia, who, after the conversion of Peada of Mercia, persuaded Sigeberht to follow his example. He was baptized by bishop Finan in the kingdom of Northumbria, near Hexham, and bishop Cedd was despatched to Essex to effect the reconversion. Bede recorded that the king was murdered *c*.660 by two of his immediate court in what sounds like a dispute about pagan marriage practices. The church at Bradwell-on-Sea in Essex, built in Sigeberht's time, survives. His conversion earned him the epithets 'the Good' and 'Sanctus'.

Swithhelm, son of one Seaxbald, succeeded *c*.660 on the murder of Sigeberht II. He was baptized at Rendlesham by Cedd, with Aethelwald of the East Anglians acting as sponsor. He died *c*.664 after a short reign.

Sigehere, son of Sigeberht I, succeeded Swithhelm *c*.664, ruling at first jointly with Sebbi, his kinsman. Bede added that they were subject to Wulfhere, king of the Mercians, and that Sigehere gave up his Christian belief. His co-ruler, Sebbi, with the help of bishop Jaruman, sent from Mercia, reconverted him. He was alive when Earconwald was made bishop of London in 675, but Roger of Wendover gives his death as 683. In the twelfth century Florence of Worcester suggested that he was married to St Osyth, a granddaughter of Penda of Mercia, but since she is said to have preserved her virginity it is unlikely that she was the mother of his son, Offa, later king of the East Saxons.

Sebbi, son of Seaxred, was joint ruler of the East Saxons with Sigehere, but seems to have outlived him. He succeeded *c*.664, ruled alone after 683, and abdicated *c*.694, dying some two years later in a monastery. Bede related that he had long wished to become a monk but that 'his wife obstinately refused to be separated from him', and that it was often said that he should have been a bishop rather than a king. He was buried in St Paul's, London.

Sigeheard and **Swaefred**, sons of Sebbi, ruled jointly after *c.*694 when their father retired to a monastery. A third brother is believed to be Swaefheard, who ruled in west Kent at the same time. Their dates of death are unknown but must have been before 709. One of Swaefred's charters is dated 704.

Offa, son of king Sigehere, may have been associated in the kingship with his kinsmen Sigeheard and Swaefred before their deaths. Bede wrote of him with great enthusiasm: 'a youth so lovable and handsome that the whole race longed for him to have and to hold the sceptre.' But *c.*709 he abdicated, left his wife, and journeyed to Rome with Cenred, king of the Mercians, 'and ended his life in a monk's habit'.

Swaefberht, who succeeded on the abdication of Offa, was presumably a member of the East Saxon royal house, since his accession does not seem to have been disputed. We have no details of his reign, during which Essex was under the influence of Mercia, but Symeon of Durham gave his death as 738. He may have reigned jointly for some time with Selered.

Selered, reputed son of king Sigeberht II, succeeded in 738, but may have been ruling jointly with Swaefberht. The *Anglo-Saxon Chronicle* reported that he was slain in 746, but gave no detail. If he really was the son of Sigeberht II, whose death is proposed for no later than 664, Selered must have been extremely old to have been killed in battle.

Swithred, a son of one Sigemund and a great-grandson of king Sebbi, succeeded on the death of Selered in 746. Florence of Worcester conceded that there were 'poor kings' of the East Saxons at this time, and little evidence is available. His date of death is not known.

Sigeric I, son of king Selered, is identified by an entry in the *Anglo-Saxon Chronicle* that he 'journeyed to Rome' in 798. It has been presumed that he had abdicated, but neither the date of his accession nor of his death is known.

Sigered, son of king Sigeric, is believed to have succeeded in 798 when his father went to Rome. He is mentioned as a sub-king in a charter of Ceolwulf I of Mercia dated 823. But after Ecgberht's great victory at Ellendun in 825, the *Anglo-Saxon Chronicle* records that the men of Kent,

Surrey, Sussex and Essex all submitted to Wessex. The rulers of Wessex then seem to have decided to wind up the Essex sub-kingship. It has been pointed out that Sigered successively attested Mercian charters as king, sub-king and, finally, as *dux* (leader). He died *c*.827.

Sigeric II may represent the last faint glimpse of the Essex kingship, since in a charter dated between 829 and 839, granting land at Braughing, a Sigeric is described as 'minister' to Wiglaf of Mercia. However, by this time the power of Mercia itself was waning, and Viking incursions increasing in weight and frequency.

East Anglia

East Anglia, the land of the north and south folk (Norfolk and Suffolk) was settled as a separate kingdom in the fifth century. Though one of the earliest Anglo-Saxon kingdoms, its name must be later, since it waited by definition on an identifiable West Anglia (and Middle Anglia). The Fens to the west gave it a measure of protection but also inhibited expansion, save possibly through Essex to the south. In the eighth century it fell under Mercian control and in the following century was overrun by Viking invaders. It was reconquered by kings of Wessex in the early tenth century and incorporated into the kingdom of England.

Raedwald, the most famous of East Anglian kings, is said by Bede to have been the son of Tytil and grandson of Wuffa; the dynasty was hence known as the Wuffingas. He is placed as fourth in the line of bretwaldas of southern Britain, and though that probably overstates his authority, it indicates that East Anglia's period of influence came early. His reign can be dated roughly, since Bede related that he gave refuge to Edwin, and helped him to recover Northumbria by defeating Aethelfrith at the battle of the river Idle, *c*.616. Raedwald's son, Regenshere, was killed in the victory, which suggests that Raedwald must by then have been middle-aged or elderly. Bede complained that though Raedwald had been converted to Christianity in Kent, he had subsequently reneged, erecting altars to both faiths, 'so that his last state was worse

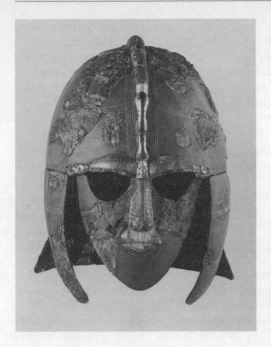

Sutton Hoo Helmet. This remarkable iron helmet, found at Sutton Hoo in 1939, shows strong Scandinavian influence. The burial was probably of Raedwald, king of the East Angles, c.625.

than his first'. His date of death is not known, but was probably soon after his great victory, and certainly before 627. His burial place is uncertain, but it has plausibly been argued that he was the great king for whom the elaborate and remarkable ship-burial at Sutton Hoo, near Woodbridge, was prepared. If the Merovingian coins found there can correctly be dated no later than 625, the possibility seems very strong.

Earpwald, son of Raedwald, succeeded probably c.622. According to Bede, he was converted to Christianity by Edwin, who had been restored to the throne of Northumbria by Raedwald. Soon after his accession, Earpwald was murdered by a pagan named Ricberht, who may possibly have seized the throne. After three years of confusion, Earpwald's half-brother, Sigeberht, established his rule.

Sigeberht is reputed to be the half-brother of his predecessor, Earpwald, sharing the same mother, whose name is not known. He was in exile in Gaul before succeeding, suggesting that there were family tensions. He is credited with founding the see of Dunwich, c.631, with

Felix as bishop. Bede's account is that he retired to a monastery, handing over the kingdom to his kinsman Ecgric, who had previously ruled a part. When the East Anglians were attacked by the redoubtable Penda of Mercia, they persuaded Sigeberht to leave his cell and lead them once more into battle. He refused to bear arms and was killed, staff in hand, together with Ecgric, in the subsequent defeat.

Ecgric. There is little information on this ruler, save that he shared power for a time with Sigeberht, and was killed *c*.635 fighting against Penda, king of the Mercians.

Anna, who succeeded when both Sigeberht and Ecgric were killed by the Mercians *c*.635, was a son of Raedwald's brother Eni, suggesting that he was middle-aged when he became king. He was killed in 654 by Penda of Mercia. Bede called him 'a very religious man and noble both in mind and deed', and reported that he converted Cenwealh of Wessex when he took refuge with the East Anglians. He is said to have been buried at Blythburgh in Suffolk. His family was notable for piety: of his daughters, Aethelfryth married Ecgfrith of Northumbria and became abbess of Ely; Seaxburh married Earconberht of Kent and succeeded her sister as abbess of Ely; Aethelburh was abbess of Faremoûtier-en-Brie, near Meaux; Wihtburh was a nun at Ely; Saethryth, a stepdaughter, was also abbess at Faremoûtier.

Aethelhere was the brother of Anna and succeeded him after he had been killed by the Mercians in 654. He then appears to have changed sides, since Bede was very specific that Aethelhere was killed at the battle of the Winwaed (15 November 655) fighting for Penda of Mercia. The marriage to Hereswith, a daughter of Herewith of Deira, and a sister of the abbess Hild, has been shown to be incorrect, as has the reference in Bede to him as 'the author of the war', which has convincingly been demonstrated to apply to Penda himself.

Aethelwald was a brother of both king Anna and Aethelhere, his predecessors, and took the throne when the latter was killed in 655. He stood sponsor for Swithhelm, later king of the East Saxons *c*.656, at his palace of Rendlesham in Suffolk, not far from Sutton Hoo. He died *c*.663.

Aldwulf succeeded to the East Anglian throne *c*.663, but is not easy to identify. Bede, whose early years were spent during Aldwulf's reign, noted that his mother was Hereswith, a sister of Hild, who became abbess of Whitby; that would make her the daughter of Herewith of Deira, a nephew of both Edwin of Deira and Aethelwald of East Anglia. One source gives his father as Aethelric, son of Eni, and a brother of king Anna: another says that his father was Aethelhere. The first East Anglian coins were minted during his reign, but politically East Anglia seems to have remained under Mercian influence. He died in 713 after a reign of fifty years.

Aelfwald succeeded his father Aldwulf in 713. The family seems to have been devout, and his sister Ecgburh was an abbess. Aelfwald asked Felix to write the life of St Guthlac of Crowland, which was dedicated to him, and in a letter towards the end of his reign to Boniface, Aelfwald assured him that he was prayed for in all the East Anglian monasteries. Symeon of Durham gave his date of death as 749.

Hun, **Beonna**, and **Alberht** are reported by Symeon of Durham to have shared rule in East Anglia after the death of Aelfwald in 749. He ran the first two together, producing a composite king called 'Hunbeanna'. Florence of Worcester recorded that in 758 Beonna was king of East Anglia, and coins inscribed 'Beorna' have been found, particularly at Butley in Suffolk. The three were presumably sub-kings under Mercian overlordship.

Aethelberht, whose date of accession in East Anglia is given as 779, was said by Florence of Worcester to have been the son of Aethelred by Leofruna. It is not clear whether his father had been king. In 794 he was captured by Offa of Mercia and executed at Sutton in Herefordshire, presumably for leading a revolt against Mercian overlordship. A number of legends circulated, particularly that he had been treacherously slain while seeking the hand of Offa's daughter. His body was taken to Hereford for burial; he was subsequently canonized, and the cathedral took his name.

Eadwald is known only by a coin which has been dated between 819 and 825. Presumably he was a Mercian sub-king.

Athelstan. A number of Athelstan's coins have been found and dated between 825 and 837. No details of his reign are known, but it is possible that he led an East Anglian revival. The *Anglo-Saxon Chronicle* recorded that after the Mercians were defeated at Ellendun in 825, the East Anglians turned to Ecgberht of Wessex, killing Beornwulf of Mercia. Two years later, according to Florence of Worcester, they slew Ludeca of Mercia, who was trying to avenge his predecessor.

Aethelweard is known only by his coins, which have been dated between 837 and 850.

Beohtric. Coins of Beohtric have been dated c.852. Since the name of Beohtric is found as witness to charters of Berhtwulf of Mercia, and described as the king's son, it is probable that he was a Mercian sub-king.

Edmund succeeded to the throne of East Anglia in 855, it is said at the age of fifteen. After his martyrdom, elaborate legends circulated suggesting that he was the son of a king Alkmund of Saxony and adopted as his heir by an (unknown) king Offa of East Anglia. In fact, there is little evidence for his ancestry or his reign, though coins have been found. The *Anglo-Saxon Chronicle* reported that a large Viking army reached East Anglia in 865, removed to York, but returned in 869; it gave a bald account of how Edmund fought the Danes and was killed in 869. But soon stories were spreading that he had been tied to a tree at Hoxne and shot to death with arrows when he refused to abandon his faith. His body was taken to Beodericsworth (Bury St Edmunds), where miracles were claimed. Aelfric wrote a celebrated account of St Edmund c.992. His saint's day is 20 November.

Guthrum is the first identifiable Viking king of East Anglia, after the death of Edmund. In the 870s he campaigned mainly in central and southern England until in 878 he was defeated by Alfred of Wessex at Edington and forced to terms. By the treaty of Wedmore, Guthrum accepted baptism, under the name of Athelstan, but took a large slice of territory east of Watling Street and the river Lea. According to the *Chronicle of St Neots*, he died in 890 and was buried at Hadleigh in Suffolk. All his surviving coins were minted after his conversion.

Oeric is named by the *Anglo-Saxon Chronicle* as the king of the Danes killed at the battle of the Holme in 903 by the men of Kent. He had been persuaded by Aethelwald, atheling of Wessex and a fugitive, to take up his cause. William of Malmesbury recorded that he succeeded Guthrum, which would make his succession 890.

Lindsey

Lindsey, which had its own kings, was never strong enough to play an independent role and was usually dominated by Mercia or Northumbria. It subsequently became part of the Danelaw. A list of its kings was given by Florence of Worcester in the early twelfth century where, as usual, descent was traced back to Woden; the last one, Aldfrith, appears to have been a contemporary of and sub-king to Offa of Mercia in the late eighth century. Lindsey retained its identity as a tri-thing or division of Lincolnshire.

Deira

Deira was an early Anglo-Saxon kingdom, running from the Humber to the Tees, and including York and Whitby. Its main preoccupation was with its northern neighbour Bernicia, and in the seventh century it was taken over to form the substantial power of Northumbria.

Aelle was said by the *Anglo-Saxon Chronicle* to have succeeded in 560, and it gave him a pedigree going back to Woden. Bede wrote that the British boys put up as slaves in Rome, who so impressed Gregory, came from Aelle's kingdom. The *Chronicle*, reporting Aelle's death in 588, says merely that he 'passed away', but a later source reports that he was killed by Aethelfrith, the son of his northern rival, Aethelric of Bernicia. The chronology is confused and identification difficult. Aelle's young son Edwin subsequently recovered both thrones, and his daughter Acha married Aethelfrith.

Edwin, ultimately king of both Deira and Bernicia, was a child of about three when his father Aelle died in 588. Aelle's kingdom of Deira was taken over by the Bernicians, and the young child was removed for safety to Mercia. There he was married to Cwenburh, but he later moved on to seek shelter with Raedwald, powerful ruler of the East Angles. Bede related how Aethelfrith, who had taken control of both northern kingdoms, sought to have Edwin handed back. Raedwald refused and in c.616 led an army against Aethelfrith, defeating him at the battle of the river Idle near Gainsborough. Edwin was placed on both thrones. The united kingdom of Northumbria became a force in English dynastic politics and Bede credited Edwin with overlordship throughout most of Britain. That was clearly excessive, but Northumbria was a power to be reckoned with. In 625 Edwin married for a second time and his wife, Aethelburga, daughter of Aethelberht I of Kent, converted him to Christianity. He established York as an episcopal see and began building the minster. A campaign against Wessex was, according to the *Anglo-Saxon Chronicle*, highly successful, but in October 633 Edwin encountered Cadwallon of Gwynedd and Penda of Mercia at Hatfield Chase (Heathfield), near the scene of his first great victory. Edwin was killed, along with his eldest son, Osfrith. Bede related how, in a discussion at Edwin's court, the famous simile was used, comparing the life of man with that of a sparrow, flitting for a moment through a great hall, full of light and warmth, before plunging into the darkness outside. Edwin's head was buried at the minster in York, his body at the monastery at Whitby.

Osric, who attempted to hold Deira after the death of Edwin in 633, was his cousin, son of Aelle's brother, Aelfric. But the following year he was killed by Cadwallon of Gwynedd, whom he was besieging, probably at York. The territory of Northumbria was overrun and split once more into its component parts.

Oswine, son of Osric, succeeded Oswald of Bernicia in 642 on the Deiran throne. Bede described him as 'tall and handsome, pleasant of speech, courteous in manner ... a man of great piety and religion who ruled the kingdom in the greatest prosperity, beloved by all'. He was murdered at Gilling in 651 by order of Oswiu, king of the Bernicians, having been betrayed by a thegn whom he had trusted. The last of the line of Aelle, he was revered as a saint.

Oethelwald, son of Oswald, of Bernicia, was put in (possibly as sub-king) either by Oswiu, his uncle, or as a client king by the Mercians. He was patron of bishop Cedd. Bede explains that Oethelwald refused to help Oswiu at the battle of the river Winwaed in 655 against Penda of Mercia, retiring to a place of safety. After Oswiu's victory, he is not heard of again.

Aelfwine, a son of Oswiu, was a sub-king of Deira, put in by the Bernicians. He was killed at the battle of the river Trent against Aethelred of Mercia in 679, aged about eighteen.

Bernicia

The kingdom of Bernicia was formed in the fifth century by Anglo-Saxon settlers around the rivers Tyne and Wear, and expanded rapidly, mainly at the expense of its Celtic neighbours, the Votadini towards the Forth, and Rheged in the north-west around Carlisle and southern Galloway. It then began rivalry with the Anglo-Saxon kingdom of Deira to the south, which it absorbed in the seventh century. As the united kingdom of Northumbria it became briefly an important power, but the resistance of Mercia to the south and the devastating effects of Viking raids in the ninth century prevented further advance.

Ida, son of Eoppa, is the first Bernician king to be identified. Bede reported that he began to reign in 547 and ruled for twelve years. The *Anglo-Saxon Chronicle* offered a long pedigree, crediting him with the fortification of Bamburgh. Nennius recorded that by his queen, Bearnoch, Ida had six sons, and six more by his concubines. The eldest son, Adda, ruled for eight years from 560.

Aethelric, another son of Ida, succeeded his brother Adda in 568 and was said by Nennius to have ruled for four years, though the *Anglo-Saxon Chronicle* reported that Aethelric succeeded Aelle in Deira in 588 and ruled until 593. William of Malmesbury added that Aethelric succeeded to Deira in 'extreme old age' and after a life of penury. It has been plausibly suggested that Aethelric's son, Aethelfrith, killed Aelle of Deira in 588 and put in his father as a sub-king to rule Deira.

Theodric succeeded his brother Aethelric in 572 and was said by Nennius to have reigned for seven years.

Frithuwald came to the throne in 579 and is said to have ruled for six years. He was described by Nennius as another son of Ida, but the comment that he was reigning when Augustine's mission arrived in Kent (597) can scarcely be correct. The Bernician succession at this point is doubtful.

Hussa was said by Nennius to have reigned for seven years, but it is not clear how he fits into the Bernician genealogy. The regnal dates 585–92 have been suggested. The *Anglo-Saxon Chronicle* reported that his son Hering led the Bernicians to their great victory over Aedan mac Gabhráin at Degsastan in 603.

Urien, ruler of Rheged to the west, was said to have attacked the Bernicians c.580. With other warlords, including Rhydderch of Strathclyde, he then besieged Hussa on the island of Lindisfarne c.590, but was betrayed and slain. Urien was praised by the bard Taliesin as warrior and protector, but after his death Rheged slowly disappeared; a descendant Rienmelth (or Rhiainmelt) became the wife of Oswiu of Bernicia, which might have facilitated the takeover. Through Geoffrey of Monmouth and Malory, Urien was introduced into Arthurian legend, and transposed to south Wales.

Aethelfrith, son of Aethelric, became king of Bernicia in 593 and added the neighbouring kingdom of Deira. His first wife was Bebba; the second was Acha, daughter of Aelle, king of Deira, by whom he had seven sons and a daughter, Aebbe, who founded the monastery at Coldingham. Bede described him as 'a very brave king and most eager for glory . . . for no ruler or king had subjected more land to the English race or settled it, having first exterminated or conquered the natives'. He defeated the north Britons at Catterick c.600, a disaster recorded in Welsh annals by Aneirin in *The Gododdin*, and in 603 won a crushing victory over Aedan mac Gabhráin, king of Dalriada, at Degsastan, probably in Liddesdale. Towards the end of his life he is said to have inflicted a severe defeat on the Britons at Chester. Not surprisingly, references in the Welsh annals are unflattering. In c.616 he was himself defeated and killed at the battle of the river Idle by Raedwald of the East Angles, who was supporting the claims of Edwin, fugitive claimant to the throne of Deira.

Eanfrith, son of Aethelfrith, acceded to the throne of Bernicia in late 633, when Edwin was killed. Since the death of his father, he had been a fugitive with the Picts who, according to Bede, had converted him to

Christianity, but he reneged on becoming king. He was killed by Cadwallon in 634, apparently while seeking peace, and was succeeded by his brother Oswald. His son Talorgan was king of the Picts, the presumption being that Eanfrith had married a Pictish princess while in exile.

Oswald, son of Aethelfrith, reunited Deira and Bernicia when he succeeded his brother Eanfrith in 634. He defeated and killed the redoubtable Cadwallon at a battle on the Deniseburn, known as Heavenfield, near Hexham. Bede recorded many instances of Oswald's trust in Christianity. Having been in exile among the Picts and Irish in his youth, he brought in Aidan as bishop, who established his see on Holy Island (Lindisfarne). Bede included Oswald as the sixth bretwalda of southern Britain. On 5 August 642 he was killed by Penda of Mercia at Maserfield, near Oswestry, west of Shrewsbury. Bede listed miraculous cures at the place where he fell, and he was revered as a saint. His body is said to have been buried at the monastery of Bardney in Lindsey; his head and hands, which Penda exhibited on a stake, were recovered by his brother, Oswiu, and buried at Lindisfarne and Bamburgh. His wife was a daughter of Cynegils of Wessex, and his son Oethelwald became king of Deira.

Oswiu, younger brother of Oswald, was born in 612 and took the throne of Bernicia after the defeat at Maserfield in 642. He was hailed as the seventh bretwalda of southern Britain. He is said by Bede to have hunted down and killed Oswine of Deira in 651, taking over the kingdom. His greatest victory was in 655 at the Winwaed, when he killed Penda of Mercia. For a time he exercised considerable control over Mercia, his son Ahlfrith marrying Penda's daughter Cyneburh, and his daughter Ahlflaed marrying Penda's son, Peada, who agreed to convert to Christianity. Bede also records that Oswiu brought about the conversion of Sigeberht of the East Saxons. He was responsible for summoning the Synod of Whitby in 664 to decide between the Irish and Roman computations of Easter, and for the consecration of bishops Chadd and Wilfrid. Oswiu was twice married, first to Rienmelth (or Rhiainmelt), said to have been descended from Urien of Rheged, then to Eanflaed, a daughter of Edwin. He died on 15 February 670, intending, had he lived, to make a pilgrimage to Rome, and was buried at Whitby.

Ahlfrith, son of Oswiu, was a sub-king from 655 when Oethelwald (of Deira) was deposed. He married Penda's daughter Cyneburh, helped to persuade his brother-in-law Peada to become a Christian, and was a patron of Wilfrid and the Roman religious party. In 664, though, he took up arms against his father, was deposed, and perhaps killed.

Ecgberht I, whose ancestory is unknown, was established by the Danes as a client king of the north part of Bernicia in 867, after their occupation of York. He was driven out by a rebellion of the Northumbrians in 872, took refuge with the Mercians, and died the following year.

Ricsige succeeded Ecgberht as king of north Bernicia in 873, according to Roger of Wendover, and is said to have reigned for three years. He was presumably under Danish control, since archbishop Wulfhere of York, who had fled with Ecgberht, was recalled to his see.

Ecgberht II followed Ricsige as king of northern Bernicia in 876 but died two years later. He is known only by a reference in Symeon of Durham.

Eadwulf succeeded in northern Bernicia in 878 and is said to have been a supporter (*dilectus*) of Alfred of Wessex. He ruled from Bamburgh until 913 when he was succeeded by his son. The chronicle of Aethelweard reported that he ruled as reeve (*actori*), though he is sometimes referred to as an ealdorman. The *History of St Cuthbert* suggests that he may have been killed by Edred, a son of Ricsige.

Aldred, son of Eadwulf, succeeded as ruler of northern Bernicia in 913. He found difficulty in sustaining his position against the Vikings of York, and was twice forced by Ragnall I to take refuge with the Picts, first in 914, again 918–20. But his father Eadwulf had been under the protection of Alfred of Wessex, and Aldred submitted to Edward the Elder in 923, and at Eamont Bridge in Cumbria to Athelstan in 927. His date of death is not known.

Northumbria

Northumbria was a composite kingdom, made up of Deira (between the Humber and the Tees) and Bernicia, which, at its greatest, stretched from the Tees to the Firth of Forth. It included much of Cumbria and the north-west and, for a short time, the kingdom of Lindsey. United first under Aethelfrith (d. 616), its period of military predominance was short. Its literary and religious influence lasted much longer, but from 793, when Lindisfarne was sacked, it suffered severely from Viking depredations. Deira and its capital York fell under Danish kings, and only the northern part of Bernicia maintained a shaky independence, relying heavily on help from Wessex and from the Scottish kings.

Ecgfrith, son of Oswiu (of Bernicia), was born in 645 and succeeded his father in 670. At the time of his father's great victory over the Mercians in 655 he was said to be a hostage at the court of queen Cynewise of Mercia. His first wife was Aethelfryth, daughter of Anna, king of the East Anglians, from whom he was separated and who retired to an abbey; his second was Eormenburh, related to the wife of Centwine of Wessex. His reign was dominated by warfare. It began with a victory over the Picts in 672, which was followed c.674 by a defeat of the Mercians, giving him temporary control of Lindsey. Five years later he was himself defeated, and his brother Aelfwine killed, on the Trent by Aethelred of Mercia, forcing him to give up his new territory. At home, his stormy relations with bishop Wilfrid led to the latter journeying to Rome to seek redress; on his return, Ecgfrith imprisoned him and his successor Aldfrith expelled him in 691. Ecgfrith was killed on 20 May 685 while campaigning against the Picts at Nechtansmere, near Forfar, and the military decline of Northumbria began. He is the first Northumbrian monarch whose coins are extant, and is said to have been buried on Iona.

Aldfrith, son of Oswiu, succeeded in 685 when his brother, Ecgfrith, was killed in battle against the Picts. He was said by Bede to be illegitimate, possibly by an Irish princess, and to have been brought up on Iona, 'a self-imposed exile', to gratify his love of learning. His wife, Cuthburh, was a sister of Ine of Wessex, but they parted 'during their lifetime'. His coins have his name on one side and a rather pantomime dragon on the other. Aldfrith's reign, which covered the middle years of

Bede's life, saw Northumbria's cultural and religious influence at its peak, though the king's relations with bishop Wilfrid were often strained. He is said by the *Anglo-Saxon Chronicle* to have died at Driffield on 14 December 705.

Eadwulf was king of Northumbria for no more than a few weeks after the death of Aldfrith in 705. He was dispossessed by a party led by Berhtfrith, an ealdorman, on behalf of Aldfrith's young son, Osred. It was suggested by Symeon of Durham that Arwine whose death was recorded in 740 was Eadwulf's son.

Osred I, first son of Aldfrith, was no more than eight when he was placed on the throne in 705 after an attempted coup by Eadwulf. In a later letter, St Boniface denounced Osred, accusing him of debauching nuns and of a 'contemptible and despicable death'. In 716, at the age of nineteen, he was killed and replaced by Cenred.

Cenred, son of Cuthwine and a descendant of Ida (of Bernicia), became king after Osred in 716. His death after only two years suggests a violent end.

Osric, if a second son of Aldfrith, cannot have been much older than eighteen when he succeeded Cenred in 718, since his elder brother, Osred, had died in 716 aged nineteen. Though Osric reigned for eleven years during Bede's lifetime, we are told little about him save that he died on 9 May 729 after naming Ceolwulf, brother of Cenred, as his successor. The *Anglo-Saxon Chronicle* says that he was slain.

Ceolwulf, son of Cuthwine and brother of Cenred, succeeded to the Northumbrian throne in 729. Since Bede dedicated his great *Ecclesiastical History of the English People* to him, he is better known than most contemporary rulers, but he reigned for a comparatively short time, since in 731 he was seized and forced to become a monk, before being reinstated. A second coup or an abdication removed him finally in 737, though he was allowed to live out his life in the monastery on Lindisfarne, dying in 764. He was credited with introducing his fellow monks to the pleasures of wine and beer instead of milk and water. Writing about him in 731, Bede remarked, circumspectly, that 'both the beginning and the course of his reign have been filled with so many and such serious commotions and setbacks that it is as yet impossible to know what to say about them'.

Eadberht was a first cousin of his predecessor Ceolwulf and a son of Eata, said to be a descendant of Ida. He was presumably chosen as a more effective battle-leader than Ceolwulf. His brother, Ecgberht, was archbishop of York from 734 to 766, and the closeness of their collaboration is indicated by the existence of a coin inscribed with both their names. Under Eadberht something of the glory and influence of Northumbria was restored. In 740, while he was campaigning against the Picts, his own territories were devastated by Aethelbald of Mercia. In 750 he was reported to have added the plain of Kyle in Ayrshire to his kingdom. He joined forces in 756 with the Picts in a successful campaign against the Britons of Strathclyde, capturing their capital at Dumbarton, but Symeon of Durham, without sufficient explanation, recorded that, within ten days, his army had been utterly destroyed. Two years later he became a monk at the monastery of St Peter at York, making over his throne to his son Oswulf. He died on 20 August 768 and was buried, with his brother, in York Minster.

Oswulf, son of Eadberht, succeeded when his father retired to a monastery in 758, but died within a few months, on 24 or 25 July 759. The *Anglo-Saxon Chronicle* recorded that he was killed 'by members of his household', the continuator of Bede that he was 'treacherously killed by his thegns'. Later sources give his place of death as Market Weighton, east of York.

Aethelwald Moll, whose ancestry is unknown, became king after the murder of Oswulf in 759, 'elected by his people' according to the continuator of Bede. On 1 November 762 he was married at Catterick to Aethelthryth. The previous year he had gained a victory near Melrose over Oswine, presumably a rival candidate for the throne, and possibly the second son of Eadberht. The British Museum has two coins struck by Ecgberht, archbishop of York, but bearing Aethelwald's name. He was said by the *Anglo-Saxon Chronicle* to have abdicated after six years, but Symeon of Durham implied that he was driven out (*amisit*).

Ahlred, son of Eanwine, was said by Symeon of Durham to have been descended from Ida. He replaced Aethelwald Moll in 765, and in 768 married Osgearn or Osgifu, possibly the daughter of king Eadberht and a sister of king Oswulf. He was driven out by the son of Aethelwald Moll in 774 and died in exile among the Picts. Northumbria was now victim of disputed successions and short reigns, while facing increasing danger.

Aethelred I was the son of Aethelwald Moll, who had reigned 759–65. He drove out Ahlred in 774, but his period of effective rule was brief. By 779 he had himself been driven out, and though he was restored in 790, he was killed 'by his own court', probably at Corbridge, on 19 April 796. He is said to have been avenged by his minister Torhtmund, who slew the murderer. It is also reported that he put away his first wife, possibly to facilitate a grand second marriage on 29 September 792 to Aelfflaed, daughter of Offa of Mercia. Meanwhile, in 793 Lindisfarne's monastery was destroyed by a Viking raiding party.

Aelfwald I, son of Oswulf, dispossessed Aethelred I c.779, at a period when the Northumbrian crown was prey to coups by noble factions. He ruled until 23 September 788, when he was murdered by a close adviser, Sicga, and buried at Hexham. His sons Oelf and Oelfwine were murdered in 791 by order of Aethelred I, restored to power. The British Museum has coins from Aelfwald's reign.

Osred II was the son of Ahlred, who reigned 765–74, and possibly nephew to Aelfwald I, 779–88. He succeeded the latter but was driven out by Aethelred I, the former king, in 790. On returning from exile, he was seized and murdered 14 September 792, and buried at Tynemouth.

Osbald, who succeeded Aethelred I in 796, lasted a mere twenty-six days before he was expelled. He took refuge with the Picts, but his death is reported by Symeon of Durham for 799. He was buried at York.

Eardwulf, son of Eardwulf, succeeded 14 May 796, dispossessing Osbald. In 798 he defeated a conspiracy against him by Wada, and in 800 captured and murdered Ahlmund, son of former king Ahlred. The following year he was reported to be campaigning against Cenwulf of Mercia. About 806 he was himself driven out by Aelfwald II, but pope Leo III and the emperor Charlemagne came to his assistance and he was reinstated for a brief period c.808–10. The British Museum has coins from his reign.

Aelfwald II succeeded Eardwulf c.806 but died within two years. His ancestry has not been identified and no coins from his reign have been found.

Eanred, son of king Eardwulf, gained the throne *c.*808 and held it until his death *c.*840. Though his reign of about thirty-two years is the longest in Northumbrian or Bernician history, little is recorded, save his submission to Ecgberht of Wessex in 829. This suggests that the kingdom had ceased to play a major role in English affairs. Many coins from his reign have survived.

Aethelred II was the son of king Eanred and succeeded him *c.*840. He was driven out by Raedwulf in 844, but restored later that year, dying *c.*848. Symeon of Durham reported that he had been murdered. A number of his coins are extent.

Raedwulf seized the throne from Aethelred II in 844 and survived long enough to issue coins, many of which are extant. However, he was killed the same year by Danish raiders.

Osberht, whose ancestry is not known, took the throne of Northumbria on the death of Aethelred II *c.*848. He was driven out *c.*862, restored 867, but killed on 21 March 867 by the Danes at York, in a fierce battle, described at some length by Symeon of Durham.

Aelle, said by Symeon of Durham to be the brother of king Osberht, dispossessed him *c.*862. Civil war followed but in 867 the two united in the face of the Danish occupation of York. An onslaught on the city made some progress but, in the end, both kings were killed 21 March, the survivors submitting to the Danes.

Mercia

Mercia was one of the most powerful of the Anglo-Saxons kingdoms and at one period seemed likely to become the nucleus of a kingdom of England. But its central position, while affording many lines of advance, forced it to fight on many fronts. The heart of the kingdom was the valley of the Trent: Lichfield, founded in 669, was its episcopal see, Repton and Tamworth its royal towns. Under Penda, Aethelbald, and Offa, in the seventh and eighth centuries, Mercian power was at its height, but the defeat by Wessex at Ellendun in 825 was followed by shattering Viking incursions, and supremacy passed to Wessex.

Cearl is mentioned by Bede, who recorded that his daughter Cwenburh married Edwin of Northumbria while he was a fugitive and before his victory at the river Idle in 616. That implies that Cearl was probably ruling in the late sixth and early seventh centuries. On the assumption that Penda succeeded him, he died 626.

Penda was clearly a great king, but since he was a pagan and almost all the information about him comes from Bede, a devout monk, the account is not flattering. A Mercian genealogy gave him as the son of Pybba, grandson of Creoda, and then traced the line back to Woden, the heathen battle-god of the Germanic peoples. His wife was Cynewise, of whom nothing is known. The commonly accepted date of Penda's accession, given in the *Anglo-Saxon Chronicle*, is 626: it adds that he was then fifty, which seems an overestimate. Bede implies his accession in 633, when he joined Cadwallon of Gwynedd in defeating and killing Edwin of Northumbria.

Penda already had one successful campaign to his credit. In 628 he had defeated Cynegils of Wessex at Cirencester, wresting from him much of the territory of the Hwicces in the Avon valley. The son and successor of Cynegils, Cenwealh, married a sister of Penda, presumably as part of a negotiated settlement. After Edwin's death at Hatfield in 633, Penda suffered some setbacks. His ally, Cadwallon, was defeated and killed at Heavenfield in 634 by Oswald (of Bernicia), who reconstructed Northumbrian power. It has been suggested that Penda's murder of Edwin's son, Eadfrith, who had taken refuge in Mercia, was an attempt to buy off Oswald. Penda's campaign against the East Anglians, when he killed both their kings, Ecgric and Sigeberht, cannot be dated precisely, but was probably soon after Hatfield. Penda's greatest triumph came in 642 when Oswald moved against him, but was defeated and slain at Maserfield, near Oswestry. The battle was fierce since, according to Nennius, Penda's brother Eobba (Eowa), a co-ruler or sub-king, was killed on the victorious side. Oswald's limbs were staked out on the field of battle, presumably in honour of Woden. Penda now wielded as much power in southern England as any of the recognized bretwaldas could have claimed. The *Anglo-Saxon Chronicle* reported that in 645 Penda

expelled Cenwealh from Wessex, explaining that he had repudiated
Penda's sister; Cenwealh then sought refuge in East Anglia, where Anna
ruled. Cenwealh's return after three years may indicate some
weakening of Penda's position, particularly since the Wessex king had
been converted and baptized in the meantime. Penda also continued to
wage war against the Northumbrians, devastating their lands, since
Bede recorded that Oswiu, Oswald's successor, suffered 'savage and
insupportable attacks'. Penda's last victory came in 654 when Anna
moved against him but was killed. The following year, Oswiu attacked
him. Despite gathering together a large army—'thirty princes ... some
of them kings', according to the *Anglo-Saxon Chronicle*—Penda was
defeated and killed on 15 November at the battle of the Winwaed. His
son Peada then turned Mercia into a Christian kingdom.

Peada, son of Penda, is an interesting king of whom we know too little.
He was made king or *princeps* of the Middle Angles (Leicestershire) by his
father *c*.653. Bede reported that he asked Oswiu of Bernicia for the hand
of his daughter, Ahlflaed, but was told that he must first accept baptism;
though his father was a pagan, Peada was permitted to go through the
ceremony. He escaped the debacle of the defeat at the Winwaed in 655,
possibly through the good offices of his brother-in-law, Ahlfrith of
Northumbria. The victorious Oswiu installed him as a sub-king in
southern Mercia. The *Anglo-Saxon Chronicle* recorded in some detail the
foundation of the monastery at Peterborough. However, Bede related
that the following year (656) he was 'foully murdered' through the
treachery of his wife.

Wulfhere was a young son of Penda and a brother of Peada. After
the defeat at the Winwaed, Mercia fell under Northumbrian control,
but in 658 three ealdormen, whom Bede named, raised a rebellion
and placed Wulfhere on the throne. He lost little time in restoring
Mercian power: Christianity and conquest went hand in hand.
Florence of Worcester praised his zeal in supporting the Christian
faith, 'utterly rooting out the worship of idols', and tells us that his
wife was Eormenhild, a Kentish princess, of great devoutness. Essex
was under his overlordship and he intervened to restore Christianity
there after a period of apostasy. By 661 he was reported to be
campaigning against Wessex, seized the Isle of Wight, and gave it to
Aethelwald of Sussex, for whom he had stood sponsor in baptism. He
seems to have repaid a Welsh raid on Lichfield by destroying Pengwen,

near the Wrekin, and killing the prince Cynddylan. But towards the end of his reign, his power faltered. Though he initiated an attack upon Northumbria, he suffered a sharp defeat at the hands of Ecgfrith and was obliged to cede Lindsey. He was reported to have given battle to Aescwine of Wessex in 675, and though the outcome is not on record, Wulfhere died shortly afterwards.

Aethelred I was the third son of Penda to succeed to the throne of Mercia, after the death of his brother Wulfhere in 675. He married Osthryth, a daughter of Oswiu, king of Bernicia, whom Bede said tersely was 'murdered by her own Mercian nobles' in 697. In 676 Aethelred was said to be ravaging Kent, presumably to prevent it shaking off Mercian overlordship. Mercia and Northumbria were soon at war again and fought on the Trent in 679, when Aelfwine, brother of Ecgfrith of Northumbria, was killed. Bede related that archbishop Theodore restored relations between the two kings, but Mercia reclaimed Lindsey. Aethelred founded a number of churches and monasteries, and Eddius Stephanus called him 'Wilfrid's faithful friend'. He abdicated in 704 in favour of his nephew Cenred and is reported to have died in 716 as abbot of the monastery at Bardsey.

Cenred, son of king Wulfhere, succeeded his uncle, Aethelred, in 704. It was clearly an agreed arrangement, since Aethelred subsequently appealed to Cenred to welcome back bishop Wilfrid. Bede recorded that Cenred abdicated in 709 and, accompanied by Offa of the East Saxons, went to Rome; the fact that he had a royal companion suggests that his exile was not forced. He died as a monk, soon after his arrival. Florence of Worcester tells us that Cenred was married, but does not give the name of his queen. A number of charters attributed to him are extant but should be treated with caution.

Ceolred was a son of king Aethelred and succeeded when his cousin Cenred abdicated in 709. Though he supported bishop Wilfrid, St Boniface gave him a bad character, using him as an example of wickedness, accusing him of attacking the privileges of the church and of 'horrid and unspeakable crimes'. In 715 he was reported to be at war with Ine of Wessex. He died in 716, going mad in the middle of feasting (according to Boniface), and was buried at Lichfield. The *Anglo-Saxon Chronicle* reported that his queen, Werburh, died as the abbess of a monastery in 782, after a widowhood of sixty-six years, which sounds unlikely. The suggestion that she was a daughter of king Wulfhere is even more unlikely since that would make her at least 107 years old at her death.

Aethelbald, son of Alwih, succeeded Ceolred in 716. The direct line from Penda having expired, recourse was had to a grandson of Penda's brother, Eowa. Once again, the chronology is difficult, since Eowa died in 642, and Aethelbald in 757: a great-grandson seems more plausible. Aethelbald had been forced into exile by his predecessor, but took refuge in the Fens, where he met St Guthlac at Crowland. He proved to be one of the strongest Mercian rulers, claiming in charters to be king of the southern English. In this period London passed from Essex to Mercia. The rivalry with Wessex was carried on fiercely but with fluctuating fortunes. The *Anglo-Saxon Chronicle* reported that he seized Somerton from Aethelheard of Wessex in 733, and he was soon at war with Aethelheard's successor, Cuthred, in 740. In 752 he suffered a setback in a severe defeat at Burford, described by Henry of Huntingdon at suspicious length. Aethelbald's benefactions to the church did not prevent Boniface from sending him a letter of reproof, complaining that he had never contracted a lawful marriage, but 'debauched holy nuns and virgins consecrated to God'. Aethelbald was murdered in 757 at Seckington, near Tamworth, by his own guards, and buried in the royal crypt at Repton.

Beornred. Little is known of this king, who ruled Mercia for only a few months: no charters or coins have been found. He may have been implicated in the murder of his predecessor, Aethelbald, in 757, but was soon dispossessed by Offa, a kinsman of Aethelbald. Florence of Worcester called him a tyrant who lost his kingdom and his life at the same time.

Offa was one of the great kings of Mercia, descended through his father, Thingfrith, from Eowa, a brother of Penda. He was therefore a younger cousin of Aethelbald, murdered in 757. Offa seized the throne from Beornred a few months later and held it until his death in 796. His queen, Cynethryth, outlived him, her name appearing on charters and coins. Offa is known for his introduction of the silver penny, with his portrait on it, and for the construction of the 149-mile Offa's Dyke, a bulwark and frontier against the Welsh, running from Prestatyn to Chepstow.

Offa succeeded in extending Mercian power over the smaller kingdoms of Sussex, Kent, Essex, and East Anglia. Against Northumbria and Wessex he launched diplomatic as well as military offensives. One daughter, Eadburh, married Brihtric, king of Wessex (789), and a second, Aelfflaed, married Aethelred I of Northumbria (792). Proposals to Charlemagne for marriage alliances came to nothing, though the two rulers treated each other with respect, exchanging gifts.

At an early stage, Mercian power was reasserted against Kent, whose kings became sub-kings. Offa may have lost control for some years after a battle at Otford in 776, but by the end of his reign, his authority had been restored. Sussex was under his control after 771. The struggle against Wessex tipped in Mercia's favour after a victory at Benson in Oxfordshire in 779, and he succeeded in advancing the Mercian border against the Welsh. It may be that an attempt by the East Anglians to escape Mercian domination lay behind the capture and execution of their king, Aethelberht, in Herefordshire in 794.

Offa succeeded in persuading pope Hadrian to grant archiepiscopal status to Lichfield, to counterbalance the prestige of Canterbury; however, the grant was rescinded soon after his death. In 787, his only son, Ecgfrith, was crowned king of the Mercians, but after Offa's death in July 796, the position deteriorated rapidly. Ecgfrith did not even survive the year. Alcuin blamed Offa, seeing it as retribution for the crimes he had committed to secure Mercia for his son—'it was the vengeance of the father's blood that fell upon Ecgfrith . . . it proved the undoing not the making of his reign'.

Ecgfrith, Offa's son, was made king of the Mercians by his father in 787, presumably to give him experience and ensure his succession. In the event, when his father died in 796, Ecgfrith lasted only 141 days, dying in December. The circumstances of his death are unknown but the timing must arouse suspicion. Negotiations for marriage to a daughter of Charlemagne, begun c.789, had broken down, and no queen is reported. The existence of coins struck in the name of his mother, Cynethryth, and her witness to Ecgfrith's charters, confirm that she was a power in the land before and after Offa's death.

Cenwulf was another in the line of formidable Mercian warrior-kings. His father, Cuthberht, claimed descent from Penda's brother, Cenwalh. The circumstances of Cenwulf's accession in 796 are not known, but the death of his predecessor, Ecgfrith, a young man, so soon after taking the throne, must raise suspicion. Cenwulf's queen, Aelfthryth, is referred to in a charter: the existence of a previous queen, Cynegyth, is doubtful. Faced early in his reign with a Kentish rebellion against Mercian domination, Cenwulf responded ruthlessly, devastating the region, capturing the new king, Eadberht II, mutilating and deposing him. The East Saxons were also brought under Mercian control once more. Next he was involved in a feud with Eardwulf, king of the Northumbrians, who led an expedition against him in 801. The matter was settled without a decisive battle, but Cenwulf was thought to have had a hand in Eardwulf's subsequent expulsion.

At his accession, Cenwulf had received an exhortatory letter from Alcuin, begging the king 'never to forget him who raised you from poverty to be a ruler over the princes of his peoples'. His bequests to the church were numerous and he was the founder of the abbey of Winchcombe, in the sub-kingdom of the Hwicces. His daughter Cwenthryth was an abbess. His son, Cynhelm, died young and was buried at Winchcombe, and Cenwulf himself was buried there in 821. Though Cynhelm was a young man when he died, a legend spread that he had been murdered as a boy by a wicked sister, and he became a popular local saint as St Kenelm.

Ceolwulf I was a brother of Cenwulf, whose only son predeceased him. He succeeded in 821 and resumed Cenwulf's campaign against the northern Welsh. However, he was expelled from the kingdom two years later, and his date of death is not known.

Beornwulf seized power from Ceolwulf in 823. His ancestry is unknown, and his reign short but eventful. In 825 he fought Ecgberht of Wessex at Ellendun, near Swindon, and was badly beaten. This induced the smaller kingdoms of the south-east to throw off Mercian domination and ally with Wessex. To bring them to heel, Beornwulf advanced against the East Anglians, but was killed.

Ludeca. The origins of Ludeca are not known, but Florence of Worcester believed that he was a kinsman of Beornwulf, whom he succeeded in 825. When he advanced against the East Anglians to avenge his predecessor, he was himself killed. No charters are extant, but coins of indifferent quality have been found.

Wiglaf took the throne of Mercia after Ludeca had been killed by the East Anglians, but Mercian power was in decline: Viking raids were increasing, and Wiglaf's reign was difficult. Within two years he had been attacked by Ecgberht of Wessex, who drove him out and declared himself king. Wiglaf managed to regain the kingdom in 830 and held it until his death in 840. His queen, Cynethryth, is identified in charters. His son, Wigmund, married Aelfflaed, daughter of king Ceolwulf I, but did not succeed to the throne. His grandson, Wigstan, was murdered in 849, possibly by king Berhtwulf's son, and venerated as St Wystan.

Berhtwulf succeeded Wiglaf in 840. In view of the unsettled state of Mercia, a coup cannot be ruled out. His origins are not known but he might have been related to king Beornwulf. His queen, referred to in a charter, was Saethryth. By this time Viking raids were becoming severe, and Berhtwulf was driven out by 'a great host', which stormed Canterbury and London in 851.

Burgred. The reign of Burgred saw the virtual annihilation of Mercia, not at the hands of its old enemies, Wessex and Northumbria, but by the new menace of the Vikings. Burgred became king c.852 after Berhtwulf had been driven out by the Danes. He restored some temporary stability, begging the help of Aethelwulf of Wessex against the Welsh and then marrying his daughter, Aethelswith. In 867 he appealed once more to Wessex for help, this time against the Danes, but was forced to allow them to winter in Nottingham. For some years he held them in negotiation, but in c.874 they occupied Repton and drove him out of the kingdom. Burgred retired to Rome where he died soon after and was buried. His queen, Alfred's sister, died in 888 and was buried in Pavia.

Ceolwulf II, whose ancestry is not known, was described by the *Anglo-Saxon Chronicle* as 'a foolish thegn', set up by the Danes when they overran Mercia c.874. Nevertheless, he granted charters and minted coins. Under 877, the *Chronicle* reported that the Danes 'share out' Mercia, giving a portion to Ceolwulf—presumably the western part. His reign did not last much longer, since by 879 Aethelred II was in control of Mercia.

Aethelred II, whose origins are unknown, seems to have been placed in control of Mercia by Alfred of Wessex after much of it had been recovered from the Danes c.878. In charters he is variously described as *dux et patricius* (leader and nobleman), ealdorman, procurator, and 'lord of the Mercians'. He does not appear to have struck his own coins, suggesting the status of a sub-king. In 883 Alfred put him in charge of London, which had been a Mercian town until occupied by the Danes, and c.889 he married Alfred's eldest daughter, Aethelflaed. Her mother was Ealhswith, of the Mercian royal house, and she was therefore a niece of Burgred, king of the Mercians until c.874. Much of his time was spent campaigning with Alfred against continued Danish attacks. Aethelweard the chronicler described the part played by Aethelred in repelling Danish raids from their bases at Thorney Island and Benfleet c.893. Asser related that Aethelred pursued the Mercian onslaught against the Welsh with such vigour that they appealed directly to Alfred for protection. He remained on good terms with Alfred, who left him a sword in his will. Aethelred died in 911 and was buried at Gloucester. His work was continued by his widow Aethelflaed.

Aethelflaed ('the lady of the Mercians'), was a daughter of Alfred 'the Great'. Her mother was from the Mercian royal house and c.889 she married Aethelred, ealdorman of Mercia. After the death of her husband in 911, she took over his position as ruler of the Mercians on behalf of Wessex, collaborating closely with her brother, Edward. She extended Alfred's policy of constructing fortified burhs, including Chester, Bridgnorth, Tamworth, and Stafford. In 916 her troops defeated the Welsh at Llangorse lake, near Brecon, capturing the king of Gwent's wife. Afterwards she turned her attention to reconquering the parts of Mercia still under Danish control, storming Derby and Leicester. She died at Tamworth on 12 June 918 and was buried with her husband at Gloucester.

Aelfwynn, daughter of ealdorman Aethelred and of Aethelflaed, 'the lady of the Mercians', was a granddaughter of Alfred the Great and a niece of Edward the Elder. She became queen of Mercia on the death of her mother in June 918 but was soon dispossessed by Edward, 'deprived of all authority', and removed to Wessex. Her later life is not recorded, but if she survived, she was probably sent to a monastery.

Hwicce

This small kingdom led an obscure existence in the seventh and eighth centuries. It comprised present-day Worcestershire, part of west Warwickshire, and part of north Gloucestershire. It was in the end absorbed by Mercia, but its existence is reflected in the diocese of Worcester, established in 675 to look after the spiritual needs of the Hwicces.

Eanhere, the first king of the Hwicces to be identified, was ruling in the mid-seventh century. His niece, Eafa, daughter of his brother Eanfrith, married Aethelwald, king of the South Saxons. Bede reported that Eanhere and his brother were both Christians.

Osric is known from a charter of 676 granting land at Bath for a nunnery. Bede noted that Oftfor replaced Bosel as bishop of Worcester during this reign, which would date it about 691. Osric is credited with the foundation of the monastery of St Peter's at Gloucester. It has been suggested that he was the nephew of Eanhere, and son of Eanfrith, his brother.

Oshere is dated by charter evidence as king of the Hwicces by 693, probably at the start of his reign. He was dead before 716. His son Aethelric issued a charter in 706 and was king in the 730s.

Aethelheard made a grant of land in present-day Warwickshire in a charter dated *c.*704. He is associated with Aethelweard, suggesting that they were joint rulers. They also attested a charter granted in 692 by Aethelred, king of the Mercians, to whom they were clearly sub-kings.

Aethelric, a son of Oshere, was beneficiary of a grant from Aethelbald, king of the Mercians, which has been dated between 716 and 737. He was presumably a sub-king to Mercia.

Eanberht was a joint ruler with Uhtred and Aldred. His existence is confirmed by a charter of 757 giving land to the bishopric of Worcester, and a second, in 759, to abbot Headda. He seems to have died before his fellow kings.

Uhtred is identified by charters as a joint ruler with Eanberht and Aldred in 737 and 759, but made grants alone in 767 and 770. Since Aldred granted alone in 778, it has been suggested that Uhtred may have excluded Aldred from power in the 760s, but that Aldred resumed the sub-kingship after Uhtred's death. A charter of 770 refers to the need to strengthen defences.

Aldred, joint ruler of the Hwicces with Eanberht and Uhtred in the 750s, made a grant by himself in 778 to St Mary's, Worcester, which suggests that he outlived them. He was then acting as sub-king for Offa of Mercia. No more kings or sub-kings of the Hwicces have been identified, but Aethelmund is described as *princeps* (prince) in a charter of Ecgfrith of Mercia in 796, and his son, Aethelric, granted lands in 804. The *Anglo-Saxon Chronicle* for 802 identified Aethelmund as an ealdorman of the Hwicces, killed in battle near Kempsford by the men of Wiltshire, who were fighting for Wessex.

Wessex

Wessex, which became the nucleus of the kingdom of England, was one of the last Anglo-Saxon kingdoms to be settled, and did not attain pre-eminence until the decline of Mercia in the ninth century. It began in the sixth century with migrations of German settlers into Hampshire, augmented by Jutes moving across from Kent, and expanded westwards against the Britons into Somerset, Devon, and Dorset. Its people were then known as the Gewisse. The legendary founder of the dynasty was Cerdic, and Winchester became the main royal town. Wessex gained greatly from the damage inflicted on its rivals, Mercia, East Anglia, and Northumbria, by Viking incursions in the ninth century, and became the spearhead of Saxon reconquest in the tenth century.

Cerdic was claimed as the founder of the Wessex dynasty, but little is known for certain about him. The *Anglo-Saxon Chronicle* declared confidently that Cerdic and his son Cynric landed at Cerdicesora with five ships in 495, and had established their kingdom by 519, with Cerdic dying in 534. This is suspiciously detailed for an account written four centuries after the event. Alliterative legendary heroes are very common: 'Cerdic' sounds like Caratacus—i.e. Ceretic, a Celtic name. The dates have been challenged, and a reign of Cerdic between 538 and 555 has been counter-proposed. Much of Hampshire was settled, not by Saxons from overseas, but by Jutes moving west from Kent. Cerdic must be viewed with the eye of faith.

Cynric, son of Cerdic, is said by the *Anglo-Saxon Chronicle* to have landed with his father in 495. Until his father's reputed death in 534, every reference is an alliterative pairing, suggesting that we are dealing with legend rather than fact. In 552 he is said to have defeated the Britons at Old Sarum, and in 556, with his son Ceawlin, at Barbury castle. His death is given as 560. Since this is sixty-five years after his first fighting appearance, he was either remarkably fit and lucky, or part of a founding myth. Other sources give him as the son of Creoda, and grandson of Cerdic, which would be chronologically more probable.

Ceawlin, son of Cynric, succeeded his father in 560, according to the *Anglo-Saxon Chronicle*, having helped him defeat the Britons in 556. He is reported to have defeated the men of Kent in 568, and the Welsh (i.e. the Britons) at Dyrham in 577, giving him possession of Bath, Gloucester, and Cirencester. Expelled from his kingdom in 591, he 'perished' two years later. Bede described him as the second bretwalda of southern England, which overstates his power.

Ceol is reported to have succeeded in 591 and to have ruled for five or six years; a later entry in the *Anglo-Saxon Chronicle* notes that he was the son of Cutha and the grandson of Cynric. Cutha is said to have been killed in 584 at Fethanleag fighting alongside Ceawlin, 'who departed in anger'. If the detailed story has any validity, it may be that Ceawlin, an ageing king, was expelled by his nephew.

Ceolwulf is said to have succeeded his brother Ceol in 597. The chroniclers remark, vaguely, that he 'ever fought against the Angles, or against the Welsh, or against the Picts, or against the Scots'. Since he is also reported fighting against the South Saxons in 607, he was clearly busy. His death is given as 611.

Cynegils, son of Ceol, came to the throne c.611 on the death of his uncle, Ceolwulf. He was presumably too young to have succeeded on the death of his father c.597. He was the first king of the West Saxons to be baptized, with Oswald of Bernicia as his godfather, and he founded the see of Dorchester for bishop Birinus (634). One of his daughters was married to Oswald. Cynegils shared the kingdom with Cwichelm, described by the *Anglo-Saxon Chronicle* as his son. But since Cynegils and Cwichelm are said to have fought side by side in 614, it seems more likely that he was, as William of Malmesbury reported, his brother. About three years later, he was involved in war against the young kings of the East Saxons, both of whom were killed. In 626 he campaigned against Edwin of Deira, and two years after that he fought against Penda of Mercia. He died c.642.

Cenwealh succeeded his father Cynegils c.642. His first wife is said to have been a sister of Penda of Mercia, but when he repudiated her in favour of Seaxburh c.644, Penda drove him out and he sought refuge in the Fens. There he was baptized, and three years later recovered his throne. Cenwealh's reign was one of incessant warfare. In 652 he was fighting at Bradford-on-Avon, presumably against the Mercians; in 658 at Penselwood against the Britons; in 661 at Posentesburh, near Shrewsbury, also against the Britons, while his own territories were being ravaged by Wulfhere of the Mercians. He died in 672.

Seaxburh was the widow of Cenwealh and took over the government of his kingdom for two years after his death in 672. Bede observed that Wessex had fallen into the hands of sub-kings. It is not clear on whose behalf Seaxburh was acting, since she does not appear to have had surviving children.

Aescwine, who succeeded in 674, was the son of Cenfus, and a descendant of Cerdic. This seems to have been a period of instability for Wessex, and Aescwine died two years later.

Centwine, the son of king Cynegils, succeeded in 676 and must have been middle-aged at the time. He was married to a sister of Eormenburh, queen of Northumbria. The *Anglo-Saxon Chronicle* reported that in 682 he 'drove the Britons to the sea', i.e. he pushed further into west Somerset and Devon. However, in 685 he was dispossessed by Caedwalla, a distant kinsman, and retired to a monastery, where he soon died.

Caedwalla was a great-great-grandson of king Ceawlin and the son of Cenberht (whom the *Anglo-Saxon Chronicle* for 661 described as king, i.e. a sub-king). His reign was brief and eventful. He was born *c*.659 and was therefore twenty-six when he forced Centwine from the throne in 685; the Celtic-sounding name suggests that his mother may have been a British princess. His wife was Cynethryth. Before he gained the throne, he had spent some time in exile in the Chilterns and the Sussex weald, where he had met and been befriended by bishop Wilfrid, though he remained a pagan. He and his brother Mul campaigned against the men of Kent and Sussex, killing Aethelwald, king of the South Saxons, *c*.680, and taking the Isle of Wight (686), where they killed the last king and his two brothers. Bede recorded, with some satisfaction, that Caedwalla 'endeavoured to wipe out all the natives by merciless slaughter', in order to replace them by Christians. When his brother was captured and burned by the men of Kent, Caedwalla returned to devastate the kingdom and avenge his death. Suddenly there was a dramatic change of heart, perhaps brought about by the onset of illness. In 688 he abdicated in favour of a kinsman, Ine, and journeyed to Rome. In a long and detailed passage, Bede related that Caedwalla was baptized by pope Sergius, took the name Peter, but survived only seven days, dying 20 April 689. He was buried in St Peter's.

Ine, one of the most famous of the Wessex kings, came to the throne in 688 when Caedwalla abdicated and left for Rome. He was a son of Cenred and a great-great-great grandson of Ceawlin. His wife, Aethelburh, is said to have been a sister of his successor, Aethelheard. Ine's first task was to restore Wessex's authority over its smaller neighbours. Wihtred of Kent in 694 agreed to pay a substantial wergeld for the death of Mul. Essex and East Anglia were brought under control, giving possession of London. In 710 he waged war against Geraint of Dumnonia, extending his rule into parts of Devon. An invasion in 715 by Ceolred of Mercia was beaten off, and rebellion by two Wessex princes, Cynewulf and Eadberht, dealt with.

Ine's charters show numerous grants to the church, particularly at Abingdon, Malmesbury, and Glastonbury, and a new see was established at Sherborne in 705 for Aldhelm, one of the greatest scholars of the age. The law code for which he is celebrated was composed early in his reign. Ine records the help of his father, Cenred, and of 'a great assembly of the servants of God'. It was intended to introduce greater uniformity among the peoples under his rule and was concerned largely with the appropriate compensation for injuries and crimes. The Welsh were given protection, though not at the same rate as the Saxons.

After a reign of thirty-seven years, Ine abdicated in 725 and went to Rome, in company with queen Aethelburh. She was probably younger than Ine, since the *Anglo-Saxon Chronicle* records her campaigning during the rebellion of 725 and destroying Taunton, which presumably the rebels had captured. One of his sisters, Cwenburh, became abbess of Wimborne; another, Cuthburh, married Aldfrith of Northumbria before also taking the veil. Ine died soon after arriving at Rome and the kingship passed, by agreement, to Aethelheard.

Aethelheard. The ancestry of Aethelheard is not established, and though he is said by some sources to have been the brother of Ine's queen, Aethelburh, there is no direct confirmation. He married Frithugyth, mentioned in charters. Succeeding Ine in 726, he was soon in difficulties, facing a rival candidate, Oswald, who claimed descent from Ceawlin. Though Oswald died in 730, Aethelheard was confronted by Aethelbald of Mercia, who captured Somerton in 733 and seems to have reduced Wessex temporarily to client status. Aethelheard died in 740 according to the *Anglo-Saxon Chronicle*, in 739 according to the continuator of Bede.

Cuthred, who succeeded Aethelheard c.740, was described by the *Anglo-Saxon Chronicle* as his kinsman, and by Symeon of Durham as his brother. He had considerable success in restoring Wessex's prestige. In 743 he was reported to be fighting the Welsh in alliance with Aethelbald of Mercia, but the understanding soon broke down. In 750 he was in conflict with 'a presumptuous ealdorman', Aethelhun; however, only two years later, when he defeated an ageing Aethelbald at Burford, we are told by Henry of Huntingdon that Aethelhun fought valiantly in the Wessex vanguard. Cuthred's son, Cynric, was killed in battle in 748. In 755, he resumed his campaign against the Welsh, but died the following year.

Sigeberht, a kinsman of Cuthred, came to the throne in 756; Florence of Worcester adds that his father was Sigeric. His brother was Cyneheard. Sigeberht survived only a year and the *Anglo-Saxon Chronicle* offers a detailed and plausible story. He was deposed by Cynewulf 'and the counsellors of Wessex' for 'unlawful actions', but was allowed to remain in the Hampshire region as a sub-king. There he quarrelled with and killed one of his previous supporters, an ealdorman called Cumbra, fled into the woods, and was slain by a herdsman at Privett. There is a village of that name in modern Hampshire.

Cynewulf, claiming descent from Cerdic, deposed Sigeberht in 757. He continued the advance of Wessex against the Britons in the south-west, and in 779 was defeated at Benson by Offa of Mercia, losing territory to the south of the Thames in modern Berkshire. The *Anglo-Saxon Chronicle* gives an extraordinary account of his death in 786. Cyneheard, brother of Sigeberht, hatched a plan to seize the throne by surprising Cynewulf on a visit to his mistress, protected by only a small bodyguard. Cyneheard's men fought their way in and killed the king, but his guard refused to surrender, and were cut down. The following day a large relief force burst in, and the slaughterers were slaughtered in turn. Cyneheard was buried at Axminster, Cynewulf at Winchester.

Brihtric succeeded in Wessex on the murder of Cynewulf in 786. Of the family of Cerdic, his parentage is unknown: the *Chronicle of Abingdon* suggested that he was Cynewulf's brother. Soon after his accession, he married Eadburh, a daughter of Offa of Mercia, partly one may suppose as an insurance. About 789 he joined with Offa in expelling Ecgberht, a rival claimant, who was given refuge by Charlemagne. Brihtric had to deal with the first Viking attacks. Asser tells a melodramatic story that Eadburh, jealous of one of Brihtric's young favourites, poisoned them both. He died in 802 and is buried at Wareham.

Ecgberht has a special place in Wessex history as the ruler who began that kingdom's drive towards supremacy. He was descended from Ingild, a brother of Ine, and the *Anglo-Saxon Chronicle* gave his father as Ealhmund, who had ruled in Kent before the Mercian takeover. As a young man, Ecgberht was driven into exile by Brihtric of Wessex and Offa of Mercia, but was given shelter by Charlemagne. He succeeded Brihtric in 802, apparently without violence. The early years of his reign were spent campaigning against Dumnonia (Cornwall): he is reported devastating the region in 815, and fighting the Cornish Welsh at Galford (perhaps Camelford) in 823. Next, in 825, he faced an invasion from Beornwulf of Mercia, whom he defeated at Ellendun (near Swindon) in a savage encounter. Ecgberht's victory enabled him to recover Kent, driving out Baldred. The East Anglians and the men of Surrey, Sussex, and Essex also accepted his overlordship, and Wiglaf of Mercia was temporarily driven out of his kingdom. When the Northumbrians also submitted at Dore, the *Chronicle* acknowledged him as the eighth bretwalda of England. Such superiority was difficult to sustain. Wiglaf was able to recover his kingdom, and towards the end of his reign Ecgberht was fully employed in beating off Viking raids. Though the grand claims for Ecgberht's power may be doubted, the political and military balance had tipped decisively in favour of Wessex. He died in 839.

Aethelwulf, who succeeded Ecgberht in 839, had previously served as sub-king in Essex, Kent, Surrey, and Sussex, issuing charters. Though lacking the drive of his predecessor, he managed to hold on to most of Wessex's gains. His first wife was Osburh, daughter of ealdorman Oslac; his second, whom he married on 1 October 856, was the young princess Judith, daughter of Charles 'the Bald', king of the Franks, whom he saw when visiting the French court on his way back from Rome. His reign saw an ominous increase in the frequency and weight of Viking raids, though in 851 at Aclea (Ockly?), south of the Thames, he defeated one band in what the *Anglo-Saxon Chronicle* called 'the greatest slaughter of a heathen host that we have ever heard tell of'. Aethelwulf died on 13 January 858 and was buried at Winchester.

Aethelbald was the second son of Aethelwulf. His elder brother, Athelstan, who had acted as sub-king in Kent, Essex, Surrey, and Sussex, died c.850. Aethelbald took over the kingship of Wessex when his father made a protracted visit to Rome 855–6, though Asser hints at a conspiracy to oust the old king completely. On Aethelwulf's death in 858, Aethelbald married his young widow, Judith, which Asser declared to be a disgrace. Aethelbald died in 860 and was buried at Sherborne.

Aethelberht succeeded his brother Aethelbald in 860, having previously ruled as a sub-king. During his reign, a Viking band is said to have raided Winchester but to have been driven off. The *Anglo-Saxon Chronicle* says that otherwise he ruled 'in good peace and in great tranquillity', and Asser confirms that he 'governed in peace, love, and honour'. However, he died in 865, and was buried with his brother at Sherborne.

Aethelred I, fourth son of Aethelwulf, was the third brother to hold the throne of Wessex, succeeding Aethelberht in 865. His reign, spent in incessant warfare against the Vikings, was one of mixed fortunes, though with the aid of his younger brother, Alfred, he won one notable

Ring of Queen Aethelswith of Mercia, sister of Alfred of Wessex, who married king Burgred of Mercia in 853. The gold ring was found in Yorkshire in 1870 by a ploughman, who thought so little of it that he tied it to his dog's collar.

victory at Ashdown. He died on 15 April 871, possibly from wounds received in battle, and was buried at Wimborne.

Alfred, b. 849, 5th s. of Aethelwulf and Osburh; acc. Apr. 871; m. Ealhswith, da. of Aethelred 'Mucill', ealdorman of Mercia, and Eadburh; issue: Aethelflaed, Edward, Aethelgifu, Aelfthryth, Aethelweard; d. 26 Oct. 899; bur. Winchester.

Alfred is the only English king to be called 'the Great', and is by far the best known of the pre-Conquest monarchs. He owes much of his fame to the biography by bishop Asser, composed in the king's lifetime c.893. Consequently we know much more about him than about other kings of the period, some of it imaginary, all of it respectful. Nevertheless, he had solid achievements to his credit. The fifth son of king Aethelwulf, it was by chance that all four brothers died while Alfred was still a young man: Athelstan c.850, Aethelbald 860, Aethelberht 865, and Aethelred I in 871. Born at Wantage, Alfred was an experienced soldier when he came to the throne, having fought alongside Aethelred, particularly at Ashdown, near Hungerford, in January 871. Asser gave Alfred credit for the victory, relating that he 'fought like a wild boar'.

The first months of his reign were spent campaigning against the Vikings, and the *Anglo-Saxon Chronicle* recorded nine encounters, excluding mere skirmishes. At the end of the year, Alfred was forced to come to terms, and the Viking attacks were diverted to Mercia and Northumbria. The respite lasted until 875, when fresh bands attacked Wareham, then Exeter and Gloucester. Alfred's strategy was circumspect rather than audacious, and he made several agreements to move the invaders on. Early in 878, when they re-entered Wessex, Alfred could offer little resistance and retired to the marshes of Athelney in Somerset to regroup. Around this desperate moment, legends accumulated, especially the story of Alfred and the cakes, first found in a a late-tenth-century *Life of St Neot*. From Athelney he emerged in May 878 to win a great triumph over the Danes at Edington, near Westbury. Their leader, Guthrum, was forced to accept baptism and to give hostages, and by a subsequent division of territory, the Danes retired east of Watling Street and the river Lea, leaving London in Alfred's possession. 'Never before', wrote Asser jubilantly, 'had they made peace with anyone on such terms.' Edington proved to be a turning-point. Much Viking activity moved to northern France, and many of the Danes who remained in England were more concerned to settle than to continue raiding. Alfred's counter-measures stiffened resistance and discouraged attacks. The reorganization of the fyrd, the building of more than thirty fortified towns or burhs as strongpoints, and the commissioning of large warships to deal with coastal raiders meant that total destruction had been ruled out.

Alfred's reputation is much more than that of a warrior king. He made himself a scholar, learning Latin in middle age. He translated works by Gregory the Great, Boethius, and Augustine, as well as the Psalms. The *Anglo Saxon Chronicle* was started during his reign, possibly at the king's suggestion. His law code showed knowledge of the previous codes of Aethelberht of Kent, Ine of Wessex, and Offa of Mercia. His own writings were part of a larger plan to restore learning throughout his lands. In his preface to Gregory, Alfred lamented the pitiful state of knowledge in the kingdom at his accession: 'there were very few men on this side of the Humber who could understand their divine services in English, or even translate a single letter from Latin into English.' His remedy was to bring in scholars from Mercia and Wales, and from the continent, to appoint 'learned bishops', and to establish a school at court for the sons of the nobility.

As a small boy, Alfred was taken twice to Rome, where he was received with respect by pope Leo IV. At the age of nineteen he married Ealswith, a Mercian princess, consolidating the understanding between Mercia and Wessex which the Viking raids were bringing about. It was reinforced in *c*.889 when his eldest daughter, Aethelflaed, married Aethelred II, ealdorman of Mercia, to whom Alfred had entrusted London. The reconciliation of these old enemies, Wessex and Mercia, was the foundation for the general acceptance in 886 of Alfred as king of 'all the English people save those who were under the power of the Danes'. At his daughter's wedding, Alfred was struck down by a mysterious illness which plagued him all his life, and which has been variously diagnosed as porphyria, gallstones, Crohn's disease, or epilepsy; the affliction of piles did not prevent him from hunting with great enjoyment. Of his personal piety there is no doubt.

Revisionist attacks upon Alfred's reputation have usually taken the form of assailing Asser's biography, and it has even been dismissed as a forgery. Though it was clearly hagiographical, and suffered much from later interpolations and from slipshod editors, it has nevertheless retained the confidence of most scholars. Under Alfred's children, Edward the Elder and Aethelflaed, 'the lady of the Mercians', the great counter-attack against the Vikings developed and ensured that the new kingdom of England would be basically Saxon rather than part of a great Scandinavian sea-empire. He died on 26 October 899, aged fifty, and was buried at Winchester.

ABELS, R., *Alfred the Great* (1998).

Edward the Elder, b. c.870, s. of Alfred and Ealswith; acc. 26 Oct. 899; m. (1) Ecgwynn; issue: Athelstan, da.; (2) Aelfflaed, da. of ealdorman Aethelhelm; issue: Aelfweard, Edwin, Aelfgifu, Aethelhild, Eadflaed, Eadhild; (3) Eadgifu, da. of ealdorman Sigehelm; issue: Edmund, Edred, Eadburh, Eadgifu (i), Eadgifu (ii),   · Eadgyth; d. Farndon, 17 July 924; bur. Winchester.

Edward the Elder, so-called to distinguish him from Edward, king 975–8, succeeded his father in 899. Almost all Edward's life was spent campaigning. In the 890s he was his father's first lieutenant, winning important victories over the Danes at Farnham (893) and at Buttington-on-Severn (near Chepstow) (894). His succession was contested by his cousin, Aethelwald (son of Aethelred I), who seized the manors of Wimborne and Christchurch. When Edward drove him out, he took refuge with the Vikings of York, who accepted him as their king. In 903 Aethelwald persuaded Oeric, king of the East Anglian Vikings, to invade Wessex on his behalf. Edward's response was swift, with a raid on East Anglia, in which Aethelwald was killed. Freed to undertake a general advance against the Danes, and assisted by his brother-in-law, Aethelred II of Mercia, and by his sister Aethelflaed, Edward won a great victory at Tettenhall in Staffordshire in 910, following it with another in 911 at Wednesfield, when an invading Viking host was intercepted returning laden with booty. While Aethelred consolidated the Mercian border, Edward pushed into Essex and East Anglia, constructing burhs at Hertford and Witham, and later at Buckingham and Bedford. A further victory at Tempsford on the Ouse, in which the Danish king Guthrum II was killed, caused Viking resistance in East Anglia to collapse.

On the death of Aethelflaed ('the lady of the Mercians') in 918, Edward dispossessed her daughter, Aelfwynn, and incorporated Mercia into the kingdom of Wessex. The fall of the five Danish boroughs and submission of the Welsh after he had captured and fortified Chester allowed Edward to push towards the Humber. At Dore, in Derbyshire, he is said to have received the submission in 923 of the York Vikings, the Northumbrians, and of the kings of Scotland and Strathclyde. He died at Farndon in Cheshire and was buried at Winchester. In a reign of twenty-five years, he had almost doubled the size of his kingdom.

Aelfweard was a son of Edward the Elder by his second wife Aelfflaed and succeeded his father 17 July 924. But by 2 August he was dead at Oxford, no more than twenty-five years old. So brief a reign and the fact that his successor Athelstan had a different mother may suggest a family feud or coup. The absence of any comment on Aelfweard as a prince (in contrast to the achievements of his father at the same age) may mean that he was not in robust health or of a military disposition. He was buried at Winchester.

Viking York

The kingdom of Jorvik lasted for nearly a hundred years, from 867 to 954. Politically, it seems chaotic, with frequent coups and changes of ruler, but excavations at Coppergate have revealed a thriving and bustling city, and the continuation of its archbishopric lent it status. Though based on the old kingdom of Deira, it is not clear how extensive was its effective control. The connection between York and the Viking city of Dublin was a potential source of strength, but also a distraction. The kingdom was nearly taken over by Athelstan in the 930s, and finally integrated with England under Edred in the 950s.

Ivar ('the Boneless'), brother of Halfdan I, was a son of Ragnar Lodbrog ('Hairy-breeks'), a Danish leader who had harried the France of Charles 'the Bald' in 845. Ivar established himself in Dublin in the 850s; in 865 he and his brother invaded East Anglia, and two years later switched their onslaught to Northumbria, capturing York. Northern England seems to have been left to Halfdan while Ivar returned to Ireland in 871, to die there in 873. A late source accuses him of killing Aelle, captured at York, as a blood-sacrifice, and of martyring Edmund, king of the East Angles, in 869.

Halfdan I, brother of Ivar 'the Boneless', took control of Deira in 867, killing both Northumbrian kings, and putting in Ecgberht I as puppet ruler of Bernicia, north of the Tyne. The following year was spent campaigning against Mercia, 871 against Wessex. In 874 he drove out Burgred, king of the Mercians, and installed Ceolwulf II there. After 875 he settled his followers in Northumbria, founding the Danish kingdom of York. It has been suggested that his men were weary of fighting, and he seems to have been ill-supported when he moved to Ireland in 877, seeking to recover his brother's kingdom of Dublin. He was reported killed at Strangford Lough.

Guthrith I, son of Harthacnut, became king of York by 883. The chronology of his reign is not easy to establish, and the literary and numismatic evidence hard to reconcile. He is said to have been rescued from slavery by abbot Eadred and baptized with the name of Cnut, but it has also been suggested that Cnut was a different ruler at that period. Legend reports that Guthrith was chosen by the spirit of St Cuthbert as a Christian ruler, and the bishopric of Chester-le-Street, where the saint's remains had a temporary resting-place, gives some support. Coins from his period are found under the name of Cnut. He reigned until 14 August 895 and was buried, according to the chronicler Aethelweard, at York.

Sigfrid established himself as ruler of Viking York in 895 on the death of Guthrith I. Previously he had been reported leading raiding parties against Wessex. A considerable number of his coins, most of them struck at York and of good quality, have been found. Neither the date nor the circumstances of his death are known, but by 901 Aethelwald was ruling at York.

Cnut or **Knutr** is something of a mystery. There is no reference to his reign in literary sources, yet in 1840 a very large horde of coins was found at Cuerdale in the Ribble valley bearing his name, some combining the names of Cnut and Sigfrid. They were struck at York and could not have been buried later than 905–10. Since no coins of Guthrith I, who ruled at York 883–95, have been found, it has been assumed that the 'Cnut' coins must be his, and it is pointed out that his father's name was Harthacnut. Another suggestion is that Cnut was another name for king Sigfrid. A third identification is with a Danish noble, mentioned in Norse sources, who invaded Northumbria c.900 and established a brief rule—too brief, perhaps, for the quantity of coins produced, since he was assassinated in 902. What is clear is the comparative isolation of Northumbria at this time and the volatility of its kingship.

Aethelwald, son of king Aethelred I of Wessex, had a brief but spectacular career. At his father's death in 871 he was a small boy, so the throne was taken by his uncle, Alfred. On Alfred's death in 899, Aethelwald claimed the throne, but was driven out by his cousin Edward (the Elder), who besieged him at Badbury, near Wimborne. Aethelwald escaped by night and fled to the Danes at York who, according to the *Anglo-Saxon Chronicle*, received him as their king. Some of his coins have been found. In 903 Aethelwald began an attempt to regain Wessex, landing first in Essex and East Anglia, where he persuaded the Danes under king Oeric to take up his cause. A harassing raid on Wessex across the Thames at Cricklade provoked Edward to counter-attack across East Anglia. On the retreat, Edward's Kentish allies became separated, and were engaged in a fierce conflict by the Danish forces at the Holme, believed to be near Swaffham in Norfolk. Aethelwald was killed, along with Oeric.

Halfdan II seems to have been joint ruler at York with Eowils after Aethelwald had been killed c.903. His ancestry has not been established. For 909, the *Anglo-Saxon Chronicle* reported that Edward the Elder, king of Wessex, had raided and devastated Northumbria, presumably in retaliation for Danish incursions. Halfdan and Eowils led a counter-raid the following year but, on the way back, loaded with spoils, were intercepted at Tettenhall, near Bridgnorth, on 5 August 910 and killed. The defeat was a severe blow to Viking York's power.

Eowils is known through the *Anglo-Saxon Chronicle* and the chronicle of Aethelweard as joint ruler of York with Haldan II, and shared his fate at Tettenhall in 910. The balance had tipped decisively towards Wessex.

Ragnall I was probably a grandson of Ivar 'the Boneless'. The severe defeat at Tettenhall had removed many of the leaders of Danish York, enabling Ragnall to seize the throne after he had re-established his position in Dublin. In 914 he was reported with a fleet at the mouth of the Tyne, and seems to have gained Bernicia after defeating Edred, reeve of Bamburgh, and Constantine, king of the Scots, at Corbridge. The following year he campaigned in Ireland, but returned in 918, winning a second encounter at Corbridge. He then moved south and in 919 captured, or recaptured York. The *Anglo-Saxon Chronicle* related that he submitted to Edward, king of Wessex, in 920, but the implied overlordship seems to have been nominal. He died in 921.

Sihtric, who succeeded Ragnall I at York in 921, was probably his cousin and another grandson of Ivar 'the Boneless'. His nickname 'Caech' means squinty or one-eyed. Until his attempt upon York, his activities had been mainly in Ireland, where he occupied Dublin in 917. He is said to have killed Niall, high-king of Ireland, outside Dublin in 919. The following year he launched a raid into Mercia, destroying Davenport in Cheshire, but his reign in York seems comparatively uneventful. In 925 he met Athelstan at Tamworth and, on 30 January, was given his sister in marriage. Roger of Wendover wrote that Sihtric was converted to Christianity for the occasion, but soon reneged, repudiating both his new religion and his new wife. When he died in 927, Athelstan turned out Guthrith, Sihtric's brother, and his son Olaf, and took possession of the kingdom.

Guthrith II, brother of king Sihtric, left Dublin to take over the kingdom of York in 927. However, he was moved on by Athelstan of Wessex and returned to Ireland, spending the rest of his days raiding and enslaving. He died in 934.

Olaf Guthrithsson (Anlaf Guthrithsson) was one of the more impressive Viking leaders of his day. His father (Guthrith II) had held the kingdom of Dublin and, briefly, the kingdom of York. Succeeding him at Dublin in 934, Olaf joined forces in 937 with the kings of Scotland and Strathclyde in a grand attack upon Athelstan, which resulted in their crushing defeat at Brunanburh. Olaf escaped with difficulty and restored his position in Ireland. On the death of Athelstan in 939, Olaf led another invasion, took possession of York, and began a raid on Mercia, storming Tamworth. The new young king of Wessex, Edmund, hastened to make terms, negotiated by the archbishops of Canterbury and York, whereby Olaf agreed to receive baptism but was ceded all the lands north of Watling Street. That Olaf's rule of his new territories was a reality is indicated by his coins struck at Derby. The outlines of a great new power bloc, stretching across northern England and Ireland, were visible, but in 941 Olaf died while campaigning in Northumbria. He was said by Roger of Wendover to have married Aldgyth, daughter of a Danish nobleman called Orm, perhaps as his second wife. It is clear that Olaf thought on a grand scale and was a young warrior of more than common ability.

Olaf II Sihtricsson, (Anlaf Sihtricsson), nicknamed 'Cuaran' ('Slipper'), was cousin of Olaf Guthrithsson and succeeded him in 941 in Dublin and York, and was the son of Sihtric 'Caech', who had ruled in York until 927. However, he was not able long to retain the enormous gains made by Olaf Guthrithsson at the expense of Mercia. Edmund took the opportunity at once to reconquer the territories ceded in 940 with little, if any, resistance. In 943 Olaf came to terms with Edmund, converting to Christianity and acknowledging the loss of his lands south of the Humber. It may be that his surrender cost him the support of the Danes at York, where he was temporarily replaced by Ragnall II Guthrithsson. In 944 Edmund intruded into this civil war and, according to the *Anglo-Saxon Chronicle*, drove out both kings, resuming control of Northumbria. Ragnall seems to have been killed, but Olaf returned to Dublin. He regained power in Northumbria in 949 but ran into fresh competition from Erik Bloodaxe, and was again driven out in 952. The rest of his life was spent in Ireland as king of Dublin. In 980, after a sharp defeat, he retired to Iona, ending his days there in 981. The medieval poem *Havelock the Dane* is based loosely upon his adventures.

Ragnall II Guthrithsson was brother of Olaf, who ruled at York 939–41. He seems to have disputed the succession in 943 with Olaf Sihtricsson, and came to terms with Edmund of Wessex that year, receiving baptism. The following year, though, he was driven out and killed by Edmund.

Erik Bloodaxe was one of the many sons of Harald Harfagri ('Fair-haired'), king of Norway; his wife was Gunnhildr, daughter of the king of Denmark, Halfdan Gudrodarson. He was named as his father's successor but, after two years of savage warfare, failed to consolidate that position and was driven out. Erik then took advantage of the disintegration of the kingdom of York to establish himself as king in 947. Edred, king of Wessex, who claimed overlordship, led a punitive raid into the region, forcing the Danes to abandon Erik. Olaf Sihtricsson then returned as king. Erik regained the throne in 952 but was again expelled after two years, meeting his death on Stainmore, presumably trying to escape to Cumbria or to the Scots. He is said to have been killed by Maccus (Magnus), son of Olaf Sihtricsson. The kingdom of York was then incorporated into Mercia/Wessex. Excavations at Coppergate have revealed a great deal of the economic and commercial vitality of Viking York, and Erik is one of the few kings of the period of whom we have a description: Egill the poet called him a stout, handsome man, 'hot-headed, harsh, unfriendly and silent', who ruled his people 'under the helmet of his terror'.

Erik Bloodaxe's silver penny, struck by him at York c.948. The sword confirms what we are told of a grim ruler.

Isle of Man

The island was not settled by the Romans, and little is known of its government until it came into the Norwegian sphere of influence in the ninth century. Some of its rulers were clearly Norwegian governors or sub-kings, some came from the Viking kingdom of Dublin, while others were pirates or usurpers. After the battle of Largs in 1266, the island was ceded to the kings of Scotland, but was annexed in 1333 by Edward III of England. From 1405 it belonged to the Stanley family, earls of Derby, and from 1736 to the dukes of Atholl. They sold it to the British government in 1765, and in modern times it has been ruled by a Lieutenant-governor.

Pre-conquest England

The work of Alfred, Edward the Elder, and Athelstan in driving back the Danes advanced the supremacy of Wessex, but also forged a kingdom of England, even if the component parts, particularly in the north, retained considerable autonomy. Indeed, Edgar in 973 seems to have made claims towards sovereignty over Britain, even if they were shadowy and unsubstantiated. When a fresh Danish onslaught began under Sweyn and Cnut in the early eleventh century, they took over the whole land. Edward 'the Confessor' ruled over a kingdom recognizable as the later England, and this was the country taken over by William 'the Conqueror', also by descent a 'Northman', in 1066.

Athelstan, b. c.895, s. of Edward the Elder and Ecgwynn; acc. 924; d. 27 Oct. 939; bur. Malmesbury.

Athelstan, grandson of Alfred the Great, was the third in a line of rulers who, in a period of sixty years, transformed Wessex from a kingdom on the brink of disintegration into the core of an English and, it was claimed, a British kingdom. He was educated at the Mercian court, but the circumstances of his accession are obscure. His half-brother

Aelfweard who became king is mentioned in only one version of the *Anglo-Saxon Chronicle*, and died sixteen days after the death of Edward the Elder. Athelstan dealt with the objections that he was illegitimate and was consecrated at Kingston-upon-Thames. One of his first actions was to sanction the marriage of his sister at Tamworth on 30 January 925 to Sihtric, Viking king of York. The dynastic implications were obvious. When Sihtric died in 927, Athelstan drove out his successor, Guthrith and his son Olaf, and took direct rule of the region. Next he summoned the ealdorman of Bamburgh and the kings of Scotland and Strathclyde to a meeting at Eamont Bridge, south of Penrith, on 12 July 927, where they submitted to him. He called the Welsh princes, including Hywel Dda, to Hereford, where they agreed to pay tribute and recognized the Wye as the boundary. He put down a revolt of the Britons in the south-west, reaffirming the frontier on the Tamar, and established a bishopric at St Germans. Athelstan's prestige was greatly enhanced by the marriages of his sisters to European monarchs.

Athelstan's understanding with the Scottish kings broke down in 933, and the following year he led an army to ravage Scotland as far as Kincardineshire. Three years later, the Scottish kings formed a coalition with Olaf Guthrithsson, who sought to recover the kingdom of York. They launched an invasion but were routed in 937 at Brunanburh, perhaps near York; the victory was decisive, though Athelstan's losses included two of his young cousins. Brunanburh was Athelstan's crowning victory. His charters described him as 'king of the English and ruler of all Britain', and his coins repeated the claim. He did not marry, does not seem to have had children, and was a great collector of religious relics. He died on 27 October 939 and was buried at Malmesbury, where his young cousins, killed at Brunanburh, had been interred.

Edmund I, b. 921, s. of Edward the Elder and Eadgifu; acc. Oct. 939; m. (1) Aelfgifu; issue: Eadwig, Edgar; (2) Aethelflaed; d. 26 May 946; bur. Glastonbury.

Edmund succeeded his half-brother Athelstan. Though only eighteen, he was already battle-hardened, having fought in 937 in the savage encounter at Brunanburh. Olaf Guthrithsson seized the opportunity to recover York, and in 940 was strong enough to invade Mercia and storm Tamworth. Edmund, not yet in control, was forced to temporize and cede the territories north of Watling Street. Fortunately for Edmund, Olaf died in 941, and he was to able to recover the ceded territories. However, on 24 May 946 he was stabbed to death at Pucklechurch in

Gloucestershire by Leofa over a personal grudge. He was buried at Glastonbury where his friend Dunstan was abbot. His first wife, Aelfgifu, called 'saint' by the *Anglo-Saxon Chronicle*, died in 944 and was buried at Shaftesbury; his second, Aethelflaed, daughter of ealdorman Aelfgar of Damerham, Hampshire, remarried and died many years later.

Edred, b. c.924, s. of Edward the Elder and Eadgifu; acc. May 946; d. 23 Nov. 955; bur. Winchester.

Edred succeeded when his brother was murdered, and his first priority must have been to retain his territories in the north. After Erik Bloodaxe had established himself as Viking king of York in 947, Edred led an expedition into Northumbria and expelled him. However, there was considerable resentment in York against Mercian/Wessex rule, and Edred had archbishop Wulfstan imprisoned for collaboration. Erik recovered the throne in 952 but was killed two years later. Edred was in poor health and died at Frome in 955. He was a close friend of Dunstan, abbot of Glastonbury, and his charters reveal numerous bequests to the church.

Eadwig, b. c.942, s. of Edmund and Aelfgifu; acc. Nov. 955; m. Aelfgifu, da. of Aethelgifu, c.956; d. 1 Oct. 959.

A small boy when his father was murdered in 946, Eadwig succeeded his uncle in 955. His brief reign, dominated by palace intrigue, is hard to interpret. He was crowned at Kingston-upon-Thames in January 956 and was married soon after to a cousin; it is said that at the coronation feast abbot Dunstan was obliged to rebuke him for drunken and lascivious behaviour. His marriage was annulled in 958 on grounds on consanguinity. He was soon involved in further difficulties. Dunstan, a close friend of his predecessor, was driven into exile, and Mercia and Northumbria appear to have withdrawn their allegiance, choosing Edgar as king. Since Edgar was no more than fourteen, the division may have been an agreed one, but it carried a threat to the unity of Wessex/England, built up so carefully in the previous eighty years. The danger was removed in 959 when Eadwig died, leaving Edgar as king of all England. Eadwig's character has been variously assessed. Aethelweard, a close relative, writing thirty years later, tells us that he was called 'All-Fair', and 'deserved to be loved'; a modern historian has described him, more tersely, as 'licentious and incompetent'.

Edgar, b. 943, s. of Edmund and Aelfgifu; acc. Oct. 959; m. (1) Aethelflaed, da. of ealdorman Ordmaer, c.960; issue: Edward; (2) Wulfthryth, c.963; issue: Eadgyth; (3) Aelfthryth, da. of ealdorman Ordgar, wid. of ealdorman Aethelwold, c.965; issue: Edmund, Aethelred; d. 8 July 975; bur. Glastonbury.

Though no more than sixteen years old when he succeeded his brother Eadwig, Edgar had been recognized as king in Mercia and Northumbria since 957. A factor which contributed greatly to the success of Edgar's reign was a slackening of Viking raids and a diminution of internal feuding. His coronation, postponed until his thirtieth year, took place on 11 May 973 at Bath, on the border of Mercia and Wessex, and set the pattern for all future ceremonies. Immediately after, he visited Chester, where he received the submission of at least six kings, including princes from Scotland and Wales, and was ceremoniously rowed by them on the Dee. If Edgar's ceremony at Chester implied lordship, it was exercised gently, but the freedom from constant warfare allowed him to institute a number of reforms. Dunstan was recalled to favour, promoted at once to the archbishopric of Canterbury, and supported by the king in his efforts at monastic reform. Edgar's laws permitted a good deal of autonomy to the Danes, who were allowed to retain their traditional customs. Towards the end of his life, Edgar undertook a comprehensive reform of the currency, providing more mints, and arranging for the systematic recall and reissue of worn or debased coins. The *Rule of St Benedict* accorded him heroic status: 'he ruled everything so prosperously that those who had lived in former times ... wondered very greatly.'

Coronations

As formal acknowledgement of a monarch's right to rule, the coronation confirms their accession and acceptance by their subjects. For early warrior kings, the principle of succession was by election within the ruling tribes or families, copying Roman practice, so the inaugural ceremony was both public acclamation of the new ruler and acknowledgement of military prowess. This 'election and elevation' was subsequently replaced by primogeniture (succession by first-born, usually male), and assent changed to recognition of a monarch's established right.

continued

Coronations *continued*

With the spread of Christianity there developed the practice of consecration by unction (anointing with holy oil); there was a widespread belief that anointment conferred sacredness, and the Church expected monarchs to fulfil both spiritual and secular roles. An interest in symbolism led to 'coronation', combining both crowning and unction as a liturgical ritual, well established in England by the tenth century.

The coronation ritual, organized by the clergy, came to combine all these elements: the order used for Aethelred in 978 showed clear divisions into election, oath, anointing, delivery of insignia (regalia), and blessing. By the twelfth century, the undisputed place of coronation for English monarchs was Westminster abbey, whose monks then took over and developed the order of ceremony and associated ritual. The coronation eve saw the vigil procession from the Tower of London to Westminster palace (1377–1661, except when plague was rampant), and this has been partially revived in the carriage procession from Buckingham palace. Since medieval times, it has been usual for a queen-consort to be crowned with her husband, although not all queens have been crowned (Henrietta Maria, Caroline of Brunswick) and some have had separate ceremonies (Elizabeth of York, Anne Boleyn). After the Reformation the ritual was secularized and abridged, but the modern ceremony— acclamation, oath, anointing, delivery of the insignia, crowning, enthronement, and homage—continues to reflect earlier forms even though some details have been simplified.

The coronation of Scottish monarchs was generally simpler. Inauguration involving elevation, usually at Scone, was central, but crowning and anointment were eventually granted to Robert I (1329) before use at David II's coronation (1331). Since many later rulers succeeded as children or infants, ceremonial was minimized. Changes in the oath could have considerable political significance: at the last Scottish coronation (1651), Charles II had to swear to the covenant, and anointment was omitted as being too popish a practice.

Edward ('the Martyr'), b. c.962, s. of Edgar and Aethelflaed; acc. July 975; d. 18 Mar. 978; bur. Wareham, rebur. Shaftesbury.

Edward was thirteen when his father died and the peace of the realm was soon shattered. Edgar's third wife and widow, Aelfthryth, put forward the claims of her own son, Aethelred, who was no more than six or seven. Edward did not last long. On a visit to his half-brother at Corfe in March 978, he was stabbed to death, at the instigation, it was rapidly presumed, of his stepmother. The body, hastily buried at Wareham, was subsequently transferred to Shaftesbury. Miracles were soon claimed, the young king was given the status of a saint, and known to posterity as Edward 'the Martyr'.

Aethelred II ('the Unready'), b. c.968, s. of Edgar and Aelfthryth; acc. Mar. 978; m. (1) Aelfgifu, da. of ealdorman Thored; issue; Athelstan, Ecgberht, Edmund, Eadred, Eadwig, Edgar, Eadgyth, Aelfgifu, Wulfhild, 2 das.; (2) Emma, da. of Richard I, count of Normandy, 1002; issue: Edward, Alfred, Godgifu; d. 23 Apr. 1016; bur. St Paul's, London.

Aethelred has the misfortune to be regarded as among the most inept of English kings. The son of Edgar by his third wife, Aethelred came to the throne in 978 when his half-brother Edward was murdered on a visit to him. Since he was then no more than ten years old, power was in the hands of his mother, Aelfthryth. The circumstances of his accession cast a shadow over his reign, but even more disastrous was a resumption of Viking raids on a grand scale. Attacks were directed mainly at the south coast and were, by their nature, difficult to anticipate. When he took over the reins of government Aethelred made considerable attempts to control the problem. In 991 he reached an understanding with the dukes of Normandy to reduce the help that raiders might receive in France. In 997 the Wantage Code made an appeal to the loyalty of the Danes in England by reiterating the protection of their own customs. The fortified burhs of Alfred and Edward the Elder were strengthened and more were built. However, the long period of peace had made the English less capable of resisting, and the *Anglo-Saxon Chronicle* gave many examples: 'the leaders were the first to set the example of flight' (993); 'as soon as the battle was about to begin, the word was given to withdraw' (997). When they did give battle they were often beaten. Goda the thegn was killed in Devon in 988, Byrhtnoth the ealdorman at Maldon in 993, Aethelstan, the king's son-in-law, in 1010. Other leaders became disloyal. Under these circumstances, the policy of buying off groups of Danes, with which Aethelred is associated but which had often been employed before, becomes more intelligible.

Soon after the defeat at Maldon, attempts began to pay off the Danes. Some of the Danes kept their promises, but fresh raiders returned. The situation, already bad, became desperate when Danes intent on conquest rather than booty made their appearance. Sweyn 'Forkbeard', king of Denmark, was campaigning in the 990s. On 13 November 1002 the king, complaining of a plot to assassinate him, ordered the death of all Danes living in England. The St Brice's Day massacre made it even less likely that Danish settlers would rally round a Saxon king. Exeter, Salisbury, Norwich, Sandwich, Wallingford, Oxford, and Cambridge were all sacked. Winchester was described as too strong to be assaulted, but its people watched an arrogant and confident host passing their gates on its way to the coast, carrying provisions and treasures from more than fifty miles around. In 1011 they seized Canterbury, captured archbishop Aelfheah, and in 1012 brutally murdered him. Two years later the Danelaw surrendered to Sweyn and his son Cnut, who began a massive invasion of the Wessex heartland. Aethelred fled to Normandy and Sweyn was acknowledged as king of all the land. There was one last twist to Aethelred's fortunes. Sweyn died in February 1014, and though the Danes declared for Cnut, the English begged Aethelred to return and rule justly. He led an attack upon the Danes in Lindsey, but Cnut brought his fleet to Gravesend and was once more bought off. Fighting continued, but what resistance was offered was largely the work of Aethelred's son, Edmund. When Aethelred died in April 1016, the English chose Edmund to succeed him and the fight went on.

The reign of Aethelred was perhaps the worst time that England has ever suffered, with famine to compound the misery. As king, Aethelred bore responsibility, but it was easier to sneer at him as 'Rede-less' ('Lacking in counsel', a nickname not used in his lifetime), than to suggest what he could have done. His recall in 1014 implies that he was not totally despised. His second marriage to Emma of Normandy was doubtless diplomatic in origin, but she remained with Aethelred throughout his misfortunes.

Sweyn ('Forkbeard'), b. c.960, s. of Harald 'Bluetooth' and Gunhild, acc. autumn 1013; m. Gunhild, da. of Mieszko of Poland, c.995; issue: Harald, Cnut, Gytha, Estrith; d. 3 Feb. 1014; bur. Roskilde, Denmark(?).

King of Denmark from c.985, Sweyn began raiding England in 994. It is said that his sister, Gunhild, was killed in the St Brice's Day massacre in 1002 and that Sweyn swore vengeance. In 1013, with his son Cnut, Sweyn established himself in the Danelaw and launched an invasion of the south, driving Aethelred into exile. London surrendered, resistance crumbled, and Sweyn was acknowledged as king of England. However, his reign lasted a few weeks only, since he died at Gainsborough in February 1014. The Danish version was that he fell off his horse, the English that he had been run through by the ghost of St Edmund 'the Martyr'.

Edmund II ('Ironside'), b. c.992, s. of Aethelred and Aelfgifu; m. Ealdgyth, wid. of Sigeferth, 1015; issue: Edward, Edmund; d. 30 Nov. 1016; bur. Glastonbury.

Edmund's elder brothers, Athelstan and Ecgberht, died in 1014 and c.1005. During his youth, the kingdom was subject to debilitating Viking raids and was near to dissolution. Moreover, in 1002 his father made a second marriage to Emma of Normandy, and a half-brother, Edward (later 'the Confessor'), was born soon after, who might well prove a rival. In 1015, Aethelred had the thegn Sigeferth killed and his widow Ealdgyth imprisoned at Malmesbury. Edmund rescued her and married her; her possessions gave him a territorial base in the east midlands. When Cnut invaded in 1015 seeking to recover the throne his father Sweyn had held so briefly, Edmund took the lead in opposing him. On Aethelred's death in April 1016, the English chose Edmund as king, while Cnut continued to press his claims. The summer was spent in campaigning throughout the south. Battles at Penselwood (in Kent?) and at Sherston (near Malmesbury) were indecisive, but at Ashingdon, south of the river Crouch in Essex, Cnut carried the day. Edmund fled to the west, but at Deerhurst, near Gloucester, the two kings met on an island in the Severn and reached an understanding. Edmund was to rule Wessex while Cnut took Mercia and the Danelaw. The story that they fought a personal duel there was a later invention. However, in November 1016 Edmund died, and Cnut then took the whole kingdom without opposition.

Cnut, b. c.995, s. of Sweyn 'Forkbeard' and Gunhild, da. of Mieszko of Poland; acc. 30 Nov. 1016; m. (1) Aelfgifu of Northampton, da. of ealdorman Aelfhelm; issue: Sweyn, Harold; (2) Emma of Normandy, wid. of Aethelred II, 1017; issue: Harthacnut, Gunhild; d. Shaftesbury, 12 Nov. 1035; bur. Winchester.

Cnut was a battle leader turned statesman. He came to England in 1013 with his father, who succeeded in driving out king Aethelred but died

SAXONS, DANES, NORMANS
[showing union of the Saxon and Norman lines]

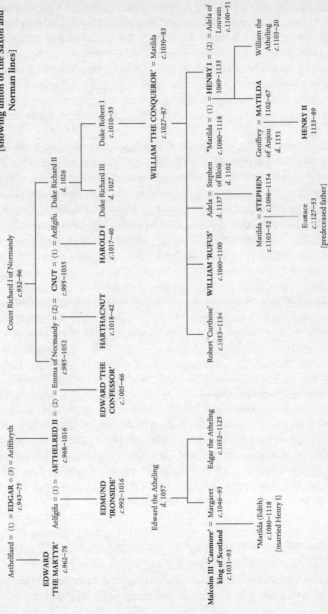
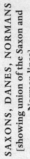

immediately afterwards. When Aethelred, briefly restored, died in April 1016, Cnut and Edmund 'Ironside' contested the succession. Cnut's victory at Ashingdon forced Edmund to yield Mercia and the Danelaw, and when Edmund died in November 1016 there was no opposition to Cnut's election as king of all England. Aethelred's son Edward by his marriage to Emma of Normandy was a boy of eleven, and Cnut neutralized his claim by marrying Emma within a few months. His previous marriage to Aelfgifu of Northampton seems to have been put on hold.

Cnut was now king of England, Denmark, Norway, and southern Sweden. He experienced considerable difficulty in retaining his Scandinavian lands and in 1030 sent out his young son Sweyn to rule Norway under the guidance of Aelfgifu. The Norwegians found their rule intolerable, and by 1034 Cnut had lost that kingdom. Another challenge came from Malcolm II of Scotland, who invaded Northumbria in 1018, inflicting a severe defeat at Carham. Cnut managed to restore the situation and in the early 1030s visited Scotland to receive the submission of three Scottish rulers.

Cnut was at pains to reconcile his English and Danish subjects. In 1020 he addressed a proclamation or letter conveying 'friendly greetings to all his subjects', and another, in 1027, was addressed to 'the whole of the English nation'. In 1023 the remains of archbishop Aelfheah, brutally murdered by the Danes in 1012, were reinterred in a solemn ceremony at Canterbury. Cnut's law codes, mainly the work of archbishop Wulfstan, repeated many of Edgar's provisions and promised protection to all subjects. Already a Christian ruler before his accession in England, Cnut became a great patron of the church, making a visit to Rome in 1027. In 1032 he visited Glastonbury, where he did honour at Edmund's tomb in an obvious gesture of reconciliation. Though his rule was strong and his tax demands heavy, Cnut gave his subjects internal peace and security. The famous story of his forbidding the waves to advance is first told by Henry of Huntingdon some hundred years later, and is a fairly conventional homily.

LAWSON, M. K., *Cnut: The Danes in England in the Early Eleventh Century* (1993).

Emma of Normandy, b. c.985, da. of Richard I, count of Normandy and Gunnor; m. (1) Aethelred II, 1002; (2) Cnut, 1017; d. 1052; bur. Winchester.

Emma, 'the jewel of the Normans', had a long and eventful life, full of vicissitudes. She was married in her teens to Aethelred as his second wife, partly to cement an understanding between the English and the Normans against Viking raiders. She bore the king a number of children and remained with him until his death in 1016. The following year she married, as his second wife, Cnut, who had defeated Edmund 'Ironside' and seized the throne. By him she had a son, Harthacnut. On Cnut's death in 1035, she took up the cause of Harthacnut but was unable to prevent his half-brother Harold 'Harefoot' taking power, and was forced into exile. She came back on Harold's death in 1040 and was very influential during the brief reign of Harthacnut. When her son Edward succeeded his half-brother in 1042, he pushed his mother firmly aside, pensioning her off to live in decent retirement in Winchester until her death. She was buried there alongside Cnut, her second husband. Her great-nephew was William 'the Conqueror.'

Harold I ('Harefoot'), b. c.1017, s. of Cnut and Aelfgifu of Northampton; acc. Nov. 1035; m. Aelfgifu; issue: Aelfwine(?); d. 17 Mar. 1040; bur. Westminster.

Harold's elder brother Sweyn died c.1036. At Cnut's death, Harold's younger half-brother and rival, Harthacnut, was in Denmark, and his mother (Emma of Normandy) could not prevent Harold seizing the crown. A compromise was reached whereby Harold acted as regent, but in practice he took control, and Emma fled to Bruges. Harthacnut was preparing an invasion in 1040 when Harold died suddenly at Oxford; his half-brother then became king.

Harthacnut, b. c.1018, s. of Cnut and Emma of Normandy; acc. Mar. 1040; d. 8 June 1042; bur. Winchester.

About seventeen when his father died, Harthacnut was in Denmark. His mother attempted to protect his interests, but was at length driven into exile by his half-brother Harold, who claimed first a regency and then the throne. Harthacnut was preparing to invade in March 1040 when his rival died; he landed at Sandwich in June and was acknowledged as king. Taxation was racked up to fierce levels. The *Anglo-Saxon Chronicle* related that Harthacnut had his predecessor's body dug up and 'cast into a marsh'; the same source added that 'he never did anything worthy of a king' and that he died in 1042, while drinking, 'with horrible convulsions'. He was buried with his father at Winchester.

Edward ('the Confessor'), b. c.1005, s. of Aethelred II and Emma of Normandy; acc. June 1042; m. Eadgyth, da. of earl Godwin, 23 Jan. 1045; no issue; d. 5 Jan. 1066; bur. Westminster abbey.

For much of his life the chance of Edward becoming king of England seemed remote. He was merely one of several claimants to a throne securely held by Cnut and his two sons, but the deaths in quick succession of Cnut (1035), Harold (1040), and Harthacnut (1042) brought Edward into the reckoning and he had powerful support from his mother's relatives in Normandy, who had given him shelter in the long years of exile. When Harthacnut succeeded his half-brother in 1040, Edward had been recalled and treated with honour. On Harthacnut's sudden death, Edward was chosen king without opposition and crowned at Winchester on 3 April 1043.

His reign was comparatively peaceful. The Viking raids which had made the reign of his father so miserable had diminished. The difficulties that arose stemmed largely from the role of the powerful Godwin family and the problem of the succession. Since he was nearly forty, marriage was a dynastic imperative, and in 1045 he chose Eadgyth, daughter of earl Godwin. Her brothers, Swegen and Harold, were for many years Edward's lieutenants, dealing with coastal raids and the incursions of the Welsh. However, since the marriage produced no children, it failed of its main purpose, and rumours soon circulated that it had not been consummated. Worse still, relations between the king and his new relatives deteriorated rapidly. Earl Swegen, Godwin's eldest son, was wild and turbulent, kidnapping the abbess of Leominster and murdering his cousin, earl Beorn: he was lucky to be forgiven. In 1051 some French followers of Eustace of Boulogne were involved in a fracas with the inhabitants of Dover; when the king instructed Godwin to punish the town, he refused. Summoned to a trial, he and his family went into exile, and the queen was sent to a nunnery. The Godwins returned in force in 1052 and, after a confrontation in London, Edward gave way and reinstated them. On Godwin's death in 1053, Harold was given his earldom.

A decision which had long-term consequences was to appoint Tostig, another of Godwin's sons, to the earldom of Northumbria. As years went by, the failure of the king and queen to have children pushed the succession question forward in significance. In 1056 the search concentrated on Edward, the surviving son of Edmund 'Ironside', a baby when his father had died back in 1016, but brought up at the Hungarian court; he could hardly be endorsed without inspection and he arrived in London the following year, only to die at once. Other candidates included Sweyn Estrithsson, king of Denmark, and a nephew of Cnut; the sons of Edward's sister Godgifu, who had married Drogo, count of Mantes; and William of Normandy, whose claims were not strong (being merely the great-nephew of Emma), but whose incentive to command both sides of the Channel was powerful. The event which brought about the climax was a revolt of the Northumbrians late in 1065 against what they termed Tostig's harsh rule. Though Edward's throne was not in danger, the revolt was formidable, and Tostig had to go. Harold did not support his brother, and Tostig took himself off to Scandinavia, swearing revenge. The king was badly shaken. When he died two months later, on 5 January 1066, naming Harold as his successor, the scene was set for the extraordinary events of that year.

Edward was buried at once in Westminster abbey, the great church he was rebuilding, but did not live to see completed. His reputation as a man of uncommon piety soon developed and, after the Conquest, he became a potent symbol of Old England, though his character is at odds with his reputation as a saintly, unworldly, and somewhat feeble man. He was well built, not particularly pious, with a passion for hunting. Though he showed some skill in balancing factions and avoiding confrontations, he had no great plans or projects. Nevertheless he gave his kingdom more than twenty years of peace and order after sixty years of turmoil and unheaval.

BARLOW, F., *Edward the Confessor* (1970).

Alfred the Atheling, second son of Aethelred II by his second wife Emma of Normandy, and younger brother of Edward 'the Confessor'. The two boys were brought up in Normandy. Alfred must have been about thirty when he travelled to England in 1036, possibly to contest the throne against Cnut's son, Harold I. He was captured by Godwin's men, sent to Ely, and blinded. The *Anglo-Saxon Chronicle* called him 'a blameless prince' and mourned his death: 'no more horrible deed was done in this land after the Danes came, and made peace with us here.'

Godwin was the greatest subject in eleventh-century England. The son of Wulfnoth, his ancestry is obscure but he married Gytha, daughter of a Danish nobleman and closely related to Cnut himself, *c*.1020. Godwin's rise was spectacular, since in 1018, as soon as Cnut was safely on the throne, he was made an earl. This suggests that he was one of the warriors upon whom Cnut relied in his struggle against Edmund 'Ironside' in 1016. On Cnut's death in 1035, Godwin initially supported the claims of Harthacnut, but was obliged to trim when Harold 'Harefoot' seized the throne. The accusation that he was responsible for the death of the atheling Alfred (Edward's younger brother) in 1036 haunted Godwin for the rest of his life, though he denied it. He served Harthacnut on his succession in 1040, and when he died in 1042 was a leading advocate for Edward as king; in 1045 his daughter, Eadgyth, married Edward. Godwin himself held the earldom of Wessex, his son Swegen that of Mercia, and Harold that of East Anglia, but by 1051 the Godwins had fallen into disfavour, partly because of Swegen's wild behaviour, partly because of their dislike of king Edward's Norman friends. Civil war was avoided but they withdrew into exile, only to return in force in 1052 and obtain reinstatement. In April 1053, while at table with the king, Godwin had a stroke, and died on the 14th. His son Tostig died at Stamford Bridge in September 1066, his sons Harold, Gyrth, and Leowine on the field of battle at Hastings the following month.

Edward the Atheling had only a walk-on part in the complicated succession question of the eleventh century. He was a son of Edmund 'Ironside', taken out of the country as a baby when his father died in 1016, and brought up at the Hungarian court. He married Agatha, a relative of the emperor Henry II. In 1056, when king Edward's marriage was still childless, Edward was sent for on approval, but died soon after reaching London the following year. His young son, Edgar, then became a possible candidate for the succession, was elected on Harold's death at Hastings, but swept aside by William of Normandy. Edward's daughter Margaret married Malcolm III of Scotland as his second wife.

Harold II, b. c.1022, 2nd s. of earl Godwin and Gytha; acc. 6 Jan. 1066; m. Ealdgyth, da. of earl Aelfgar, 1066; issue: Harold; also (illeg.) 4 s. 2 das. by Eadgyth Swanneshals ('Swanneck'); d. 14 Oct. 1066; bur. Waltham abbey.

Though Harold was king for less than a year, he is one of the best-known monarchs. Before 1066 his reputation was as a trusted supporter of Edward 'the Confessor', prominent in council, resolute in battle, tall and strong. It is often said that he had no royal blood, but he was cousin to Sweyn Estrithsson, king of Denmark, and the nephew of Cnut. The marriage of his sister Eadgyth to king Edward in 1045 strengthened his position and he was made earl of East Anglia. The escapades of his elder brother Swegen, which included the murder in 1047 of his cousin Beorn, and the Godwins' dislike of the king's Norman friends led to a breach in 1051, which forced the family into exile. Harold fled to Dublin, returned to harry the coast of Somerset, and helped to force Edward in 1052 to reinstate them. On the death of his father the following year, he succeeded as earl of Wessex. Two years later he was sent to Wales to deal with Gruffydd ap Llywelyn, who had sacked Hereford; in 1062–3, a further campaign ended when Gruffydd was killed by his own men. Harold then married Gruffydd's widow, the daughter of the earl of Mercia and an heiress.

Meanwhile, the question of the succession had come to the fore, since the royal marriage had produced no children. William of Normandy later insisted that, on a visit in 1065, Harold had sworn an oath to support his claim to the throne. The episode has been much discussed. It is far from obvious why Harold should have committed himself, unless he was acting under duress, or what he had to gain by doing so. If Edward sent him, it is odd that he should have chosen such an envoy, and that within a few months he should have changed his mind and left the crown to Harold on his deathbed. The incident which started the train of events leading to Harold's death at Hastings was a revolt, late in 1065, by the Northumbrians against the rule of their earl, Tostig, Harold's younger brother. Harold could not, or would not, protect him and, deprived of his earldom, Tostig stormed off into banishment, determined on reinstatement and revenge. Edward lasted only a few weeks after the Northumbrian revolt, dying in January 1066 and naming Harold as his successor. He was crowned the following day in the new Westminster abbey. It was clear that he would have to fight to retain his throne. The first move came from Tostig who, with the help of William of Normandy, crossed to the Isle of Wight and began harrying the coastal towns. Harold chased him off to Lindsey, where Edwin and Morcar, the new king's brothers-in-law, chased him off to Scotland. There Tostig joined forces with an enormous expedition led by Harald Hardrada, king of Norway, to whom he paid homage. Landing in the Humber estuary, they defeated Edwin and Morcar at Fulford but, five days later, were in turn defeated and killed by Harold at Stamford Bridge. While Harold was in York regrouping, news came that William had landed at Pevensey.

Harold's journey south was a remarkable feat, though its wisdom may be questioned. He and his housecarls reached London, a distance of more than two hundred miles, in four days. He was off again within a week to confront William just outside Hastings. There, on 14 October, 'by the hoar apple-tree', the issue was decided. Harold and his two brothers, Gyrth and Leowine, were killed, and his army scattered. Legend relates that Harold's mangled body was recovered by Eadgyth 'Swan-neck', his mistress, and taken for burial to Waltham abbey, the college of secular canons which he had endowed and which had been dedicated, in the presence of king Edward, in 1060.

Harold's decision not to support Tostig has been much criticized, and the split in the Godwin family did it no good. Yet the consequences may be exaggerated. The force which Tostig brought to join Harald Hardrada was small, and the Norwegian king's vast fleet would, by itself, have been a major threat. The decision to give battle so quickly may however have been an error. Though Harold probably had a larger army than William, many of his housecarls would have been exhausted; the battle itself was so closely run that a few more reinforcements, certainly available, could have made all the difference. It may be that Harold's pride, on this occasion, overcame his military judgement.

LOYN, H. R., *Harold, Son of Godwin* (1966).

Ireland

Seventh-century Ireland was divided into about 150 small kingdoms called tuatha, some becoming loosely aggregated into larger tribal units. The main tribe in the north-west was the Northern Uí Néill, in the north-east the Dál Riada; central Ulster was dominated by the Airgialla, Meath by the Southern Uí Néill, the west by the Connachta. For many centuries, the chief Irish family were the Uí Néill (named after Niall of the Nine Hostages), whose spread and attacks destroyed much of the tribal structure; their claim to the high-kingship of Ireland was not seriously challenged until the tenth century, by Brian Bóruma. Viking invaders and internecine wars were followed by Anglo-Norman incursions, and by 1171 Henry II of England had secured the submission of many of the Irish kings.

Early Ireland

Niall of the Nine Hostages, s. of Eochaid Mugmedon and Cairenna; Irish high-king c.445–53; d. c.453.

Prominent in Irish tradition, but lacking supporting documentary evidence, the semi-legendary Niall became high-king of Ireland and established a dynasty of rulers whose fame has made him one of the best-known Irish kings. He and his sons finally broke up the Fifth (Province) of Ulster, and he has been credited with raids on Britain and possibly Gaul. The most plausible explanation of Niall's epithet 'Noígiallach' is derived from the hostages sent by the nine tuatha which originally made up the Airgiallan confederation (vassal tribes of the Uí Néill), a recognized form of submission. The sagas ascribe his slaying to Eochu, a Leinster prince, and scholars have argued persuasively that this was mid-century. The O'Neills take their name from him.

Mael Sechnaill II, b. 949, s. of Domnaill of Mide and Donnflaith; high-king of Ireland 980–1002, 1014–22; d. Cro-inis, 2 Sept. 1022.

Leader of the Clann Cholmáin branch of the southern Uí Néill by 975/6, Mael Sechnaill succeeded Domnall (of the northern Uí Néill) as high-king in 980, under the alternating system of succession. In a reign dominated by battles against the Danes, and attempts to crush rivals, his struggles against the Munster king Brian Bóruma (Boru) were briefly halted at Clonfert (997), where each recognized the other's supremacy in their respective halves of the country. Although jointly defeating the Danes at Glenn Máma (999), conflict resumed and Mael Sechnaill was forced to submit to Brian in 1002. After Brian's death at the battle of Clontarf (1014), Mael Sechnaill resumed the high-kingship until his own death, when the alternating system of succession ended and a long interregnum followed.

Brian Bóruma (Brian Boru), b. 926, s. of Cennétig mac Lorcain; king of Munster 976–1014, high-king of Ireland 1002–14; d. Clontarf, 23 Apr. 1014; bur. Armagh.

Brian became chief of the Dál Cais (north Munster) on the death of his brother, and rose rapidly to become king of all Munster, attacking both rivals and Vikings. Progress was checked by the high-king Mael Sechnaill, who also wished to control Leinster, and a truce was declared in 997; this lasted only until 1002, when Mael Sechnaill was forced to submit. Politically astute and a skilled military strategist, Brian continued to enforce his authority over much of the country (acknowledged as *imperator Scotorum*, 1005) but was slain in the victory over the rebellious Leinstermen and their Norse allies at the battle of Clontarf. He had demonstrated that the high-kingship was open to the most powerful claimant rather than an hereditary right of the Uí Néill, and has become the best known of all Irish kings. The O'Briens take their name from him.

Dermot MacMurrough, b. c.1110, s. of Enna; king of Leinster 1126–66; d. Ferns, 1 May 1171.

Said to have succeeded his father while in his teens, and described by Gerald of Wales as 'of giant stature', noisy, and violent, Dermot is traditionally supposed to have been driven into exile in 1166 in consequence of abducting Devorgilla, wife of the king of Breífne. This more likely resulted from a failed bid for the high-kingship, won by Connacht's king, Rory O'Connor. Dermot successfully sought military aid from Henry II, in order to recover Leinster, and raised forces in South Wales; their principal leader was Richard de Clare, earl of Pembroke ('Strongbow'), to whom Dermot promised his daughter Aífe, and who later succeeded as king of Leinster after Dermot's death from 'an insufferable and unknown disease'. The nickname 'Diarmit na nGall' ('Dermot of the Foreigners') may refer to his association with the Anglo-Normans, or to his overlordship of the Hiberno-Norse kingdom of Dublin, recaptured in 1170. Despite his patronage of ecclesiastical reform, he is more usually blamed as the instigator of English rule in Ireland.

Rory O'Connor, b. c.1116, s. of Turlough O'Connor and Tailtiu O'Melaghlin; king of Connacht 1156–83, high-king of Ireland 1166–83; d. Cong, 2 Dec. 1198; bur. Clonmacnoise.

Ruaidhri Ua Conchobhair assumed the kingship of Connacht on his father's death in 1156, and through force of arms was inaugurated as the high-king at Dublin in 1166. His prompt banishment of the Leinster king Dermot McMurrough resulted in an Anglo-Norman invasion, to which he was initially conciliatory but then made two unsuccessful attempts to dislodge its forces from Dublin. He did not submit to Henry II in 1171, but concluded a 'treaty' at Windsor (1175), in which he was confirmed as king of Connacht and granted overlordship of unoccupied north and west Ireland, while acknowledging Henry as his liege-lord. This proved short-lived as Rory was unable to maintain effective control and Henry unable to prevent Anglo-Norman settlers from expanding beyond his claimed areas. Opposed by two of his sons, Rory was ousted in 1183, and entered the abbey of Cong.

Cathal O'Connor, b. c.1152, s. of Turlough O'Connor and Dearbhforgnill; king of Connacht 1202–24; d. Bringheol, 27 May 1224; bur. Knockmoy.

Nicknamed 'Crobderg' ('the red-handed', possibly a birthmark), Cathal unsuccessfully challenged for the kingship of Connacht before and after his half-brother Rory's death in 1198, and was driven into Ulster; he finally slew Cathal Carrach O'Connor near Boyle monastery (1202), and was inaugurated king of Connacht. He seems to have acknowledged the supremacy of John, attending him in 1210 during the English king's second expedition to Ireland, which enhanced royal control over the Anglo-Norman lords. A surviving letter from 1224 begs a charter from Henry III, as he had had from John, for possession of Connacht, which he hoped to pass on to his son Aed. Cathal founded abbeys at Knockmoy, Athlone, and Ballinter.

Picts and Early Scots

The Picts were probably the earliest nation to emerge from the unification of a number of tribal societies in northern Britain, sometime during the second or third centuries AD when southern Britain was subject to Rome. Centered on the eastern side of the country above the Forth–Clyde line, so separated from the Dalriadan Scots along the western coastal strip by the 'Spine of Britain' (North West Highlands and Grampians), Pictland was further divided into northern and southern parts by 'The Mounth' (an eastward arm of the 'Spine'). The *Pictish Chronicle* named Cruithne (with a pedigree back to Noah) as the founding father: division of the land between his seven sons may be a representation of tribal coalescence into one extended group. Since the *Cruithni* (Irish form of the Latin *Priteni* before this was modified to *Brittoni*) were indigenous, stories that the Picts were incomers from Scythia or Thrace are fanciful. It is thought that one of the tribal kings was chosen as overlord from a pool of candidates eligible through the

Kingdoms of the Picts and Early Scots

female royal line, a system encouraging political stability since no tribe was unduly favoured or threatened.

Cultural convergence between the Picts and the proto-Scots of Argyll was hindered by the latter's relative geographical isolation in the west and their ease of contact across the Irish Sea. A gradual settlement of *Scotti* from northern Ireland now seems more likely than an invasion, and by *c*.500 Dalriadan Scots and Picts were two distinct nations, with distinct languages. For much of the seventh century, the neighbouring kingdom of Northumbria was all-powerful, but the battle of Nechtansmere (near Forfar) in 685 gave the Picts, Dalriadan Scots, and Strathclyde Britons freedom from English overlordship.

Fergus, s. of Erc; king of Dalriada *c*.495–501; d. 501.

In the mid-490s Fergus and his brothers are said to have migrated from the Dalriada homeland in Ulster to Kintyre and mid-Argyll, possibly from a desire for more land. The Dalriadans had already been converted to Christianity by St Patrick, and Fergus Mor ('the Great') is accepted as the first historical king of Dalriada and dynastic founder.

Aedan mac Gabhráin, king of Dalriada 574–608; d. 17 Apr. 608.

Great-grandson of Fergus Mor, so of Irish lineage, Aedan was elected after a disputed succession and anointed at his inauguration by Columba, his spiritual adviser. Permitted to collect tribute from his Ulster territories by the Irish high-king (Convention of Drumceat, Co. Derry, 575), Aedan established a powerful kingdom, campaigning in Orkney (580) and the Isle of Man (582), but victory over the Pictish tribe of the Miathi (590) was empty, with two sons lost. His intrusion into southern Pictland led to conflict with the Bernician Angles, two sons being assassinated by the Northumbrians (598). In 603 Aedan led a great army, with some Irish allies, against Aethelfrith of Northumbria, but was heavily defeated at Degsastan (possibly Dawston Rigg, in Liddesdale), and he may have abdicated or been deposed after this, despite surviving several more years. One queen may have been from a British royal house, another Pictish.

Talorgan, s. of Eanfrith; king of Picts 653–7; d. 657.

When Aethelfrith, king of Bernicia, was slain *c*.616, his son Eanfrith was forced into exile amongst the Picts, one of whose princesses he is presumed to have married. Talorgan may thus have claimed the Pictish kingdom through his mother, but it is also likely that he acknowledged the overlordship of his uncle Oswiu of Northumbria, said by Bede to have subdued 'the greater part of the Pictish race'. Talorgan gained victory over the Dalriads at Srath Ethairt (654) when he slew their king Dunchad, and was succeeded by Gartnait son of Donnel, then his brother Drust, who were also subordinate to Oswiu.

Oengus I (Angus), s. of Fergus; king of Picts 729–61, king of Dalriada 736–50; d. 761.

The abdication of Nechtan in 724 to retire into the Church was followed by a vicious intertribal contest for overlordship, eventually won in 729 by Oengus, who proved to be one of the most powerful Pictish kings. After storming Dunadd, one of the chief fortresses of the Scots of Dalriada, he appears to have ruled as their overlord from 736–50. Challengers to his authority risked death by ritual drowning, as typified by Talorgan son of Drostan in 739. Oengus fought the Angles in Northumbria, but his power began to ebb from 750, when his army was heavily defeated by the Strathclyde Britons at Moctauc (Mugdock, north of Glasgow); it is probable that Dalriada was freed from Pictish domination by Aed Find as a result of this. Oengus continued to rule over Pictland until his death, and was succeeded by his brother Bude.

Constantine, s. of Fergus; king of Picts 789–820, king of Dalriada 811–20; d. 820.

King of the northern Picts by 782, Constantine defeated his rival Conall mac Taidg in battle in 789 to rule all Pictland, and from 811 added the Dalriada kingship (which had been held by his father 778–81). His power base at Forteviot in Fortriu or Fortren (modern Perthshire) reflected the Scottish migration eastwards at a time of intense Norse raiding on the Dalriada homeland of Argyll. He also founded or revitalized the church at Dunkeld between 811 and 820, when Iona's leaders had retreated to Ireland. Described as 'king of Fortren' at his death in 820, and one of three kings of the Cenél Gabhráin to hold the kingships of both Picts and Scots prior to Kenneth mac Alpin, Constantine was succeeded in both by his brother Oengus (II).

Alba and Early Scotland

From the early ninth century, both Picts and Scots began to recognize the same kings as their rightful rulers rather than conquerors. Recorded initially as kings of Fortren, then of the Picts, they became known at the beginning of the tenth century as kings of Alba (sometimes, 'Pictavia') as a result of the Irish annalists forsaking Latin for vernacular Gaelic. Western Gaelic, then Northumbrian English, began to diffuse into Pictish dialect and culture, to its eventual demise. The apparent disappearance of the Picts was therefore an illusion produced by linguistic change. The best-known remnants of Pictish culture are their symbol stones, but despite many suggested interpretations their meaning is still obscure. During the twelfth century Scottish writers increasingly preferred 'Scotia', which led to confusion both then and later. The numbering of Scottish kings begins with Kenneth mac Alpin, and his male descendants continued to rule the kingdom for almost two centuries.

Kenneth I mac Alpin, king of Dalriada c.840–58, king of Picts c.842–58; d. Forteviot, 13 Feb. 858; bur. Iona.

Of western Gaelic origins and possibly great-grandson of Aed Find (d. 778), Kenneth became king of Dalriada before extending his authority eastwards into Pictland. The Picts had been weakened by Viking invasion, and although circumstances remain confused, Kenneth assumed their kingship, more probably through a strong matrilinear claim than conquest. He might be regarded as having dual nationality, and thus eminently suited to rule both nations. By mid-century his control extended over a kingdom greater than Constantine's, recognizable as the ancestor of medieval Scotland, and his transfer of some of Columba's relics from Iona made Dunkeld the new ecclesiastical centre. Kenneth raided Lothian (northern Northumbria) repeatedly, but was himself assailed by the Danes and Strathclyde Britons. He died of a tumour at Forteviot (near Perth) and was succeeded by his brother Donald.

Donald I, s. of Alpin; king of Scots and Picts 858–62; d. 862; bur. Iona(?).

Donald, 'wanton son of a foreign wife', may have had a Norse mother, suggesting one of the earliest known alliances between the Vikings and

HOUSE OF ALPIN

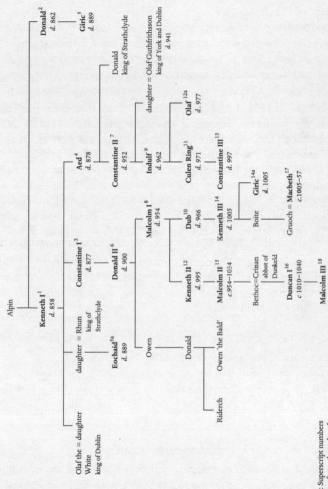

Note: Superscript numbers refer to the order of succession.

a native British dynasty. His brother Kenneth mac Alpin had already assumed kingship over the Picts, and Donald imposed the laws of an earlier Dalriada king, Aed Find (d. 778), upon both Picts and Scots; this proclamation at Forteviot brought secular law as well as church organization under Scottish control. His death, possibly by assassination, is given variously at Raith-inber-amon, Belachoir, or Scone, and he was succeeded by his nephew Constantine I.

Constantine I, s. of Kenneth mac Alpin; king of Scots 862–77; d. 877; bur. Iona(?).

For much of his reign Constantine faced repeated Viking attacks, despite the possibility that his sister may have married Olaf the White of Dublin. According to the Irish annals, Olaf laid waste to Pictavia in 866, though the 'Brechin Chronicle' has Constantine triumphant in another attack that year. After besieging and sacking Dumbarton in 871, Olaf and Ivar took large numbers of Britons, Albans, and Saxons back to Dublin as slaves; the Strathclyde king, Artgal, survived Dumbarton, but was assassinated the following year, apparently on the advice (*consilio*) of Constantine. The Danes inflicted a heavy defeat at Dollar (east of Stirling) in 875, and Constantine died at their hands at 'Inverdufata' (unidentified), possibly by remnants of Halfdan's army returning to Dublin from York via lowland Scotland (877). The anti-Strathclyde faction led by Kenneth I's sons returned to power through Constantine's son, Donald II, in 889. Thenceforth the Scottish kingship was shared by descendants of Constantine and his brother Aed in an alternating system of succession, and after 997 by new rival segments of Constantine's line alone.

Aed, s. of Kenneth mac Alpin; king of Scots 877–8; d. Strathallan, 878; bur. Iona(?).

Aed succeeded his brother Constantine I after his death in 877, but his reign was brief owing to a family feud in which his first cousin Giric (son of Kenneth's brother Donald I) staked a rival claim to the Scottish kingship. A battle at Strathallan (north of Stirling) left Aed mortally wounded.

Giric, s. of Donald I; king of Scots 878–89; d. 889; bur. Iona(?).

A nephew of Kenneth mac Alpin, Giric objected to the Scottish kingship continuing solely in the hands of Kenneth's sons and their descendants, and gained power after slaying his first cousin, Aed (878). He was supported by Eochaid, whose guardian he may have been, and who was a grandson of Kenneth I through his mother. They appear to have ruled jointly until their expulsion in 889 by Donald II (another grandson of Kenneth). After this, Giric's segment of Alpin's dynasty was excluded from the Scottish succession. At a time of struggle for the control of Bernicia, Giric has been credited with successful English campaigns. It was also claimed that he freed the Scottish church from Pictish servitude, which led to his later mythical inflation as 'Gregory the Great'.

Eochaid, s. of Rhun; king of Scots(?) 878–89.

As son of the last known native British king of Strathclyde, Eochaid may have supported his cousin Giric's struggle for the Scottish throne in order to maintain Strathclyde as a separate kingdom. Although a grandson of Kenneth mac Alpin through his mother, his paternal grandfather Artgal had been slain on the advice of one of Kenneth's sons (Constantine I), another cause for hostility against them and their descendants. After Aed's death (878), Eochaid and Giric are said to have ruled jointly until their expulsion by Donald II in 889, thereby ending the native British dynasty in Strathclyde, which became a Scottish sub-kingdom. It is possible that Eochaid was amongst the Strathclyde exiles who then settled in Gwynedd (north Wales).

Donald II, s. of Constantine I; king of Scots 889–900; d. 900; bur. Iona(?).

With the expulsion in 889 of Giric and the Briton Eochaid who appear to have ruled jointly for eleven or twelve years, and the annexation of Strathclyde by Donald II, the native British dynasty there ended. The intensity of Viking attacks lessened during Donald's reign, and he had some success against them. One account claims that he was slain by the Danes at Dunnottar (south of Aberdeen), another that he died at Forres from infirmity. In the alternating system of succession, he was followed by Constantine II, who was himself succeeded by Donald's son Malcolm I.

Constantine II, s. of Aed; king of Scots 900–43; d. St Andrews, 952; bur. St Andrews.

Constantine encouraged the Bernicians against the Danish Ragnall I of York (battles of Corbridge, 914, 918), but came to terms with the Danes and subsequently supported them against the rising power of the West

Saxons. Although he made peace with Wessex, this was broken (933) when he renewed his alliance with Olaf Guthfrithsson, Norse king of Dublin and claimant to York, to whom he gave his daughter in marriage. Athelstan then invaded as far as Dunnottar, Kincardineshire, and later inflicted crushing defeat on Olaf and Constantine at Brunanburh (possibly Aldborough) in 937, when Constantine's son is said to have been killed. Olaf eventually gained York (939), and Constantine's influence in northern England increased. He had earlier pledged to uphold the rights of the Scottish church (906), and in 943 abdicated after a long reign to retire as a monk at St Andrews, seat of the kingdom's chief bishop.

Malcolm I, s. of Donald II; king of Scots 943–54; d. Fetteresso, 954; bur. Iona(?).

Malcolm succeeded to the Scottish kingship when his long-reigning cousin Constantine II retired to St Andrews in 943. The struggles between the West Saxons and Scots for overlordship of Bernicia, and Wessex and Dublin for control of Scandinavian York, dominated his reign. Edmund of Wessex acknowledged Malcolm's overlordship of Strathclyde–Cumbria in return for defending northern England from back-door Viking attack (945), and Malcolm's plunder of the Bernicians as far south as the Tees in 949 was connected with Olaf Sihtricsson's attempt to regain York from Erik Bloodaxe. He was careful not to upset the alternating system of succession in Scotland, so appointed Constantine II's son Indulf as sub-king of Strathclyde and tanist (heir), who thus became his successor. Malcolm was slain by the men of Moray at Fetteresso (south of Aberdeen).

Indulf, s. of Constantine II; king of Scots 954–62; d. Invercullen, 962; bur. Iona(?).

Given a Scandinavian name (Old Norse *Hildulfr*), as he himself gave his sons Olaf and Culen, Indulf was appointed sub-king of Strathclyde (c.945) by Malcolm I, following the alternating system of succession that prevailed for two centuries. As tanist (heir), Indulf then assumed the Scottish kingship in 954, after which Malcolm's son Dub ruled Strathclyde. During Indulf's reign, temporary Bernician weakness enabled the Scots to occupy Edinburgh, although their annexation and rule in Lothian was not formally recognized until later. Scandinavian challenges for the mastery of Moray in the north led to his death in battle at Invercullen (north-west of Aberdeen) in 962.

Dub (Duff), s. of Malcolm I; king of Scots 962–6; d. Forres, 966; bur. Iona(?).

Appointed sub-king of Strathclyde by Indulf according to the alternating system of succession, Dub moved up to the Scottish kingship in 962 after Indulf was slain. The smooth running of this system was undermined towards the end of his reign by a third segment attempting to found a new dynasty in Strathclyde. Dub's rival and heir Culen (son of Indulf) had not been granted that sub-kingship as expected, and may have lacked patience to wait. Culen's first challenge at Duncrub, Perthshire, was unsuccessful (965), but the Scottish king was driven north where he was slain by Moray men at Forres; this is alleged to have coincided with an eclipse of the sun on 20 July.

Culen, s. of Indulf; king of Scots 966–71; d. Lothian, 971.

Culen, who bore a Scandinavian name and byname Ring (Old Norse *Hringr* = ring-giver), should have been heir to the Scottish king Dub under the alternating system of succession, but he was not given the sub-kingship of Strathclyde in the usual pattern. This may have underlain his challenge to Dub, initially unsuccessfully at Duncrub (965), but later driving him into Moray to be slain at Forres (966). Culen himself was subsequently slain by Riderch, son of Donald of Strathclyde, who had almost certainly excluded him from that sub-kingship; it is alleged that he had carried off Riderch's daughter. On Culen's death, the Scottish kingship swung back to the house of Constantine I in Kenneth II, who maintained the feud by slaying Culen's brother Olaf (977).

Kenneth II, s. of Malcolm I; king of Scots 971–95; d. Fettercairn, 995; bur. Iona(?).

Brother of Dub (d. 966), Kenneth succeeded Culen Ring but faced rivalry from Culen's brother Olaf, whom he slew in 977. He tried to engineer new succession laws to replace the old alternating system, to exclude rival segments from the kingship in order to secure it for his son Malcolm (II), but this was opposed by Culen's son (the future Constantine III) and a branch of his own house that descended from his brother Dub. At the same time, rivals needed to be kept out of Strathclyde, whose sub-kingship was usually granted to the tanist (heir) to the Scottish throne. Kenneth's relationships with the new dynasty of sub-kings there were generally friendly, and he plundered England as far as Stainmore (972) as Strathclyde rule was pushed southwards. He also consolidated the Scottish hold over Lothian, his rule being recognized by Edgar of England c.975. Kenneth was assassinated at Fettercairn (south of Aberdeen) by Fenella, daughter of the mormaer of Angus, in revenge for killing her only son.

Constantine III, s. of Culen Ring; king of Scots 995–7; d. 997; bur. Iona(?).

As Kenneth II had slain both his father and uncle (Olaf) in the power struggles for the Scottish kingship, Constantine's alleged opposition to Kenneth's plans to change the succession laws to favour his own line is not surprising. Constantine did succeed to the Scottish kingship on Kenneth's assassination, according to the prevailing alternating system, but proved to be the last of the descendants of Aed to do so. He was slain by Kenneth III (son of Dub, so a descendant of the rival line from Constantine I) at 'Rathinveramon' (unidentified, but probably near Scone). He was known to medieval historians as 'the Bald'.

Kenneth III, s. of Dub; king of Scots 997–1005; d. Monzievaird, 1005; bur. Iona(?).

Having slain Constantine III (997), his line's final victory over Aed's descendants, it remains unclear whether it was Kenneth who succeeded to the kingship, or his son Giric, or whether they ruled jointly. Both have been given an eight-year reign before being killed at Monzievaird (west of Perth) by Kenneth's first cousin, Malcolm II, who thereby realized his father's ambition of triumphing over the house of Dub; this, however, contributed to the feud which resulted in the killing in 1040 of Duncan I (Malcolm's grandson) by Macbeth who had married Kenneth III's granddaughter, Gruoch.

Malcolm II, b. c.954, s. of Kenneth II and a Leinster princess; king of Scots 1005–34; issue: Bethoc, Muldred, Donada; d. Glamis, 25 Nov. 1034; bur. Iona(?).

Having defended Cumbria from invasion by Aethelred II in 1000, Malcolm's slaying of his predecessor Kenneth III and son Giric (1005) ended the alternating system of succession and allowed a more centralized, heritable form of kingship to develop. Raids into Northumbria were repulsed at Durham by Uhtred of Bamburgh (1006), but the later victory (1018) at Carham (west of Berwick) gave him control of Lothian down to the Tweed; the death of his ally Owen of Strathclyde added this sub-kingdom to his jurisdiction. Cnut's invasion of Scotland in 1031–2 led to Bernicia being secured for England, and broadly settled the eastern end of the Scottish border. As Malcolm had no known male heir, the succession struggle resurfaced, and he slew another cousin in 1033 to ensure that his daughter Bethoc's son Duncan (I) would succeed; another daughter's marriage to Sigurd of Orkney may have been a prudent alliance in his house's feud against Moray. The last male descendant of Kenneth I to hold the kingship, and described by Irish annalists as 'the honour of all the west of Europe', Malcolm was clearly a powerful ruler.

Gwynedd

Gwynedd was one of the most prominent of the Welsh kingdoms, based upon Anglesey and Snowdonia, but with ambitions to expand. Founded in the immediate post-Roman period, it prospered in the eleventh and twelfth centuries, taking advantage of divisions in England. It was subdued by the campaigns of Edward I in 1277 and 1282–3 and incorporated into the new principality under English control. The rulers of Welsh kingdoms were usually termed 'brenin' (king) until the twelfth century. Subsequently they were more commonly called 'arglwyddi' (lords), except in Gwynedd, where they called themselves 'tywysog' (prince).

Cunedda is credited with founding the kingdom of Gwynedd, but is a very shadowy figure. According to tradition, he was a leader of the Votadini in southern Scotland who, in the early fifth century, led his people into north Wales, driving out the Irish with great slaughter. It has been suggested that the move might have been arranged by Stilicho, who was reorganizing the defences of Roman Britain c.395. The division of the newly acquired lands between Cunedda's eight sons resembles the legend of the seven sons of Cruithne and the origin of the Picts, but may have some historical foundation. In the twelfth century, Geoffrey of Monmouth offered a much more elaborate version, connecting Cunedda with Lear, and relating that he rebelled against his aunt, Cordelia, seized the kingship of the whole island, 'and ruled it in great glory for thirty-three years'.

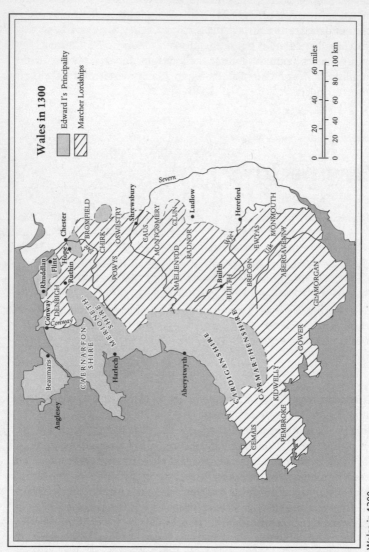

Wales in 1300

Maelgwyn Gwynedd was said by *Annales Cambriae* to have been a great-grandson of Cunedda, and to have died of plague *c*.547. He was known as Maelgwyn Hir ('the Tall'). Gildas, writing as a contemporary, launched a bitter and sustained attack upon him as Maglocunus: 'first in evil... mightier than many both in power and malice'. He accused Maelgwyn of seizing the throne by murdering his uncle, cohabiting with his nephew's wife, and retiring to a monastery but recanting to return to his 'disgusting vomit'. 'I call it scandalous', Gildas concluded, rather feebly.

Cadfan, a descendant of Maelgwyn, was the son of Iago ap Beli, reported in the *Annales Cambriae* to have died 613. Geoffrey of Monmouth offered an elaborate account that Cadfan was chosen to lead the Welsh when they were attacked by Aethelfrith of Bernicia, and that he gave shelter to Edwin, who gained the Northumbrian throne from Aethelfrith in 616. Cadfan died in 625.

Cadwallon, son of Cadfan, succeeded *c*.625. Geoffrey of Monmouth related that he was brought up with Edwin of Northumbria, then a child refugee, but after Edwin had recovered his kingdom, they fell out. In 631 Edwin headed an invasion of north Wales, which captured Anglesey and drove Cadwallon over to Ireland. He returned in 633 and, with the aid of Penda of Mercia, overran Northumbria and killed Edwin at Heathfield; he followed this by slaying both Osric of Deira and Eanfrith of Bernicia. In 634 he was himself killed at Heavenfield, near Hexham, by Oswald of Northumbria. To the Welsh, the death of Cadwallon wrecked any lingering hope of driving the Saxons into the sea; to Bede and the Saxons, he was 'the abominable leader of the Britons'.

Cadafael ap Cynfedw seems to have taken the throne of Gwynedd on the death of Cadwallon in 634, possibly because Cadwallon's son may have been young. In 655 he campaigned with Penda of Mercia against Oswiu of Northumbria. According to the *Northern History*, quoted by Nennius, he departed the night before the battle at the Winwaed in which Penda was killed. He was subsequently known as Cadafael Cadomedd ('the Battle-dodger').

Cadwaladr, son of Cadwallon, took the throne after the disastrous battle of the Winwaed in 655. His reign was brief and comparatively uneventful, though he was reported in 658 to have been defeated by the

West Saxons at Pinhoe, near Exeter. It is not clear what he was doing there. He died of plague in 664, and became a heroic figure in Welsh legend; several churches are dedicated to him.

Rhodri Molwynog. After the death of Cadwaladr in 664, the throne of Gwynedd is said to have been taken by his son Idwal and then by Idwal's son, Rhodri, who died in 754. The genealogical evidence is not good and the information very sketchy.

Hywel ap Rhodri Molwynog. The death of Rhodri is given as 754. If Hywel succeeded at once, it would give him, dying in 825, a reign of seventy-one years, which seems unlikely. In 813 the *Annales Cambriae* reports him fighting with a brother, Cynan, for control of Anglesey. Cynan gained possession in 816 but died later the same year. Cynan's daughter, Ethyllt, was the mother of Merfyn Frych and founded a new line of Gwynedd kings.

Merfyn Frych ('the Freckled'), succeeded Hywel in Anglesey in 825 and later extended his rule to the mainland. He was said to be the son of Gwriad and Ethyllt, daughter of Cynan ap Rhodri, and a descendant of Llywarch Hen, a legendary hero. He married Nest, daughter of Cadell ap Brochwel of Powys, and died in 844.

Rhodri Mawr ('the Great'), succeeded his father Merfyn Frych in Gwynedd in 844 and acquired Powys in 855 through his mother, Nest. When, in 872, he added Seisyllwg through his marriage to Angharad, daughter of Meurig ap Dyfnwallon of Ceredigion, he had brought together three of the largest Welsh kingdoms. Yet he faced severe difficulties. Viking raids on Wales increased: in 856 Rhodri defeated a Danish force under Gorm, but in 877 was forced into exile in Ireland by the Vikings. When he returned the following year, he was killed in battle with the Mercians. His territories were divided up among his sons but he retained an important place in folk memory.

Anarawd, son of Rhodri Mawr, succeeded his father in Anglesey in 878. In 881 he won a victory over Aethelred II of Mercia on the river Conwy, but, under pressure from Viking raids, turned to Alfred of Wessex for help, acknowledging his overlordship. In 895 he was reported to have had English aid in ravaging Ceredigion, probably held by his brother, Cadell. He died in 916.

Idwal Foel ('the Bald'), son of Anarawd, succeeded his father in 916. He appears to have been restless under the overlordship of Athelstan, and when Edmund succeeded in 939, Idwal rebelled. In 942 he and his brother Elisedd were killed, and control of Gwynedd passed to Hywel Dda of Seisyllwg.

Iago ab Idwal lost control of Gwynedd to Hywel Dda in 942 on the death of his father. He regained it on Hywel's death in 950, but was engaged in warfare with his brother Ieuaf until 969. Ieuaf is reported by the *Brut* to have been captured, blinded, and hanged. Four years later, Iago was one of the princes who did homage to Edgar on the Dee at Chester. However, in 979 he was dispossessed by Ieuaf's son, Hywel.

Hywel ab Ieuaf, nephew of Iago ab Idwal, seized the throne in 979. In 983 he was reported, in alliance with Aelfhere (ealdorman of Mercia), to have attacked Deheubarth, but to have been beaten off. His understanding with the English gained for him the nickname 'Ddrwg' ('the Bad'), but after six years he is said to have been killed by Saxon treachery.

Cadwallon ab Ieuaf succeeded his brother Hywel in 985. However, the following year he was killed in battle against Maredudd, prince of Deheubarth, who ruled Gwynedd until his death in 999.

Cynan ap Hywel recovered the throne when Maredudd of Deheubarth died in 999. He ruled until 1005, when his branch was once more dispossessed by a prince of Deheubarth, Llywelyn ap Seisyll, a descendant of Idwal Foel's brother, Elisedd.

Iago ab Idwal was a great-grandson of Idwal Foel and represented the older dynasty of Gwynedd. He acceded on the death of Llywelyn ap Seisyll in 1023, but was murdered in 1039 by Llywelyn's son, Gruffydd, who ruled Gwynedd until 1063. The *Brut* reports that Gruffydd 'overcame the Saxons in a multitude of battles' but was at length killed by his own men. From 1063 until 1075 Gwynedd was ruled by his half-brother, Bleddyn ap Cynfyn, killed by Rhys ab Owain, and from 1075 to 1081 by Bleddyn's cousin, Trahearn ap Caradoc.

Gruffydd ap Cynan, b. c.1055, s. of Cynan and Ragnhildr; acc. 1081; m. Angharad, da. of Owain ab Edwin; issue: Owain, Cadwaladr, Cadwallon, Susanna, Gwenllian, Marared, Rannillt, Annest; d. 1137; bur. Bangor.

Gruffydd ap Cynan began restoring the power of Gwynedd after decades of strife and disputed succession. On his father's side, he was the great-great-great grandson of Idwal Foel: his mother was Ragnhildr, granddaughter of Sihtric of the Silken Beard, king of Dublin (d. 1042). In the 1070s his campaign against Trahearn and Caradoc to recapture Gwynedd had only temporary success, but in 1081, in alliance with Rhys ap Tewdr of Deheubarth, Gruffydd killed them at Mynydd Carn. By this time, Norman pressure on Wales was developing. Gruffydd was captured by the Normans and kept in prison for some years. In 1094 he was fighting the Normans once more and in 1098 was compelled to take refuge in Ireland. He came to terms and was reinstated. Despite clashes with Henry I in 1114, he extended his kingdom and retained his throne until his death in 1137.

Owain Gwynedd, b. c.1100, s. of Gruffydd ap Cynan and Angharad; acc. 1137; m. (1) Gwladus, da. of Llywarch ap Trahearn; issue: Iorwerth Drwyndwn, Maelgwyn; (2) Christina, da. of Gronw ab Owain ab Edwin; issue: Dafydd, Rhodri; also (illeg.) Rhun, Hywel, Cynan, Angharad, Gwenllian; d. 28 Nov. 1170; bur. Bangor.

Before succeeding, Owain worked with his father and brother Cadwallon to extend the power of Gwynedd, largely to the east of the Conwy. As ruler, Owain was ambitious but circumspect. He was assisted by the civil war raging in England during Stephen's reign and won most of Ceredigion back from the Normans after defeating them at Crug Mawr, near Cardigan, in 1136. He was checked by Henry II in 1157 and agreed terms, acknowledging English overlordship. Yet he maintained his position and a second expedition led against him by Henry in 1165 ended in dismal and damp failure. A court poet praised him: 'in screaming battle, cool, yet burning war'.

Cadwaladr, b. c.1105, 2nd s. of Gruffydd ap Cynan and Angharad; m. Alice, da. of Richard Fitzgilbert, earl of Clare; issue: Cadfan, Rhicert; d. 29 Feb. 1172; bur. Bangor.

The younger brother of Owain Gwynedd, Cadwaladr's exploits took place against the background of English weakness during the reign of Stephen. After he had established a power base in Ceredigion, he entered the civil war on the side of Matilda, and fought at Lincoln in

1141 when Stephen was captured. A quarrel with his brother forced him into exile, but in 1157 Henry II insisted on his restoration. He reunited with his brother to resist Henry's second campaign against the Welsh in 1165.

Cynan ab Owain, b. c.1120, s. of Owain Gwynedd and an unknown woman; acc. 1170; d. 1174.

After the death of Owain Gwynedd in 1170 his sons, legitimate and otherwise, disputed the succession. Cynan had established a semi-independent territory in Meirionnydd in 1147, and this seems to have been the area confirmed to him in a brief understanding reached by the sons in 1171.

Dafydd ab Owain, s. of Owain Gwynedd and Christina; acc. 1175; m. Emma, daughter of Geoffrey of Anjou, 1174; issue: Owain; d. 1203.

Dafydd, son of Owain's second marriage, took a prominent part in the fighting between the brothers after 1170. Hywel was defeated and killed in Anglesey, and a share-out soon after gave Dafydd the eastern cantrefs of Gwynedd. In 1173 he drove out another brother, Maelgwyn. He strengthened his position in 1174 by marriage to the half-sister of Henry II. He seemed to have some chance of reuniting Gwynedd under his rule, but in 1175 was forced to yield Anglesey to another brother, Rhodri, and confine himself east of the Conwy. In 1194 he was attacked by a nephew, Llywelyn ab Iorwerth, and defeated in battle at Aberconwy. Three years later, he lost his remaining foothold, and spent his last six years on the English estates granted to him by Henry II.

Rhodri ab Owain, s. of Owain Gwynedd and Christina; acc. 1175; m. da. of Rhys ap Gruffydd, 1188; issue: Gruffydd; d. 1195; bur. Holyhead.

One of the many sons of Owain Gwynedd, Rhodri participated in the fighting which followed Owain's death. In 1171 he joined his brother Dafydd in killing their half-brother, Hywel, and in the subsequent share-out took the western parts of Gwynedd. He quarrelled with Dafydd, was imprisoned, but escaped and regained Anglesey and the adjacent mainland. There he was visited in 1188 by Gerald of Wales on his celebrated tour. Two years later Rhodri was attacked and dispossessed by his nephews, Gruffydd and Maredudd. He seems to have taken refuge in the Isle of Man, promising to marry the daughter of Ragnall, king of the island. Manx forces helped him to recover Anglesey briefly, but he died in 1195.

Llywelyn ab Iorwerth, b. 1173, s. of Iorwerth Drwyndwn ('Flatnose') and Marared, da. of Madog ap Maredudd; acc. east Gwynedd 1195; m. Joan, illeg. da. of king John, 1205; issue: Gruffydd (illeg.), Dafydd, Gwenllian, Helen, Gwladus, Margaret, Susanna; d. 11 Apr. 1240; bur. Aberconwy.

Known as Llywelyn 'the Great' and hailed by the bards as 'a second Achilles', he came close to uniting all Wales under his overlordship. His father seems to have taken little part in the disputes that followed the death of Owain Gwynedd in 1170, ruling Arfon and Nantconwy, and dying when Llywelyn was still an infant. Llywelyn began his career by joining in the attacks on his uncles Dafydd and Rhodri in the 1190s. By 1203 he had succeeded in reuniting the kingdom of Gwynedd, and his marriage in 1205 to the natural daughter of king John was recognition of his eminence. Later he extended his overlordship to Powys, his mother's kingdom. Relations with John deteriorated, and in 1211 two expeditions to north Wales forced him to cede the eastern cantrefs of Perfeddwlad, and to give hostages. But John's accumulating difficulties enabled Llywelyn to recover the territories a year later, and though John threatened another campaign, Llywelyn retained the cantrefs. While civil war raged in England, Llywelyn led a concerted attack upon the Anglo-Norman position in south Wales, supported by many of the Welsh princes. The supremacy he had gained was reflected in the title 'prince of Aberffraw and lord of Snowdon', which he adopted after 1230. He suffered a stroke in 1237, and his last years were disturbed by the antagonism showed by his natural son, Gruffydd, towards his half-brother Dafydd, on whom Llywelyn had tried to settle the inheritance.

Dafydd ap Llywelyn, b. c.1208, s. of Llywelyn ab Iorwerth; acc. 11 Apr. 1240; m. Isabella, da. of William de Braose V; d. 25 Feb. 1246; bur. Aberconwy.

The only legitimate son of Llywelyn the Great, Dafydd was intended by his father to inherit all his territories. The succession was guaranteed by Henry III (1220), the pope (1222) and the Welsh nobility (1226, 1238), but there was tension with Dafydd's elder brother, Gruffydd, who was illegitimate. On Llywelyn's death in 1240, Henry III decided to cut down Dafydd's power and used Gruffydd against him. When Dafydd made a bid for his father's position, styling himself 'prince of Wales', Henry led a campaign against him in 1245. Dafydd died early the following year.

Gruffydd ap Llywelyn, b. c.1200, illeg. s. of Llywelyn ab Iowerth and Tangwystyl, da. of Llywarch Goch of Rhos; m. Serena; issue: Owain Goch ('the Red'), Llywelyn, Dafydd, Rhodri, Gwladus; d. 1 Mar. 1244; bur. Aberconwy.

As an illegitimate son, Gruffydd had no formal claim to estates but could expect some consideration. He was a hostage in the hands of king John until 1215 and on release began to press for lands, involving him in frequent disputes with his father and his half-brother, Dafydd. After a period of imprisonment, Llywelyn released him in 1234 and gave him territory in Powys. His half-brother then deposed him and held him captive in Criccieth. In 1241 he obtained the help of Henry III, who transferred him to the Tower of London in honourable imprisonment. While attempting to escape, Gruffydd broke his neck when the linen sheets tore. His sons, Llywelyn and Dafydd, were the last native princes of Wales.

Llywelyn ap Gruffydd, b. c.1220, 2nd s. of Gruffydd ap Llywelyn and Serena; m. Eleanor, da. of Simon de Montfort, earl of Leicester, 1278; issue: Gwenllian; d. 11 Dec. 1282; bur. Cwm Hir.

Llywelyn was the second son of Gruffydd, and had to contend with an elder brother Owain and a younger brother Dafydd. At the death of his uncle Dafydd in 1246, he shared Gwynedd west of the Conwy with his brothers, but they quarrelled and he defeated them at Bryn Derwin, south of Caernarfon, in 1255, taking control of the whole kingdom. Owain was captured and imprisoned. The protracted dispute between Henry III and his barons offered Llywelyn a chance to consolidate his rule. By 1258 he controlled the greater part of north and central Wales, with the other native rulers doing homage to him as prince of Wales. In June 1265 at Pipton, he concluded a treaty with Simon de Montfort, pledging himself to marry de Montfort's daughter. Though de Montfort was killed soon after at Evesham, Henry III confirmed the position at Montgomery in 1267, recognizing Llywelyn as prince of Wales. However, the gradual recovery of power by the English crown was bound to cause difficulties with Llywelyn and he had alienated many of his supporters by high-handed actions. Edward I, who succeeded in 1272, was familiar with Wales, though his absence on a crusade gave Llywelyn a respite of some years. But after Llywelyn had repeatedly refused to do homage to the king, Edward declared war in 1276 and advanced on Wales with three large armies; Dafydd, Llywelyn's brother, fought on the English side. Llywelyn was forced back into

Snowdonia and, at the onset of winter, obliged to come to terms. By the treaty of Aberconwy, he surrendered his brother Owain, a prisoner since 1255, abandoned all claims to overlordship, and was confined to western Gwynedd. His brothers were reinstated in lesser lordships. His much-delayed marriage to Eleanor de Montfort took place at Worcester in 1278 in the presence of Edward I and Alexander III, king of Scotland.

The reconciliation with Edward did not last. In 1282 his brother Dafydd, this time working with Llywelyn, precipitated a rising by a sudden attack upon the castle at Hawarden. Edward led a punitive expedition into north Wales and Llywelyn, not wishing to be trapped in Snowdonia again, moved south, where he ran into the troops of Edmund Mortimer, one of the marcher barons. He was killed in a skirmish near Builth, and his head taken to London and exhibited on a pole in the Tower. His brother Dafydd was executed in 1283.

Dafydd ap Gruffydd, b. c.1230, 3rd s. of Gruffydd ap Llywelyn and Serena; m. Elizabeth, da. of Robert Ferrers, earl of Derby; issue: Llywelyn, Owain, 7 das.; d. 3 Oct. 1283.

The younger brother of Llywelyn, Dafydd followed a contorted course. One Welsh historian calls him 'a man of exceptional courage and personal attractiveness', another dismisses him as 'ambitious, treacherous, and disloyal to his elder brother'. He began, in alliance with his eldest brother Owain, by disputing Llywelyn's inheritance. Beaten in 1255 at Bryn Derwin, he was forgiven by Llywelyn, but in 1263 fled to England to seek protection from Henry III. At that time Henry was scarcely in a position to protect himself, but in 1267, after his victory at Evesham, he insisted that Llywelyn should restore Dafydd. Once more Dafydd plotted against his brother, intending to surprise and murder him. When the plot was discovered he fled to Edward I, and was again restored in 1277. He then turned against his English allies, and his action in 1282 in attacking Hawarden castle precipitated a general rising. After his brother's death, Dafydd attempted to carry on resistance, declaring himself prince of Wales. He found little support, was betrayed, and, after a trial at Shrewsbury, was executed as a traitor.

Powys

Powys was an important Welsh kingdom but its resources were limited, and it had difficulty in resisting Gwynedd to the north and Mercia to the east. Its core was the valley of the upper Severn, west of Shrewsbury; its eastern border was marked after the eighth century by Offa's Dyke; to the south it sometimes extended to the river Wye, near Hay. It enjoyed a brief prominence in the early twelfth century, being then divided into northern and southern Powys, Fadog, and Wenwynwyn.

Cadell Ddyrnllug ('the Blackfisted'), was the legendary founder of Powys in the fifth century. He is reputed to have been a swineherd, who gave hospitality to St Germanus, and was rewarded with the throne. Nennius, who recorded the story in the early ninth century, added that Cadell's descendants ruled Powys 'even to this day'.

Brochwel Ysgythrog (Brochmael Ysgythrog) ('of the Tusks') is said to have ruled Powys in the late sixth century, and to have been the father of St Tysilio. He may have been engaged in resisting the advance of Ceawlin, king of Wessex, up the Severn valley. If he is the king mentioned by Bede for his inglorious part in the defeat of the Britons at Chester c.616, he would have been very old.

Selyn ap Cynan, grandson of Brochwel, was slain in the battle near Chester won by Aethelfrith of Bernicia c.616, reported at length by Bede.

Cyngen, son of Cadell, probably inherited on the death of his father in 808. He erected a monumental pillar near Llangollen (still extant) to his great-grandfather, Elisedd, said to have checked the English advance c.725. He died in 854 at Rome on a pilgrimage, according to *Annales Cambriae*.

Bleddyn ap Cynfyn, s. of Cynfyn ap Gwerstan and Angharad, wid. of Llywelyn ap Seisyll; acc. Powys and Gwynedd, 1063; issue: Madog, Rhiryd, Cadwgan, Iorwerth, Maredudd, Gwenllian, Hunydd; d. 1075.

The half-brother of Gruffydd ap Llywelyn of Deheubarth, Bleddyn faced the advance of the Normans after the conquest of 1066. He gave support to the Mercians, assisting Edric 'the Wild' in 1067 and Edwin and Morcar in 1068. In 1070, at the battle of Mechain, he slew two sons of Gruffydd who had challenged his succession, but was subsequently under great pressure on his north-eastern border from the marcher lords. He was killed in 1075 by Rhys ab Owain of Deheubarth, but his descendants continued to rule Powys. The *Chronicle of the Princes* lavished praise on him as 'the most mild and clement of kings'.

Madog ap Bleddyn seems to have shared the throne of Powys with his brother Rhiryd after the death of his father in 1075. In 1085 they launched an attack upon Rhys ap Tewdwr, ruler of Deheubarth, and drove him into exile in Ireland. He returned very quickly with Viking allies and recovered his throne, killing both brothers.

Iorwerth ap Bleddyn ruled Powys jointly at the end of the eleventh century. He supported Robert of Bellême, earl of Shrewsbury, in the revolt of 1102, but was persuaded to change sides in exchange for promises of territory. Disappointed with his reward, he defied Henry I and was imprisoned 1103–10. The year after his release, he was murdered by a nephew, Madog ap Rhiryd.

Cadwgan, 3rd s. of Bleddyn ap Cynfyn; m. da. of Picot de Sai, lord of Clun; issue: Henry, Gruffydd, Owain, Madog, Eionion, Morgan, Maredudd; d. 1111.

Cadwgan, third son of Bleddyn, joined his elder brothers in resisting the counter-attack of Rhys ap Tewdwr of Deheubarth in 1088, but escaped when they were both killed. In 1094, with Gruffydd ap Cynan of Gwynedd, he made a sustained attempt to arrest Norman penetration of Wales winning an important victory at Coed Yspwys. It required two expeditions by William 'Rufus' to subdue the resistance. Cadwgan joined the revolt of Robert, earl of Shrewsbury, in 1102; at the settlement he was given Ceredigion, but was subsequently stripped of his lands because of the behaviour of his son Owain. Though he was restored to rule southern Powys after the murder of his brother Iorwerth in 1111, he too was murdered at Welshpool the same year, by his nephew Madog ap Rhiryd.

Owain ap Cadwgan burst on to the Welsh scene in 1109 when he abducted Nest in a daring raid on the castle of her husband, Gerald of Windsor, at Pembroke. Nevertheless, he succeeded his father as ruler of Powys in 1111. In 1114 Henry I drove him into Gwynedd and forced him to submit. He spent 1115 in Normandy, and on his return was ambushed and killed near Carmarthen by supporters of Gerald, seeking revenge.

Maredudd ap Bleddyn, 5th s. of Bleddyn ap Cynfyn; acc. Powys 1116; issue: Gruffydd, Madog, Hywel, Iorwerth Goch ('the Red'); d. 1132.

Maredudd joined in the revolt of his brothers Cadwgan and Iorwerth in 1102, but failed to change sides when they did and was handed over to the English. He escaped in 1107 and worked with his nephew, Owain. On Owain's death in 1116, Maredudd succeeded. In 1121 his raids across the English border antagonized Henry I, who led an expedition against him. He was reduced to taking refuge in Snowdonia before making peace on terms.

Madog ap Rhiryd and his brother **Ithel** were used by the English against Owain and his father Cadwgan, and encouraged to invade Ceredigion. They succeeded in driving Owain out and were rewarded with southern Powys. When Owain returned, he reached an understanding with Madog, but they were both expelled by Iorwerth. In 1111 Madog murdered Iorwerth and his successor Cadwgan, and the English then installed Madog as ruler of southern Powys. He was subsequently captured and blinded by kinsmen. Ithel died in 1124.

Madog ap Maredudd, s. of Maredudd ap Bleddyn; acc. 1132; m. Susanna, da. of Gruffydd ap Cynan and Angharad, da. of Owain ab Edwin; issue: Gruffydd Maelor, Elise, Owain Fychan, Llywelyn, Owain Brogyntyn, Marared, Gwenllian; d. 1160; bur. Meifod, near Welshpool.

Madog used the civil war taking place in England to encroach upon the eastern border, but his main task was to resist the ambition of his northern neighbour, Owain Gwynedd. In 1150 he was defeated in a battle near Coleshill. He was assisted in 1157 by Henry II but died in 1160. The last ruler of an undivided Powys, Madog was greatly praised by poets and bards.

Owain Cyfeiliog, b. c.1125, s. of Gruffydd ap Maredudd; acc. 1160; m. Gwenllian, da. of Owain Gwynedd; issue: Gwenwynwyn, Caswallon; d. 1197.

On the death of Madog (1160), Powys was divided, the southern part going to Owain, Madog's nephew. He had previously acted as underlord in Cyfeiliog in western Powys, which he had to defend against Rhys ap Gruffydd of Deheubarth. In the late 1160s he formed part of the coalition under Owain Gwynedd to resist the English under Henry II, but in 1167 switched to an English alliance, to which he adhered for the rest of his reign. In his early life he was much applauded as a warrior, later for his wisdom and moderation, and for his poetry. In 1195 he abdicated in favour of his son Gwenwynwyn, spending the last two years of his life in the monastery of Strata Marcella, which he had founded in 1170.

Gwenwynwyn, b. c.1160, s. of Owain Cyfeiliog; acc. 1195; m. Margaret, da. of Robert Corbet; issue: Gruffydd, Madog; d. 1216.

Gwenwynwyn took over from his father in southern Powys in 1195 and added the lordship of Arwystli to the south in 1197. He made an early bid for pre-eminence among the Welsh princes, launching a series of attacks upon marcher territories. He seems to have overplayed his hand, and in 1208 John deprived him of his kingdom. Restored in 1210, he was forced into a dependence upon Llywelyn ab Iorwerth. This broke down in 1216 and Llywelyn soon pushed him into exile in Cheshire, where he died.

Gruffydd ap Gwenwynwyn, b. c.1200; s. of Gwenwynwyn and Margaret, da. of Robert Corbet; acc. 1240; m. Hawise, da. of John Lestrange; issue: Owain, Llywelyn, John, William, Dafydd, Gruffydd, Marared; d. 1286.

Gruffydd's father had been dispossessed as ruler of southern Powys by Llywelyn ab Iorwerth, who ruled until his death in 1240. Gruffydd, who had been brought up in England, was then reinstated with English support, but Llywelyn's grandson, Llywelyn ap Gruffydd, drove him out again in 1257. In 1263, when England was convulsed by civil strife, Gruffydd threw in his lot with Llywelyn, did homage and was restored to part of his lands. The understanding lasted until 1274 when he quarrelled with Llywelyn, was once more driven out, and again restored in 1277 with English help. The death of Llywelyn and his brother Dafydd in 1282 and 1283 enabled Gruffydd to retain his kingdom until his death. His granddaughter Hawise married in 1309 John, first Lord Charlton (or Cherleton) of Powys, who took possession of the lordship of Powys, despite protests from his wife's uncles.

Gruffydd Maelor I, b. c.1130, s. of Madog ap Maredudd and Susanna, da. of Gruffydd ap Cynan; acc. 1160; m. Angharad, da. of Owain Gwynedd; issue: Madog, Owain; d. 1191.

At the death of Madog, Powys was divided, with Gruffydd taking most of the northern part, including Maelor. His brother Owain Fychan took

Mechain, and his brother Owain Brogyntyn took Edeyrnion. When Owain Fychan was murdered in 1187, Gruffydd took his estates. Gerald of Wales recorded that archbishop Baldwin tried to persuade him to separate from his wife, who was a first cousin. Praised as a liberal patron, his political conduct seems to have been circumspect.

Madog ap Gruffydd, b. c.1160, s. of Gruffydd Maelor and Angharad; acc. 1191; m. Isota; issue: Gruffydd Maelor, Gruffydd Ial, Maredudd, Hywel, Madog Fychan, Angharad; d. 1236; bur. Valle Crucis.

From 1191 Madog shared northern Powys with his brother Owain, and on his death in 1197 became sole ruler. His limited resources dictated a balancing act. At first he allied with Llywelyn ab Iorwerth, then opposed him 1211–15, but rejoined him in 1215. He founded in 1201 the Cistercian house of Valle Crucis, where he was buried.

Gruffydd Maelor II, b. c.1200, s. of Madog ap Gruffydd and Isota; acc. 1236; m. Emma, da. of Henry, Lord Audley; issue: Madog, Llywelyn, Owain, Gruffydd; d. Dec. 1269; bur. Valle Crucis.

Gruffydd ruled northern Powys in difficult and turbulent times. He gave support in 1241 to Henry III in his campaign against Dafydd ap Llywelyn, and was given a pension. But as the English king ran into increasing difficulties, Gruffydd was exposed. In 1256 his lands were overrun by Llywelyn ap Gruffydd and he was forced to change sides. He stayed with Llywelyn until his death in 1269, after which his territories were divided among his four sons.

Deheubarth

Deheubarth was the most powerful of the kingdoms of south Wales. It was formed in the tenth century by the marriage of Hywel Dda of Seisyllwg to Elen of Dyfed, and subsequently extended into Breichiniog. After the Norman conquest Deheubarth had to contend with strong Anglo-Norman infiltration to the south, and particularly into Pembrokeshire. It reached its peak under 'the Lord Rhys' in the late twelfth century, but soon disintegrated.

Cadell, son of Rhodri 'the Great', succeeded to Seisyllwg in 878, on the death of his father. He himself died in 909, and was succeeded by his sons Clydog and Hywel Dda, who ruled jointly until Clydog's death in 920.

Hywel Dda ('the Good'), b. c.890, s. of Cadell ap Rhodri; m. Elen, da. of Llywarch ap Hyfaidd of Dyfed, c.904; issue: Rhodri, Edwin, Owain; d. c.950.

Hywel was one of the great Welsh princes, acceding in Dyfed c.904, in Seisyllwg in 920, and gaining control of Gwynedd c.942. The *Brut* called him 'the head and glory of all the Britons'. He acknowledged the overlordship of Edward the Elder and Athelstan, and was on close terms with them, witnessing a number of charters. He visited Rome in 928. A silver penny, now in the British Museum, is inscribed 'Rex Houel' and was probably minted in Chester. The laws for which he is famous, though not written down until the thirteenth century, were probably an attempt, towards the end of his reign, to bring some uniformity to his various kingdoms.

Owain ap Hywel succeeded his brothers Rhodri (d. 953) and Edwin (d. 954) as ruler of Deheubarth, the rest of his father's territories having reasserted their independence. His sons were Cadwallon (d. 966), Idwallon (d. 975), Einion (d. 984), and Maredudd, who succeeded him in 988. Checked in a raid on Gwynedd in 954 at Llanrwst, Owain turned his attention south to Morgannwg and Gwent: his son, Einion, was killed in a raid on Gwent in 984.

Maredudd ab Owain defeated and killed Cadwallon of Gwynedd in 986 and assumed control of that kingdom. In 987 he took over the government of Deheubarth from his aged father. His son Cadwallon died in 992, and his daughter Angharad married Llywelyn ap Seisyll. Maredudd died in 999. The *Brut*, often extravagant in its praise, called him 'the most famous king of the Britons', and he appears to have dealt strongly with both Viking raids and Saxon incursions.

Llywelyn ap Seisyll was a descendant of Rhodri 'the Great' through his mother Prawst, a great-granddaughter. His marriage to Angharad, daughter of Maredudd, gave him a claim on Deheubarth. After the death of Maredudd in 999, Deheubarth was disputed and lost control of Gwynedd. Llywelyn recaptured Gwynedd from Cynan in 1005, and added Deheubarth in 1018 by killing Aeddan ap Blegywryd and his sons. In 1022, at Abergwill, he defeated an Irish adventurer, Rhain, who claimed to be a son of Maredudd. Llywelyn died shortly afterwards in 1023, leaving a son, Gruffydd, who succeeded later in reuniting Gwynedd, Powys, and Deheubarth.

Rhydderch ab Iestyn ruled Deheubarth from the death of Llywelyn in 1023 until 1033. His family came from south-east Wales and he may have taken advantage of the quarrel between Llywelyn and his son Gruffydd. Rhydderch's son Caradoc died in 1035, but another son, Gruffydd, regained Deheubarth in c.1044.

Hywel ab Edwin was a great-great-grandson of Hywel Dda and ruled Deheubarth from c.1033 until 1044. Reigning jointly at first with a brother, Maredudd (d. 1035), he was expelled by Gruffydd ap Llywelyn c.1042. He took refuge in Ireland, returned with Viking support, but was killed on the Towy.

Gruffydd ap Rhydderch. While Deheubarth was being disputed between Hywel and Gruffydd ap Llywelyn, Gruffydd ab Rhydderch made off with the prize in 1044. He succeeded in beating off a formidable challenge from Gruffydd ap Llywelyn in alliance with earl Godwin's son, Swegen, and in 1049 took the offensive, with Viking support, harassing Gwent and the Severn estuary. The *Anglo-Saxon Chronicle* reported that the English relief force, led by bishop Ealdred of Worcester, was surprised and cut up. However, in 1055 Gruffydd was overthrown and killed by Gruffydd ap Llywelyn, who took possession of Deheubarth.

Gruffydd ap Llywelyn, b. c.1000, s. of Llywelyn ap Seisyll and Angharad; acc. Gwynedd and Powys 1039, Deheubarth 1055; m. Ealdgyth, da. of Aelfgar, earl of Mercia; issue: Maredudd, Idwal, Nest; d. 5 Aug. 1063.

Gruffydd was a formidable ruler, who succeeded for some time in bringing most of Wales under his control, but pushed too hard. He did not succeed to his father's kingdom of Deheubarth in 1023 but managed to take Powys and Gwynedd in 1039, killing Iago ap Idwal. He inflicted a check near Welshpool upon the Mercians, and then turned his attention south to Deheubarth, where Hywel ab Edwin was ruling. A protracted campaign culminated in Gruffydd killing his opponent in 1044, but the

throne eluded him and was seized by Gruffydd ap Rhydderch. Fresh
fighting began, with Gruffydd ap Llywelyn assisted by Swegen
Godwinsson. Not until 1055 did he kill Gruffydd ap Rhydderch and
obtain the throne. His three kingdoms made him a powerful opponent
and for some time he terrorized the Mercian border, burning the
cathedral and town of Hereford. When Leofgar, the new fighting bishop
of Hereford, marched against him in 1056, he and the sheriff were both
killed at Glasbury. The *Anglo-Saxon Chronicle* described the disaster at
some length, and Harold Godwinsson was despatched to restore the
situation. This was not easy, but Gruffydd was forced to do homage to
Edward 'the Confessor'. When raiding continued, the English court
decided upon a showdown, and in 1063 Harold led a strong force into
south Wales. Gruffydd's half-brothers, Bleddyn and Rhiwallon, seem to
have split from him and joined the English. 'The man who had hitherto
been invincible', lamented the *Brut*, 'was now left in the glens of
desolation.' Gruffydd escaped from his palace at Rhuddlan in the nick of
time but was subsequently killed by his own men. His head was sent by
Harold as a trophy to Edward.

Maredudd ab Owain. The Welsh empire of Gruffydd ap Llywelyn fell
to pieces on his death in 1063. Maredudd, who took Deheubarth, was a
direct descendant of Hywel Dda. From 1066 he faced the earliest
incursions of the Normans into south Wales, losing Gwent to Robert
Fitzosbern. In 1170 he was given some English estates near Hereford in
compensation. Two years later he was killed near the Rhymney by
Caradoc ap Gruffydd, from Gwynllwg, who also aspired to dominate
south Wales.

Rhys ab Owain succeeded his brother in 1072 and carried on the
struggle against Caradoc. In 1075 he brought about the death of Bleddyn
ap Cynfyn, ruler of Powys and Gwynedd, but three years later was
himself defeated by Bleddyn's successor in Gwynedd and cousin,
Trahearn ap Caradoc. *Brut* recorded that he became like a timid stag,
hunted through thickets and rocks. Shortly after, Rhys and his brother
Hywel were killed by Caradoc ap Gruffydd, who had killed their
predecessor, Maredudd.

Rhys ap Tewdwr son of Tewdwr ap Cadell, another descendant of
Hywel Dda, made himself master of Deheubarth after Rhys ab
Owain's death in 1078. He married Gwladus, daughter of Rhiwallon

ap Cynfyn, and had issue Gruffydd, Hywel, and Nest. His immediate task was to hold at bay Caradoc, who had slain his two predecessors. Temporarily dispossessed by his adversary in 1081, he joined forces with Gruffydd ap Cynan of Gwynedd to defeat and kill Caradoc at Mynydd Carn. He came to terms with William 'the Conqueror' and did homage, but remained under attack from rival Welsh princes. In April 1093 he was killed near Brecon in circumstances which are not clear, probably attempting to resist the Norman advance up the Usk valley.

Gruffydd ap Rhys was too young to take over his father's kingdom in 1093, but was removed to safety in Ireland. Norman penetration of Deheubarth continued apace. He returned in 1113 but failed to recover the kingdom, and was subsequently given lands by Henry I in the upper valley of the Cothi. He married Gwenllian, daughter of Gruffydd ap Cynan and had issue Anarawd, Cadell, Maredudd, Rhys, Gwladus, and Nest. At the start of Stephen's reign, he took part in the rising of 1136, regaining much territory from the Normans, but died in 1137.

Rhys ap Gruffydd ('the Lord Rhys'), b. c.1133, s. of Gruffydd ap Rhys and Gwenllian, da. of Gruffydd ap Cynan; acc. 1155; m. Gwenllian, da. of Madog ap Maredudd; issue: Gruffydd, Maredudd Ddall ('the Blind'), Cynwrig, Rhys Gryg ('the Hoarse'), Maredudd, Maelgwyn, Hywel Sais ('the Saxon'), Maredudd, Gwenllian; d. 28 Apr. 1197; bur. St David's cathedral.

The anarchy of Stephen's reign gave the Welsh princes an opportunity to recover lost territory. Rhys, the fourth son of Gruffydd, was a small boy when his father died in 1137. His eldest brother, Anarawd, was killed in 1143 by Cadwaladr, younger brother of Owain Gwynedd; Cadell, Gruffydd's second son, made gains against the Anglo-Normans, but was so badly wounded in an ambush in 1151 that he could no longer lead; the third brother, Maredudd, then took over the kingdom, overrunning Gower and moving into Ceredigion. When he died in 1055, Rhys became sole ruler and built up a powerful position. But with Henry II he was dealing with a stronger adversary than Stephen: he acknowledged overlordship in 1158 and treated Henry with some caution. He extended his influence by diplomatic marriages—his own to the daughter of the last sole ruler of Powys, followed by those of his children. In 1062 he seized the castle of Llandovery, provoking Henry to an expedition which forced Rhys to submit, reaffirming his homage at Woodstock. The reconciliation did not last and a grand coalition of the Welsh princes, helped by bad weather and barren hills, forced Henry to retreat in 1165. It was now the turn of the English king to be circumspect. The revolt of Henry's sons 1173–4 and the diversion of Anglo-Norman advance into Ireland took much pressure off Rhys and enabled him to consolidate his power. Henry recognized his supremacy in south Wales, appointed him justice, and treated him with care. When Gerald of Wales accompanied archbishop Baldwin on his crusading tour in 1188, Rhys met them at Cardigan and, with great dignity, escorted them through his dominions. Relations with Henry's successor, Richard I, were less cordial. Fortunately Richard was absent for almost the whole of his reign, and Rhys's renewed attacks upon Norman strongholds went unpunished. Of more concern were the difficulties caused by his sons, and in 1194 'the Lord Rhys' suffered the indignity of being briefly imprisoned by his son, Maelgwyn. He died in 1197, and a fine effigy was erected in the following century over his tomb at St David's.

Gruffydd ap Rhys, b. c.1160, eld. s. of Rhys ap Gruffydd and Gwenllian; acc. 1197; m. Matilda, da. of William de Braose III; issue: Rhys, Owain; d. 25 July 1201.

The position of Deheubarth built up by Rhys was partly personal and could not be sustained. His sons quarrelled incessantly. Gruffydd took cantref Mawr on his father's death. He had for years been at odds with his younger brother, Maelgwyn, who was strong in Ceredigion. Soon after his accession, Maelgwyn captured him and handed him over to Gwenwynwyn of Powys, who passed him on to the English. On his release, Gruffydd was gaining the upper hand when Maelgwyn came to terms with king John, who confirmed his control of Ceredigion in exchange for the key castle at Cardigan, captured by his father. After only four years, Gruffydd died of illness.

Rhys Gryg ('the Hoarse'), b. c.1162, 4th s. of Rhys ap Gruffydd and Gwenllian; acc. 1204; m. Joan, da. of Richard, earl of Hertford; issue: Rhys, Maredudd; d. 1234; bur. St David's cathedral.

Rhys usually acted with his eldest brother Gruffydd against their volatile younger brother, Maelgwyn. On Gruffydd's early death, he took control of cantref Mawr. At first he supported king John, but in 1211 changed sides, joined Llywelyn ab Iorwerth, and stormed the royal castle at Aberystwyth. John retaliated by supporting Rhys's nephews, Rhys and

Owain (sons of Gruffydd), against him, and an expedition from Brecon moved into Rhys's heartland, defeating him near Llandeilo. Rhys was captured and imprisoned at Carmarthen. He was not released until 1215 and promptly threw in his lot with Llywelyn, who restored him to cantref Mawr and cantref Bychan to the west; Deheubarth was divided up. He took part in Llywelyn's revolt of 1231, seizing the castle at Cardigan, and was still campaigning in 1234, when he was mortally wounded besieging Carmarthen.

Maelgwyn ap Rhys, b. c.1168, 6th s. of Rhys ap Gruffydd and Gwenllian; issue: Maelgwyn Fychan ('Junior'); d. 1231; bur. Strata Florida.

Maelgwyn, short, restless, ambitious, and a sixth son, struggled all his life to construct a territorial base for himself. This involved frequent campaigns against his father and his brothers. As early as 1187 he conducted a raid on Tenby and acquired a following in Ceredigion. In 1188, when archbishop Baldwin conducted his recruiting mission to Wales, Maelgwyn pledged himself to join the crusade though, like many others, he did not do so; instead, he waged war on his father. His surplus energy was devoted to fighting his eldest brother, Gruffydd. Deheubarth's influence declined apace. On Rhys's death in 1197, Maelgwyn seized Ceredigion and managed to capture Gruffydd. When Gruffydd was released and began to do well, Maelgwyn did a deal with king John, handing over Cardigan castle in exchange for lands in Ceredigion. In 1211 he was attacked and defeated by his nephews, Rhys and Owain, before John's increasing difficulties in England persuaded him to change tack once more, joining Llywelyn ab Iorwerth. At Llywelyn's distribution of territories in 1216, Maelgwyn was given extensive lands in west Wales, including Carmarthen and Llandovery. In 1222, when Gruffydd's son Rhys died, Llywelyn gave Maelgwyn half the estates in Ceredigion. He died in 1231 and was succeeded by his son, Maelgwyn Fychan.

Smaller Welsh Kingdoms

In the conditions of Wales, geographically divided by mountains and valleys, much depended on the prowess and sagacity of individual rulers, and kingdoms could expand and contract at speed. GWENT took its name from Caerwent, the Roman base, and lay between the rivers Usk and Wye. By the ninth century it had been taken over by Morgannwg, and after 1066 most of it fell quickly to the Norman advance. To the west was GLYWYSING, ruled over c.600 by Meurig ap Tewdig. It became part of MORGANNWG which, after the Conquest, formed the lordship of Glamorgan. West again was the kingdom of DYFED. Ruled by Llywarch ap Hyfaidd until 904, it became part of SEISYLLWG when his daughter married Hywel Dda, and was eventually incorporated into Deheubarth. Norman penetration into Pembroke-shire was rapid. North of Gwent lay BRYCHEINIOG, up the Usk valley to Brecon, and reputedly founded by Brychan, son of an Irish chieftain of the fifth century. Brychan was reported to have had twenty-four daughters and to have led his men to a devastating victory over their neighbours from Deheubarth. But in the tenth century it fell to Deheubarth and soon after the Conquest became part of the Norman lordship of Brecknock. North of Brycheiniog was BUILTH, which dwindled from a small kingdom into a cantref. Nennius, in the *Historia Brittonum*, compiled in the early ninth century, named Ffernfeal as the ruler, adding that he also reigned in Gwerthrynion to the north-east, and tracing his ancestry back to Vortigern. It was absorbed into Gwynedd and, after the Conquest, much of it became the lordship of Radnor. To the west was CEREDIGION, a coastal kingdom between the rivers Teifi and Dovey. It was said to be the region to which Cunedda moved after his migration from southern Scotland, and to have been ruled by his son, Ceredig. Seisyll, king in the eighth century, gained territory to the south, but the expanded kingdom of Seisyllwg became part of Deheubarth.

Another small kingdom with strong links to south Wales was DUMNONIA (Cornwall), which included for a time Devon and part of Somerset. In the early eighth century its king, Geraint, received a letter from Aldhelm, bishop of Sherborne, advising him on the correct date of Easter. The region was incorporated into Wessex in the early ninth century by Ecgberht, and rebellions in 825 and 838 failed to restore its independence.

House of Dunkeld

The absence of a male heir to Malcolm II meant that the succession passed to the issue of his daughter Bethoc, who had married Crinan, lay abbot of Dunkeld. Known alternatively as the House of Canmore (from 1158), it survived until the death of 'the Maid of Norway' in 1290.

Duncan I, b. c.1010, s. of Crinan, abbot of Dunkeld, and Bethoc, da. of Malcolm II; king of Strathclyde *ante* 1034, king of Scotland 25 Nov. 1034–40; m. a kinsw. of Siward, earl of Northumbria; issue: Malcolm, Donald, Maelmuire; d. Elgin, 14 Aug. 1040; bur. Iona(?).

Duncan's path to the Scottish kingship had been cleared by his grandfather Malcolm II's elimination of rivals, and he succeeded him in 1034. Already king of Strathclyde, and the last to be so called, Duncan thus became overlord of Cumbria, Lothian, and Alba, but not the northerly Moray, Caithness, or Sutherland. Attempts to reclaim the two latter regions led to two defeats by his cousin Thorfinn, earl of Orkney, and heavy losses were incurred also at an unsuccessful siege of Durham (1039). Contrary to Shakespeare's portrait of him as a wise old man, Duncan was young (*immatura*), headstrong, and lacked his grandfather's ability. As discontent grew, opposition focused on another challenger to the Scottish throne, Macbeth, mormaer of Moray, whose allegiance to Duncan had waned. Although weakened, Duncan marched north on the offensive in 1040, only to be fatally wounded at Pitgaveny (near Elgin), whence his sons (the future Malcolm III and Donald Bane) escaped.

Macbeth, b. c.1005, s. of Findlaech of Moray and Donada; mormaer of Moray 1032–57, king of Scots 1040–57; m. Gruoch c.1032; d. Lumphanan, 15 Aug. 1057; bur. Iona(?).

The Moray dynasty had been weakened by internal feuding which climaxed in 1020 with the murder of the hereditary mormaer Findlaech by his nephews Malcolm and GilleComgáin; Macbeth, possibly a grandson of Malcolm II and encouraged by the Scots king to avenge his father's death, burnt GilleComgáin to death in his own hall (1032) to reclaim the mormaership. Allying himself through marriage to the house of Kenneth III which bitterly opposed that of the ruling king (Duncan I), Macbeth slew Duncan near Elgin in 1040 and assumed the

HOUSES OF DUNKELD
BALLIOL, AND BRUCE

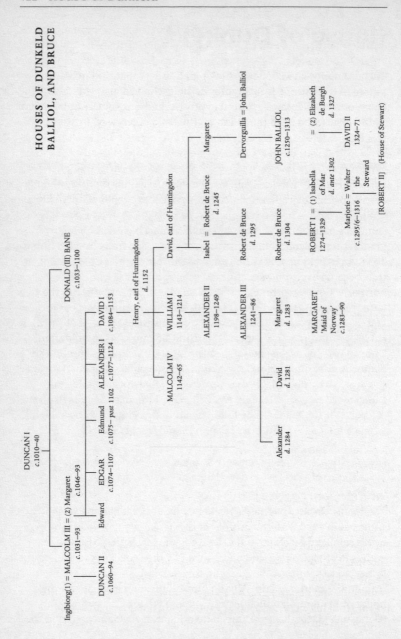

Scottish kingship. He was unable to prevent Norsemen from taking control of Sutherland and Caithness, but crushed Crinan, lay abbot of Dunkeld and Duncan's father, when faced by southern opposition (1045). An indecisive battle at Dunsinnan near Scone prevented Duncan's son Malcolm, returned from exile, from gaining the throne in 1054, but lost Macbeth territorial control of Perth and Fife; Malcolm finally prevailed at Lumphanan in Mar (west of Aberdeen).

Shakespeare's portrayal of Macbeth as vile usurper and tyrant employs generous dramatic licence. Succession struggles still persisted at that period, the northern house of Moray was as old as that of the southern mac Alpins, and Duncan's claim through his mother weak. A seventeen-year reign, which included a pilgrimage to Rome in 1050 (where Macbeth is said to have 'scattered money like seed' to the poor), implies strength and stability, and was remembered as a time of plenty. He was also a generous friend to the church, and his likely burial on Iona suggests further acknowledgement of his kingship.

Gruoch, da. of Boite (s. of Kenneth III); m. (1) GilleComgáin; (2) Macbeth, c.1032.

Gruoch was wife first of GilleComgáin, who ruled Moray after murdering Findlaech, and bore him Lulach, who was later king of Scots (1057–8). Findlaech's son, Macbeth, avenged his father's death and took the widowed Gruoch as his own wife, thereby healing the internal Moray feud. As granddaughter of Kenneth III, she was a descendant of a rival line which Malcolm II had tried to destroy; the feud between Macbeth's Moray dynasty and the house of Kenneth mac Alpin was thereby intensified, as was that between the houses of Kenneth II (father of Malcolm II) and Kenneth III. Shakespeare's depiction of Lady Macbeth as scheming and ambitious has no historical foundation.

Thorfinn, b. c.1009, s. of Sigurd Hlodvisson, jarl of Orkney, and a da. of Malcolm II of Scotland; m. Ingibjorg, da. of Finn Arnuson; issue: Paul, Erlend, Ingibiorg; d. 1065; bur. Birsay.

On Sigurd's death at Clontarf (1014) at the hands of Brian Bóruma, Thorfinn, still only a small boy, was sent to his grandfather's Scottish court, where he was given Caithness and Sutherland. Forceful, ambitious, and described as black-haired and ugly, he slowly wrested power from his elder brothers until he controlled the whole of Orkney and also the Hebrides. He fought against his cousin Duncan I

with his other cousin Macbeth, and they may have divided the
Scottish kingdom between them. Thorfinn is said to have
accompanied Macbeth on his pilgrimage to Rome in 1050, and
established Orkney's first bishopric at Birsay, where he built a minster.
Remembered after his death as 'the Mighty', his daughter became
Malcolm III's first wife, and his sons fought alongside Harald Hardrada at
Stamford Bridge (1066).

Lulach, b. c.1032, s. of GilleComgáin and Gruoch; king of Moray 15 Aug. 1057
and Scotland 8 Sept. 1057–1058; d. Essie, 17 Mar. 1058; bur. Iona(?).

Son of the mormaer of Moray, then stepson of Macbeth under whose
guardianship he was reared, Lulach was chosen to succeed him in the
Scottish kingship even though Malcolm 'Canmore' held sway over
much of southern Scotland by then. Named 'Lulach *fatuus*' ('the Simple')
in the Latin king-lists, and dwelling at Loch Deabhra, he reigned only
nominally and briefly, being ambushed and slain at Essie in Strathbogie
(west of Aberdeen), possibly by one of Malcolm's sons. His own son, Mael
Snechta, succeeded him in Moray, but no further Scottish overlords
came from Moray dynasts.

Malcolm III, b. c.1031, s. of Duncan I and a kinsw. of Siward, earl of
Northumbria; acc. 17 Mar.1058; m. (1) Ingibiorg, da. of Thorfinn, jarl of Orkney,
c.1059; issue: Duncan, Malcolm, Donald; (2) Margaret, da. of Edward the Atheling,
1070; issue: Edward, Edgar, Edmund, Ethelred, Alexander, Edith, Mary, David; d.
Alnwick, 13 Nov. 1093; bur. Tynemouth, rebur. Dunfermline.

On the death of his father in 1040, the boy Malcolm sought shelter in
England, where he remained during Macbeth's reign. Backed by Edward
'the Confessor', Malcolm and Siward, earl of Northumbria, invaded
Scotland in 1054, regaining the southern parts for Malcolm at
Dunsinnan on the day of the Seven Sleepers (27 July); Macbeth was
eventually defeated at Lumphanan in 1057, and his stepson Lulach slain
the following year. Peace with the north was cemented by Malcolm's
marriage to Ingibiorg, daughter of Macbeth's former ally, Thorfinn, jarl
of Orkney. This home stability enabled Malcolm to turn his attention to
neighbouring Northumbria, but if this region had helped make him
king, in the end it destroyed him.

These Northumbrian incursions produced plunder but no territory.
With Malcolm taking advantage of any power vacuum, the first raid was
prompted by Tostig's absence in Rome in 1061. William I's devastation

of the north then suggested benefits to be gained in the aftermath, and the Scots harried as far down as the Tees (1068-70), but with no real achievement. Edgar the Atheling had, meanwhile, fled north from William, and Malcolm's subsequent marriage to his sister Margaret generated a real threat of Scottish intervention in England. In a preemptive invasion, William crossed the border, less for conquest than to bring Malcolm to heel, and, in the Abernethy agreement (1072), the Scottish king swore fealty and agreed to expel Edgar and his supporters. Two further English raids by Malcolm (1079, 1091), followed by submissions, showed little regard for oaths, and William II's construction of Carlisle castle may have reflected his awareness of this. Responding to a summons to Gloucester in August 1093 (laying the foundation stone for a new cathedral at Durham *en route*), Malcolm was angered by the English king's failure to restore certain manors as promised, and led a retaliatory invasion into Northumbria in the November. Alnwick castle agreed to surrender to the Scottish siege, but Malcolm was treacherously and fatally speared in the eye at the gates; his eldest son by Margaret, Edward, was mortally wounded and died in nearby Jedburgh Forest.

Known as 'Canmore' (*ceanmor* = great head, chief), Malcolm was very much an opportunist, ready to attack others though subservient if attacked himself, forgetful of submissions, but failing to extend his kingdom. Able to speak English, Gaelic, and Latin, though apparently unable to write, he was devoted to his second wife, but the claims of anglicization and religious reform during his reign have been inflated. His dynastic line (three sons became kings) continued for two centuries.

Margaret, queen of Scotland, b. c.1046, da. of Edward the Atheling and Agatha, poss. da. of Liudolf, margrave of Westfriesland; m. Malcolm III, 1070; d. Edinburgh, 16 Nov. 1093; bur. Dunfermline.

Granddaughter of Edmund 'Ironside' (killed 1016), Margaret was born at Castle Reka near Mecseknadasd, in southern Hungary, and raised at its court where her father and uncle had settled in exile. Still a child, she came to England when her father, Edward the Atheling, was recalled in 1057 as a possible successor to the childless Edward 'the Confessor'. Her arrival in Scotland in 1068, after the Northumbrian revolt, has been heavily romanticized, though Symeon of Durham implied that her first meeting with Malcolm III may not have been until 1070, after William I's harrying of the north.

She is said to have reformed the somewhat stagnant Celtic church through her familiarity with European Christian practices (ritual, location of Lent, marriage prohibitions), though her piety and personal endowments, pilgrims' shelters, and introduction of Benedictine monks to Dunfermline, suggest reformation of religion rather than church organization. Her confessor Turgot's biography, written at daughter Edith's request, was hagiographic but emphasized Margaret's Anglo-Saxon lineage: her children's names are noticeably non-Celtic. Her death, coming after severe fasting and ascribed to hearing of her husband's and eldest son's slaughter, was followed by canonization in 1250.

Edinburgh castle

Standing high on Castle Rock, this was one of the strongest and most important fortresses in Scotland, but also served as royal residence, seat of government, and prison, and now houses the Honours (regalia) of Scotland. There is no trace of the earliest fortifications, and the eleventh-century St Margaret's Chapel (named for the queen of Malcolm III) is all that remains of their castle. Occupied by Edward I between 1296 and 1313 during the wars of independence, the foundations were demolished by Robert Bruce in 1314, but rebuilt by David II (1367–71) whose great tower was modelled on Edward III's new works at Windsor. The castle was besieged many times over the following centuries, though the giant bombard 'Mons Meg' (presented by Philip of Burgundy in 1457 to his niece's husband, James II) proved so heavy to haul around that it became restricted to firing salutes. The great hall restored by James IV was used as a Parliament hall and for state banquets, later serving as barracks and military hospital before restoration in 1887–91. Mary of Guise died at the castle (1560), and James VI was born there (1566), but no monarch after Charles II visited it until George IV in 1822. Daring escapes were hazarded by internees and Napoleonic prisoners held in the vaults, though less severely than earlier captives. The castle defences were periodically renovated, and a large parade ground (the Esplanade) constructed in the early nineteenth century, now used for the annual military tattoo.

Edinburgh Castle. A fine view showing the castle's strength on its rock. It was held for the Hanoverians throughout the occupation of the city by the Jacobites in 1745–6.

Donald III, b. c.1033, 2nd s. of Duncan I; acc. 13 Nov. 1093, dep. May 1094, rest. 12 Nov. 1094, dep. Oct. 1097; issue: Bethoc; d. Rescobie(?); bur. Dunkeld, rebur. Iona.

The younger brother of Malcolm III, Donald Bane ('the Fair') lived quietly in the Hebrides during Macbeth's and his brother's reigns, but emerged to claim the Scottish kingship through the custom of tanistry when Malcolm and his son Edward were slain in Northumberland. Later described as 'an old Celtic reactionary', Donald immediately expelled the English followers at the Scots court, pleasing those who resented their country's increasing anglicization but annoying William 'Rufus'. With the English king's aid, Malcolm's eldest son Duncan (II) ousted his uncle in May 1094, but was killed a few months later, so enabling Donald to resume the throne; it is thought that he shared government with Edmund, another of Malcolm's sons. In 1097, further military support from William 'Rufus' led to Donald's defeat by Edgar (second son of Malcolm and Margaret). Donald was imprisoned, said to have been later blinded, and died in prison.

Duncan II, b. c.1060, eldest s. of Malcolm III and Ingibiorg; acc. May 1094; m. Octreda, da. of Gospatric, earl of Northumberland and Dunbar, c.1090; illeg. issue: William; d. Mondynes, 12 Nov. 1094; bur. Dunkeld, rebur. Iona(?).

Given as hostage by his father to William I of England following the treaty of Abernethy (1072), Duncan was released on William's death (1087) and knighted by Robert 'Curthose' in Normandy. He swore fealty to William 'Rufus', and, with an Anglo-Norman force, deposed his uncle Donald Bane who had assumed the throne on Malcolm III's death in 1093. Scottish resentment of Duncan's foreign supporters led to many deaths amongst them, and he had to promise never again to harbour Englishmen or Normans. This so weakened his position that, after a very few uneasy months, he was slain by the mormaer of Mearns, near Dunnottar, while fighting his brother Edmund who had backed Donald Bane. The earliest genuine Scottish charter extant is that granted by Duncan to Durham in 1094.

Edmund, b. c.1075, 3rd s. of Malcolm III and Margaret; ruled Lothian 1094–7; d. Montacute, *post* 1102; bur. Montacute.

The only one of Malcolm's sons by his second marriage to have supported his uncle Donald Bane and rejected alien Anglo-Norman influences, Edmund defeated his half-brother Duncan II in 1094, enabling his uncle to regain the throne. He is said to have shared power with Donald III, governing the more southerly Lothian, and may have been Donald's designated successor. They were ousted by his older brother Edgar, with support from William 'Rufus', in 1097. Both were imprisoned, but Edmund is thought to have been released, become a monk in England, and died in the Cluniac priory at Montacute, Somerset, supposedly requesting burial in chains, in sign of eternal penitence for Duncan's death.

Edgar, b. c.1074, 2nd s. of Malcolm III and Margaret; acc. Oct. 1097; d. Dundee, 8 Jan. 1107; bur. Dunfermline.

Driven out with his younger brothers Alexander and David by Donald Bane after Malcolm III's death in 1093, Edgar sought refuge in England under the protection of his maternal uncle Edgar the Atheling. In 1095, William 'Rufus' invested Edgar with the Scottish kingdom, as his vassal, but it was two years before he provided the military support that enabled Edgar to overthrow Donald Bane and re-establish himself. His treaty with Magnus 'Barefoot', in which the Norseman secured control of the Western Isles (1098), and the marriage of his sister Edith to Henry I of England (1100), gave the kingdom some much-needed peace.

Edgar introduced the sealed writ into Scotland (examples survive at Durham), and his influences appear to have been pre-Conquest English rather than Celtic or Anglo-Norman, reflected by the resemblance of his seal to that of Edward 'the Confessor'. Described by Ailred of Rievaulx as 'a sweet-tempered and amiable man', he died unmarried and was succeeded by his brothers Alexander I and David I.

Alexander I, b. c.1077, 5th s. of Malcolm III and Margaret; acc. 8 Jan. 1107; m. Sybilla, illeg. da. of Henry I of England; illeg. issue: Malcolm; d. Stirling, 25 Apr. 1124; bur. Dunfermline.

Taking refuge in England against Donald Bane after his father's death in 1093, Alexander's years there underlaid the modest reforms of his eventual reign, though the seeds of later Scottish struggle for independence may also be observed. When Edgar regained the kingdom from Donald, Alexander received the earldom of Gowrie. On his childless brother's death in 1107, he succeeded to the throne, reluctantly honouring Edgar's deathbed gift of southern Lothian, Teviotdale, and Strathclyde to their youngest brother David; this had the effect of moving the centre of the Scottish kingdom further north, around Scone, Perth, and Stirling. About this time, he strengthened ties with England by marrying the illegitimate daughter of Henry I, Sybilla, who lacked both modesty and beauty ('morus modestia...corporis elegantia').

Apart from aiding Henry I in his Welsh campaigns in 1114, Alexander's main concern was a gradual modernization of Scotia. Faced with northern Celts opposing anglicization, he drove the men of Mearns and Moray back into Ross (acquiring the nickname 'the Fierce'), and is thought to have founded the monastery at Scone (1115) in thanksgiving. He continued his mother Margaret's interests in church life and practice—'a lettered and godly man, very humble and loving towards clerics and monks', according to Fordun—laying the basis for a diocesan episcopate on the Roman model (completed by David I), and introducing English ecclesiastics and Augustinians, though determined to keep the Scottish church independent from Canterbury and York. Reform of civil government was limited, but the earliest known Scottish coins have been attributed to his reign, as also the offices of chancellor, constable, and sheriff; the new designation of *comes* (transitional between mormaer and earl) appeared on charters.

Stirling castle, Central Scotland

Controlling from a high volcanic crag the main ford of the River Forth, a link between the Scottish Highlands and Lowlands, the castle has always had strategic importance. The earliest recorded fortification was used by Malcolm III in the eleventh century, but from the time of Alexander I (who died there in 1124, as did William I in 1214), it was an important royal centre, rivalling Edinburgh. Changing hands many times during the wars of independence, it was dismantled by Robert Bruce after Bannockburn (1314) because of his fear of losing it, but rebuilt by Edward III during his support of Edward Balliol. James III was born there (1452), James IV completed the great hall and developed the inner courtyard and defences, James V had the royal apartments remodelled in French Renaissance style, Mary, queen of Scots, was crowned in the old chapel in 1543, and the future James VI was baptized (1566) and his son Henry born there in 1594.

continued

Stirling castle, Central Scotland *continued*

The 'Kings Knot', an ornamental garden with a pleasure canal, was laid out in the seventeenth century, but the castle surrended to Monck for Cromwell after a short siege in 1651. Although in a poor state of repair in the eighteenth century, it was able to withstand and harry the Jacobites in the 1715 and 1745 risings, before being subdivided to serve as barracks; the army remained until 1964.

David I, b. c.1084, 6th s. of Malcolm III and Margaret; acc. 25 Apr. 1124; m. Matilda (Maud) de Senlis, da. of Waltheof, earl of Northumbria, and wid. of earl of Northampton and Huntingdon, c.1114; issue: Malcolm, Claricia, Hodierna, Henry; d. Carlisle, 24 May 1153; bur. Dunfermline.

As the youngest of Malcolm III's many sons, David might not have been expected, initially, to accede to the kingship. His early adult years were spent at the English court of Henry I, who had married his sister Edith (unpronounceable to the Normans, so usually called Matilda), and David served him as a justice. The lands gifted by his brother Edgar were achieved only by standing up to the next brother Alexander but, through marriage to Matilda de Senlis (a great-niece of William 'the Conqueror'), he acquired the earldom of Huntingdon with extensive lands in Bedfordshire and Northamptonshire.

Ruling as 'earl' during Alexander's reign, David succeeded his childless brother in 1124, and continued his introduction of Anglo-Norman legal and administrative practices, integrating with rather than imposing upon Celtic patterns. The 'Davidian revolution' included grants of land throughout southern Scotland to noble Anglo-Norman incomers, whose dependants rapidly anglicized local society and culture; church reform resulted in the creation or renewal of several bishoprics, with a parochial system, and the personal founding of ten major monasteries, particularly for Augustinian canons and Cistercian monks; town development led to the formation of burghs, and a Scottish coinage system was established.

His grafting of new with old, native with newcomer, and the introduction of Normanesque feudalism, enabled David to call upon vast armies for territorial conquest. The ever-rebellious men of Moray were suppressed in 1130, and a string of castles between Aberdeen and Berwick controlled the north. Through his English title and lands, David had sworn to accept his niece, the empress Matilda, as successor to Henry I, she being his only surviving legitimate issue; when Stephen (husband of another niece, Matilda of Boulogne) challenged for the English crown, involving that kingdom in civil war, David did not remain neutral but supported the empress and invaded England on three occasions. Despite defeat at the battle of the Standard (1138) near Northallerton in Yorkshire, and an ignominious expulsion from London in 1141 (the intended coronation of empress Matilda), a Scottish peace reigned in Cumberland and Northumbria which markedly contrasted with the uncertainty further south.

David died at Carlisle in 1153, after a rule which had transformed the kingdom and strengthened the monarchy. His son, Henry, had died the previous year, leaving the succession to an inexperienced grandson, Malcolm.

Dunfermline palace and abbey, Fife

The Benedictine abbey was founded by David I (1150) on the site of a small church endowed *c.* 1072 by his mother Margaret, wife of Malcolm III, both of whom were buried there, as were their sons and the body (though not the heart) of Robert Bruce. There seems to have been an associated palace from the late thirteenth century since Edward I spent the winter of 1303–4 there before taking Stirling castle; David II was born there (1324), but it was devastated by Richard II in 1385. After rebuilding, it continued as a royal residence, and was the birthplace of James I in 1394.

By the Reformation much of the abbey's land and revenue had passed into private hands, but after 1587 the remainder was annexed to the crown, and James VI granted it to his bride, Anne of Denmark. The abbey guesthouse was enlarged to become an occasional residence for royalty, and was the birthplace of their daughter Elizabeth (1596) and son Charles I (1600). The palace was used by Charles II in 1650 but thereafter abandoned, becoming roofless by 1708.

Malcolm IV, b. 20 Mar. 1142, s. of Henry, earl of Northumbria and Huntingdon, and Ada, da. of William de Warenne, earl of Surrey; acc. 24 May 1153; d. Jedburgh, 9 Dec. 1165; bur. Dunfermline.

The death of earl Henry in 1152 left Scotland with a boy-king the following year, and the earldom of Northumbria in his younger brother's hands. Malcolm's slender affinity with his Celtic subjects, and continued trust in foreign incomers and their Normanizing policies, resulted in rebelliousness amongst the native earls in areas formerly held quiescent. Henry II of England, newly enthroned, power-hungry, and sensing a vulnerability absent under David I, moved quickly and, in a treaty at Chester (1157), reclaimed northern England, settling the Scottish border on the line of the Solway and Tweed. In return, the honour of Huntingdon (removed from earl Henry by Stephen in 1141) was restored to Malcolm, and the lordship of Tynedale bestowed upon his brother William. After they had assisted Henry in bringing the count of Toulouse to heel, in Aquitaine (1159), Malcolm was knighted by his cousin; this suggestion of vassaldom so annoyed six of the Scottish earls that they besieged Malcolm, unsuccessfully, at Perth castle. Resistance in Ross, Argyll, Moray, and Galloway failed to unseat him, and Somerled, 'lord of the Isles', was slain when invading Renfrew in 1164. Malcolm's power advanced into Clydesdale (where a Flemish colony was installed), Kyle, and Renfrew, where the Stewart dynasty was built up; a single kingdom—the 'kingdom of Scotland'—was emerging out of a single kingship. Known from the fifteenth century as 'the Maiden' for his chastity, Malcolm continued many of his grandfather's innovative practices, founding Cupar Angus abbey in 1162, but died unmarried three years later.

Somerled, ('lord of the Isles') 1158–64; several marriages, incl. Ragnhild, da. of Olaf, king of Man c.1140; issue incl. Dugald, Gillebrigte, Olaf, Angus, Bethag, Ranald; d. Renfrew, 1164; bur. Iona, or Sadell abbey in Kintyre(?).

Claiming descent from the founder of Dalriada, though most probably of mixed Celtic–Norse ancestry, Somerled resisted Norse supremacy in the western isles, and became master of the greater part of Argyll and Kintyre. He may personally have supported David I at the battle of the Standard (1138), but turned against his young successor, Malcolm IV, in 1153, possibly through Celtic opposition to continuing Normanizing policies. In the mid-1150s, Somerled's aid was sought by the chiefs of the Isles in their opposition to his brother-in-law Godred, king of Man

(Olaf's son and successor); Godred was forced to share his kingdom, retaining Man, Lewis, and Skye, but ceding Mull, Jura, and Islay (1156). The quarrel was renewed in 1158, when Godred was driven out to Norway, Man plundered, and Somerled made himself 'king of the Isles'. Although making peace with Malcolm IV in 1160, Somerled resented the expanding Stewart lordship (through fiefs) in the west of Scotland, and declared war in 1164, sailing up the Clyde to Renfrew, where he and his son Gillebrigte were killed. Godred regained possession of Man, but the Isles were divided between Somerled's remaining sons, Dugald (Lorn, Mull, Tiree), Ranald (Kintyre, Islay, Jura), and Angus (Bute, Arran, Skye). The lordship of the Isles was held by their descendants until 1493 when James IV appropriated the vast MacDonald estates.

William I ('the Lion'), b. 1143, 2nd s. of Henry, earl of Northumbria and Huntingdon, and Ada, da. of William de Warenne, earl of Surrey; acc. 9 Dec. 1165; m. Ermengarde, da. of Richard, vicomte de Beaumont, 5 Sept. 1186; issue: Alexander, Margaret, Isabella, Marjorie; illeg. issue: 2s., 4das.; d. Stirling, 4 Dec. 1214; bur. Arbroath.

Succeeding his celibate elder brother, William reigned for forty-nine years, the longest span in medieval Scotland, but had to acknowledge English overlordship for fifteen years of it, while uncertainties over succession may have contributed to much of the unrest. Originally granted the earldom of Northumbria by his grandfather David I, he resented its re-appropriation by Henry II of England (1157), and in 1174 rashly attempted to regain it while Henry was preoccupied with the 'Great Rebellion', only to be captured at Alnwick, led to Northampton with his feet tied beneath his horse, and imprisoned at Falaise in Normandy. The subsequent treaty (Falaise, December 1174; ratified in York, August 1175) released William from custody at the cost of acknowledging Henry as feudal overlord; Scottish nobles and churchmen also had to acquiesce, the church of Scotland was to be subject to that of England, and five key fortresses were surrendered, to be garrisoned by English troops at Scottish expense.

This humiliation triggered a revolt in Galloway which lasted until 1186, and prompted construction of a castle at Dumfries. In 1179, meanwhile, William and his younger brother David personally led a force northwards into Easter Ross, establishing two further castles, and aiming to discourage the earls of Orkney from expanding beyond Caithness. A further rising in 1181 involved Donald Macwilliam, a direct descendant of Duncan II, and briefly took over Ross; not until the death of the claimant Donald (1187) was William able to reclaim Inverness, and further royal expeditions were required in 1197 and 1202 to neutralize Orcadian threat.

Constant reminders of English suzerainty persisted. Apart from the English garrisons at Roxburgh, Berwick, and Edinburgh castles, Henry arranged in 1186 for William to marry the daughter of a French vassal—William was by then in his forties but lacked legitimate issue—and insisted on cognizance of all his activities in Scotland. Not until 5 December 1189, when Richard I needed finance for his crusade, was the treaty of Falaise abrogated by a formal quit-claim at Canterbury, which cost 10,000 merks. Although Scotland regained its formal independence, Anglo-Scottish relations remained tense, and king John eventually brought a large army to Norham (near Berwick) in August 1209, to exploit the flagging Scottish leadership. As well as promising a large monetary sum, the aged and ailing William agreed to his two elder daughters marrying English nobles and, when the treaty was renewed in 1212, John apparently gained the right to arrange the marriage of William's young son, the future Alexander II.

Despite continued dependence on English goodwill, William's reign showed much achievement. He threw himself into the government of his kingdom with energy, following the lines laid down by David I. Anglo-French settlements and feudalization were extended, new burghs founded, criminal law clarified, the responsibilities of justices and sheriffs widened, and trade grew. Arbroath abbey was founded (1178), and the bishopric of Argyll established *c.*1192, the same year as papal confirmation that the Scottish church was free of all external authority save the pope's. A contemporary epithet for William as 'the lion of justice' developed in the fourteenth century into the byname 'the Lyon'; the less familiar 'the Ruddy' tallies with a chronicler's description of *garbh* (brawny).

Ermengarde de Beaumont, da. of Richard, vicomte de Beaumont-sur-Sarthe; m. William I, 5 Sept. 1186; d. 11 Feb. 1234; bur. Balmerino, Fife.

Daughter of a comparatively minor vassal to Henry II of England, her marriage to William, at Woodstock near Oxford, was arranged by Henry and emphasized his superior position; Edinburgh castle (appropriated under the treaty of Falaise) was returned to William for her as part of her tocher (dowry). The chroniclers indicate some public prominence in

1212, perhaps because her husband was ill. During a long widowhood, spent mainly at Forfar, she founded the Cistercian abbey at Balmerino, where she was buried.

Alexander II, b. 24 Aug. 1198, s. of William I and Ermengarde; acc. 4 Dec. 1214; m. (1) Joan, da. of John, king of England, 19 June 1221; (2) Marie de Coucy, da. of Enguerrand de Couci, 15 May 1239; issue: Alexander; (illeg.) Marjorie; d. Kerrera, 8 July 1249; bur. Melrose.

From the outset, Alexander aimed to regain independence from England and recover its border counties. Taking advantage of the struggles between its king (John) and his barons, Alexander laid claim to Northumberland, Cumberland, and Westmorland, controlling Carlisle by 1216 in response to John's burning from Berwick to Haddington (to 'smoke out' the 'little fox-cub'—a reference to Alexander's red hair). The Scots then marched to Dover, where Alexander met prince Louis of France (claimant to the English throne) and did homage for Northumberland. However, after John's death in October 1216, the royalist success at Lincoln persuaded Louis to return home, and Alexander was forced to make peace with Henry III in December 1217. Scottish expansion southwards was abandoned, and Henry accepted their separate sovereignty, though the frontier was not finally established along the Solway–Tweed line until the treaty of York (1237). Alexander's marriage to Henry's sister Joan (1221) reinforced the new realism that had entered Anglo-Scottish relations, and enabled him to concentrate on domestic issues.

Unlike his two predecessors, whose French influences were marked, Alexander aimed for better balance between Gaelic and Norman cultures, and a new balance of power between crown and magnates, whether native Scots, Northumbrian, or Anglo-Norman in origin. Reorganized administration and expanding trade generated wealth, and underpinned the process of bringing the whole kingdom under royal control. Loyal earldoms enabled him to suppress disorder and insurrections in Moray, Argyll (1220s), Ross and Caithness (early 1230s), and, eventually, Galloway (1234–5). The Western Isles were still under the suzerainty of Norway, but when diplomacy failed, Alexander led an expedition in 1249, only to succumb unexpectedly to a fever while on the island of Kerrera in Oban Bay.

Joan (Joanna), b. 22 July 1210, eldest da. of John, king of England, and Isabella of Angoulême; m. Alexander II of Scotland, 19 June 1221; d. London, 5 Mar. 1238; bur. Tarrant Kaines abbey, Dorset.

A marriage between the young lord Alexander and any future daughter of king John had been mooted as early as 1209, at the treaty of Norham, with Northumbria as possible tocher, but it was not until 1221 that such a union was solemnized at York. Joan's younger brother Henry (III) was by then on the English throne, and the alliance helped ease Anglo-Scottish relations, though any influence over husband or brother appears minimal; failure to produce a child may have contributed. After both kings met at York in September 1237, Joan continued south, on pilgrimage to Canterbury with Henry's wife, Eleanor, but she was taken ill that winter in London, where she died.

Marie de Coucy, 2nd da. of Enguerrand de Couci; m. (1) Alexander II of Scotland, 15 May 1239; (2) John de Brienne; bur. Newbottle.

Daughter of a Picard lord, and related to the French crown, Marie seems to have settled better in Scotland than her predecessor, and gave Alexander his desired heir and successor. She left Scotland for France after his death, in the autumn of 1250, but though she may have planned to return the following spring, she did not do so for several years; she visited York at Christmas 1251, however, when her boy-king son was knighted, then married. Squabbles between the Comyns and Durwards during Alexander's minority encouraged her return to Scotland in June 1257, with her second husband, though she had to swear to Henry III that she would do nothing to upset the government of 1255. In 1258, agreement was reached that the care of the kingdom would be in the hands of a council, in which queen Marie and John de Brienne were factionally neutral.

Alexander III, b. 4 Sept. 1241, s. of Alexander II and Marie de Coucy; acc. 8 July 1249; m. (1) Margaret, da. of Henry III of England, 26 Dec. 1251; issue: Margaret, Alexander, David; (2) Yolande de Dreux, da. of the comte de Dreux, 14 Oct. 1285; d. nr. Pettycur, Fife, 19 Mar. 1286; bur. Dunfermline.

Aged eight on accession, Alexander was Scotland's first boy-king for almost a century, and his minority almost inevitably saw some faction-fighting, notably between the high-ranking Comyn family and the lesser Durwards. Alexander's marriage to the daughter of the English king (1251) enabled Henry III to interfere, imposing his choice of council in

1255, but by 1258 (when Henry had his own political difficulties) the nobility had reached a compromise in which royal interests prevailed over their own. In 1259–60, Alexander assumed full power, and his reign became one of relative peace and growing prosperity. He worked with the magnates rather than subduing them, balancing old and new rivalries, and relations with England were friendly, all of which enabled him to complete his father's expedition to the Western Isles. Negotiations having failed, Scottish raids provoked Norwegian response, till by September 1263 their fleet had reached the Firth of Clyde; the subsequent skirmishes, dignified into the Battle of Largs, were in reality less conclusive than the death of king Haakon, overwintering in Orkney, and the treaty of Perth (1266) finally saw the formal transfer of overlordship of the Western (though not the Northern) Isles and Man to the Scots.

Later Scottish chroniclers came to regard Alexander's reign as a 'golden age', when the name Scotland became definitively synonymous with the whole kingdom of the Scots, not just lands north of the Forth and Clyde, and the realm itself robust and autonomous. This success became jeopardized, though, by the deaths of both of Alexander's sons in the early 1280s, prompting a second marriage to Yolande (Yoleta) de Dreux, daughter of a Gascon vassal of Edward I. Five months later, while travelling to her across the Forth from Edinburgh to Kinghorn, in a storm, he was thrown from his horse and killed. If Yolande was pregnant, no living issue resulted, and the kingdom faced the uncertainty of unprecedented female succession.

Margaret, b. 5 Oct. 1240, eld. da. of Henry III of England and Eleanor of Provence; m. Alexander III, 26 Dec. 1251; d. Cupar, 27 Feb. 1275; bur. Dunfermline.

Marriage to the Scottish heir had been suggested while both were still infants, but the death of Alexander II expedited matters, and Margaret's marriage to Alexander III took place at York at Christmas 1251. Her early years in Scotland were unhappy and solitary, affected by the squabbles surrounding Alexander's minority, and both parents were concerned for her welfare. Release from Edinburgh castle in 1255 was followed by visits to the English court, though Scottish wrath was incurred by the delivery of her first child at Windsor rather than on home soil. A lady of great beauty, chastity, and humility, according to the Lanercost chronicler, she attended her brother Edward's coronation in London in 1274, but died soon after at Cupar castle.

Margaret ('Maid of Norway'), uncrowned queen of Scotland, b. c. Apr. 1283, da. of Erik II of Norway and Margaret, da. of Alexander III; acc. 19 Mar. 1286; d. c.26 Sept. 1290; bur. Bergen.

The death of Alexander III's sons, David (1281) and Alexander (January 1284, without issue), meant that the only Canmore successor was a sickly baby girl by his daughter Margaret, who had died in childbirth. Known as the 'Maid of Norway', she had been acknowledged heir to the Scottish throne on 5 February 1284, and succeeded her grandfather unexpectedly two years later. The broad-based government set up to rule in her absence faced the diplomatic problem of her marriage and settled upon Edward of Caernarfon (the future Edward II), the alliance being confirmed at the treaty of Birgham (July 1290). In the September, Margaret sailed from Norway but died in or near Orkney, leaving the kingdom without an obvious successor.

Balliol and Bruce

The lack of provision for the succession after the death of the 'Maid of Norway' left the kingdom without a monarch for two years. The close family connections between the English and Scottish royal houses, and Edward I's political experience, resulted in a series of meetings at Norham and Berwick before him, to determine which of the eventual thirteen claimants had the best right to the throne. This affair has become known as the 'Great Cause'. Some of the 'competitors' were descendants of the illegitimate offspring of William 'the Lion', but the main choice lay between three men—John Balliol, Robert Bruce, and John Hastings, all descended from David, earl of Huntingdon (youngest brother of Malcolm IV and William I). Laws of inheritance were still ambiguous, but judgement was finally given on 17 November 1292 to John Balliol, as the most senior line.

After Balliol's abdication in 1296, Edward I took the control of Scotland into his own hands, but his hold was illusory. National resistance developed from skirmishes into the first war of independence, in which William Wallace played a leading role, but the Scots were forced to submit to Edward in 1304, after which he began reorganization of government with the support of many of the Scottish nobles. This was soon to be swept away by the revolt of Robert Bruce, grandson of the competitor, but the second interregnum had lasted for a decade.

John Balliol, b. c.1250, 3rd s. of John Balliol and Dervorguilla, da. of Alan of Galloway; acc. 17 Nov. 1292; abdic. 10 July 1296; m. Isabella de Warenne, da. of John de Warenne, earl of Surrey, c. Feb. 1281; issue: Edward, Henry, das.; d. Château Gaillard, Normandy, Apr. 1313.

Of Picard descent but with a mother who was a great-great-granddaughter of David I, and succeeding to Galloway in 1290, John Balliol was selected from the competitors by Edward I, with a warning to rule Scotland justly lest he should have to intervene against him; Balliol swore fealty, was enthroned at Scone (30 November), and paid homage in December. Throughout his reign, he was repeatedly humiliated, even being summoned to appear at Westminster (1293) to explain his judgements. Edward's demand for military service in France the following June stiffened opposition resolve, but as Balliol had become compromised by his submissions, a council of twelve took power out of his hands (July 1295), and then allied with Edward's French enemies under Philip IV. Hostilities began in March 1296, but after Edward sacked Berwick, Balliol was forced to surrender, ritually stripped of royal symbols—the arms torn from his surcoat left him as 'Toom Tabard' (empty coat)—and consigned to the Tower of London. Declaring formally to have nothing more to do with Scotland, he was transferred into papal custody in 1299, before being released to his ancestral lands in Picardy (1301) for the remainder of his life.

Robert I ('the Bruce'), b. 11 July 1274, s. of Robert Bruce and Marjorie, acc. 25 Mar. 1306; m. (1) Isabella, da. of Donald, earl of Mar, c.1295; issue: Marjorie; (2) Elizabeth, da. of Richard de Burgh, 1302; issue: Matilda, Margaret, David, John; illeg. issue: 2s., 3 das.; d. Cardross, 7 June 1329; bur. Dunfermline.

Grandson of the competitor Robert Bruce, and given the earldom of Carrick by his father in 1292, Robert Bruce became involved in the 1297 uprising and continued his resistance even after Wallace's army was crushed at Falkirk the following year. Family ambitions, though, took precedence over loyalty to the deposed king, and the arrangement whereby Bruce and John Comyn of Badenoch became joint guardians (later joined by bishop Lamberton) was destabilized by regular Bruce–

Comyn antagonism; the Comyns were Balliol's leading supporters and remained steadfastly loyal. Bruce stayed on the Scottish side until 1302, when he submitted to Edward, who had just agreed a nine-month truce. This was Scotland's loss rather than England's gain, but the surrender may have been prompted by realistic fears about his lands and honours, especially if a Balliol restoration occurred with French aid.

Bruce's *coup d'état* of 1306 was carefully planned. He fatally stabbed John Comyn in a church at Dumfries, and hastened to Scone for enthronement and coronation as Robert I (25 March), but his position was weak and he was defeated by English forces at Methven (19 June) and forced into hiding. He returned to Carrick early the following year and, gaining a breathing space from the death of Edward I and Edward II's financial problems, began to deal with his own internal concerns. The earl of Ross was badly scared, the Comyns were defeated at Inverurie and Buchan laid waste, Edward Bruce ravaged Galloway to reduce English authority there, and Robert himself tackled the west in the Brander campaign. By the autumn of 1308 ceaseless campaigning was giving way to settled administration. Robert I was now widely accepted as rightful king, and his authority was enhanced by the decisive victory at Bannockburn (24 June 1314) against a large English force, and the flight of Edward II. Edward continued to refuse to consider peace despite repeated Scottish raids into northern England, and it was not until his deposition in 1327 that negotiations could properly commence. The treaty of Edinburgh, ratified at Northampton (May 1328), set the seal on Robert's achievements; Edward III recognized the full independence of Scotland, relinquished his claim to Berwick and the borders, and agreed to the marriage of Robert's young son David to his daughter Joan.

Robert's concern with the succession—he had no male heir until 1324—led to three successive tailzies of the crown. The papacy eventually recognized his title as king of Scotland (1324), despite two brief episodes of excommunication, one after the sacrilege of Comyn's murder, the later one in 1320 lifted by the nobles' appeal usually known as the 'declaration of Arbroath'. Robert died at his house at Cardross after two years' serious illness, described by chroniclers as 'leprosy', and whilst his body was taken to Dunfermline, his heart (at his request) was embalmed, carried on crusade, and eventually interred at Melrose abbey.

BARROW, G. W. S., *Robert Bruce and the Community of the Realm of Scotland* (1976).

Isabella, da. of Donald, earl of Mar, and Helen (Elen), wid. of Malcolm, earl of Fife; m. Robert Bruce, earl of Carrick (later Robert I), c.1295; d. ante 1302.

Links between the Mar and Bruce families were close, and Robert's sister, Christian, had wedded the earl's son and successor, Gartnait (or Gratney). Isabella's marriage took place about the time Robert went over to the English, and appears to have been tragically short, though it produced Marjorie, eventual ancestress of the Stewart kings.

Elizabeth, 2nd da. of Richard de Burgh, earl of Ulster, and Margaret; m. Robert Bruce, earl of Carrick (later Robert I), 1302; d. Cullen, 26 Oct. 1327; bur. Dunfermline.

Daughter of one of Edward I's staunchest Anglo-Irish supporters, Elizabeth married Robert Bruce after his submission to the English king, but the union also strengthened Bruce ties with the Stewarts, since she was James Stewart's niece by marriage. After the battle of Methven (1306), she was sent north for safety to Kildrummy castle, possibly aiming for Orkney, but was seized from the sanctuary of St Duthac at Tain and taken before Edward I. Sentenced less harshly than some of the other royal ladies, she was confined in the manor house at Burstwick in Holderness, being allowed two elderly pages and two servantwomen, 'elderly and not at all gay'; release came only after Bannockburn (1314), as part of the exchange for the earl of Hereford. Elizabeth eventually bore Robert his hoped-for legitimate male heir.

Edward Bruce, b. c.1276, 2nd s. of Robert Bruce and Marjorie, titular king of Ireland 1315–18; illeg. issue: Alexander, Thomas(?); d. Faughart, nr. Dundalk, 14 Oct. 1318.

Younger sibling of Robert I, Edward became one of his brother's foremost military commanders, ravaging Galloway in 1308 to reduce English authority there and subsequently created its lord. Further campaigns preceded the siege of Stirling castle (1313), where his impatient agreement with the English commander that it would surrender if not relieved within a year forced the hand of Edward II and precipitated the battle of Bannockburn (1314), where Bruce commanded the leading brigade; a subsequent raid into north-east England caused widespread damage. Having been named as heir presumptive to the Scottish throne in 1315, he embarked on an expedition to Ireland, but despite forcing the Ulster nobles to acknowledge him as king, there was less than expected support, and

Robert had briefly to come to his aid in 1317. Arrogance also prompted him to contact the Welsh, suggesting he join them in expelling the English, and become additionally prince of Wales. Described (understatedly) by a chronicler as 'a little headstrong and impetuous', Edward Bruce became unable to sustain his position, was killed at the battle of Dundalk by an Anglo-Irish army, and his body quartered and dispersed.

Marjorie Bruce, b. c.1295/6, da. of Robert I and Isabella of Mar; m. Walter the Steward, 1315; issue: Robert; d. nr. Paisley, Mar. 1316.

The only child of Robert I's first marriage, and named after her grandmother who had brought the earldom of Carrick into the Bruce family, Marjorie's surrender as a hostage had been a condition of her father's submission in August 1297, though he complied in neither. After Methven (1306), she was sent north with her stepmother and other royal ladies, but was seized at Tain and escorted to Edward I; the order to place Marjorie incommunicado in a cage in the Tower of London, like her aunt Mary and the countess of Buchan (at Roxburgh and Berwick castles respectively), was revoked, and she was sent to the Gilbertine nunnery at Watton, Yorkshire. Eventually exchanged for the earl of Hereford after Bannockburn, she agreed to her uncle Edward becoming heir presumptive (1315), before being given in marriage to Walter the Steward (or Stewart), the younger son but eventual heir of James the Steward. In the fatal fall from her horse in March 1316, she gave birth to a son, Robert (later Robert II), so was the joint founder of the royal house of Stewart.

David II, b. 5 Mar. 1324, s. of Robert I and Elizabeth de Burgh; acc. 7 June 1329; m. (1) Joan, da. of Edward II of England, 17 July 1328; (2) Margaret Drummond, da. of Sir Malcolm Drummond, Apr. 1363; d. Edinburgh, 22 Feb. 1371; bur. Holyrood.

The only surviving son of Robert Bruce, David was five years old on accession, and his reign was disrupted by both exile and imprisonment. The death of the guardian of Scotland, Thomas Randolph, earl of Moray, in 1322 left the kingdom vulnerable to attack by Edward Balliol, backed by Edward III, and the 'disinherited'; the boy-king and his young wife were sent to Dumbarton castle, then France for safety in 1334, where they were graciously received by Philip VI. It was not until 2 June 1341 that they landed at Inverbervie, and were received by the people 'with blythnes', but faced a kingdom suffering the effects of widespread invasion and baronial feuding. Edward III's campaign in Normandy encouraged David to lead a large force of Scots across the border to pressurize the English, but after stripping Hexham, it succumbed to local forces at Neville's Cross, west of Durham (17 October 1346); David was wounded in the face by an arrow, then taken prisoner.

During his eleven years' imprisonment in England, from which he was released by the treaty of Berwick (October 1357), on payment of a ransom of 100,000 merks (to be paid at the rate of 10,000 merks per year), the kingdom was governed by Robert the Steward as guardian, but suffered badly from the 'first pestilence' (Black Death) in 1349–50. On David's return, this time no longer a pleasure-loving youth, much was undertaken to restore the Scottish economy. He governed with vigour, dealing firmly with recalcitrant nobles and a wider baronial revolt (1363), and continued to pursue the goal of final peace with England. By the time of his death, the monarchy was stronger, and the kingdom and royal finances more prosperous than might have seemed possible.

His private life has been criticized, but despite two wives and several mistresses—the murder of Katherine Mortimer in 1360 stiffened his attitude to his nobles—he died childless, and the throne passed to the Steward by the tailzie of 1318.

Joan, b. 5 July 1321, 2nd da. of Edward II of England and Isabella of France; m. David Bruce (later David II), 17 July 1328; d. nr. London, 14 Aug. 1362; bur. church of the Friars Minor, London.

Born in the Tower of London, hence sometimes referred to as 'Joanna of the Tower', she was married at Berwick at the age of seven to the son and heir of Robert I of Scotland, but was to spend relatively little time in that country. Driven into exile in 1334, passed mainly at Château Gaillard in Normandy, they returned in 1341, but after David's capture at Neville's Cross (1346), she visited him in the Tower of London, and later resided at Hertford castle for a while. After David's release in 1357, she found a mistress ensconced, so sought refuge at her brother Edward III's court. Her prolonged absence in England affected relations between the two countries, and her childlessness shadowed the succession.

Margaret Drummond, da. of Sir Malcolm Drummond; m. (1) Sir John Logie; issue: at least 1 s.; (2) David II, Apr. 1363; d. Avignon, 1375.

After the death of queen Joan (1362), Margaret Logie was openly recognized by the king as his 'beloved', but the royal grants to her son and the possibility of an heir if David and she did marry may have fuelled the restiveness of Robert the Steward and his allies. In the event, David and Margaret were married at Inchmurdoch, Fife, where the rebels were then humiliated. By 1369, Margaret had fallen out of favour, presumably because there were no signs of children, and David divorced her the following March, to leave himself free to marry again—Agnes Dunbar was already in prospect. Furious, Margaret fled to France, to appeal to the papal *Curia* at Avignon against the sentence, but her death removed the threat of Scotland being placed under an interdict.

Edward Balliol, b. c.1283, s. of John Balliol and Isabella de Warenne; crowned 24 Sept. 1332, expelled Dec. 1332, rest. 1333–6; d. Wheatley, nr. Doncaster, Jan. 1364.

Son of the king of Scots chosen by Edward I from the thirteen claimants in 1292, Edward de Balliol's prospects seemed good until the wars of independence marginalized the family, and he stayed in his Picardy lands after his father's death in 1313. With David II only a small boy on accession in 1329, and the death of his regent in July 1332, Edward resumed the Bruce–Balliol civil war the following month, landing at Kinghorn (Fife) with the 'disinherited' and other land-hungry nobles, and supported by Edward III of England. Defeating the Scots at Dupplin, Balliol assumed the title 'king of Scots' and was crowned at Scone on 24 September. He was compelled to seek refuge in Carlisle within three months, but was joined by Edward III in a siege of Berwick the following May, the relieving Scots being massacred (through use of the long-bow) at nearby Halidon Hill in July. Balliol's subsequent parliament at Edinburgh (1334), which acknowledged English help and surrendered Berwick 'forever' to England, was followed by his homage to Edward and grant of southern counties from Haddington to Dumfries to direct English rule. Edward III's incursions to support his puppet king ceased only with the start of the French wars, and by 1341 David II had returned from exile. Balliol, meanwhile, had spent much of his time in England, but did not surrender his claim to the Scottish crown to Edward III until 20 January 1356, in return for a pension.

Stewarts

The house of Stewart ruled Scotland in direct descent for over three centuries, and inherited the thrones of England and Ireland in 1603. The family was of Breton origin, holding the office of seneschal or steward of the counts of Dol and Dinan, but Walter was recruited by David I and appointed high steward in 1138. The title became heritable, and by 1300 the family had become one of the most powerful in the west Highlands. 'Stewart' gradually replaced 'the Steward' as a surname. The sixth high steward married the daughter of Robert I, so when the Bruce male line failed, the succession passed to their son as Robert II. Despite several periods of minority rule, rebellion, assassination (James I) and deposition (Mary), the dynasty proved more durable than its English counterparts, and ended only with the 'Glorious Revolution' of 1688.

Robert II, b. 2 Mar. 1316, s. of Walter the Steward and Marjorie Bruce, da. of Robert I; acc. 22 Feb. 1371; m. (1) Elizabeth Mure, da. of Sir Adam Mure of Rowallan, c.Nov. 1347; issue: John, Walter, Robert, Alexander, Margaret, Marjorie, Elizabeth, Isabella, Jean; (2) Euphemia Ross, da. of Hugh, earl of Ross, c.May 1355; issue: David, Walter, Egidia, Jean; illeg. issue: 8s., 1 da.; d. Dundonald, 19 Apr. 1390; bur. Scone.

Grandson of Robert Bruce, but lacking his courage and vigour, Robert the Steward was recognized as heir presumptive by the tailzie of 1318, after the death of Edward Bruce at Faughart, though this was modified after the birth of David Bruce (1324) to succession only if David had no male heirs. Escaping to Dumbarton after the battle of Halidon Hill (1333), Robert became joint guardian with the earl of Moray the following year, and tried to regain some of the lands ceded by Edward Balliol, but subsequently made peace with Edward III. Aged twenty-two, he took over as guardian in 1338, but during David II's captivity was styled instead as king's lieutenant. On David's return, Robert was rewarded with the earldom of Strathearn, but was at the heart of the baronial rebellion of 1363. Forced to submit, he nevertheless remained heir presumptive despite the growing power of the Drummonds.

David's unexpected death in 1371, without heirs, made Robert king at the age of fifty-five, and one of his first acts was to define the succession, since there was some dubiety about the legitimacy of his children by his first wife. Described by a chronicler as impressive in appearance, humble, and affable, he had never really attempted to elevate himself above the other nobles, and later commentators have condemned him as weak, senile, and responsible for the decline in power and prestige of the crown. Most of the English-occupied lands had been recovered by the early 1380s, but by then England was less of a problem than internal concerns: law and order were breaking down, and in 1384 Robert submitted to the Holyrood general council and agreed that his heir John, earl of Carrick, should enforce the law throughout the realm. There was no attempt to displace Robert, but in 1388, Carrick was similarly relieved of authority because of his own bodily weakness.

BOARDMAN, S. I., *The Early Stuart Kings: Robert II and Robert III, 1371–1406* (1996).

Elizabeth Mure, da. of Sir Adam Mure of Rowallan; m. Robert the Steward (later Robert II), c.Nov. 1347; d. c.1353.

The Mure family had held the estate of Rowallan in Cunningham (northern division of Ayrshire) from the thirteenth century. Elizabeth bore Robert nine children before the papal dispensation of 22 November 1347 permitted their marriage and, by canon law, the legitimization of their issue. Contention arose later as to whether this legitimization could apply to children born of parents who were within the 'forbidden degrees' of consanguinity, implying that their descendants' claims to the Scottish throne were suspect.

Euphemia Ross, da. of Hugh, earl of Ross, and Margaret Graham; m. (1) John Randolph, earl of Moray; (2) Robert the Steward (later Robert II), c.May 1355; d. c.1387.

Euphemia's first husband had defeated Edward Balliol at Annan, and been a joint guardian of the realm in 1334 during David II's minority, before imprisonment by the English and death at Neville's Cross (1346). A papal dispensation of 2 May 1355 permitted marriage to Robert, by then earl of Strathallan as well as Strathearn, and her sons were thought by some to have stronger claims to the succession than their half-brothers by Robert's first marriage to Elizabeth Mure. Euphemia Ross should not be confused with her niece of the same name, who became countess of Ross in her own right in 1372 and died in 1395.

Robert III, b. c.1337, eldest s. of Robert the Steward (later Robert II) and Elizabeth Mure; acc. 19 Apr. 1390; m. Annabella Drummond, da. of Sir John Drummond,

1367; issue: David, Robert, James, Margaret, Mary, Elizabeth, Egidia; illeg. issue: 2s.; d. Dundonald, 4 Apr. 1406; bur. Paisley.

Christened John, created earl of Carrick on his father's accession, and confirmed as heir-apparent (1371), he was given authority to enforce the law throughout the realm on Robert II's submission in 1384, for a period of three years. He too failed to maintain order and, after a kick from a horse belonging to Sir James Douglas incapacitated him, was removed from authority in 1388 by the three estates, his younger brother Robert being appointed guardian. Although some of the physical damage may have improved, he was left very timid and retiring.

He was crowned in 1390 as Robert III, since the name of John for a monarch was reckoned to be ill-omened, but his brother continued as guardian until 1393, when Robert took back the government into his own hands. The reign was beset by problems: a steep decline in crown finances; the continuing 'Highland problem', which included freelance Stewart activities, and growing disaffection of the lords of the Isles; rivalry within the royal house, notably between his son David and brother Robert, whom he had created dukes of Rothesay and Albany respectively in 1398. Inability to control matters led to censure by the general council (1399) for 'mysgovernance of the realm', and appointment of Rothesay as lieutenant throughout the kingdom.

A brief intervention in Scotland by the newly enthroned Henry IV of England occurred in 1400; demanding homage, he came to Edinburgh, but Robert does not appear to have acquiesced. Albany was restored to power after the death of Rothesay (1402), but the ageing king must have had some presentiment of danger, since he arranged to send his twelve-year-old son, James, to France at the end of 1405, ostensibly for his education. The news of the boy's capture at sea by the English hastened Robert's death, only weeks later. His allegedly self-written epitaph reflected an enduring sense of failure: 'Here lies the worst of kings and the most wretched of men in the whole realm.'

BOARDMAN, S. I., *The Early Stuart Kings: Robert II and Robert III, 1371–1406* (1996).

Annabella Drummond, queen of Scotland, b. c.1350, da. of Sir John Drummond; m. Robert Stewart, earl of Carrick (later Robert III), 1367; d. Scone, 1401.

The Drummond family rose to prominence in the 1360s as kin of David II's second wife, Margaret, and Annabella was the queen's niece. It was she rather than Robert who corresponded with Richard II of England in

1394 about a possible marriage of their eldest son David with an English princess, and she took a significant part in the Anglo-Scottish courtly interchanges at that time. She strongly supported her son, the duke of Rothesay, against the duke of Albany, and formally (and successfully) complained in 1399 that Albany's deputies were obstructing the levying of the huge pension granted earlier for 'her adornment and other things necessary for her rank and livelihood'. When Henry IV came to Edinburgh in 1400 to receive Robert's homage, his sparing of the countryside was reputed to have been out of reverence for her. Annabella, 'faire, honorabil and pleasand', died at Scone in the autumn of 1401.

Robert Stewart, duke of Albany, b. 1339, 3rd s. of Robert the Steward (later Robert II) and Elizabeth Mure; m. (1) Margaret, countess of Menteith, c. Sept. 1361; issue: Murdac, Janet; (2) Muriella, da. of Sir William Keith, Marischal of Scotland, 1380; issue: John, Andrew, Robert; also (which mother uncertain): Maria, Margaret, Isobel, Marjory, Elizabeth; d. Stirling, 2 Sept. 1420; bur. Dunfermline.

Although a younger son, Robert controlled Scotland for over thirty years during the reigns of three kings. Acquiring the earldoms of Menteith and Fife through marriage and inheritance, he took over as chamberlain (1382), this post being retained until 1407, during which time direct taxation was allowed to lapse—Robert thereby gaining the 'innumerable blessings of the common folk'—customs revenues fell and, even though expenditure diminished, there were occasional heavy deficits. On the earl of Carrick's incapacity after injury in 1388, Robert Stewart was chosen by the estates to act as guardian for his father, and he continued as such for a year or two after Carrick succeeded as Robert III. Animosity developed between David, the headstrong new earl of Carrick, and his uncle, which Robert III tried to placate by creating both dukes in 1398: Carrick became duke of Rothesay, and Robert Stewart chose Albany, a name hinting at the ancient kingdom of Alba and suggesting royal rather than baronial pretensions. Rothesay's behaviour eventually led to his arrest, but his subsequent death at Falkland (1402) provoked accusations against Albany and Douglas until the king publicly exonerated them.

Albany became heir presumptive on Robert III's death in 1406, but the young James I was prisoner of the English and uncrowned, and fears about the powerful Albany–Douglas faction exacerbated civil unrest; Albany was appointed governor of the realm, and assumed far more royal trappings than his predecessors. Relations with Henry IV in England were unsteady; he failed to secure James's release, and maintained the imposter 'Richard II' in Scotland for several years. Albany was talented and politically astute, but has been regarded as a master of chicanery who avoided controversial measures and failed to punish powerful offenders. He died aged eighty, in full possession of his faculties, without ever fulfilling his ambitions for the throne.

Alexander Stewart, earl of Buchan, b. c.1342, 4th s. of Robert II and Elizabeth Mure; m. Euphemia, countess of Ross, 1382; illeg. issue: 6s., 1 da.; d. c.1405; bur. Dunkeld.

Alexander Stewart first intervened in Moray politics in 1370, and became king's lieutenant in the north two years later. Lord of Badenoch and earl of Buchan in 1382 through his marriage to the widowed countess of Ross, he continued his reign of violence (including feuds, cattle-raids, and protection rackets) at a time of marked Highland lawlessness, until sacked as justiciar by the three estates in 1388. He deserted his wife in 1389 for a woman named Mariota, and was censured by the bishops of Moray and Ross. Since there had been other quarrels with the bishop of Moray, Alexander, with the help of 'wyld wykkyd Heland-men', burned the burgh of Forres (May 1390), then Elgin and its cathedral (17 June) in revenge, becoming known as 'the Wolf of Badenoch'. Forced to appear before Robert III's council, he subsequently did penance and helped repair the cathedral.

Murdac Stewart, duke of Albany (Murdoch Stewart), b. c.1362, s. of Robert, duke of Albany, and Margaret, countess of Menteith; m. Isobel, da. of Duncan, earl of Lennox, 17 Feb. 1392; issue: Robert, Walter, Alexander, James, Isobel; d. Stirling, 25 May 1425; bur. Blackfriars church, Stirling.

Serving for a year as justiciar in 1389, soon after his father had become governor of Scotland, Murdac was captured at Homildon Hill (1402), delivered to Henry IV, and held at his court despite several negotiations for ransom and release. Henry V, on his accession, had him sent to the Tower for security, but Murdac was eventually released in exchange for Hotspur's son and a ransom of £10,000 (1416). He was heir presumptive, and succeeded to both dukedom and governorship in 1420, but lacked his father's political touch and popularity; under him, lawlessness grew apace, with his own sons amongst the worst offenders. Agreement was finally reached in London (1423) to secure the release of James I, who returned as 'a king unleashed'. Reprisals did not materialize until 1425, probably because Murdac's half-brother John was still commander of the Scottish army in France, but the arrests of Murdac's eldest surviving son, Walter, and brother-in-law were soon followed by those of himself, his wife, son Alexander, and octogenarian father-in-law. At their trial on 24 May, before an assize of nobles at Stirling, conviction was aided by the youngest son's burning of the burgh of Dumbarton in protest. Walter was beheaded immediately, in front of Stirling castle; Murdac, Alexander, and the earl of Lennox met the same fate the following day.

John Stewart, earl of Buchan, b. c.1381, eldest s. of Robert, duke of Albany, and Muriella Keith; m. Elizabeth, da. of Archibald, earl of Douglas, 1413; issue: Margaret; d. Verneuil, 17 Aug. 1424.

Created earl of Buchan by his father, by then acting as governor, John Stewart was also granted the earldom of Ross (1406), and appointed chamberlain in place of his father the following year. In 1418, the dauphin requested Scottish aid, and an expeditionary force led by Buchan and his brother-in-law disembarked at La Rochelle in October 1419. A small engagement at Baugé in Anjou (22 March 1421), where the Franco-Scottish forces prevailed, proved that the English were not invincible, and Buchan was made constable of France. The dauphin became recognized as Charles VII, but after his setback at Cravant, Buchan recruited a fresh expeditionary force that landed in France in the spring of 1424. Their combined forces were cut to pieces at Verneuil (17 August) by the English under the duke of Bedford, and Buchan was slain. His death enabled James I, at last back in Scotland, to commence reprisals against the Albany clan.

James I, b. 25 July 1394, 3rd s. of Robert III and Annabella Drummond; acc. 4 Apr. 1406; m. Joan Beaufort, da. of John Beaufort, earl of Somerset, 2 Feb. 1424; issue: Alexander, James, Margaret, Isabella, Joan, Eleanor, Mary, Annabella; d. Perth, 21 Feb. 1437; bur. Perth.

The only surviving son of Robert III, acceding at the age of twelve but uncrowned, James I spent the first eighteen years of his reign as a prisoner at the English court. His father had dispatched him to France for safety at the beginning of 1406, but a month's delay at Bass Rock allowed news to reach England, and his ship was boarded off Flamborough Head by merchants and 'pirates' of Great Yarmouth;

Henry IV restituted the captured cargo but not the heir apparent, who was lodged in the Tower. Robert, duke of Albany, acted as governor of Scotland meanwhile, but did little to negotiate a ransom for his king's return. During his time in England, James observed a royal government that was the most intensive and centralized in western Europe, served under Henry V in France in 1420-1, and was knighted, but his fears about Albany ambitions were heightened by the release of Albany's son Murdac and his succession to the governorship. English attitudes changed after Henry's death (1422), and eighteen months later James was released upon payment of 60,000 marks (in English coin) at 10,000 marks per year to cover the 'costs and expenses' of his stay in England. One year's worth was remitted as dowry for Lady Joan Beaufort, whom he married before leaving London, and twenty-seven Scottish nobles were to remain in England as hostages.

James was now nearly thirty, intellectual, artistic, athletic, and decisive. With power at last, he took a strong stand against the prevalent lawlessness, and was determined to improve royal revenues from their near-bankrupt state. Scotland was so unused to strong leadership that complaints soon arose, but there still remained insufficient revenues for him to sustain his position easily. One solution was the forfeiture of lands held by rebellious nobles, and the Albany Stewarts fell in consequence. Social and economic legislation was unprecedented, contrasting sharply with the Albanys' *laissez-faire* approach, and covered trade, public health, order, fire precautions, and dress.

The king's acquisitiveness was related to the cultivation of a powerful monarchy. In 1427 he defaulted on his ransom and abandoned the hostages, investing the money in projects such as rebuilding Linlithgow as a splendid setting for the court, founding the Charterhouse of Perth, and importing luxuries for the court. By 1435, James had become 'thick-set and oppressed by too much fat'; despite a genuine desire to aid the common weal, he had also become greedy and ruthless, and disaffection was growing. His failure to retake Roxburgh (August 1436) was humiliating, and the earl of Atholl (who was thought by some to have been the rightful king if the descendants of Robert II and Elizabeth Mure were of illegitimate descent) was involved in the planning of a coup. James fought the conspirators manfully by torchlight in the Dominican friary at Perth, but was assassinated.

BROWN, M., *James I* (1994).

Linlithgow palace, Lothian

Initially a timber manor house built at the lochside by David I, lodging Edward I of England in 1301 during his support of John Balliol, it was subsequently strengthened by him during the wars of independence. Returned to Scottish hands after Bannockburn (1314), it was repaired for David II, but after the 1424 fire was rebuilt in stone by James I with a great hall. Repairs and additions by his successors culminated in James IV closing off the open side to the west and transforming it into a fashionable residence. It remained unused after Flodden until the 1530s when work recommenced to suit James V's rather extravagant tastes; his queen, Mary of Guise, compared it favourably to the noblest French châteaux, and bore Mary, queen of Scots, there (1542). After considerable disrepair the north range was finally rebuilt in 1618–24 as one of the finest Renaissance façades in Scotland, but the palace was never used by James VI after the court's move to London in 1603.

Charles I was the last king to sleep there, though his son (the future James VII and II, then still duke of York) used it while Commissioner to the Scottish Parliament. The 5th earl of Linlithgow later forfeited his titles and hereditary keepership by supporting 'the Old Pretender'. Roofless since an accidental fire in 1746, the palace has never been restored, and is currently cared for through the Scottish Development Department.

Joan Beaufort, queen of Scotland, b. c.1400, da. of John Beaufort, earl of Somerset, and Margaret, da. of Thomas, earl of Kent; m. (1) James I, 2 Feb. 1424; (2) James Stewart, 1439; issue: John, James, Andrew; d. Dunbar, 15 July 1445; bur. Perth.

Granddaughter of John of Gaunt, and described by James I in his *Kingis Quair* as having 'beautee eneuch to mak a world to dote', Joan married the captive Scottish king two months before his release, and bore him twin sons which, though the elder died in infancy, secured the succession. Wounded when the conspirators arrived to assassinate James—she 'fled yn hir kirtill, her mantell hongyng aboute hir'—she acted as custodian of the new boy-king with the earl of Douglas and bishop Cameron of Glasgow. Her second marriage, to a minor noble (the

'Black Knight of Lorne'), was controversial and threatened to reshape court politics. Support dwindled, and she took refuge in Dunbar castle, dying there while the castle was under siege.

James II, b. 10 Oct. 1430, s. of James I and Joan Beaufort; acc. 21 Feb. 1437; m. Mary, da. of Arnold, duke of Gueldres, 3 July 1449; issue: s.(?), Mary, James, Alexander, David, John, Margaret; illeg. issue: John; d. Roxburgh, 3 Aug. 1460; bur. Holyrood.

The younger twin son of James I, and disfigured by a large birthmark (giving rise to the nickname 'Fiery Face'), James was only six when his father was murdered in 1437, and a long minority ensued. Sentence was passed against the claimant earl of Atholl and his co-conspirators, and the boy-king and his sisters were entrusted to the queen dowager at Stirling. The reduction in noble families through execution or forfeiture had created political imbalance, and in the absence of a strong ruler, three rival families fought for control: the Livingstons, Crichtons, and Black Douglases. William, eighth earl of Douglas, eventually became the most powerful magnate, was created lieutenant-general for the kingdom in 1444 and, with his brothers whom he had honoured, dominated the political scene from then until 1452.

James married Mary of Gueldres in 1449 and, with a confidence enhanced by his sisters' prestigious European marriages, set about re-establishing his authority; unlike his father, he had spent his youth in Scotland, and understood prevailing conditions. The Livingstons were arrested and their estates taken over (1449–50), and for a while there was uneasy peace. Douglas had relinquished his lieutenant-generalship, and visited Rome in late 1450, the pope having proclaimed it a jubilee year; during his absence, two of the Crichtons allegedly encouraged James to attack the Douglas estates. Something of a compromise was subsequently reached between king and earl, but though the earldom of Wigtown remained in royal hands, James had not prevailed and Douglas continued high-handed. The great crime of the reign came in February 1452, when Douglas (with a safe-conduct) attended Stirling castle to discuss with the king the agreement between the Black Douglases and the earls of Crawford and Ross; faced with Douglas's refusal to break this bond, James personally stabbed him to death. Civil war erupted again, but parliament justified the king's action, and James carefully built up strength until in 1455 he was able to shatter Douglas power.

Jacob·von·gots·
genauen·küng·
von·schottland·

James II of Scotland. Painted in the 1450s by a German visitor, Jörg von Ehingen. His facial birthmark is clearly visible.

Master of his realm at last, James, in the spirit of his father, filled and created new earldoms, reinvigorated central government, improved the administration of justice, aided the foundation of a new university at Glasgow, and revived direct taxation. His talents as a military leader found outlet through continuing stormy Anglo-Scottish relations; he played off Yorkists against Lancastrians, and border raids gave way to preparation for outright war, including imported iron (for guns) and gunpowder from Flanders. With a large army, James laid siege to Roxburgh towards the end of July 1460, and ordered his bombards to fire a salvo to greet the arrival of his queen; standing too close to a gun which exploded, he was fatally struck in the thigh by a flying shard, and Scotland was left again with a boy-king.

Mary of Gueldres, queen of Scotland, da. of Arnold, duke of Gueldres, and Catherine, duchess of Cleves; m. James II, 3 July 1449; d. Edinburgh, 1 Dec. 1463; bur. Holy Trinity church, Edinburgh.

Mary's marriage to James was arranged with an eye to improving Scottish commercial interests in the Low Countries. Niece of Philip 'the Good' of Burgundy, and brought up at his court, she sailed from Flanders with a deliberately magnificent retinue which had been funded by Philip, who also promised a dowry of 60,000 crowns. Holyrood palace was commenced for her reception, and she was crowned soon after the marriage. In August 1460 she arrived at the siege of Roxburgh to encourage the troops, only to suffer the loss of her husband unexpectedly. Appointed as one of the seven regents for the new young king, she became head of the faction of 'young lords', but all were drawn into the English conflict between Lancastrians and Yorkists. Mary entertained Margaret of Anjou at Lincluden abbey in 1460, and later sheltered Henry VI and Margaret after their defeat at Towton. Her diplomacy enabled Scotland to regain Berwick, but after the fiasco of the Norham castle siege (1463), the Scots switched sides to support the victorious Yorkists. Mary had sufficient wealth from her dower lands to improve amenities at Stirling and Falkland, build a new castle at Ravenscraig in Fife, and found Trinity College, Edinburgh, and a hospital in Stirling.

James III, b. May 1452, eldest surviving s. of James II and Mary of Gueldres; acc. 3 Aug. 1460; m. Margaret, da. of Christian I, king of Denmark, 13 July 1469; issue: James, James, John; d. Miltoun, 11 June 1488; bur. Cambuskenneth.

Crowned at Kelso at the age of eight, James was a weak monarch when compared with his two predecessors; regarded as the most unpopular of the fifteenth-century Stewart kings, he faced two rebellions, failed to attend to the administration of justice, and debased his coinage. While still a minor, the deaths of his mother (1463) and the bishop of St Andrews (1465) resulted in his seizure by a group of lesser nobles headed by the Boyds of Kilmarnock, but there was no repetition of the chaotic

power struggles of his father's minority. Lord Boyd concluded the treaty
of Copenhagen in 1468 whereby James would marry the daughter of the
Danish king, but after her arrival at Leith, the Boyds sought safety in the
Low Countries while the estates obligingly found them guilty of treason.
James, now governing for himself, travelled little and proved unable to
restore strong central power: parliaments repeatedly exhorted him to
cease granting remissions and respites for crime, and to hold justice-
ayres throughout the realm. He did, though, commence a policy of
rapprochement with England by betrothing his son James to Edward IV's
daughter Cecily (1474).

James's suspicious nature saw his adult brothers as potential rivals:
Alexander, duke of Albany, fled to France but, perhaps sensibly,
parliament allowed the charges against him to lapse; John, earl of
Mar, was arrested (1479) and died in unclear circumstances. Edward
IV, interested in recovering Berwick, acknowledged Albany in 1482 as
'king of Scotland', and provided troops for support. James assembled
an army to oppose them, but dissident nobles seized him at Lauder,
imprisoned him in Edinburgh castle (July 1482), and executed two of
the lesser men in his household whom the chroniclers later
transmogrified into low-born favourites. The English regained
Berwick but the invasion threatened to descend into farce, and James
emerged from the castle for a general reconciliation. Crown-magnate
mistrust continued, however, and the king found himself in
increasing conflict with disaffected, mainly lowland nobles, including
the Humes and Hepburns, powerful Border families. The earl of Argyll
defected in the spring of 1488, and dissent began to coalesce around
James's fifteen-year-old son, the duke of Rothesay, now proclaiming
himself 'prince of Scotland'. Something of an agreement was patched
up at Aberdeen, the northern lords generally remaining faithful, but
this proved short-lived, and the two sides met near Stirling. The king,
bearing the sword of Robert Bruce, and his forces were subsequently
routed at Sauchieburn (near Bannockburn field) on 11 June, and James
fled, allegedly to Miltoun, where he was fatally stabbed by a man
masquerading as a priest.

James had an exalted view of monarchy, reflected in the imperialistic
schemes for conquest of Brittany, Gueldres, and Saintonge that he
presented in his early parliaments, and in his introduction of the earliest
Renaissance coin portrait north of the Alps, with its arched imperial
crown. His later portrayal as a committed patron of the arts is not well

supported, although he appears on the Trinity College, Edinburgh altarpiece with his queen.

MACDOUGALL, N., *James III: A Political Study* (1982).

Margaret of Denmark, queen of Scotland, b. c.1457, da. of Christian I of Denmark and Norway, and Dorothea, princess of Brandenburg; m. James III, 13 July 1469; d. Stirling, 14 July 1486; bur. Cambuskenneth.

The treaty of Copenhagen (1468) had included a proposed marriage between James III and the Danish king's only daughter. Christian agreed to a dowry of 60,000 Rhenish florins, but was unable to raise this in full, so the isles of Orkney and then Shetland, which had been pledged as security, passed into Scottish ownership. James and Margaret were married at Holyrood, and made a royal progress the following year as far as Inverness. Probably in thanksgiving for the safe delivery of an heir in 1473, the queen, who was notably pious, then made a pilgrimage to St Ninian's shrine at Whithorn in Galloway. She seems to have had some political involvement after James's incarceration in Edinburgh castle in 1482, but their subsequent living apart may have been less of a question of personal estrangement than of security: the young duke of Rothesay (as heir) would have been safer apart from his father, as had been the case when James I was assassinated. After Margaret's death, James III unsuccessfully attempted to obtain her canonization.

Alexander Stewart, duke of Albany, b. c.1454, 2nd surviving s. of James II and Mary of Gueldres; m. (1) Catherine Sinclair, da. of William, earl of Orkney and Caithness; issue: Alexander, Andrew, s., Margaret; (2) Anne de la Tour, da. of Bertrand, comte d'Auvergne and de Bouillon, 19 Jan. 1480; issue: John; d. Paris, 1485; bur. Paris.

Created earl of March and lord of Annandale by his father in 1455, and duke of Albany sometime before July 1458, Alexander was appointed admiral of Scotland, march warden, and then lieutenant of the kingdom, but there was animosity between James III and his brothers; John, earl of Mar, died c.1479/80, while Albany was said to have been imprisoned in Edinburgh castle, with a dramatic escape via a French ship lying off Newhaven, near Leith. His first marriage had been dissolved on grounds of propinquity, and while in France he married the comte d'Auvergne's daughter; their son John would eventually become governor for the young James V. On return to England, Albany made an alliance with Edward IV, agreeing to surrender Berwick in return for the title 'king of Scotland'. Joining the English invasion (1482), he marched to Edinburgh but was persuaded to make peace with James III, whom he subsequently liberated from Edinburgh castle. Albany was created earl of Mar and Garioch the following year, but almost immediately resumed his English alliance. In 1484 he raided Lochmaben with the earl of Douglas and English forces, but was routed and escaped to France. Said to have been of mid-stature, well-proportioned, and with a 'verie awful countenance' when facing his enemies, he was killed by a splinter from a lance while watching a tournament in Paris.

John MacDonald, earl of Ross and lord of the Isles, b. c.1434, s. of Alexander, 3rd lord of the Isles, and Elizabeth, da. of Alexander Seton, lord of Gordon and Huntly; m. Margaret, da. of Robert II and Elizabeth Mure, c.1450; illeg. issue: 2 s.; d. Dundee, 1498; bur. Paisley.

Still a minor when he succeeded his father in 1449, and described later as a 'meek, modest man...and a scholar more fit to be a churchman than to command so many irregular tribes of people', John MacDonald was affected by his father's league with the earls of Douglas and Crawford against the young James II, but eventually came to terms with the king, and was appointed a warden of the marches. He joined James against the English, but after Roxburgh (1460) became re-involved with the Douglases. In 1462 he made the secret treaty of Westminster–Ardtornish with Edward IV, who was hoping to regain some of his lost influence in Scotland, whereby Ross and Douglas would become his vassals and share all lands north of the Forth; the 'Wars of the Roses' prevented English help, and the rebellion collapsed. Knowledge of this treaty eventually emerged and Ross was attainted (1475), but on the queen's intercession his lands except Ross (which went to the crown) were restored, though he resigned them immediately into the king's hands, and was formally created 'lord of the Isles'. Subsequent rebellion in Ross under MacDonald's sons and nephew led to forfeiture again, but his voluntary surrender of the lordship (1493) enabled him to remain at court, with a pension, before retiring to the monastery of Paisley.

James IV, b. 17 Mar. 1473, s. of James III and Margaret of Denmark; acc. 11 June 1488; m. Margaret, da. of Henry VII of England, 8 Aug. 1503; issue: James, da., Arthur, James, da., Alexander; illeg. issue: 2 s.; d. Flodden, 9 Sept. 1513; bur. Sheen, head at St Michael's, Wood Street (?).

James succeeded to the throne with two advantages: he was no babe-in-arms and, as focus of the dissent against his father, he had the acceptance of a wide range of magnates. The taint of patricide and regicide, though, resulted in many penances, even to wearing an iron belt around his waist. He has been regarded as a Renaissance prince, 'the glory of all princely governing' according to Sir David Lindsay, and much has been made of his encouragement of learning and the arts. A third university (Aberdeen) was founded in 1495, an Education Act passed (1496) relating to law administration, and a printing-house licensed in Edinburgh. The court was cosmopolitan and multilingual—James is credited with speaking six languages, including Gaelic—and centred on a cult of honour which may have contributed to the remarkable unity of purpose amongst his nobles. He spent lavishly on clothes, buildings, and fittings; the palace of Holyroodhouse was commenced for his bride, Margaret Tudor, and new halls built at Edinburgh and Stirling castles.

Although not assuming personal rule until 1495, James was concerned to improve the processes of law. Unlike his father, he travelled widely to hold justice-ayres, and tackled Border lawlessness. Edinburgh had become the principal burgh, and the supreme courts of justice were centralized there, which encouraged its growth as the kingdom's capital. Annual parliaments gave way to greater use of council and session for administrative, political, and legal business, and a civil service began to develop; by the end of the reign, the royal council was more broadly based than it had ever been. James intervened in major feuds, sometimes playing off his nobles and clans against each other; the authority he commanded enabled him to tackle the turbulent MacDonalds of the Western Isles, which ended with the final forfeiture of the lord of the Isles (May 1493) and annexation of his lands. Liberality, as well as diplomatic and military expenses, required funding, but though James utilized many of his father's techniques to fill the coffers, he did not acquire the accompanying unpopularity, and by 1513 the annual royal revenue had almost tripled from that of the early 1490s.

In foreign matters, James's support of the Yorkist pretender Perkin Warbeck, who arrived in Scotland in late 1495, and raids into northern England provoked military response from Henry VII, but a truce was declared in 1497, which by 1502 had become a treaty of 'perpetual peace'. This was sealed by James's marriage the following year to Henry's eldest daughter—Dunbar's 'Marriage of the Thistle and the Rose'—and managed to endure for a decade despite some strain. France began to supply James with timber, tackle, and shipwrights as well as soldiers and munitions. Royal men-of-war such as the *Margaret* and the *Michael* were developed and tested, as were bombards (siege guns) and other artillery, and the king himself acquired no fewer than five hand-guns. Finding himself in the strange position of peace/alliance with both England and France, James's position became increasingly difficult as European politics became more convoluted. Eventually, in 1512, the old alliance was renewed with Louis XII of France. James, excommunicated by the dying pope, assembled his forces for war with England, and crossed the border in August 1513 to take the castles of Norham, Wark, Etal, and Ford. As sickness and desertion began to take their toll of the Scots, English forces were mustered under the earl of Surrey, and the two sides met at Flodden on 9 September. The Scottish guns and long spears were less manoeuvrable than hoped, and in the near-massacre, the king, eight earls, and fourteen greater lords perished. His body was taken to Berwick and embalmed, but its subsequent fate remains disputed.

MACDOUGALL, N., *James IV* (1989).

Margaret Tudor, b. 29 Nov. 1489, da. of Henry VII of England and Elizabeth of York; m. (1) James IV, 8 Aug. 1503; (2) Archibald Douglas, earl of Angus, Aug. 1514; issue: Margaret; (3) Henry Stewart (later Lord Methven), Mar. 1526; d. Methven, 18 Oct. 1541; bur. Perth

As elder sister to Henry VIII, Margaret's marriage to James IV meant that her Scottish descendants were in close line of succession to the English throne. Her marriage at the age of thirteen sealed a treaty of 'perpetual peace', and James began to build a splendid new palace of Holyroodhouse in preparation. Of their six children, only one survived to adulthood, and he succeeded to the throne (at seventeen months) as James V. James IV had already named her as regent in the event of his death, but the appointment was resented as she was seen as a representative of the victorious enemy at Flodden, and the duke of Albany (next in line) was invited to come over from France to act instead. Margaret meanwhile had remarried, and after Albany's arrival, when the young king was taken from her keeping, she fled to England, where she gave birth to a daughter before proceeding south to her brother's court.

Ordered back to Scotland by Henry in early 1517, in an attempt to reassert English influence there and to make peace with her husband Angus, she was formally though briefly reconciled, and eventually allied with the earl of Arran to favour England rather than France, and to rule in James V's name. Angus and Margaret became bitter enemies, and her decision to seek a divorce so shocked Henry that he ceased to respect his headstrong and capricious sister. After her divorce in 1526, Margaret married Henry Stewart, younger son of Lord Avondale, who was later created Lord Methven by James V to honour his mother. She enabled her son to break free from Douglas control in 1528, continued her involvement in national politics (keeping her brother well-informed), unsuccessfully attempted to gain a divorce from Methven (1537), and died intestate at Methven castle after being stricken with palsy.

John Stewart, duke of Albany, b. c.1484, s. of Alexander, duke of Albany, and Anne de la Tour; m. Anne de la Tour, comtesse d'Auvergne and de Lauragais; illeg. issue: Eleonora; d. Mirefleur, 2 July 1536; bur. chapel of Vic le Comte.

Half-French, born and brought up in France, Albany was nevertheless heir presumptive to the Scottish throne, being a grandson of James II. After Flodden (1513), he was invited to assume the regency during the minority of his young cousin, and arrived in splendour at Dumbarton in May 1515 with a fleet of eight ships. Parliament restored title and lands, and declared him the only legitimate issue of his father. Albany's governorship was competent though intermittent because of repeated visits to France, striving to restore the Franco-Scottish alliance, and he negotiated the treaty of Rouen (1517) whereby James V would marry a French princess. Henry VIII claimed that Albany was endangering the young king's life and 'working the perdition of his sister', and prepared for war, but a truce was agreed near Carlisle and Albany's army disbanded. He returned again from France (1523) to renew hostilities, but an attack on Wark, in Northumberland, misfired, and his prestige collapsed. He left Scotland for good in 1524, to serve Francis I of France, and died at his castle of Mirefleur in Auvergne.

James Stewart, earl of Ross, b. Mar. 1476, 2nd s. of James III and Mary of Gueldres; d. Edinburgh, 12 Jan. 1504; bur. St Andrews.

Younger brother of James IV, similarly named in case of possible succession, and preferentially favoured by his father, he was given the earldom of Ross in 1481 after its forfeiture to the crown by John MacDonald, lord of the Isles, and named bishop of St Andrews six years later. Negotiations had begun for a marriage to Edward IV's third daughter, Katherine, but they came to nothing, and he was raised to duke of Ross in 1488. Although nominated to the newly vacant archbishopric of St Andrews in 1497, which would remove him as an opposition focus, the canonical minimum age for a bishop was thirty, which was some years away; while in Rome seeking confirmation of this appointment, he seems to have been instituted to the commendatorship of Holyrood abbey. Translated to the commendatorship of Dunfermline in 1500, Ross became Chancellor of Scotland (in name only) the following year, and then commendator of the extremely rich abbey of Arbroath, but died shortly afterwards, before consecration.

James V, b. 10 Apr. 1512, s. of James IV and Margaret Tudor; acc. 9 Sept. 1513; m. (1) Madeleine de Valois, da. of Francis I of France, 1 Jan. 1537; (2) Mary of Guise, 18 June 1538; issue: James, Arthur, Mary; illeg. issue: 7 s., 2 das.; d. Falkland, 14 Dec. 1542; bur. Holyrood.

Scotland faced yet another minority rule after James IV's death at Flodden and, as on previous occasions, the magnates struggled for control. Although another son (Alexander) was born to James IV posthumously, the heir presumptive was John, duke of Albany, who was invited to come from France and assume the governorship. The next in line was the earl of Arran, but greater challenge arose from the Douglas earls of Angus. Archibald Douglas had married the queen dowager Margaret Tudor within a year of James IV's death, but her capriciousness and Albany's return to France in 1524 led to an alliance between Arran and Margaret, who invested the twelve-year-old James with the symbols of sovereignty. It had been arranged (July 1525) that the king would reside with the leading nobles in rotation, but Angus declined to give him up and, with a household dominated by Douglases, he became a virtual prisoner. Despite a coalition of alienated earls, it was not until the end of May 1528 that James effected an escape from Edinburgh to Stirling castle, which his mother had put at his disposal.

James's personal rule spanned fourteen years, and was characterized by forthright assertion of royal authority and a perhaps unexpected diplomatic importance. He needed to recover crown lands and revenue to replenish noticeably scant royal coffers. With the help of a team of lay lawyers, such as the Pavia-trained Sir Thomas Erskine, three areas were exploited: the wealth of the church, the dowry a bride would bring with her, and proceedings against the nobles. At a time when ecclesiastical reformation was spreading throughout northern Europe, and the

James V of Scotland. He has been called 'the most unpleasant of the Stewarts'—an unwelcome victory in a fiercely competitive field. The painting, showing him aged about 28, was done posthumously.

Scottish clergy's hold on legal and administrative procedures was considerable, James was able, with pope Clement's agreement, to control appointments to major benefices, and raise monies from the church to endow a college of justice for civil causes. Much of the money levied from the church, though, went into his building schemes, such as the courtyard at Falkland, the palace block at Stirling, and Linlithgow.

Although Albany had negotiated the treaty of Rouen (1517), whereby James would marry a French princess, this had yet to materialize, and he had become one of the most eligible bachelors in Europe. The delicate political balance between England, France, and the empire, with Rome a nervous spectator, was reflected by courtship of the Scottish king in high quarters. With an eye to dowry, James eventually settled on a French bride. Rejecting the duke of Vendôme's daughter after inspection, he married Francis's delicate eldest daughter Madeleine at the beginning of 1537, but she died only months later; Mary of Guise then brought a further generous dowry, but the strengthened alliance with France resulted in eventual war with England.

James's domestic policy reflected his determination to show authority as well as replenish royal coffers. The Borders were forcefully brought under control in 1530–1, and subsequently the West Highlands and Islands. Justice-ayres were held regularly, his severity to malefactors endeared him to the law-abiding, and his mixing with commoners prompted the nickname 'the poor man's king'. It was in James's dealing with his nobles, however, that severity slid into the vindictiveness with which he is frequently associated: his hatred of the Douglases, his former captors, led to exile for the earl of Angus and the burning of Lady Glamis (1537). Forfeitures for treasonable alliances were nothing new, but raised rents and some expropriation fuelled discontent.

It was international events that brought the final crisis. James's council forbade his meeting with Henry VIII at York in September 1541, perhaps from fear that Henry might encourage James towards protestantism, and this caused Henry to mobilize a northern force. The Scottish defeat at Solway Moss (24 November 1542) has often been claimed to have created such shame and despair in James that he died only three weeks later, but this is unsupported by contemporary reports: further campaigns were being planned, and administration continued as usual. His death at Falkland is now thought to have been most probably due to 'pestelence'—epidemics were recurrent—or cholera.

CAMERON, J., *James V: The Personal Rule, 1528–1542* (1998).

Falkland palace, Fife

Used as a royal hunting seat from the twelfth century, and owned by the earls of Fife in the fourteenth, Falkland castle was destroyed by the English in 1327. Passing to the dukes of Albany after rebuilding, it was acquired by James II whose 1450s extensions became the north range of the palace, with further chambers being added by his widow, Mary of Gueldres. James IV added the east and south ranges, which were remodelled by James V's French craftsmen in the 1530s to transform it into the first Renaissance building in Scotland, now regarded as amongst the finest work of its period in Britain and marking the height of the 'auld alliance'. The ornamented gatehouse, garden and tennis court (1539) contributed further to this favourite royal residence.

The north range was burnt, possibly accidentally, when Cromwell's troops were quartered there (1654), and only its foundations remain. Although no monarch has stayed there since Charles II, it continues a royal property, and much restoration has been undertaken by the Crichton Stuarts in their role as hereditary constable, captain, and keeper of Falkland. The National Trust for Scotland has now assumed responsibility for the building.

Madeleine de Valois, b. Aug. 1521, da. of Francis I of France and Claude, da. of Louis XII of France; m. James V, 1 Jan. 1537; d. Holyrood, 7 July 1537.

The French king had resumed war with the emperor Charles V and, fearing a renewal of Anglo-Imperial relations, sought a strengthening of Scottish friendship. Madeleine, Francis's eldest surviving daughter, favoured the proposed match with James, and they were married in Notre-Dame. After visiting Chantilly, Compiègne, and Rouen (where she fell ill), they embarked for Scotland on 10 May, but fears for her delicate health were justified as she died of consumption only weeks later.

Mary of Guise, b. 20 Nov. 1515, da. of Claude, duke of Guise, and Antoinette de Bourbon; m. (1) Louis d'Orléans, duc de Longueville, 4 Aug. 1534; issue: Francis, Louis; (2) James V, 18 June 1538; d. Edinburgh, 11 June 1560; bur. Rheims.

A tall, handsome girl with reddish-gold hair, and unexpectedly widowed at twenty-one just before the birth of her second son, Mary was selected by Francis I to marry the recently widowed James V and so maintain the Franco-Scottish alliance. Henry VIII had also expressed an interest in Mary—Jane Seymour had just died—but she reluctantly agreed to marriage with her third cousin (through a Gueldres connection) and landed in Scotland in June 1538. Their two sons died in infancy, and a subsequent daughter, Mary, was only six days old when James died. Using her intelligence and diplomacy, Mary appeared to acquiesce to Henry VIII's idea of her daughter's marriage to his son Edward, but her continuous defence of Catholic and French interests in Scotland during the internal struggle for power and Henry's 'rough wooing' led to the treaty of Haddington (7 July 1548); the five-year-old queen was to marry the dauphin, and France would help defend Scotland.

With the child Mary's departure, and after a year-long visit to the French court and her family in 1550–1, Mary of Guise determined to rule Scotland herself. Imperious now, though still subtle, she replaced Arran as regent in 1554, but the growing protestant movement added a religious element to political problems. She had a genuine desire to restore stability and prosperity, and improve law and order, but she underestimated the Scots' independent nature and a growing anti-French feeling; her increasingly repressive policies after 1558 sparked a protestant rebellion in May 1559—John Knox had just returned from exile, and was to become her bitterest critic—but this was inconclusive. The return of the young earl of Arran encouraged her opponents and she was forced to retreat to Leith; her authority was transferred to a regency council, but a fortnight after her return to Holyroodhouse she fell seriously ill. In the treaty of Berwick (February 1560), the recently acceded Elizabeth of England agreed to support the rebellious (protestant) lords of the Congregation, but French help for Mary was unforthcoming, and she retreated into Edinburgh castle, swollen with dropsy but still resolute. After her death in June, an English-backed administration was led by Lord James Stewart until his half-sister Mary returned to Scotland.

Margaret Douglas, countess of Lennox, b. 8 Oct. 1515, da. of Archibald Douglas, earl of Angus, and Margaret Tudor; m. Matthew Stewart, earl of Lennox, 6 July 1544; issue: Henry, Henry, 1s., 3 das., Charles; d. Hackney, 9 Mar. 1578; bur. Westminster abbey.

Niece to Henry VIII and half-sister of James V, Margaret Douglas became all too aware of the hazards of close proximity to two crowns. Her first imprisonment in the Tower arose from betrothal to Sir Thomas Howard (Anne Boleyn's uncle), whom Henry thought was aiming for the throne. Eventually serving two princesses and some of Henry's queens, her marriage was arranged by Henry to his ally, Matthew Lennox, and their eldest surviving son, Henry Darnley, became the focus for their ambitions. In favour during Mary I's reign, but subsequently retiring to Yorkshire, Margaret Lennox's outspokenness and the probability of catholic intrigues led to confinement at Sheen, but Lennox was subsequently allowed to return to Scotland, with Margaret remaining at the English court as surety. A further spell in the Tower followed her son's marriage to Mary Stewart (1565), but she regained liberty after his murder, and supported her husband as regent to the young James VI. Her third sojourn in the Tower resulted from the precipitate marriage of her son Charles to the daughter of 'Bess of Hardwick', whose husband, the earl of Shrewsbury, was custodian to the imprisoned Mary, queen of Scots, and Elizabeth suspected intrigue. Although Margaret was pardoned before Charles's death in 1577, she died soon after in poverty. A woman of forceful character and ambition, the desire to see her line unite both thrones was fulfilled only posthumously.

James Stewart, earl of Moray, b. 1531, s. of James V and Margaret Erskine, da. of John, Lord Erskine; d. Linlithgow, 23 Jan. 1570; bur. Edinburgh.

Illegitimate son of James V, made prior *in commendam* of St Andrews (1538) and educated there, James was legitimized with his brother John early in 1551. Subsequently appointed one of the commissioners to negotiate the marriage of his half-sister Mary with the dauphin, he was sent to France again in 1561 to invite her to return home. Having brought the Borders back under control, Mary rewarded him with the earldoms of Moray, then Mar (1562). Although chief adviser to the queen, he failed to prevent her marriage to Darnley, and was denounced after his involvement in the Chaseabout raid—he was a strong calvinist—but was given asylum in England by Elizabeth; the rebel protestant lords were summoned to trial, but Moray was subsequently restored to favour. Whilst not directly involved in Darnley's murder, he judiciously left for France soon afterwards. On Mary's abdication in 1567, he was appointed regent to her young son James VI, but his two years in office until murdered by James Hamilton of Bothwellhaugh, staunch supporter of the exiled queen, were riven by civil war between the Queen's party and the King's party, and he had difficulty in keeping the latter stable. Moray was ambitious and intensely self-controlled but, despite depiction as a 'Good Regent', his political acumen was poor, and his successes rare.

Mary, queen of Scots, b. 7 Dec. 1542, da. of James V and Mary of Guise; acc. 14 Dec. 1542, abdic. 24 July 1567; m. (1) Francis, dauphin of France, 24 Apr. 1558; (2) Henry Stewart, Lord Darnley, 29 July 1565; (3) James Hepburn, earl of Bothwell, 15 May 1567; d. Fotheringhay, 8 Feb. 1587; bur. Peterborough, rebur. Westminster abbey.

Mary, queen of Scots, continues to be the most heavily romanticized of the Stewart monarchs. On the thrones of Scotland and France, and with a strong claim to that of England, her vicissitudes were shaped more by political circumstances than her occasional impulsiveness and folly. Three husbands, long exile, and imprisonment, then execution ordered by her cousin Elizabeth, have spawned plays, novels, and opera, portraying her as catholic martyr or papist plotter, and increasing the mythology.

Succeeding to the throne when barely a week old and crowned at nine months, Mary spent most of her first five years at Stirling, while England and France sought to gain control. Following the peace negotiated after Solway Moss, Mary's marriage to the young son of Henry VIII was agreed at Greenwich (July 1543), but pro-French Scottish opposition led to rejection of this treaty and alliance instead with France. Henry, furious, replied with devastating invasions of south-east Scotland (the 'rough wooing'), but despite a resounding victory at Pinkie Cleugh (1547), the English could not sustain their position. The assistance of French troops had come on condition of Mary being sent to France, since she was now betrothed to the young dauphin. In August 1548, she sailed from Dumbarton castle to be brought up and educated with Henri II's children. Marriage to Francis when she was fifteen was followed by unexpected accession to the French throne the following year (1559) after the death of Henri II from a splintered lance at a tournament. Mary was now queen of two kingdoms, but any dynastic potential was short-lived as Francis died in December 1560, and, despite her long absence from Scotland, she chose to return there as queen regnant rather than remain as queen dowager.

Mary Queen of Scots. This portrait by François Clouet shows her aged sixteen as Dauphiness of France. Pierre Brantôme called her 'a true goddess', and the Venetian ambassador to France thought her 'the most beautiful princess in all Europe'.

During her absence in France, much had changed in Scotland: the catholic and French causes had collapsed with the death of her mother, Mary of Guise; English and French troops had agreed in the treaty of Edinburgh to withdraw all troops (July 1560); the following month, parliament agreed a series of protestant reformist measures. Mary, strongly catholic, trod carefully and, with her half-brother James as her adviser, was able to engineer a unity amongst the nobles barely seen since 1513. Many thought her policies fair, and she travelled widely throughout the country between 1562 and 1566.

The question of succession remained a matter of concern, and Mary still had eyes on the English throne. Various suitors were considered and dropped, until she fell in love with Henry, Lord Darnley, himself in line to both crowns. It was soon realized that this second marriage was a mistake. Not only did it alienate Elizabeth, but the marriage was by catholic rites, and Mary's advisers saw themselves displaced by a youth ill-suited to bear the title of 'king'. No longer on good terms with Darnley, the pregnant Mary seemed to be spending too much time with her Italian-born secretary, David Rizzio; the atrocity of his murder in front of the queen (9 March 1566) is well documented, and the assassins' return from England was tantamount to a death-warrant for Darnley. The future James VI was delivered safely in Edinburgh castle in June, but the following February Mary was again a widow after Darnley's murder at Kirk o'Field. She may not have been directly involved in the plot, but was certainly affected by the suspicion that fell on James Bothwell, with whom she had become infatuated and whom she married in May. This third marriage proved too much. They were forced to flee, and on 15 June 1567 were confronted at Carberry Hill, east of Edinburgh. Bothwell fled north, but Mary surrendered, was imprisoned in Lochleven castle and, after miscarrying twins, was compelled to abdicate on 24 July in favour of her infant son James.

Mary remained imprisoned in Lochleven until her escape on 2 May 1568, and rapidly raised a substantial force, but they were defeated at Langside (13 May). Her subsequent flight across the Solway sealed her fate. Elizabeth found her presence an embarrassment, yet felt it wiser to keep her in England under restraint. For the next nineteen years, Mary was moved around central England, ending finally at Fotheringhay; she plotted obsessively, but her involvement in a series of catholic intrigues at last persuaded Elizabeth to sign the warrant for her execution.

FRASER, A., *Mary, Queen of Scots* (1969).

Holyroodhouse, Edinburgh

The palace, now the official residence in Scotland of the reigning monarch, commenced as the guest range of Holyrood abbey (founded *c*.1128 by David I), which James III found more comfortable than Edinburgh castle. James IV converted it into a royal residence fit for his bride, Margaret Tudor, and they were married there in 1503. Subsequently extended by James V, but burnt by the English in 1544 and 1547, it was the scene of the brutal murder of David Rizzio, secretary of Mary, queen of Scots (1566). After the union of crowns in 1603 the palace was left in charge of a keeper, but was used briefly by Charles I before being accidentally burnt down in 1650; rebuilt by Cromwell, it was finally remodelled in the 1670s for Charles II, with exteriors in French style and interiors Anglo-Dutch, though he never saw it.

Charles Edward Stuart ('the Young Pretender') occupied Holyroodhouse in 1745, where he gave a celebrated ball after his victory at Prestonpans. The palace's revival began after George IV held a royal levee there, masterminded by Sir Walter Scott, in August 1822, and Victoria completed its transformation.

Francis II of France, b. 19 Jan. 1544, s. of Henri II and Catherine de Médicis; acc. 10 July 1559; m. Mary Stewart, queen of Scots, 24 Apr. 1558; d. Orléans, 5 Dec. 1560; bur. Paris.

A sickly adolescent, who became a tool of the powerful Guise family, Francis married Mary in great splendour at Notre-Dame while still dauphin, and was voted the Scottish crown matrimonial by that parliament in November. His accession the following year offered a potential dynastic inheritance of France, Scotland, England, and Ireland, but his early death from the spread of an ear infection at Orléans thwarted any such hopes, leaving Mary without an obvious place at the French court.

Henry Stewart, Lord Darnley, b. 7 Dec. 1545, s. of Matthew Stewart, earl of Lennox, and Margaret Douglas; m. Mary Stewart, 29 July 1565; issue: James; d. Edinburgh, 10 Feb. 1567; bur. Holyrood.

Descended from James II on his father's side, and grandson of Margaret

Tudor on his mother's, Henry Stewart was next to Mary in line to the English throne, but since he had been born and brought up in England as a result of his father's forfeiture, many thought his claim the stronger. Darnley had been spoken of as a possible husband for Mary, and when Lennox returned to Scotland and rehabilitation in 1564, his nineteen-year-old son soon followed. Mary found him 'the lustiest and best proportionit lang [tall] man sche had seen', and their marriage was celebrated before papal dispensation arrived. Darnley's elevation to kingship prompted a minor rebellion among the protestant lords, but more serious was the realization that he was unfit for a real share in power, being vain and irresponsible. Darnley was not the only one to feel threatened by Rizzio, but it was his dagger that was left prominently in the secretary's corpse. His reconciliation with Mary was short-lived, and indifference turned to loathing: he withdrew to Stirling, failed to attend his son's christening, then went to Glasgow to his father, to recover from what was euphemistically termed 'smallpox'. Eventually returning with Mary to Edinburgh, badly disfigured, he convalesced at Kirk o'Field, which was healthier than Holyrood, but was never to return to public life.

The real truth about Darnley's murder may never be known, and there was probably more than one conspiracy behind it. A reasonable reconstruction postulates that he tried to escape semi-naked from the Old Provost's Lodging, was caught by the men below, and smothered; with the realization that the house would shortly explode from the gunpowder in the cellars, his body was laid in the nearby orchard, where it was found later uninjured. Mary's complicity in the deed has never been wholly established.

James Hepburn, earl of Bothwell, b. c.1535, s. of Patrick, earl of Bothwell, and Agnes Sinclair, da. of Henry, Lord Sinclair; m.(1) Jane Gordon, da. of George Gordon, earl of Huntly, 24 Feb. 1566; (2) Mary Stewart, 15 May 1567; illeg. issue: William; d. Dragsholm, Denmark, 14 Apr. 1578; bur. Faarvejle.

Succeeding to the earldom in 1556, Bothwell loyally served the dowager Mary of Guise, despite being protestant, and was sent by her to France in 1559, to become briefly gentleman of the chamber to the newly acceded Francis II. A man of action rather than a statesman, Bothwell became one of the most powerful magnates in the Borders, strongly anti-English, and described by Throckmorton as 'a [vain]glorious, rash and hazardous young man'.

He had no part in the murder of Rizzio, but as Darnley became an increasing problem, the queen's predilection for Bothwell grew noticeably. If he did not personally murder Darnley, he was generally believed to have planned the death, but when placed on trial, the absence of submitted evidence could only result in acquittal. Bothwell's abduction of the queen and conveyance to his castle at Dunbar (21 April) was almost certainly collusive, and led to considerable revulsion. Conveniently, his first marriage was deemed to have been with the 'forbidden degrees' of consanguinity, so was annulled, and marriage to Mary took place on 15 May, three days after his creation as duke of Orkney. Even Mary was aware he could not be created king, but the nobles' hostility forced an encounter at Carberry Hill. Bothwell went first to Shetland, then Norway, where he was arrested and detained as a state prisoner. Escaping execution and extradition, he wrote a brief vindication of his actions, *Les Affaires du Comte de Boduel*, and was moved between prisons, ending at Dragsholm on Zealand, where he died insane and was buried in the nearby church of Faarvejle.

James VI, king of Scotland, b. 19 June 1566, s. of Henry Stewart, Lord Darnley, and Mary Stewart. See JAMES I OF ENGLAND, pp. 278–82.

Normans

The reigns of the first four post-Conquest kings were dominated by the establishment of their dynasty and by the succession question, complicated by the connection between England and Normandy. The characteristic of Norman rule has often been identified as firmness, but there was little alternative for a small group of military adventurers, unsupported by mass immigration, and in the midst of a resentful populace. Highly significant was William I's promulgation of 'Englishry': that if a murdered man could not be proved to be English, it would be presumed that he was a Norman, and the hundred fined accordingly. A more lasting consequence of the Conquest was the impetus given to expansion within the British isles, into southern Scotland, south Wales, and the east of Ireland. Welsh chroniclers, inclined at first to welcome the newcomers as an alternative to the hated Saxons, soon came to realize that 'the French' were, if anything, more ruthless and disagreeable.

William I ('the Conqueror'), duke of Normandy and king of England; b. c.1027, illeg. s. of Robert I, duke of Normandy, and Arlette, da. of Fulbert the Tanner of Falaise; acc. 25 Dec. 1066; m. Matilda, da. of Baldwin V, count of Flanders, c.1051; issue: Robert, Richard, Adelaide, Cecilia, William, Constance, Adela, Henry, Matilda; d. 9 Sept. 1087; bur. Caen.

William was about thirty-nine when he triumphed at the battle of Hastings and took the throne of England. His claim was remote, being merely that his great-aunt Emma had once been married to both king Aethelred and king Cnut. William insisted that Edward 'the Confessor' had promised him the succession in 1051, but both the event and its validity have been challenged. The dukes of Normandy were, by origin, of Viking descent, the founder of the dynasty being Rolf or Rollo, a raider who, c.911, was given land in the lower Seine valley. William was only eight or so when he inherited the duchy and his early years were difficult. Not until 1047 was he in command of the situation when he defeated his cousin, Guy of Brionne, at Val-ès-Dunes. His marriage c.1051 strengthened his hand diplomatically but he had to face a formidable coalition in Geoffrey of Anjou to the south and Henry I, king of the Franks, to the east. He defeated them in 1057 at Varaville, and in 1062 added the valuable county of Maine to his dominions, again using the pretext of a private promise. By 1066 he had shown himself a brave and resourceful soldier, a wily diplomat and an ambitious, ruthless and determined ruler. The timing of his landing was impeccable and his conduct of the battle adroit, courageous, and resolute.

Once London had surrendered to him, after a feeble attempt to rally round Edgar the Atheling, William's policy was to reconcile English and Normans to his rule. However, the continued resistance outside London made the policy difficult to sustain. The subjugation of England took six years. Exeter defied the king in person and sustained a siege; the Welsh attacked the new castle at Hereford and burned it; Edwin and Morcar rebelled; Hereward 'the Wake' led the resistance in the Fens; Edgar the Atheling joined forces with Sweyn Estrithsson to raise the north. William's response was swift retribution, relentless harrying, and the building of castles to give Norman garrisons some protection. Having established control in England, in 1072 he marched into Scotland to

The Bayeux Tapestry. Probably commissioned by Odo of Bayeux, half-brother of 'the Conqueror', partly as propaganda (stressing Harold taking the oath to support William), partly to record a great event. This scene shows Harold, 'king of the English' enthroned, holding sceptre and orb. Stigand, his archbishop of Canterbury, stands at his side.

induce Malcolm III to stop supporting Edgar, and the Scottish king was forced to do homage. Norman lords replaced English ones and the last English earl, Waltheof, was executed in 1076 for conspiracy. His earldom of Northumbria went to Walcher, bishop of Durham, a Frenchman, and when he was murdered at Gateshead in 1080 the reprisals left their mark for years.

William's later years were dominated by family discord, and he spent most of his time in Normandy. After 1072 he made only four visits to England. He did not speak the language, mistrusted the people, and regarded the country chiefly as a source of revenue. In his absence, England was ruled by his half-brother, Odo of Bayeux, and by archbishop Lanfranc. In 1073 he had to campaign to retain his authority in Maine, and in 1076 he was badly beaten by Philip of France while besieging Dol. A more enduring problem was the deterioration of his relations with his eldest son Robert 'Curthose', who had long been regarded as heir to Normandy and Maine. During 1078–9 there was open warfare, in which Robert wounded his father at the siege of Gerberoi. A compromise was worked out in 1080 and they crossed to England together; Robert led an expedition to Scotland to remind Malcolm III of his promises, while William advanced across the Wye in a show of force into south Wales. In 1083, he quarrelled with Odo and imprisoned him at Rouen, and by 1084 Maine was once more giving trouble. On his last visit to England, in 1085, William wore his crown at Christmas at Gloucester and gave orders for the Domesday survey. A draft was presented to him in August 1086 at Old Sarum, where the leading landowners of the kingdom took the Salisbury oath of loyalty. When he returned to France he found Robert again plotting with king Philip, and he had embarked once more on the weary business of campaigning when he fell ill. He died in September 1087, leaving Normandy to Robert, and England to be administered by his second son, William 'Rufus'. He was buried at Caen in the church of St Étienne.

William was a sturdy, well-built man, corpulent in middle age. His manners were plain, his tastes austere, and he had no great claim to cultivation; his conduct was usually stern and sometimes brutal. Like most rulers, his great relaxation was hunting, and the New Forest was created as his private estate. England was for him less an acquisition in its own right than a resource in the feuds and rivalries of northern France. His legacy was Norman administration and Norman justice, together with twenty years of comparative peace and security; his reign took England out of the Scandinavian orbit into a connection with France which lasted, in some form, until the fall of Calais in 1558. The Norman Conquest itself can be traced in French place-names—Chester-le-Street, Houghton-le-Spring, Mary-le-bon—and the great castles through which the English people were subdued: the White Tower of London, Windsor, Chepstow, Warwick, Dover, Lincoln, Newcastle, and York.

BATES, D., *William the Conqueror* (1989).

Tower of London

William 'the Conqueror' first erected a simple fort within the south-east corner of the Roman city walls, but transformed it into a massive palace-fortress, and the name originally given to the central limestone tower soon stood for the whole complex. As London increased in importance, successive monarchs progressively enlarged its defences, and Henry II improved royal accommodation as well as establishing a menagerie. Following Edward I's expansion, the Tower contained one of the royal treasuries, housed official documents and the largest of the royal mints, and became the kingdom's main arsenal. It also served as a place of confinement for state prisoners and those who had offended politically or religiously; many were detained only briefly, but a few (such as Anne Boleyn) were executed on Tower Green. Henry VIII was the last monarch to use the Tower as a royal residence, but the traditional coronation procession from there to Westminster continued until 1661 for Charles II. Buildings and character then changed, with the establishment of a large permanent garrison, expanded arsenal, and public exhibition of the coronation regalia.

On appointment as Constable of the Tower in 1826, the Duke of Wellington wished to restore its military importance, fearing that the country was on the brink of revolution. This passed, and with Albert's encouragement, the Tower began to assume the character of a national monument. The mint and public records had already been moved out, ordnance buildings were gradually demolished, and tourism and tradition began to play increasing roles: the Yeomen of the Guard, ravens, and Crown Jewels have contributed to its becoming one of the world's great tourist attractions.

Tower of London. William began a castle on the site immediately after his conquest to keep an eye on his new subjects. The White Tower, core of the Tower of London, was probably not finished until the reign of William 'Rufus'. In the early 14th cent., the Mint and crown jewels were moved there. Among the dozens of state prisoners were Henry VI, Richard III's nephews, Anne Boleyn, Catherine Howard, Walter Ralegh, Strafford and Laud.

Matilda, duchess of Normandy and queen of England, b. c.1030, da. of Baldwin V of Flanders; m. William, duke of Normandy, c.1051; d. 3 Nov. 1083; bur. Caen.

After an initial difficulty over consanguinity had been overcome, by the couple agreeing to found two abbeys at Caen, Matilda's marriage to William I proved fruitful and close. Matilda frequently acted as regent during her husband's absences in England and did her best to keep the peace between him and their quarrelsome sons.

Odo of Bayeux, half-brother of William I (by the same mother), was the effective ruler of England in the early years of the Norman Conquest. Born c.1036, he was made a bishop in 1049, which did not prevent him fighting at the battle of Hastings. After the Norman victory he was created earl of Kent, and served as viceroy during William's frequent absences in Normandy. His reputation was as an acquisitive man and a severe ruler, and he presided over the devastation of the north-east in retaliation for the murder of Walcher, bishop of Durham, in 1080. Arrested by William in 1083, he was not released until the king's death in 1087. He was then restored to his earldom, plotted against William 'Rufus', and was sent into exile in 1088, but continued to play an important role under Robert 'Curthose' in Normandy until his death in February 1097. He was responsible for commissioning the Bayeux Tapestry, recording the events of the Conquest.

Robert 'Curthose', duke of Normandy, b. c.1053, eldest s. of William I and Matilda; acc. 9 Sept. 1087; m. Sibyl, da. of count of Conversans; issue: William; d. Cardiff, 10 Feb. 1134.

Robert, recognized as heir to Normandy and Maine, was short, fat, mercurial, impulsive, unstable, and known as 'Short-boots'. He quarrelled with his father and waged war on him 1078–9, wounding him in the process. Reconciliation followed and he succeeded as duke in 1087, but greatly resented his younger brother William's succession in England. In 1088 he made a half-hearted and abortive attempt to expel him. 'Rufus' counter-invaded Normandy in 1091 but the two brothers then joined forces against the third, Henry, attacking him at Mont-St-Michel. In 1096 Robert went on crusade, acquitting himself with valour. He returned to Normandy in 1100, invaded England in 1101, but was briefly reconciled with Henry. The *rapprochement* did not last long and in 1106 he was decisively beaten and captured at Tinchebrai. He spent the rest of his life in comfortable imprisonment, possibly for his own protection, and died at Cardiff in 1134.

Edgar the Atheling had a strong claim to the throne of England but spent his long life on the fringe of great events. The grandson of Edmund Ironside (d. 1016) and son of Edward the Atheling (d. 1057), he was about five when his father came to England and promptly died. Edgar's election as king in October 1066, after the shattering defeat at Hastings, was a desperate attempt to find a rallying-point and was brushed aside by William 'the Conqueror'. Edgar fled to Scotland, but made his peace with William in 1074 and spent the rest of his life at court. His eldest sister Margaret married Malcolm III of Scotland in 1070 and was the mother of king Edgar; his niece Edith (known as Matilda) married Henry I in 1100. The Atheling is reported to have died c.1125.

William II ('Rufus'), king of England, b. c.1060, 3rd but 2nd surviving s. of William I and Matilda; acc. 26 Sept. 1087; d. 2 Aug. 1100; bur. Winchester.

William was the favourite son of the 'Conqueror', stockily built, with a reddish complexion, hot-tempered, sharp, and sarcastic in speech. On his father's deathbed he was given England, while Robert, his elder brother, was named for Normandy. Each then tried to take over the other's territory. An attack in Kent by Robert's men, aided by Odo of Bayeux, was beaten off in 1088, and William launched his own attack in Normandy in 1091. The fighting was inconclusive and later that year William and Robert agreed to partition the lands of their younger brother Henry in the Cotentin peninsula. This accomplished, William returned to England and set out against Malcolm III of Scotland, who had invaded Northumbria. Malcolm was forced to do homage and cede Cumbria.

Fighting resumed between Robert and William in Normandy in 1094, but the following year William returned to England to deal with Robert of Mowbray, earl of Northumberland, and the Welsh insurgents. In 1096, when Robert decided to go on crusade, he raised money by pawning Normandy to William, who took over the administration of the duchy. For the rest of his life he was king of England and *de facto* duke of Normandy. In England his incessant demands for revenue provoked great discontent, and he quarrelled with archbishop Anselm who remonstrated with him. In 1097, when the archbishop left for Rome, William seized his property. Anselm did not return until after William's death, when he resumed his quarrel with the next king.

William's death was unexpected. While hunting in the New Forest in August 1100, he was shot dead with an arrow, fired, it is said, by Walter Tyrrell. He was hastily buried at Winchester, and his younger brother Henry was crowned two days later. The episode has attracted much comment, including lurid suggestions of magic and witchcraft, but there is little reason not to believe it an accident. Monastic chroniclers, who were not fond of William because of his demands on the church and his treatment of the archbishop, saw in it God's vengeance, and hunted for sinister portents; they accused William of tyranny, avarice, blasphemy, and sodomy. His lasting memorial is the Great Hall at Westminster, remodelled by Richard II.

BARLOW, F., *William Rufus* (1983).

Palace of Westminster, London

The Benedictine abbey on Thorney Island, known as the 'Minster in the West' to distinguish it from St Paul's, suffered heavily during Danish incursions, and when Edward 'the Confessor' rebuilt it he commenced a new palace close by on the riverside, later occupied by William I. The great hall was erected by William 'Rufus' (1097), heightened and given a hammerbeam roof by Richard II (1397–9), and was used increasingly as an administrative centre, since both Treasury and Exchequer were by then centred at Westminster; parliaments, law courts, impeachment trials, coronation and other royal banquets continued to function despite recurrent flooding from the Thames and fires (notably 1263, 1298). St Stephen's Chapel was added to the east, domestic quarters were built by Henry II for the household, and Henry III spent lavishly on both abbey and palace: this was his favourite residence, and the Painted Chamber, covered with biblical scenes, was impressive. Although Westminster was the main royal residence, it was also a ceremonial palace, developing into a warren of corridors swarming with royal retainers and lawyers, and sprawling over several acres. Shortly after exuberant celebrations for the birth of a (short-lived) son to Henry VIII in early 1512, a major fire destroyed the greater part of the palace. Henry consequently moved to Whitehall, and Westminster was never used again as a royal residence.

After the Reformation, St Stephen's Chapel was secularized and assigned to the lower house of Parliament, its crypt being used as a parliamentary storehouse; the Lords settled in the White Chamber, with the Jewel House built for Edward III (1365–6) housing their records. Only Westminster Hall, the cloisters, and the Jewel House survived the conflagration of 1834, after which new Houses of Parliament were constructed to Barry's designs and Pugin's ornamentation.

Henry I, king of England, b. 1068, 4th but 3rd surviving s. of William I; acc. England 5 Aug. 1100, Normandy Sept. 1106; m. (1) Edith (known as Matilda), da. of Malcolm III of Scotland, 11 Nov. 1100; issue: Matilda, William; (2) Adela, da. of Godfrey VII, count of Louvain, 29 Jan. 1121; d. 1 Dec. 1135; bur. Reading abbey.

Henry's achievement was to begin the task of reconciling English and Normans. He had certain advantages: he had been born in England, probably at Selby, after his father had become king, and spoke the language. Almost his first action on taking the throne was to marry the daughter of the king of Scotland who, as the great-granddaughter of Edmund Ironside (d. 1016), represented the old English dynasty. His coronation charter promised to uphold the laws of Edward 'the Confessor', who was fast acquiring an undeserved reputation as a wise and just ruler.

At the death of his father in 1087 Henry's chances of succeeding in either England or Normandy did not look good. His erratic eldest brother, Robert, was reconciled to the Conqueror and given Normandy; his next brother, William 'Rufus', was given England. Henry, aged nineteen, received very little land but was able to buy estates in Cotentin. At one stage it looked as though he would lose even these since, in 1091, his two elder brothers settled their differences and agreed to join forces in expelling him. This they accomplished, but the sudden death of William in the New Forest in 1100 gave Henry his chance to seize the crown. His coronation charter disavowed the misconduct of his predecessor, and promised justice and good government. He was faced, as William had been in 1088, with the attempt of his eldest brother to take the throne of England and unite it with Normandy. Robert landed at Portsmouth in July 1101, but the dispute was compromised. In 1104 Henry prepared for a counter-attack, and at Tinchebrai in 1106 defeated and captured Robert. He declared himself ruler of Normandy, and Robert was held in safe custody for the remaining twenty-eight years of his life.

Short, restless, fat in middle age, with a formidable sexual appetite, Henry proved a capable ruler. He put an end to most Welsh raids and kept Scotland under control. The *Anglo-Saxon Chronicle* wrote that 'in his days, no man dared to wrong another. He made peace for man and beasts.' Better educated than his father or brothers, he had a genuine interest in learning, and though he soon fell out with Anselm, whom he had recalled from exile, he remained a benefactor of the church. He was cruel, even by the standards of his day: two of his own small granddaughters, retained as hostages, were blinded on his instructions. Though Robert 'Curthose' was safe in custody, his late and unexpected marriage had produced a son (c.1102), William 'Clito' (prince). As he grew up, ambitious neighbours in France and discontented subjects clustered around him; Louis VI of France took up his cause and promised him Normandy. Henry defeated his opponents at Brémule in 1119, though the issue was not resolved until 1128 when William was killed in a siege.

By this time the succession in England was becoming urgent. Though he had nearly twenty illegitimate children, Henry's marriage to Edith (usually called Matilda) had produced only one surviving son and daughter, William and Matilda. At the age of seventeen, while leaving Normandy to return to England, William was drowned in the *White Ship*. Since queen Matilda had died in 1118, Henry was free to marry again and did so at once. But his bride, Adela, produced no children, and in 1127 Henry declared his daughter Matilda his successor in both Normandy and England. For good measure, she was married in 1128 to young Geoffrey of Anjou, whose territories were adjacent to Maine, now part of Normandy; a son, the future Henry II, was born to the marriage in 1133. However, Henry's diplomacy produced, at his death in 1135, not an undisputed succession, but civil war.

GREEN, J. A., *The Government of England under Henry I* (1986).

Matilda, queen of England and duchess of Normandy, b. c.1080, da. of Malcolm III of Scotland and Margaret; m. Henry I, 11 Nov. 1100; d. 1 May 1118; bur. Westminster abbey.

Matilda (christened Edith, a name unpronounceable to the Normans) was the niece of Edgar the Atheling, and thus represented the pre-Conquest English dynasty. The marriage to Henry, which took place within three months of his accession, was intended to reinforce his claim to the throne, and help to reconcile English and Normans. A cultivated and pious woman, who revered and corresponded with Anselm, she acted as regent during her husband's many absences in Normandy.

Adela, queen of England and duchess of Normandy, b. c.1103, da. of Godfrey VII, count of Louvain and duke of Brabant; m. (1) Henry I, 29 Jan. 1121; (2) William d'Aubigny (later earl of Arundel), c.1138; d. 23 Apr. 1151; bur. Reading abbey.

The death of William, his only son, in the *White Ship* disaster in

November 1120 made it imperative for Henry I to marry again, which he did at speed. The continuator of Florence of Worcester's *Chronicle* called Adela 'a young maiden of great beauty and modesty', which was not, it seems, a purely conventional tribute. The marriage failed to produce children but, on Henry's death, Adela married William d'Aubigny and had a sizeable family. In 1150 she retired to a nunnery in Brabant and died the following year.

William the Atheling, b. c.1102, s. of Henry I and Matilda; d. 25 Nov. 1120.

Henry I produced only one legitimate son, on whom great hopes were pinned, but he perished at the age of seventeen in one of the great disasters of the age. The *White Ship*, in which he was travelling with a distinguished party, struck a rock after leaving Barfleur for England and sank with almost all on board; two of Henry's illegitimate children drowned with their half-brother. The crew were said to be drunk. The consequence, fifteen years later, was a disputed succession and civil war.

Robert of Gloucester, illeg. s. of Henry I, b. c.1090; cr. earl of Gloucester 1122; m. Matilda, da. of Robert Fitzhamon; d. 31 Oct. 1147; bur. St James's church, Bristol.

Robert was the mainstay of the forces of the empress Matilda during the civil war of Stephen's reign. He was born in Caen, fought in his father's French wars, and had the custody of Robert 'Curthose', erstwhile duke of Normandy. He acquiesced at first in the choice of Stephen as king in 1135, but by 1138 had joined Matilda's party. In 1141 he succeeded in capturing Stephen at Lincoln, but was himself taken shortly afterwards by the queen's troops. The two prisoners were exchanged. He was still campaigning against Stephen when he died at Bristol in 1147.

Stephen, king of England and duke of Normandy, b. c.1096, 3rd s. of Stephen of Blois and Adela, da. of William I; acc. 22 Dec. 1135; m. Matilda, da. of Eustace III, count of Boulogne, 1125; issue: Baldwin, Eustace, William, Mary, Matilda; d. 25 Oct. 1154; bur. Faversham, Kent.

A brave and capable commander, Stephen had a streak of generosity which sometimes made him not press home his advantage: 'lenient to his enemies and easily placated, courteous to all', commented William of Malmesbury. As a consequence, although he acquired the throne in a brilliant coup, he spent the following nineteen years trying to retain it, and his reign became famous as a time of anarchy.

A nephew of Henry I, he was in constant attendance at his uncle's court and well treated. His marriage to the heiress of Boulogne in 1125 gave him a valuable strategic base; his younger brother Henry was made bishop of Winchester in 1129 which enabled him to keep an eye on the royal treasure. Along with other magnates, Stephen swore an oath to support the succession of Matilda, the only surviving legitimate child of his uncle. When Henry died in 1135, Matilda was in Normandy. Stephen seized his opportunity, crossed from Boulogne, took Winchester with his brother's help, and was welcomed by the Londoners. Supported by many magnates who feared the rule of a woman, or domination from Anjou, Stephen was crowned by the archbishop of Canterbury at Westminster within the month. A short visit to Normandy won him widespread acceptance there. Armed opposition came from Matilda's uncle, David I of Scotland, who invaded Northumbria on her behalf. Stephen advanced to meet him, and the matter was compromised. Though David continued to support Matilda, his power was shattered in 1138 by a defeat in the battle of the Standard, near Northallerton, by the local forces of Yorkshire.

Stephen's hold on power began to falter when Robert of Gloucester, an illegitimate son of Henry I and Matilda's half-brother, took up arms on her behalf. Reducing Robert's castles took time, and in 1139 Matilda arrived to claim her kingdom. In February 1141 her supporters captured Stephen at Lincoln, where he fought with great courage, strength, and determination, and for eight months he was imprisoned at Bristol. However, when his wife's men captured Robert, the two were exchanged and Stephen regained his freedom. Matilda occupied London, but her arrogance alienated the citizens, who drove her out. The war then developed into march and counter-march, siege and relief, until Matilda returned to the continent in 1148. Conduct of Matilda's campaign passed to her young son, Henry, but he was no more successful than Stephen at bringing the war to a conclusion. The death in 1152 of his wife, Matilda of Boulogne, followed in 1153 by that of his son, Eustace, broke Stephen's spirit, and he came to terms with his adversaries. By a treaty at Winchester, he was to remain king, but Henry was to succeed him. Stephen's last year was comparatively peaceful and he made a number of royal progresses in some state. He was buried with his wife at Faversham, of which abbey he had been a great benefactor.

Stephen has been much blamed for the anarchy of his reign—'a mild, soft and good man, who did no justice', in the words of the *Anglo-Saxon Chronicle*—but there are pleas in mitigation. Although some key regions

suffered repeatedly, the warfare was neither widespread nor continuous: other parts of the country never saw an army. The reduction of castles is a slow business, and the standard method of devastating the surrounding countryside in order to starve the garrison out was one which Stephen was reluctant to employ against his own people. Matilda had strong support and the two sides were well matched, Matilda holding much of the west around Gloucester, while Stephen held the east, including London. Though Stephen raised formidable armies, his opponents were not obliging enough to offer pitched battles, and the resultant chases often seem pointless.
DAVIS, R. H. C. *King Stephen* (1987).

Matilda, queen of England and duchess of Normandy, b. c.1103, da. of Eustace III, count of Boulogne, and Mary of Scotland; m. Stephen of Blois, 1125; d. 3 May 1152; bur. Faversham, Kent.

Marriage to Matilda of Boulogne strengthened Stephen's links with royalty, since her mother was a daughter of Malcolm III of Scotland and granddaughter of Edward the Atheling, as well as sister of Henry I's queen, Matilda. When Stephen seized the throne in 1135 the resources of Boulogne were of great value to him, and Matilda worked tirelessly for his cause. After Stephen had been captured at Lincoln in 1141, queen Matilda refused to come to terms, and when her men captured Robert of Gloucester she was able to secure her husband's release in an exchange. After her death in 1152 Stephen seems to have lost heart.

Henry of Blois was the son of Stephen, count of Blois, and younger brother of king Stephen. Entering the church, he became abbot of Glastonbury in 1126 and bishop of Winchester in 1129; he retained both offices for forty years and became the wealthiest prelate of the age. His assistance in 1135 was critical in helping Stephen to gain the throne, but in 1138, when the civil war was about to begin, he was on bad terms with his brother, who had passed him over for the archbishopric of Canterbury. His appointment as papal legate was not a full compensation. After Stephen's death in 1154 he withdrew to Cluny but returned to serve under Henry II as a senior adviser until his death in 1171.

Matilda, empress claimant to the throne of England, b. Feb. 1102, da. of Henry I and Matilda; m. (1) emperor Henry V, Jan. 1114; (2) Geoffrey, count of Anjou, 17 June 1128; issue: Henry; d. 10 Sept. 1167; bur. Bec, rebur. Rouen.

After the death of his only legitimate son, William, in a shipwreck in 1120, and the failure of his second marriage to produce children, Henry I declared his only legitimate daughter, Matilda, heir to the thrones of Normandy and England. At the age of seven she had been betrothed to the emperor Henry V (hence the title by which she was known). He died in 1125. Her father then arranged for her to marry in 1128 Geoffrey of Anjou, a boy of fourteen. The marriage was soon in difficulty but after a reconciliation in 1131 a son, the future Henry II, was born in 1133.

Her father's death in December 1135 found her in Normandy, and her cousin Stephen seized both thrones with little difficulty. Pointing out that the new king had previously taken an oath of allegiance to her, Matilda then mounted a protracted attempt to oust him. In September 1139 she landed at Arundel and received widespread support, and in 1141 Robert of Gloucester (her illegitimate half-brother and chief ally) captured the king at Lincoln. This was the high point of her success. She entered London in triumph as queen, but alienated support by severe financial demands and her imperious and overbearing manner. Later in 1141, she lost her advantage when Robert of Gloucester was captured by her opponents and exchanged for the king. In December 1142 she made a dramatic escape from Oxford castle in a snowstorm, camouflaged in a white sheet, but though she remained in England until 1148 her cause languished. It was rescued by the death in 1153 of Stephen's son, Eustace, which prompted him to come to terms and recognize Matilda's son, Henry, as his heir. From 1154, she exercised considerable influence in the new reign and died in Rouen in 1167. Indefatigable and resourceful, of striking appearance, she helped to ruin her own cause in the 1140s by hasty temper, but mellowed with age and finished as a great benefactor to the church.

CHIBNALL, M., *The Empress Matilda* (1991).

Eustace, **prince**, b. c.1127, 2nd s. of Stephen and Matilda; cr. count of Boulogne 1146; m. Constance, da. of Louis VI of France, 1140; d. 10 Aug. 1153.

The death of his elder brother, Baldwin, *c.*1135 made Eustace heir to his father, who was engaged in a desperate civil war. In the later 1140s he campaigned on his father's behalf, earning a reputation for ferocity: 'an evil man' was the terse comment of the *Anglo-Saxon Chronicle*. His death in 1153 dispirited his father, who came to terms with his adversary, Matilda, recognizing her son, Henry, as his successor.

Angevins and Plantagenets

The Angevin empire took its name from the county of Anjou, which Henry II inherited from his father, Geoffrey. With Normandy, Aquitaine, and England in addition, and claims of suzerainty over Brittany, Scotland, Wales, and Ireland, it was a major European power. The three rulers from Henry II to John, who lost Normandy and much of France, are often known as the Angevins. The emblem of Geoffrey of Anjou was the *planta genesta* or broom, and the name was borrowed to apply to the five monarchs from Henry III to Richard II.

Henry II, king of England, lord of Ireland, duke of Normandy, count of Anjou, b. 5 Mar. 1133, s. of Geoffrey, count of Anjou, and Matilda; acc. Normandy 1150, Anjou 1151, England 19 Dec. 1154; m. Eleanor, da. of William, duke of Aquitaine, 18 May 1152; issue: William, Henry, Matilda, Richard, Geoffrey, Eleanor, Joan, John; d. 6 July 1189; bur. Fontevrault.

Henry took over the claim to the throne of England of his mother, the redoubtable empress Matilda, and proved a more acceptable choice. He secured his territories in three moves before he was twenty-one. First, his father conquered Normandy and handed it to him in 1150; secondly, at the age of nineteen, he married the divorced wife of Louis VII of France and through her acquired Aquitaine; thirdly, after three visits to England during the civil wars—a strange mixture of royal progress, commando raid, and Grand Tour—he was recognized in 1153 as Stephen's heir, succeeding him in 1154. He proved to be a formidable ruler, with many of the characteristics of his grandfather, Henry I. Gerald of Wales, writing about the time of Henry's death, left a vivid description: 'a reddish complexion, rather dark, and a large round head. His eyes were grey, bloodshot, and flashed in anger. He had a fiery countenance. His body was fleshy, and he had an enormous paunch, rather by the fault of nature than by gross feeding... He took little rest.' Gerald went on to praise his eloquence and learning.

He took over from Stephen with little opposition, though his widespread commitments meant that he spent more than half his reign in France. His first task was to re-establish royal authority in England, in which he was greatly helped by two remarkable Justiciars, Richard de Lucy and Ranulf Glanvill, who held the office between them for thirty years. He began by tackling the problem of castles, which had

The Angevin Empire

proliferated during the civil wars, demanding the immediate surrender of all those belonging to the crown. At the same time he began building or strengthening other castles, Dover, Newcastle, and Orford being among the best surviving examples.

Having introduced better order among his subjects, Henry moved to deal with his neighbours, who had profited from England's misfortunes. Unwilling to see Northumberland and Cumbria permanently in the hands of the Scots, he called Malcolm IV south in 1157 and persuaded him to surrender, in exchange for confirmation of the earldom of Huntingdon. Later that year he marched against Owain Gwynedd, the strongest of the Welsh princes, and though the campaign was troublesome, Owain capitulated and did homage. An expedition to Toulouse in 1159 proved too much, but in 1166 he extended his empire by taking in Brittany. Henry also laid the foundations for England's conquest of Ireland when he crossed to Waterford in 1171 to demand submission.

Towards the latter part of his reign, Henry experienced as much trouble from friends and family as from his foes. Thomas Beckett, his closest friend, served as Chancellor from 1155 and was made archbishop of Canterbury in 1161, but the cordiality did not last. Beckett's quarrel with the king over the rights of the church was important, but could have been resolved. First, Beckett fled into exile in 1164, issuing excommunications as he retreated. This was an embarrassment but no more until, in 1170, Henry decided to have his son, 'the young king', crowned as an insurance. The ceremony demanded the presence of the archbishop of Canterbury, but Henry employed the archbishop of York, who was at once suspended by the papacy. Beckett returned to England on 1 December 1170, on the understanding that there would be a second coronation, at which he would preside, but in less than a month he was cut down by four knights in his own cathedral. The scandal rocked the courts of Europe, and in 1174 Henry did public penance at Canterbury.

It transpired that the coronation had, in any case, been a mistake. It enflamed the ambitions of the young Henry, who was fifteen at the time, and made him very difficult to deal with. His grievances were assiduously fanned by Louis VII of France, to whose daughter the young king had been married in 1160, at the age of five. In 1173, young Henry, accompanied by his fifteen- and fourteen-year-old brothers, Richard and Geoffrey, fled to his father-in-law's court; Eleanor, the boys' mother, would have joined them but was apprehended. Louis pretended to believe that Henry II had abdicated in his son's favour. This was the signal for all the king's enemies to take heart, and the king of Scotland, William 'the Lion', saw his opportunity to recover Northumberland. Louis of France was joined by the counts of Flanders, Boulogne, and Blois. Henry himself conducted the war on the continent, leaving the defence of England to his subordinates. His victory at Verneuil in August 1173 knocked Louis out of the war. The English loyalists, headed by Richard de Lucy, did even better: Robert, earl of Leicester, leading an invasion force, was defeated and captured at Fornham St Genevieve, just outside Bury St Edmunds, in October 1173. What remained of the hostile coalition was smashed when troops led by Ranulf Glanvill came across the king of Scotland and a few knights sunning themselves outside Alnwick castle in July 1174 and took them prisoner. William 'the Lion' was released from captivity only after he had sworn homage to Henry.

The rest of Henry's life was less fraught. Risings and rebellions continued, but they were spasms of faction rather than deadly onslaughts. The young Henry died in 1183, once more in rebellion; his brother Geoffrey died in 1186. This left Richard and John to uphold the family tradition of baiting their father and fighting against each other. Henry was believed to favour John, who repaid him by joining with Richard in yet another plot against their father. News of John's perfidy was the last communication Henry received on his deathbed in July 1189. Whether the great empire he had built up was viable may be doubted, and it has been suggested that he would have been better employed extending his authority in Britain.

WARREN, W. L., *Henry II* (1973).

Windsor castle, Berkshire

The premier castle of England and oldest royal residence still in use, Windsor was founded by William I as a motte with two baileys (wards) overlooking the Thames. It was rebuilt in stone by Henry II (1165–79), who constructed a prominent round tower and outer walls which later withstood two sieges; the walls were repaired by Henry III before he turned to the domestic

continued

Windsor castle, Berkshire *continued*

quarters and St George's Chapel in the lower ward. Edward III continued the conversion into royal residence, using William of Wykeham's design of apartments ranged around a quadrangle, rebuilding the chapel (headquarters of Edward's newly founded Order of the Garter) and the round tower. The present chapel, notable for its fan vaulting, was commenced by Edward IV in 1475, and the old chapel converted into a lady chapel (later remodelled by Victoria into a memorial to Albert). Eleven monarchs are buried at Windsor.

Few changes were made under the Tudors, but Charles II lavishly rebuilt the upper ward apartments in baroque style, and laid out the three-mile long walk, planted with elms, as a vista for his successors. Anne, who initiated Ascot Races, relished 'Garden House' (Queen's Lodge) in the Home Park, this being used later by George III when his family outgrew Richmond, and he spent his last bleak years there. Modern Windsor is the creation of George IV, who demolished Queen's Lodge, rebuilt the private apartments in neo-Gothic, and raised the Round Tower by one storey. Edward VIII made his abdication speech from Windsor castle (1936), and it has become a regular weekend home for Elizabeth II. A fire which commenced in the private chapel destroyed the north-east corner of the Upper Ward in 1992: St George's Hall and the Grand Reception Room were devastated but restored by 1998.

Eleanor of Aquitaine, queen of England and duchess of Normandy, b. c.1122, da. of William, duke of Aquitaine; m. (1) Louis VII of France, 4 July 1137; (2) Henry II, 18 May 1152; d. 1 Apr. 1204; bur. Fontevrault.

Heiress to the duchy of Aquitaine, Eleanor was much sought after, and at the age of fifteen was married to Louis VII of France. The marriage produced only two daughters, and perhaps little pleasure, since he was pious and she was vivacious. It was dissolved in 1152. Henry, then still a claimant to the throne of England, married her at once, since Aquitaine would be a superb addition to his dominions in Normandy, Maine, and Anjou. He was then nineteen, his wife thirty. She bore him a large family. In 1173, when her three eldest sons, Henry, Richard, and

Geoffrey, took up arms against her husband, she supported them; king Henry had her arrested, and she was kept in honourable confinement until 1184. She played a prominent part during the reign of Richard, organizing the payment of his enormous ransom. On Richard's death in 1199, she transferred her support to her youngest son, John. In 1202, at the age of eighty, she withstood a siege at the castle of Mirebeau in Brittany, and was rescued by John.

OWEN, D. R., *Eleanor of Aquitaine: Queen and Legend* (1993).

Henry, ('the young king'), b. 28 Feb. 1155, 2nd s. of Henry II and Eleanor; m. Margaret, da. of Louis VII of France, 1160; issue: William (d. at birth); d. 11 June 1183; bur. Rouen

On the death of his elder brother William in 1156, the infant Henry was recognized as heir to the throne. His diplomatic marriage was arranged when he was five. Crowned at Westminster in 1170, he became dissatisfied with his treatment, sought refuge with his father-in-law, and made war on his father. A temporary reconciliation took place in 1174. Next, he quarrelled with his brother Richard, and was again at war with his father when he caught dysentery and died, with melodramatic piety. Though engaging and excelling in tournaments, he proved factious and extravagant, and the experiment of crowning an heir within his father's lifetime was not repeated.

Richard I, king of England and duke of Normandy, and lord of Ireland, b. 8 Sept. 1157, 3rd s. of Henry II and Eleanor; acc. 3 Sept. 1189; m. Berengaria of Navarre, 12 May 1191; d. 6 Apr. 1199; bur. Fontevrault.

The reputation of Richard 'Cœur de Lion' ('Lion-heart') has fluctuated wildly. The Victorians were divided. Many of them admired him as a crusader and man of God, erecting an heroic statue to him outside the Houses of Parliament; Stubbs, on the other hand, thought him 'a bad son, a bad husband, a selfish ruler, and a vicious man'. Though born in Oxford, he spoke no English. During his ten years' reign, he was in England for no more than six months, and was totally absent for the last five years.

The death of an infant brother left Richard second in succession to Henry, 'the young king'. His father intended that Henry should inherit England, Normandy, and Anjou, while Richard took his mother's duchy of Aquitaine. In 1173, at the age of fifteen, he joined the younger Henry and their mother, Eleanor, in a revolt against their father. Supported by the kings of France and Scotland, the rebellion threatened Henry II's throne, but eventually collapsed. Nevertheless, at the end of the conflict, Henry appointed Richard governor of Aquitaine, which he brought under control with difficulty. His reputation was as a brave and resourceful but savage warrior.

Fortunes changed dramatically in 1183 when his older brother Henry died, leaving him chief heir to England and Normandy. However, he did not take kindly to the proposal that he should hand over Aquitaine to his younger brother, John, and there was spasmodic fighting between them. Richard was still holding it when he succeeded his father in 1189 as king of England. He had already resolved to go to the Holy Land, where Jerusalem had been recaptured from the crusaders in 1187 by Saladin, so after visiting England for his coronation and to collect funds, Richard departed within four months. The first half of 1190 was spent in France, preparing for the expedition. *En route* for Palestine, he became betrothed to Berengaria of Navarre, partly to safeguard his southern dominions from attack, but before he reached the Holy Land, he rescued her from shipwreck and captivity in Cyprus and married her. He landed at Acre, which the crusaders were besieging, bringing with him siege-engines and sappers. The city fell in just over a month. When negotiations with Saladin stalled, Richard had three thousand prisoners murdered in cold blood. Marching towards Jerusalem, he defeated Saladin in a desperate pitched battle at Arnuf, but, weakened by bad weather and dissensions among the crusaders, he never reached his goal.

In 1192 Richard resolved to return home, but he fell into the hands of Leopold of Austria, who sent him to the emperor Henry VI. Though the pope had begged Christian rulers not to take advantage of crusaders in their absence, there was little response, and Richard remained a prisoner for more than a year while a vast ransom was being raised; the story of Blondel, Richard's devoted minstrel, who searched for his master in the dungeons of Germany, is a later legend. After his release in 1194 he paid his second and last visit to England, leaving after two months to recover his French dominions. He had made great progress in restoring the position when a chance wound in the shoulder while he was besieging the castle of Châlus-Chabrol turned gangrenous and killed him. His apologists have pointed to the stability shown by his arrangements for the governance of England in his absences, and refuse to accept that he was no more than the ultimate fighting machine of his day.

GILLINGHAM, J., *Richard I* (1999).

Berengaria, queen of England and duchess of Normandy, b. c.1164, da. of Sancho VI, king of Navarre; m. Richard I, 12 May 1191; d. c.1230; bur. l'Épau, France.

The purpose of Richard's marriage was to produce an heir and to provide protection for the southern border of his French dominions while he was on crusade. The circumstances of the marriage were more romantic than the diplomacy. After betrothal, Berengaria was sailing to the Holy Land following Richard, when she was shipwrecked off Cyprus; its ruler threatened her with captivity, whereupon Richard stormed the island and forced its surrender. He and Berengaria were married and crowned at Limasol in May 1191. Berengaria never visited England, did not speak the language, saw little of her husband, and had no children. Her long widowhood was spent in Le Mans, France, where she gained a reputation for piety and good works.

Geoffrey, count of Brittany, b. 23 Sept. 1158, 4th s. of Henry II and Eleanor of Aquitaine; m. Constance, da. of Conan IV, duke of Brittany, July 1181; issue: Eleanor, Arthur (posthumous); d. 19 Aug. 1186; bur. Notre-Dame.

Another of the turbulent sons of Henry II, and brother to Richard I and John, Geoffrey was given Brittany as a boy when Henry conquered it in 1166. He took part in the revolt against his father in 1173–4. His death was the result of an accident during a tournament. Gerald of Wales wrote of him as an oily hypocrite.

John, king of England, duke of Normandy, lord of Ireland, b. 24 Dec. 1167, 5th s. of Henry II and Eleanor; acc. 27 May 1199; m. (1) Isabella of Gloucester, 29 Aug. 1189; (2) Isabella of Angoulême, 24 Aug. 1200; issue: Henry, Richard, Joan, Isabella, Eleanor; d. 18/19 Oct. 1216; bur. Worcester.

John's reign saw important developments: first, the loss of all the continental possessions of the Angevin empire, secondly, the long struggle with the barons, which culminated in the promulgation of Magna Carta. As the youngest son, John's prospects were not good, but his elder brothers died early, leaving him in 1189 the chief heir to his brother king Richard. Even then, his accession was not assured, since Richard married in 1191 and might produce a son, while the young son of his brother Geoffrey, Arthur of Brittany, was a possible rival. It had not proved easy to provide estates for John. His father had suggested that Richard, on becoming prospective duke of Normandy in 1183, should hand over Aquitaine; Richard did not agree and the brothers quarrelled. In 1176 John had been betrothed to an heiress, Isabella of Gloucester, and marriage followed in 1189. Meanwhile he was known as John 'Lackland'.

His early career was inauspicious. To give him employment and experience, Henry sent him to Ireland in 1185 as viceroy, with the title 'lord of Ireland'. The four-month visit was a disaster. John did not conceal his contempt for what he thought the uncouthness of the native Irish chieftains with their long beards, the Anglo-Norman Irish remained suspicious, and John's expeditionary force took to looting and desertion. In 1189, when his father died, John was plotting with Richard, who was in open rebellion, and it was said that the revelation of John's treachery embittered the old king's end.

Richard set out on crusade within months of taking the throne, naming Arthur of Brittany as his heir. During Richard's captivity in Germany, John joined forces with Philip 'Augustus' of France to undermine him, but Richard forgave him, and for the next five years John played a useful part in helping to recover the lands in France lost during Richard's imprisonment. On Richard's deathbed, in 1199, he named John as heir. Philip 'Augustus' then urged the claims of Arthur, still only a ten-year-old boy. John retaliated with a campaign which led to a temporary settlement at Le Goulet: Arthur's claim to Brittany only was confirmed, and John agreed to do homage to Philip for his brother's lands. 'John Softsword' was a scornful comment. He sought to strengthen his position in 1200 by a second marriage to Isabella of Angoulême, a county in the heart of Aquitaine. His twelve-year-old bride, with whom John was said to have been much taken, produced a sizeable family.

Fighting between Philip and John soon broke out again, the French king stripping him of his continental titles which went to Arthur. John's response was vigorous and, for a time, successful, capturing Arthur at Mirebeau. Arthur's subsequent death in captivity was widely attributed to John and, after that, his position crumbled at alarming speed. John began to see disloyalty everywhere and in December 1203 suddenly left Normandy, never to return. In 1204, in a systematic campaign, Philip took Caen, the ancient capital of Normandy, and then the great eastern town of Rouen. John's vast expedition in 1205 which assembled at Portsmouth to reconquer his lost dominions, did not sail. All that remained were parts of Aquitaine and the Channel Islands.

Until this point, John had experienced little difficulty in England, but military defeat usually brings trouble and John guaranteed it by his tyrannical conduct. The incessant demands of war meant that taxation was racked up and every opportunity taken to exploit feudal rights. The de Braose family, once his staunch allies, incurred his wrath and were hunted down relentlessly: the wife and son of William de Braose were imprisoned and never seen again—starved to death according to one rumour. For good measure, John became involved in a protracted, bitter, and unnecessary controversy with pope Innocent III, when he refused to accept the papal nominee, Stephen Langton, as archbishop of Canterbury. The outcome was first an interdict in 1208, and then John's personal excommunication in 1209. Though John's counter-measures against the clergy were characteristically vigorous, the breach offered advantages to the growing number of the discontented.

Military successes in Scotland, Wales, and Ireland prompted John to reopen the continental question in 1212, and he gathered another expedition at Portsmouth. Once more, it did not sail. Llywelyn, prince of Gwynedd, again rose in rebellion. The king's response was to divert the army for France and to hang twenty-eight Welsh hostages in his custody. However, rumours of a baronial conspiracy caused the Welsh campaign also to be cancelled. John hastily came to terms with the pope, who agreed to lift the interdict in exchange for Langton's installation, and John's promise to accept his kingdom as a papal fief. Turning the tables, Philip now prepared his own invasion fleet, but it was caught unprepared and smashed to pieces in harbour at Damme by an English squadron. It seemed that John had once again wriggled out of his difficulties.

He was adept, however, at inventing new ones, and concluded that he could now bring his struggle against Philip to a triumphant end. He landed at La Rochelle in the spring of 1214. In the north, his allies, Otto of Brunswick and the counts of Flanders and Boulogne, were to launch a simultaneous attack, catching Philip on two fronts. After initial success, John's attack was beginning to falter when, in July, his allies gave battle to the French at Bouvines and were routed. The English commander, the earl of Salisbury, and both counts were captured.

John returned to England, blaming lack of support, but his barons retorted by demanding their own rights. With civil war looming in March 1215, John suddenly declared himself a crusader, thus putting himself under the protection of the church. The barons retaliated by occupying London, and the situation was stalemate. The moderates brought both sides together at Runnymede in June 1215, where the barons were granted their charter of liberties, the Great Charter, or

Magna Carta. Far from being a general statement, it was a highly specific reaffirmation of feudal rights, designed to offer the baronage some protection against ruthless royal exploitation.

The Great Charter lasted ten weeks. John at once sent off an appeal against it to his new ally, the pope, and Innocent obliged by declaring that Magna Carta was 'shameful, base, illegal, and unjust'. Civil war

King John's tomb in Worcester Cathedral. In his will in 1216 king John specifically asked to be buried at Worcester, out of respect for St Wulfstan. His statue is flanked by two bishops. It was a pious end for a man not noted for his religious zeal.

could no longer be avoided. The rebels offered the crown of England to Philip's son, Louis, if he would come and seize it. The Scots crossed the border. John began a march of devastation, capturing Berwick and slaughtering the inhabitants. Louis landed in May 1216. In the autumn, campaigning in the Fens, John lost part of his baggage train in the Wash (perhaps including some regalia), reached Newark, and died of dysentery.

The denunciations of John by contemporary chroniclers, many of them indignant at his treatment of the church, verged on the ludicrous. 'Foul as it is,' wrote Matthew Paris, 'hell itself is defiled by the fouler presence of John.' But modern revisionists, impressed by the conscientious way he administered justice, also seem extreme. 'A very intelligent and able man', writes one distinguished historian, 'a ruler of consummate ability', comments another. That is surely excessive. John was not without cunning and was well-versed in duplicity. He showed considerable adroitness in extricating himself from the crises he had created, but there is little evidence of any capacity to learn. He was ruthless, vindictive, and cruel. To Henry II he was a treacherous son, to Richard an untrustworthy brother. As king he was fertile in expedients, but seemed to have no concept of the dignity of the office, a small artful man.

WARREN, W. L., *King John* (1961).

Isabella of Gloucester, b. c.1160, da. of William FitzRobert, 2nd earl of Gloucester; m. (1) John (later king of England), 29 Aug. 1189; (2) Geoffrey de Mandeville, earl of Essex, 1214; (3) Hubert de Burgh, 1217; d. 14 Oct. 1217; bur. Canterbury.

Isabella's marriage to John seems to have been purely nominal, and she was never crowned. She was betrothed to John in 1176, when he was nine, in order to provide him with some estates. There were no children, and the couple do not seem to have lived together. As soon as he came to the throne, John obtained a divorce and remarried. Isabella was still a valuable asset and seems to have been held in comfortable captivity. In 1214, John gave her and the earldom of Gloucester to Geoffrey de Mandeville in a straightforward cash deal. On Geoffrey's death in a tournament in 1216, Isabella was placed in the charge of Hubert de Burgh, earl of Kent, who married her a few days before her death. All three marriages seem to have been commercial transactions.

Isabella of Angoulême, queen of England and duchess of Normandy, b. c.1188, da. of Aymer, count of Angoulême; m. (1) John, 24 Aug. 1200; (2) Hugh de Lusignan, count of La Marche, 1220; d. 1246; bur. Fontevrault.

Isabella, John's second wife, was a girl of twelve and betrothed to Hugh of Lusignan when John met her in July 1200. Passion seems to have been a factor in the marriage, but John needed an heir, and the county of Angoulême was of strategic importance in the middle of Aquitaine. Hugh's protests were brushed aside, but when he appealed to Philip 'Augustus' as his overlord, the French king found in his favour and used the episode as a pretext to make war on John. Later chroniclers blamed her for the loss of John's French territories, but he was quite capable of losing them without her assistance. Their testimony cancels out, since Roger of Wendover accused the king of wasting time in idle dalliance with his new bride, while Matthew Paris reported that they detested each other; the latter can scarcely be true since their fifth child was born in 1215, within a year of John's death. Isabella then withdrew to France where, in 1220, she married the son of her previous betrothed.

Arthur, count of Brittany, b. 1187, s. of Geoffrey, count of Brittany, and Constance; d. Rouen, 3 Apr. 1203.

The posthumous son of John's elder brother, Arthur had a plausible claim to the English throne. He was named in honour of the legendary Breton hero, and succeeded in Brittany at a time when the duchy was attempting to maintain its autonomy against France and England. Richard I, at the beginning of his reign, may have done Arthur a disservice by naming him as his heir. He was then in the care of his mother Constance, but his cause was taken up by Philip 'Augustus' of France, who recognized him in 1199 as heir to all Richard's French possessions. After the death of his mother in 1201, Philip had Arthur betrothed to his young daughter, Marie. Open warfare with John resulted, and Arthur was captured at Mirebeau on 1 August 1202. He was then seventeen. He was removed to Rouen and there murdered; the evidence is largely circumstantial, but since John is known to have been there on the day of the murder, it is difficult to acquit him. In Shakespeare's play *King John*, Arthur is represented, for dramatic purposes, as a small boy.

Henry III, king of England and lord of Ireland, b. 1 Oct. 1207, elder s. of John and Isabella; acc. 28 Oct. 1216; m. Eleanor, da. of Raymond Berenger IV, count of

Provence, 20 Jan. 1236; issue: 3 s., Edward, Margaret, Beatrice, Edmund, Katherine; d. 16 Nov. 1272; bur. Westminster abbey.

John's death left his heir aged nine and his kingdom in the throes of civil war. Much of the south-east was held by Louis, son of Philip of France, claiming the throne as husband of Blanche of Castile, granddaughter of Henry I. William Marshall was declared regent, Hubert de Burgh continued as Justiciar, and a number of the rebel barons transferred allegiance back to the young king. Two swift victories—one at Lincoln, the other a naval battle off Sandwich—persuaded Louis to abandon his claim. Henry reached his personal majority in 1223 at the age of sixteen, and declared himself independent in 1227. The new king was very different from his father. Though personally brave, he had neither taste nor ability for warfare. He was a generous patron to the church and devout in his personal religious life. His appearance was agreeable, his manner gentle, and he had a genuine interest in art and architecture. For all his political faults, he brought to the English monarchy a sense of dignity and a more heightened ceremonial.

In line with tradition, his first difficulties were with his own family. In July 1227, his eighteen-year-old brother, Richard, earl of Cornwall, seized a manor belonging to a royal servant and refused to yield it. He was supported by a number of barons and the king was obliged to give way. An early example had been set that the king might be defied. Two factors created unrest. There was much dislike among the English of the Poitevins whom Henry favoured and, after his marriage to Eleanor of Provence in 1236, to her Provençal relatives. Secondly, Henry had little success in warfare. He found Llywelyn ab Iorwerth, prince of Gwynedd, very difficult to deal with, and expeditions against him in 1228, 1231, and 1232 were near-disasters. Nor were his attempts to reconquer the lost territories in France any more successful: an expedition in 1228 had to be aborted, and that of 1230, led by the king himself, achieved little. The cost of these campaigns was heavy, Henry's way of life was lavish, and his great respect for the papacy meant that papal exactions were severe. A quarrel in 1232 with Hubert de Burgh deprived him of an experienced and steadfast supporter. Henry resumed the war against Louis IX of France in 1242, but was chased back into Bordeaux. From 1248 he entrusted Gascony to his new brother-in-law, Simon de Montfort, who had married his sister, Eleanor, in 1238.

The crisis of Henry's reign began with foreign policy. In 1255 the pope offered the kingdom of Sicily to be held as a papal brief, which Henry accepted on behalf of his second son, Edmund. Few of Henry's subjects saw any advantage to themselves in it, and the baronage refused to make any grant in support. At the Parliament of April 1258, many of the barons appeared in armour, demanding the exile of foreign favourites, and a committee to control the king; at the head of the baronial claims was de Montfort, a brave and resourceful soldier. Henry submitted but, like his father, appealed to the pope to absolve him from his pledges. In 1263 the issue was put for arbitration to Louis IX who, in the interests of royal solidarity, found totally in favour of the king. Recourse to arms was then inevitable. In May 1264, at Lewes, Henry's troops were routed by de Montfort's men, and both the king and his young son, Edward, captured. For a year Henry was a puppet king, taken around in de Montfort's entourage. He was restored to power in August 1265 when Edward escaped, defeating and killing de Montfort at Evesham. In 1269 Henry attended a magnificent ceremony at Westminster abbey, which had been completely rebuilt, during which the shrine of Edward 'the Confessor' was dedicated. His last years were spent in failing health, and he died in 1272. Although, in the end, Henry triumphed over his adversaries, the long-term implications of his reign were that there were limits within which monarchs must work, and the constitutional safeguards against the abuse of power imposed upon him and his father, John, were not forgotten.

CARPENTER, D. A., *The Reign of Henry III* (1996).

Winchester palace, Hampshire

A motte-and-bailey castle had been constructed in the late eleventh century, but since medieval Winchester functioned as a national administrative centre (housing the royal treasury and Domesday Book) before being superseded by Westminster, Henry II rebuilt the castle in stone, extensively altering it from 1155 to include 'the king's houses'. Accounts relating to the queen's chamber, royal chapels, and mews for the king's falcons suggest considerable outlay. Henry III was born there, and during his minority much work was undertaken to repair the damage incurred during the siege by prince Louis of France in 1216; the

continued

Winchester palace, Hampshire *continued*

great hall was rebuilt and foundations laid for a new tower. Henry subsequently spent heavily on Winchester castle, improving its defences and remodelling or redecorating most of the buildings, with the king's and queen's chambers being panelled, paved, and painted. When Edward I and his second queen, Margaret, were in residence in 1302 fire gutted the royal chambers, but Edward's preoccupation with the Scottish war meant that they were never replaced, although some repairs were ordered by Edward III for his Parliament there in 1330. The great hall was partially rebuilt in 1394, and this is the only part of the medieval palace still standing.

In 1683 Charles II commissioned Wren to build a large palace close by, but this was never completed. The shell was variously used to house prisoners of war, shelter refugee French clergy, and serve as military gaol, but was finally destroyed by fire in 1894.

Eleanor of Provence, queen of England, b. 1223, da. of Raymond Berenger IV, count of Provence; m. Henry III, 20 Jan. 1236; d. 25 June 1291; bur. Amesbury, Wilts.

Part of the purpose of the marriage of Henry III and Eleanor was diplomatic, to counter the influence of Louis IX of France, who had married Eleanor's elder sister, Margaret, in 1234. The influence of Eleanor's Provençal relatives was much resented. An uncle, Boniface, was made archbishop of Canterbury in 1241 and held the office until 1270; another sister, Sancia, married Henry's brother, Richard, earl of Cornwall, in 1243. Eleanor gave strong support to her husband during the baronial wars, going to the continent to raise men and money. After his death in 1272 she spent her long widowhood in a convent at Amesbury, where she died in 1291.

Richard, earl of Cornwall, b. 5 Jan. 1209, 2nd s. of John and Isabella; cr. earl of Cornwall 1227; elected king of the Romans 1257; m. (1) Isabella, da. of William Marshal, earl of Pembroke, and wid. of Gilbert de Clare, earl of Gloucester, 30 Mar. 1231; issue: John, Isabella, Henry, Nicholas; (2) Sancia, da. of Raymond Berenger IV, count of Provence, 23 Nov. 1243; issue: Henry, Edmund; (3) Beatrice of

Falkenburg, niece of Engelbert of Cologne, 16 June 1269; d. 2 Apr. 1272; bur. Hailes abbey, Glos.

Richard was the only brother of Henry III. Until the birth of his nephew Edward in 1239, he was heir to the throne, and his marriage to the queen's sister in 1243 confirmed his influence. He was made earl of Cornwall and count of Poitou, and gained a considerable reputation as a crusader in 1240; his earldom gave him great wealth through its tin-mines. He declined an offer from the pope of the throne of Sicily, but in 1256 was persuaded to come forward as papal nominee for the throne of the Holy Roman Empire. He was crowned at Aachen, but found it difficult to establish his authority against a rival candidate, Alfonso of Castile. Returning to England in 1259, he found his brother at odds with a powerful baronial party, but when open warfare broke out in 1264 he took the king's side, fought with him in the defeat at Lewes, and was captured hiding in a windmill. He was still in captivity when his nephew, prince Edward, rescued the royal cause at Evesham in 1265. He did not abandon his German ambitions and revisited that country in 1268-9. He died seven months before his brother in 1272.

Simon de Montfort, b. c.1208, s. of Simon de Montfort III; cr. earl of Leicester, 11 Apr. 1239; m. Eleanor, da. of John and wid. of William Marshal, earl of Pembroke, 7 Jan. 1238; issue: Henry, Simon, Guy, Amauri, Richard, Eleanor; d. 4 Aug. 1265; bur. Evesham abbey.

De Montfort was French by birth and upbringing. On his father's death in 1218, Simon agreed with his brother Amauri that he would pursue the family claims in England, leaving the French lands to Amauri. He arrived in England in 1230 to beg the young king to grant him the earldom of Leicester, established a position at court, fought with Henry in the Aquitaine campaign of 1230, married the king's sister in 1238, and was recognized as earl of Leicester in 1239. But complications arose out of his appointment in 1248 as governor for seven years of the threatened province of Gascony. De Montfort ruled by strong methods, which he insisted were necessary against rebels and traitors, but his adversaries appealed for justice to the king, and in 1252 de Montfort was forced to defend his actions at a public trial. Though he escaped condemnation, his power was curtailed.

At the Parliament of 1258, a group of magnates demanded financial reform and the expulsion of foreign favourites, and de Montfort soon acquired a leading role in the baronial party. In 1263 it was agreed to submit the points at issue to the arbitration of Louis IX of France, but when, in the mise of Amiens, he found totally in favour of the king (save for the traditional liberties of the realm), the baronage took up arms. At Lewes, on 14 May 1264, de Montfort's supporters were triumphant, capturing the king, his brother Richard, and his son Edward. For a year, de Montfort was the effective ruler of England, and the king was taken around in his entourage. In January 1265 de Montfort summoned the famous Parliament in which the counties were represented by two knights and certain boroughs by two burgesses. London gave him powerful support. But in May 1265 prince Edward escaped and raised a formidable army; at Evesham in August, de Montfort, expecting reinforcements from his son Simon, was confronted by a vastly superior royalist force, and cut down.

De Montfort has always been a controversial figure. He was acquisitive, self-seeking, hot-tempered, and combative, but he was also deeply religious, punctilious in his observances, a close friend of the great cleric Robert Grosseteste, and wearer of a hair shirt. Within weeks of his burial, miracles were reported at his tomb. He was neither a constitutional statesman nor an unprincipled ruffian but a man who, like Cromwell, climbed to greatness, step by step, a natural leader of men.

MADICOTT, J. R., *Simon de Montfort* (1994).

Edward I, king of England and lord of Ireland, b. 18 June 1239, 4th but 1st surviving s. of Henry III and Eleanor; acc. 20 Nov. 1272; m. (1) Eleanor, da. of Ferdinand III of Castile, Oct. 1254; issue: Eleanor, John, Henry, Isabel, Joan, Alfonso, Margaret, Berengaria, Mary, Elizabeth, Edward; (2) Margaret, da. of Philip III of France, 10 Sept. 1299; issue: Thomas, Edmund, Eleanor; d. 7 July 1307; bur. Westminster abbey.

With the loss of Normandy and only a fitful grasp on Gascony, the focus of the English monarchy after two hundred years moved from France to the British Isles. Though on his tombstone at Westminster Edward was described as 'the hammer of the Scots', a more apt description would have been 'the hammer of the Welsh'.

Edward was much taller than average ('Longshanks'), an imposing figure on horseback. As a military man he was a brilliant jouster, but as a strategist he was careful, painstaking, and efficient. His manner was stern, often harsh, sometimes brutal. He matured early, perhaps because his father was an unpredictable ruler who needed a reliable lieutenant. His marriage, at fifteen, to Eleanor of Castile was diplomatic, but proved congenial and loving; his second marriage in 1299, to a woman more than forty years younger, was also successful. His earliest military experience was attempting to deal with Welsh incursions in 1256–7. During the early part of the struggle between his father and the baronial party, Edward had some sympathy with the reformers, and an understanding with de Montfort, his uncle by marriage, but as soon as open warfare began in 1264 he became a champion of the royalist cause. Captured at Lewes in May 1264, he escaped a year later and, in a brilliant campaign, trapped de Montfort's main force at Evesham and annihilated it. From 1270 he was on crusade, and gained a reputation for courage. On his father's death in November 1272 he was able to take his time returning home, reaching Dover on 2 August 1274, and was crowned in Westminster abbey on 19 August.

His first task was to improve the administration and governance of England, which had caused great discontent under his father's capricious and self-indulgent rule. The evidence of widespread corruption and misgovernment led to the Statute of Westminster in 1275, which attempted reform. There was undoubtedly an improvement in the application of the law, and strong action against corrupt judges and administrators, though many of them were subsequently pardoned. A popular policy in 1290 was the expulsion of the Jews, a decision which appealed to a crusader, and was rewarded by generous grants from both Parliament and Convocation.

Edward himself took little part in the details of justice and administration, preoccupied as he was with England's policy towards her neighbours. First to feel the king's strength were the Welsh, who had profited from the dissensions of Henry III's reign. Llywelyn ap Gruffydd was at odds with his brother Dafydd: Edward's determined advance in north Wales in 1277 forced Llywelyn to cede lands east of the Conwy and confine himself largely to Snowdonia. A second war, in 1282, in which Llywelyn and Dafydd joined forces, proved a disaster for the Welsh, with Llywelyn killed in battle and Dafydd executed as a traitor. The principality was taken over, and Edward's grip was confirmed by the impressive series of castles, including Caernarfon and Harlech, built at great expense.

The Scottish difficulties were more protracted. Whereas the Welsh wars were the culmination of border disputes which went back well beyond the Norman Conquest, the Scottish were in part accidental and stemmed from what might have seen, with good fortune, the peaceful unification of the two kingdoms. In 1286 Alexander III of

Scotland, whose first wife had been Edward's sister, Margaret, was killed in a riding accident. Heir to the Scottish throne was Alexander's granddaughter, Margaret, the 'Maid of Norway', aged three. By the treaty of Birgham in 1290, it was agreed that she should marry Edward's infant son, Edward of Caernarfon. Two months later, the 'Maid' died after crossing from Norway, leaving a disputed succession, the 'Great Cause'. Edward I, as overlord, neighbour, and head of the family, presided over an adjudication between thirteen competitors, which found for John Balliol. Edward, foolishly, treated him as an underling, and a group of Scottish magnates appealed to Philip IV of France for protection. Edward headed an invasion in 1296, took Berwick, slaughtered the inhabitants, deposed Balliol, and imposed direct rule on Scotland; the removal of the coronation stone from Scone was a gesture intended as a final settlement. The result was very different. First, William Wallace raised Scottish resistance, and after he had been defeated and killed the cause was taken up by Robert Bruce, grandson of one of the competitors. Bruce was crowned king in March 1306, and though his close relatives were hunted down, killed, or imprisoned, Edward was still trying to establish his authority on his last expedition in 1307.

He also experienced difficulty in Gascony. In the earlier part of his reign, relations with Philip III were cordial, though Gascony always required attention, and Edward spent three years there, 1286–9. His nephew, Edward, earl of Cornwall, acted as regent in England. However, clashes between Norman and English sailors led to worsening relations between Edward and Philip IV who, as overlord, confiscated the duchy in 1294. An expedition the following year could not prevent the French from overrunning the northern parts of Gascony. The papacy negotiated a truce, whereby the status of Gascony as a fief held by Edward from Philip was reaffirmed, Edward married Philip's sister, Margaret, and his son, Edward, was betrothed to Philip's daughter, Isabella.

Warfare against the Welsh, Scots, and French imposed severe burdens upon Edward's subjects. In 1297, when he appealed to his barons to fight in Gascony while he led a diversionary attack in Flanders, they refused and brought forward a list of grievances. He was obliged to show some political caution, confirming the Great Charter and the Forest Charter. Persistent demands for revenue stimulated the growing importance of Parliament, which alone had full powers to consent to taxation. The need for as wide a representation as possible contributed to the 'Model' Parliament of 1295, long regarded as a uniquely important example.

Edward's achievements were mixed. His settlement in Wales endured, even if risings and incursions persisted, but the heavy-handed treatment of Scotland, not so easily subdued, poisoned relations between the two countries for centuries to come. In Gascony, he could do little save hold his own. Even with a ruler of more than common efficiency and a remarkable tenacity of purpose, the resources of England did not look adequate for the tasks Edward laid upon it.

PRESTWICH, M., *Edward I* (1988).

Eleanor of Castile, queen of England, b. c.1242, da. of Ferdinand III of Castile; m. prince Edward (later Edward I), Oct. 1254; d. 28 Nov. 1290; bur. Westminster abbey.

Prince Edward was fifteen when he was married at Burgos to Eleanor, aged about twelve, who brought with her the inheritance of two counties in Gascony and the Castilian renunciation of any claim to the province. From 1270 to 1274 she accompanied her husband on crusade, and was crowned with him in August 1274. She had a large family, but her only surviving son, Edward, was not born until 1284, when she was over forty. After her death at Harby in Nottinghamshire, the king commissioned the sequence of stone crosses which marked where her funeral cortège had rested, and of which three remain. There is a remarkable tomb and brass effigy in Westminster abbey.

PARSONS, J. C., *Eleanor of Castile: Queen and Society in Thirteenth-Century England* (1995).

Margaret of France, queen of England, b. c.1282, da. of Philip III of France; m. Edward I, 9 Sept. 1299; d. 14 Feb. 1318; bur. church of the Franciscans, London.

Margaret's marriage to Edward I, who was more than forty years older than his wife, was part of the peace settlement with France in 1298. Her first son, Thomas, was born at Brotherton in Yorkshire in June 1300. She was never crowned, but accompanied her husband on many of his journeys, and bore him two more children. She remained in England after his death in 1307 and devoted herself to charitable and religious works. If the effigy on the Alard tomb at Winchelsea is to be trusted, she was of uncommon beauty.

Eleanor Cross at Hardingstone, Northants. One of the three surviving crosses erected by Edward I in the 1290s to mark the stages of the funeral cortège of his wife, Eleanor. The others are at Geddington, near Kettering, and at Waltham Cross. The cross outside Charing Cross station in London is a replica erected in 1863.

Edmund, earl of Leicester and earl of Lancaster, b. 16 Jan. 1245, 2nd surviving s. of Henry III and Eleanor; cr. earl of Leicester 26 Oct. 1265, earl of Lancaster 30 June 1267; m. (1) Aveline, da. of William, count of Aumale, Apr. 1269; (2) Blanche, da. of Robert, count of Artois, and wid. of Henry, king of Navarre, 1276; issue: Henry, Thomas, John, 1 da.; d. 5 June 1296; bur. Westminster abbey.

Known as 'Crouchback', Edmund was the younger brother of Edward I and one of his chief lieutenants. The decision by his father, Henry III, to accept the throne of Sicily on his behalf when he was ten precipitated the baronial wars of his youth. During the campaigns of 1264 and 1265, he was in France, but on returning after the royalist triumph at Evesham, he was given the forfeited earldom of Simon de Montfort. His second marriage in 1276 was prestigious and brought him the county of Champagne as his wife's dowry. He was employed by Edward chiefly as a military commander, against the Welsh (1282), in Scotland (1291–2), and in Gascony (1296), where he died; his tomb in Westminster abbey is beside that of his brother. Henry IV, when seeking the throne, claimed that Edmund, his ancestor, had been the eldest son of Henry III but passed over because of deformity: nobody believed him.

Thomas, earl of Leicester and earl of Lancaster, b. c.1278, s. of Edmund, earl of Leicester and of Lancaster, and Blanche, da. of Robert, count of Artois; m. Alice, da. of Henry, earl of Lincoln, c.1294; succ. as earl 5 June 1296; d. 22 Mar. 1322; bur. Pontefract priory.

Thomas of Lancaster was first cousin to king Edward II, the greatest magnate of his day, and a persistent opponent of the crown. His early opposition was to Piers Gaveston, a favourite whom the king had created earl of Cornwall. Gaveston was seized in 1312 and beheaded in Lancaster's presence. In 1321 his animosity was transferred to the Despensers, whom the king was forced to banish. The following year, open warfare ensued but, after a defeat at Burton, Lancaster was captured at Boroughbridge, taken to Pontefract, and executed as a traitor. His supporters hailed him as a great champion of liberty but he seems a better example of baronial faction.

MADDICOTT, J. R., *Thomas of Lancaster, 1307–22* (1970).

Edward II, king of England and lord of Ireland, b. 25 Apr. 1284, 4th but 1st surviving s. of Edward I and Eleanor; acc. 7 July 1307; m. Isabella, da. of Philip IV of France, 25 Jan. 1308; issue: Edward, John, Eleanor, Joan; deposed 20 Jan. 1327; d. Berkeley, 21 Sept. 1327; bur. Gloucester cathedral.

Edward's reign is the tragedy of a man who threw away great advantages. His succession was undisputed. He was well built, good on horseback, strong, articulate, interested in music, theatre, and craftsmanship, and not unintelligent. In character he resembled his grandfather, Henry III, more than his father, but his anger could degenerate into petulance, and he had no military ability—a serious drawback in a medieval ruler.

His first act as king was to complete the marriage to Isabella of France. Despite rumours of the king's homosexual proclivities, the marriage, though diplomatic in origin, seems to have been tolerable until late in Edward's life: a son was born in 1312, followed by three other children, the last in 1321. Edward's coronation hinted at future difficulties. A new clause was added to the royal oath, that the king would observe 'the rightful laws and customs which the community of the realm shall have chosen'. This was vague enough but suggested that the barons had not forgotten their grievances against Edward's father and were mistrustful. Moreover, at the ceremony, Edward's favourite, Piers Gaveston, was ostentatious and provocative, bearing St Edward's crown and carrying the left spur. Many of the great magnates were deeply affronted, since Gaveston was no more than the son of a Gascon knight; in less than a month from the old king's death, he had been given the earldom of Cornwall. For good measure, Gaveston had a sharp tongue and a high opinion of himself. He acted as regent during Edward II's short absence in France, was appointed chief governor in Ireland, and was given the king's niece in marriage. In 1310 the magnates, remembering the baronial controls on Henry III, demanded limitations on the king to be supervised by a group of Ordainers, with powers to regulate finance and justice. Edward was forced to agree to Gaveston's banishment. When he returned in 1312, he was captured at Scarborough, surrendered on a safe conduct, and then beheaded near Warwick.

The regime of the Ordainers continued to operate, with effective power in the hands of Thomas of Lancaster, the king's first cousin. In 1314 a fresh disaster overtook Edward. The Scottish war was going badly and he decided on a major expedition to revive the English cause, but, at the hands of Robert Bruce at Bannockburn, Edward's large army received a crushing defeat. In 1319 an attack upon Berwick had to be abandoned after a Scottish marauding force had decimated local levies at Myton in Yorkshire. Meanwhile, the gap in Edward's favour left by the death of Gaveston was filled by the two Despensers, father and son. Lancaster and his supporters succeeded in procuring the banishment of the Despensers in 1321, but in a campaign in the marches of Wales later that year, Edward gained the upper hand and recalled them. Lancaster fled north, but was captured at Boroughbridge, hastily tried in Edward's presence, and executed at Pontefract. The king then summoned a Parliament at York, which declared the Ordinances illegal and restored him to full authority.

For four years, Edward and the Despensers were in control. Domestic opposition was crushed in a novel burst of savagery. Many of Lancaster's men were hunted down and hanged in their own localities in what has been called a reign of terror. The Despensers prospered, Hugh the elder being created earl of Winchester six weeks after Lancaster's execution. The efficiency of the regime, however, did not noticeably improve. A fresh attempt upon Scotland had to be aborted, and Edward was lucky to escape capture by the Scots at Byland. The sight of a king of England chased into York by invading Scots did not impress his English subjects.

Edward's downfall started through the convergence of three lines of action: a daring escape from the Tower of London by one of the Despensers' adversaries, the outbreak of war with France, and the alienation of queen Isabella. Roger Mortimer, a marcher baron under sentence of death, drugged his guards and escaped in August 1324 by rope-ladder, fleeing to France. A dispute about a castle at Saint-Sardos in October 1323 roused passions and led to war between Edward and Philip V of France, in which many parts of Gascony were overrun. In March 1325 Isabella, sister to both Philip and the new king, Charles IV, was sent to France to negotiate a settlement. She was joined in September by her thirteen-year-old son, prince Edward.

In France, Isabella and Mortimer became lovers. After Edward had repeatedly sent demanding her return, she arrived with a small army, landing at Orwell, and the king's supporters deserted in droves. The elder Despenser was captured at Bristol, hanged, and beheaded; his son was savagely butchered in Hereford market-place. Edward himself, captured in south Wales, was taken to Kenilworth. In January 1327 a Parliament, summoned in the name of the young prince, declared his father deposed. He was removed to Berkeley castle in Gloucestershire, where he was brutally murdered in September 1327. It was said that his screams could be heard throughout the small town of Berkeley, and a later source added that a red-hot poker had been thrust up him.

The explanation of Edward's catastrophe is not difficult—he had no judgement and little capacity. He was abject in defeat and truculent in victory; his military enterprises were as expensive as they were ill-fated.

It is less easy to explain the downwards spiral into wanton cruelty and unfeeling brutality. Contempt for Gaveston's lowly origins and distaste for his apparent homosexuality meant that he could be treated without pity, and helped to produce a counter-movement of revenge. Marlowe, in his famous play, made Edward exclaim, before his murder, 'O Gaveston, it is for thee that I am wronged'.

FRYDE, N., *The Tyranny and Fall of Edward II, 1321–26* (1979).

Eltham palace, Kent

The bishop of Durham, Anthony Bek, acquired the original manor house in 1295, granting its reversion in 1305 to the future Edward II, who bestowed it upon his wife Isabella of France soon after Bek's death in 1311; it was then developed and enlarged by Edward III to become a favourite residence for both monarch and court throughout the fourteenth and fifteenth centuries. Edward IV rebuilt the impressive great hall, and Henry VIII, whose boyhood home it had been, built a study and a new chapel in the 1520s, and commissioned the construction of a network of underground sewers. After Greenwich palace grew in royal favour, Eltham fell into disrepair and was sold after the civil war; buildings were dismantled and the site became a farm. The picturesque decay of the great hall, then used as a barn, attracted artists such as Turner and Girtin, but it was eventually rescued in the 1930s by the Courtaulds as part of a spectacular contemporary private home (now managed by English Heritage).

Isabella of France, queen of England, b. c.1289, da. of Philip IV of France; m. Edward II, 25 Jan. 1308; d. Hertford 23 Aug. 1358; bur. Franciscan church at Newgate, London.

Isabella was promised to prince Edward in 1298 as part of a *rapprochement* between France and England. Soon after succeeding to the throne, Edward went ahead with the marriage, crossing to Boulogne for the ceremony, which suggests a certain enthusiasm. The marriage produced four children. Isabella is said to have disliked her husband's friendship with Piers Gaveston, and she was certainly on bad terms with the Despensers, who succeeded him in the king's favour. When war broke out with France in 1324, Isabella was in an awkward position, and the king took possession of her estates and placed her under some restraints. She then carried out or presided over a coup of extraordinary efficiency. The following year she was sent to France to negotiate with her youngest brother, Charles IV, but while there became the lover of Roger Mortimer, a marcher baron at odds with the Despensers. When she was joined by her son, the young prince Edward, she negotiated a betrothal for him with Philippa of Hainault. In September 1326 she landed at Orwell in Suffolk with a small army of supporters, including Mortimer, the prince, and the king's youngest half-brother, the earl of Kent. They were joined at once by another of the king's half-brothers, Thomas, earl of Norfolk. The Despensers were captured and executed, her husband imprisoned, and her son proclaimed king.

For four years she and Mortimer ruled the country, making peace with France and Scotland. Mortimer took many of the Despensers' manors, and in 1328 was created earl of March. In October 1330 the young king carried out his own coup, surprising Mortimer at Nottingham Castle by means of a secret passage, and taking him off for execution. Isabella was treated with respect, and her long retirement at Castle Rising and other estates was not one of hardship. Though the poet Thomas Gray called her the 'she-wolf of France', it is more likely that she was a woman of some taste and cultivation, driven to defiance by the habits and folly of her husband.

Roger de Mortimer, b. 1287, s. of Edmund de Mortimer; m. Joan, da. of Piers de Geneville, c.1306; cr. earl of March, Oct. 1328; d. 29 Nov. 1330; bur. Shrewsbury(?).

Mortimer succeeded his father, a marcher baron, in 1304 at the age of seventeen. From 1316 to 1318 he served as the king's lieutenant in Ireland. On his return, he engaged in disputes over land with the Despensers, favourites of Edward II, and in 1322 was placed in the Tower of London under threat of execution. He made a daring escape in August 1324 and fled to France, where he became the lover of Edward's estranged queen, Isabella. Together they launched a successful invasion in September 1326, executed the Despensers, and proclaimed prince Edward king as Edward III. The deposed king was murdered in September 1327 at Berkeley castle. From 1327 Mortimer and Isabella

ruled England on behalf of the young king. They took most of the estates
of the Despensers, and in 1328 Mortimer was created earl of March. In
October 1330 the young king launched his own coup, surprising
Mortimer in Nottingham castle. He was attainted for treason and
hanged at Tyburn.

Edward III, king of England and lord of Ireland, b. 13 Nov. 1312, s. of Edward II
and Isabella; acc. 25 Jan. 1327; m. Philippa, da. of William, count of Hainault, 24 Jan.
1328; issue: Edward, Isabella, Joan, William, Lionel, John, Blanche, Edmund, Mary,
Margaret, William, Thomas; d. 21 June 1377; bur. Westminster abbey.

The inscription on Edward III's tombstone was lavish in its praise:
'the glory of the English, the flower of kings past, a pattern for kings
to come.' Later historians, as is their wont, began to cut him down to
size. Stubbs declared majestically that he was no statesman, Oman
that he was no strategist; others found his interest in chivalry
'adolescent'. It is true that he outlived his triumphs, but even the most
sceptical would scarcely deny that he achieved two things of
importance, the restoration of some stability and dignity to the English
monarchy, and the recovery of England's prestige and standing in the
eyes of his contemporaries.

  In the decade before Edward began his personal rule in 1330, one
English king (his father) had been murdered, one half-brother (earl of
Kent) and one first cousin (Thomas of Lancaster) to the king had been
executed. The royal family had been hideously divided, father against
son, brother against brother, wife against husband. Edward III's reign
lasted fifty years, with scarcely a serious challenge to his authority,
and he achieved the almost miraculous feat (for a monarch) of remaining
on good terms with five surviving sons. English forces had been
repeatedly humiliated by the Scots and the French; in 1356, by contrast,
Edward held both the kings of Scotland and France prisoner.

  He was a boy of twelve when sent to France in September 1325 to do
homage in place of his father. He fell under his mother's influence and
returned with her army in 1326 to overthrow his father and be
proclaimed king; he was crowned in January 1327. The following
January, he took part in the marriage to Philippa of Hainault which his
mother had arranged; he was then sixteen, and his bride fourteen. On
the death of Charles IV of France, a claim to the French throne was put
forward on his behalf, since his mother, Isabella, was a daughter of
Philip IV.

The young king had no reason to be attached to Mortimer, and can hardly have been unaware of the jeers directed at his mother. He showed courage in 1330 in surprising Mortimer at Nottingham and arresting him. Mortimer's execution was hardly avoidable, but his mother was treated with dignity and respect. Abroad, the pattern which dominated most of his reign had already been set, unfinished conflict with Scotland and France. Though technically there was peace with both countries, border incidents and incursions continued. When Robert Bruce died in 1329, leaving a five-year-old son, David, Edward III gave covert support to Edward Balliol, son of the claimant to the Scottish throne supported by his grandfather, Edward I. The English victory at Halidon Hill in 1333 was a warning that their young king was of sterner stuff than his father. The Scots appealed for French help and, in May 1337, Philip VI declared Gascony forfeit: in retaliation, Edward resurrected his claim to the throne of France.

An early indication of Edward's skill as a commander came in 1340 when he destroyed a large French fleet in harbour at Sluys. Both French admirals were killed. He followed it up in 1342 by occupying the duchy of Brittany, where there was a disputed succession. Next he turned his attention to Normandy, but was forced to give battle to a superior French force in 1346 at Crécy. The outcome was a devastating French defeat, gained largely by English and Welsh archers. Those slaughtered amongst the king of France's allies included the blind king of Bohemia, the count of Flanders, and the count of Blois. After his victory, Edward moved on to besiege Calais; its fall after a year in August 1347 gave the English a most valuable port and foothold. Meanwhile, David II of Scotland had been defeated and captured at Neville's Cross, near Durham, and Charles of Blois, the French candidate for Brittany, was captured at La Rocke-Derrien and lodged in the Tower.

Success on this scale could scarcely be repeated. The cost was intimidating, and, from 1348, England suffered from the effects of the Black Death, which reduced the population by at least a third. However Edward's son, the 'Black Prince', who had fought at Crécy at the age of sixteen, had begun building his own reputation with a series of harassing raids through French territory. In 1356 he faced disaster when he was intercepted on the way home to Gascony with booty by a superior French army. He gave battle at Poitiers and, once more, the English were overwhelmingly successful, capturing the king of France, John II. After this, Edward III overreached himself, trying for peace terms which no French monarch could accept. His response in 1359 was to lead what was intended as a knock-out force, threatening Rheims and Paris. The French sensibly refused to give battle, and fatigue, disease, poor supplies, and bad weather took their toll. The treaty of Brétigny later in the year arranged for the ransom of the French king, and confirmed the English in their great territorial gains from Calais south to Gascony.

Brétigny allowed an uneasy peace between England and France for ten years, though conflict continued in Castile, where the 'Black Prince' won a famous victory at Najerá in 1367. In 1369, the main struggle was reactivated, Charles V of France confiscating Gascony, and Edward once more stating his claim to the French throne. Edward was now nearly sixty and prematurely aged, the English commanders struggled to find the golden touch, and the English government was happy to negotiate another truce in 1375.

Domestic policy was largely concerned with issues arising from the wars. Repeated campaigning, on sea and land, was inordinately expensive, and the king's coffers were soon exhausted. A sharp crisis developed in 1340–1 when the Commons complained of excessive taxation. Edward responded with some adroitness, giving ground, only to recover it when Parliament was dissolved. More serious was the crisis of 1376, at a time when the king's prestige had waned. The 'Good Parliament' impeached his chancellor, Lord Latimer, and demanded an enquiry into the finances of Edward's mistress, Alice Perrers. Latimer was dismissed, but soon reinstated, and the 'Bad Parliament' of 1377 acquiesced.

Edward's institution of the Order of the Garter in 1348 has been much criticized as ostentatious and irrelevant, though it was as much a political move as a ceremonial one. No doubt vanity and love of display came into it, but it bound knights to support the king's claims on France, and was an attempt to uphold the dignity of the monarchy and to encourage ideals of chivalry. It should be contrasted with the squalid butchery which had disfigured the reign of Edward's father. As a young man, Edward had been praised for his bravery and good looks, his conviviality and approachability. In later life, and particularly after the death of queen Philippa in 1369, he became lethargic, and fell under the influence of Alice Perrers. One source gave him a dismal deathbed when, abandoned by his courtiers, he was stripped of the rings on his fingers by his mistress. Chivalry had its limits.

ORMROD, W. M., *The Reign of Edward III* (1990).

Royal Maundy

This ceremony is traditionally held on the Thursday before Easter ('Maundy Thursday'), the name possibly deriving from commemoration of Christ washing his disciples' feet and his injunction to them 'Mandatum novum do vobis' ('A new commandment I give you'). Following episcopal example, the practice was adopted by English kings before the Norman conquest, and foot-washing of the poor continued until 1754, though with occasional delegation to the royal almoner or similar deputy. In its abridged survival (the gift of Maundy Pennies), four officials still wear symbolic linen towels during the service, and the monarch carries a nosegay traditionally regarded as protection against disease.

The medieval tradition of giving alms to thirteen poor people, the number representing Christ and the twelve apostles, was modified in 1363 when the fifty-year-old Edward III presented his maundy to fifty men, and the number of recipients subsequently reflected the monarch's age. George I increased these to equal numbers of men and women. Since 1952 the ceremony has no longer been confined to the Chapel Royal or Westminster abbey in London, but has taken place in various provincial cathedrals. The silver coins, legal tender in 1p, 2p, 3p, and 4p denominations, are given to those with a lifetime of service to church and community.

Philippa of Hainault, queen of England, b. c.1314, da. of William, count of Hainault; m. Edward III, 30 Jan. 1328; d. 15 Aug. 1369; bur. Westminster abbey.

Philippa's marriage to the young prince Edward was arranged in 1326 by his mother, Isabella, who was on the continent looking for support against her estranged husband. However, it took place soon after Edward had been declared king, suggesting some personal affection. She had seven sons and five daughters, the last child (Thomas of Woodstock) born in 1355. She is credited with pleading with her husband to spare the lives of the six burghers of Calais who surrendered in August 1347 with halters around their necks. A patron of Froissart, the chronicler of chivalry, Philippa has been called 'a paragon among English queens'.

Edward, 'the Black Prince'. This tomb in Canterbury cathedral commemorates his death as the fighting man he was in life. Above the tomb hung his helmet, shield and gauntlets. His wife Joan was countess of Kent.

Edward, prince of Wales, b. 15 June 1330, eldest s. of Edward III and Philippa; cr. prince of Wales, 1343; m. Joan, da. of Edmund, earl of Kent, 10 Oct. 1361; issue: Edward (d. 1371), Richard; d. 8 June 1376; bur. Canterbury.

The 'Black Prince' (called subsequently from his armour) established a European reputation as one of the bravest warriors of his day. He fought at Crécy at the age of sixteen, and, given independent command in 1356, won a sensational victory at Poitiers, capturing the French king. In 1362 he was made prince of Aquitaine, where his authority was almost total. In 1367, helping Pedro I in an attempt to regain the throne of Castile, he won another victory at Najerá in northern Spain. Returning from Spain to defend Aquitaine, attacked by the French in his absence, he retook Limoges in 1370, ordering that no quarter be given to traitors; by that time he was suffering severely from dysentery. He died aged forty-six, leaving his nine-year-old son Richard as heir to the English throne.

Duchy of Cornwall

Cornwall had links with the crown before Domesday, and its tin-mines generated considerable revenue. Richard, younger brother of Henry III, was granted the earldom of Cornwall amongst other estates, which made him one of the richest men in the kingdom; on his death (1272), his son Edmund made Lostwithiel the administrative centre of the earldom instead of Launceston castle, since it was more central to the Blackmoor tin-producing area and at the navigable head of the river Fowey. In March 1337 Edward III created the duchy of Cornwall for the support of his son Edward the 'Black Prince', and for such of his heirs as would become kings of England. Henry VI later ordered that the inheritance of the duchy, the oldest in England, was either at birth (as the sovereign's son) or on his parents' accession to the throne (as heir apparent). If there was no eligible son, as was the case for much of the Tudor period, the duchy reverted to the crown.

The estate, which is mainly agricultural and consists of property predominantly in the south-west of England, continued to be administered for many years from Duchy Palace at Lostwithiel. In 1863 its management was clarified (26 & 27 Vict. c.49), and the council is now presided over by the lord warden of the stannaries who, with the sheriff of Cornwall, is appointed by the duke. The primary purpose remains the provision of revenue for the prince of Wales.

John of Gaunt, b. Mar. 1340, 4th s. of Edward III and Philippa; cr. duke of Lancaster, 13 Nov. 1362; m. (1) Blanche, da. of Henry of Grosmont, duke of Lancaster, 19 May 1359; issue: Philippa, John, Elizabeth, Henry, Edward; (2) Constance, da. of Pedro I of Castile, Sept. 1371; issue: Katherine, John; (3) Katharine, da. of Sir Paon Roet and wid. of Sir Hugh Swynford, Jan. 1396; issue: John, Henry, Thomas, Joan (all b. before marriage); d. 4 Feb. 1399; bur. St Paul's cathedral.

Born in Ghent when his father was on campaign, fortune smiled on John. At the age of nineteen, he married the co-heiress of Henry of Grosmont, duke of Lancaster; his father-in-law died in 1361, and when his wife's sister died in 1362 he inherited vast estates and was made a duke. The death of his three older brothers by 1376 left him the oldest of Edward's sons and uncle to Richard, heir to the throne. His second marriage, in 1371, to the heiress of Castile enabled him to claim that throne, but repeated efforts to establish his claim failed, and in 1388 he abandoned it in exchange for handsome compensation. He steered a careful course in the contorted domestic politics of his nephew's reign, though he was unpopular with Londoners, and his great palace of the Savoy was sacked in 1381 during the Peasants' Revolt. He was a patron of Chaucer and a protector of Wyclif. Fortune continued to smile after his death: his son Henry became king as Henry IV; his family by his mistress Katharine (married 1396) was legitimized and, as the Beauforts, played a prominent part in the politics of fifteenth-century England. In his play *Richard II*, Shakespeare wrote for John of Gaunt one of his most magnificent patriotic speeches.

Duchy of Lancaster

The origins of the duchy lie in Henry III's wish to provide for his youngest son Edmund 'Crouchback' after failure of a scheme for him to receive the Sicilian throne: lands seized from Simon de Montfort, earl of Leicester, during the barons' war were granted to Edmund in 1265, and augmented by all the royal holdings in the county of Lancaster and title of this earldom (1267). In March 1351 Edward III created his cousin Henry of Grosmont (who had succeeded as 4th earl in 1345) duke of Lancaster, and as a mark of special favour transformed Lancashire into a county palatine like

continued

Duchy of Lancaster *continued*

Chester and Durham; Henry thus had the right to his own chancery with his own justices, and to appoint his own sheriff. He died in 1361 without a male heir, but his daughter Blanche married John of Gaunt, Edward III's younger brother, and their son Henry Bolingbroke (as Henry IV) merged his Lancaster inheritance with the crown in 1399 after he had seized the throne from Richard II.

This 'heritage of Lancaster' (as Gaunt described it) is a compound of estates and jurisdiction, which although merged with the crown, retains a separate administration. The chancellor of the duchy is responsible for its administration, including appointment of justices of the peace in Lancashire and (now) Greater Manchester and Merseyside, and his post has frequently been filled by an elder statesman, often in the cabinet.

Thomas, duke of Gloucester, b. 7 Jan. 1355, youngest s. of Edward III and Philippa; m. Eleanor, da. of Humphrey, earl of Hereford and Essex, c.1375; issue: Humphrey, Anne, Joan, Isabel, Philippa; d. 9 Sept. 1397; bur. Westminster abbey.

Also known as Thomas of Woodstock, he was brother of John of Gaunt and uncle of Richard II. He was twenty-two when his nephew succeeded, and during Richard's minority he prospered, receiving the Garter in 1380 and a dukedom in 1385. The following year he led the attack upon Richard's favourite, Michael de la Pole, earl of Suffolk, who was impeached, and in 1387 took up arms against another favourite, the earl of Oxford. For a few months he exercised great power, but Richard reasserted himself, and the *rapprochement* was always insecure. In the summer of 1397, the king carried out a coup, arresting Gloucester in person at his own mansion. He was taken to Calais, forced to confess, and then either strangled or smothered.

Richard II, king of England, and lord of Ireland, b. 6 Jan. 1367, 2nd but 1st surviving s. of Edward the 'Black Prince' and Joan of Kent; acc. 21 June 1377, dep. 29 Sept. 1399; m. (1) Anne of Bohemia, da. of emperor Charles IV, 20 Jan. 1382; (2) Isabella, da. of Charles VI of France, 12 Mar. 1396; d. c.14 Feb. 1400; bur. King's Langley, rebur. (1413) Westminster abbey.

Richard was particularly interested in the life and death of his great-grandfather, Edward II, for whom he tried to initiate canonization, and the parallels between the reigns are remarkable. Each king was overthrown by an invasion and murdered soon after; neither had any claim to military skill, and each was accused of favouritism (a fairly common charge); in both cases, the overthrow came at a moment when the king appeared to be well in control. However, the similiarities must not be forced. Edward was accused of preferring unkingly pursuits (boating and handicraft) while Richard revelled in ceremony, spending lavishly on costume, and had, if anything, an excessively exalted view of regal dignity. He was interested in painting and in building, and was responsible for renovating Westminster Hall, which proved a drag on his finances.

Richard succeeded his grandfather at the age of ten, and his political baptism came in 1381 when he met the rebels in London during the Peasants' Revolt, acting with considerable courage. If it is true, as Froissart related, that he offered them a general pardon and assured them he would be their leader, it is certain that retribution once the rebels had dispersed was savage: more gibbets had to be erected, remarked the chronicler of Westminster, since the existing ones were too few to cope.

Richard's activity in government increased after the Revolt, and his friends were granted high honours. Michael de la Pole, son of a Hull merchant, was made Chancellor in 1383 and earl of Suffolk two years later; Robert de Vere, earl of Oxford, was made marquis of Dublin in 1385 and duke of Ireland in 1386. But financial demands by the government were heavy and the war against France did not go well. A great campaign against the Scots in 1385, led by the young king, was expensive and achieved nothing. In 1386 Parliament impeached Suffolk. The king retorted that he would not dismiss a scullion in his kitchens on such a demand; though Suffolk was forced to resign and imprisoned, he was reinstated as soon as Parliament was dissolved. The following year, the attack was resumed and Suffolk fled. A group of five noblemen, the Appellants, took over control of the government. The 'Merciless Parliament', under Appellant control, indicted many of the king's supporters, putting to death the Lord Chief Justice and the Lord Mayor of London.

As soon as he could, Richard freed himself from the Appellants, announcing to the council in May 1389 that, since he was twenty-two, he was fit to take charge. The following years were calmer. The king's policy of winding up the war with France, though unpopular among the knightly classes, permitted some lessening of tax demands. Some of his attention was taken with the problem of Ireland, where English control had deteriorated, and to which Richard paid visits in 1394–5 and 1399. Nevertheless, he could not forgive the humiliations heaped upon him in 1386–9 and remained determined to take his revenge on the Appellants.

The postponed counter-attack on the Appellants produced the melodramatic climax of Richard's reign, in which most of the combatants, including the king, fell by the wayside, leaving John of Gaunt's son, Henry Bolingbroke, as the ultimate victor. The five Appellants were Gloucester (the king's uncle), Bolingbroke (first cousin), Arundel (great-grandson of Edward I), Nottingham, and Warwick. Three of them went down in 1397, accused of treason: Gloucester was arrested at his own home by Richard himself, sent to Calais, and murdered; Arundel was beheaded; Warwick was exiled to the Isle of Man. Nottingham, a fourth Appellant, was prominent against them, shared in their forfeited estates, and was promoted duke of Norfolk. The following year, the two surviving Appellants, Norfolk and Bolingbroke, quarrelled violently, and agreed to settle their dispute by battle in front of the king. Before the joust could begin, Richard exiled Norfolk for life and Bolingbroke for ten years. With all five Appellants out of action, Richard no doubt felt that he could safely make a second visit to Ireland.

It was a fatal misjudgement. There was strong feeling among the nobility that the king was out of control, and that Bolingbroke's punishment was excessive. When Henry returned from France with a small force, ostensibly to reclaim his inheritance, Richard's support melted away. His uncle, the duke of York, acting as regent, raised a small army, but came to terms with Bolingbroke. Richard returned from Ireland only to surrender. In September, a new Parliament heard his renunciation of the throne and accepted Bolingbroke as Henry IV. Richard was taken to Pontefract castle and an abortive rising on his behalf sealed his fate. He died five months after abdicating, probably of starvation.

Richard's appearance is well known from his effigy and portrait in Westminster abbey. He was above average in height, with long yellow hair, and a small double-pointed beard. Shakespeare represented Richard as a man of deep sensitivity and intelligence, but when his body was examined in 1871, the consultant reported, laconically, that the skull was smaller than average, 'not distinguished by the size of his brain'.

SAUL, N., *Richard II* (1997).

Anne of Bohemia, queen of England, b. 11 May 1366, da. of emperor Charles IV and Elizabeth of Pomerania; m. Richard II, 20 Jan. 1382; d. Sheen, 7 June 1394; bur. Westminster abbey.

Though Anne's marriage was very much a matter of state, it became one of deep affection. The chronicler of Westminster remarked sourly that England had paid a great deal for 'this tiny scrap of humanity'. Her early death, possibly from plague, was a great blow to Richard, who ordered the manor house at Sheen where she died to be pulled down, and erected a magnificent tomb in Westminster abbey.

Isabella of France, queen of England, b. 9 Nov. 1389, da. of Charles VI of France and Isabella of Bavaria; m. (1) Richard II, 12 Mar. 1396; (2) Charles, count of Angoulême, 1406; d. 13 Sept. 1409; bur. St-Laumer, Blois.

Richard II's second queen was scarcely more than a visitor to England. The marriage, soon after the death of his first wife, was partly to facilitate a *rapprochement* with France, partly to provide an heir. However, the bride was only six. Richard treated her with kindness, showering her with gifts, but since he was dead within four years, the marriage was never consummated. She returned to France in 1401, and in 1406 married Charles, count of Angoulême, dying in 1409 giving birth to a baby daughter.

Lancastrians and Yorkists

The descendants of John of Gaunt, duke of Lancaster, held the throne of England from 1399, when Henry IV deposed Richard II, until 1461 when Henry VI was dispossessed by Edward IV, the son of Richard, duke of York. The Yorkists held it with some difficulty until 1485, when Henry VII killed Richard III at the battle of Bosworth. Henry's marriage to Elizabeth of York, daughter of Edward IV, united the rival claims and established the House of Tudor. The term 'Wars of the Roses' to describe the conflict of Lancaster and York was invented by Sir Walter Scott in the nineteenth century, but many subjects supported neither house and a good many others changed sides. Campaigns were brief, and the battles, though bloody, were occasional.

Henry IV, king of England and lord of Ireland, b. 30 May 1366, s. of John of Gaunt and Blanche, da. of Henry of Grosmont; acc. 30 Sept. 1399; m. (1) Mary, da. of Humphrey Bohun, earl of Hereford, c.1380; issue: Henry, Thomas, John, Humphrey, Blanche, Philippa; (2) Joan, da. of Charles, king of Navarre, 7 Feb. 1403; d. 20 Mar. 1413; bur. Canterbury.

The son of John of Gaunt, duke of Lancaster, by far the wealthiest magnate of his day, Henry (called Bolingbroke after his birthplace in Lincolnshire) added to his expectations by his early marriage to the heiress of the Hereford earldom. As first cousin to Richard II, he could look forward to an influential role. He was brave, shone in tournaments, and was a competent soldier; he was given the Garter by his grandfather Edward III in April 1377, and three months later bore the sword Curtana at his cousin's coronation.

His entry into politics came while his father was in Spain, pursuing his claim to the throne of Castile. Henry joined his uncle Gloucester as one of the five Appellants who demanded the dismissal of the king's favourite, the earl of Oxford. In 1387, when Oxford raised an army, Henry met him at Radcot Bridge after a skilful campaign and defeated him. For two years the Appellants controlled the king until, in May 1389, Richard was able to resume direction. The return of Henry's father may have facilitated at least an outward reconciliation with the king, and Henry prudently spent much of his time abroad in the early 1390s. He fought with the Teutonic Knights against the Lithuanians on two occasions (technically crusades), paid a brief visit to Jerusalem, and returned home in 1393.

In 1397 Richard moved against three of the five former Appellants, accusing them of treason: Arundel was executed, Gloucester murdered, and Warwick banished. Henry and Nottingham supported the king and in September 1397 were rewarded with dukedoms, as Hereford and Norfolk, though a few weeks later Norfolk confided to Henry that he wondered how long the king's favour would last. This conversation with Norfolk became known, a violent quarrel between the two developed, and preparations were made for the matter to be resolved by a great joust at Coventry in September 1398. At the last minute, with the combatants armed and ready, Richard intervened, forbade the duel, banished Norfolk for life and Henry for ten years. Gaunt died in February 1399, whereupon the king banished Henry for ever and confiscated his estates. Faced with total ruin, he had little choice but to fight. To compound the folly, Richard left for Ireland. Henry's invasion of July 1399 was quickly successful, since very few were prepared to fight for Richard. Parliament received his renunciation and declared Henry king in his place: his claim was not one of conquest but of descent from Henry III through Edmund 'Crouchback'. His coronation in October was exceptionally lavish.

Retaining the crown turned out to be harder than acquiring it. In January 1400 Richard's supporters belatedly managed a small rising, which ensured that the former king would be put to death. The French and the Scots protested at Richard's deposition, and the Welsh rose under Owain Glyn Dwr. Expeditions to Scotland and Wales had little effect, and enthusiasm for the new king waned rapidly as taxation began to bite. A victory over the Scots at Homildon Hill in September 1402 was a dubious gain, since it was won by the Percies, whose loyalty was suspect. In July 1403 Hotspur, son of Northumberland, rebelled and marched to Shrewsbury to make common cause with Glyn Dwr, but in another good campaign, Henry reached Shrewsbury first; Hotspur was defeated and killed in a battle in which the king fought with outstanding courage. Even then he was not safe. Glyn Dwr proved extremely elusive; Northumberland, who had wriggled out of the Shrewsbury fiasco, joined Nottingham and archbishop Scrope in a plot in 1405, and the execution of the archbishop gave ammunition to Henry's enemies. Once more Northumberland escaped, but in 1408, when he tried an invasion from Scotland, he was killed at Bramham Moor.

Though the new dynasty was safe at last, Henry himself was increasingly ill, suffering strokes and a painful skin complaint. Power slid towards the young prince of Wales, sixteen years old at the battle of Shrewsbury, and there were clashes between father and son. Parliament, too, was assertive in the face of a ruler who owed his throne to its endorsement, but improvements in foreign affairs allowed taxation to be reduced. By a stroke of luck, the twelve-year-old king of Scotland, James I, fell into Henry's hands in 1406 and was held captive for eighteen years. Glyn Dwr's rebellion burned itself out, and he was reduced to seeking refuge in caves. Henry died aged forty-six and was buried at Canterbury, presumably because Westminster was too closely associated with his predecessor.

KIRBY, J. L., *Henry IV of England* (1970).

Owain Glyn Dwr, b. c.1359, s. of Gruffydd Fychan (s. of Gruffydd ap Madog) and Elen, da. of Thomas ap Llywelyn; m. Margaret, da. of Sir David Hanmer, c.1383;

issue: 6 s., 4 das., including Gruffydd, Maredudd, Catherine, Alice, Margaret; d. c.1415; bur. (poss.) Monington, near Vowchurch, Herefordshire.

A prosperous gentleman from Merioneth, with estates near Oswestry and Llangollen, Owain claimed descent from the princes of both Powys and Deheubarth, but there was little in his early life to suggest a potential rebel or a national hero. He studied law at the Inns of Court, became a follower of the earl of Arundel, married the daughter of a judge, and fought in Richard II's campaign of 1385 against the Scots. A dispute over property with Lord Grey of Ruthin led Owain in September 1400 to launch a raid on Ruthin itself, which rapidly turned into a Welsh uprising. Its initial success induced Owain to declare himself prince of Wales and an expedition by the new king, Henry IV, failed to check him. The rising spread to south Wales and Henry undertook a second punitive march. In 1402 Owain inflicted a sharp defeat at Pilleth on Edmund Mortimer, who was captured, changed sides, and married Owain's daughter, Catherine. When Henry Percy ('Hotspur') and his father the earl of Northumberland joined the rebellion, it became menacing. The young prince Henry (the future Henry V) was sent to the borders to deal with the situation. In July 1403 the king, after a forced march, defeated and killed Hotspur at Shrewsbury. If Owain had deliberately held back his forces, it was a serious error. He retained his hold on Wales, burning Cardiff, negotiated with the French, and summoned a Parliament at Machynlleth. In negotiations with the pope in 1406 Owain demanded two universities, one each for south and north Wales, and the recognition of St David's as an archbishopric. But already his power was waning. In March 1405 prince Henry defeated him at Grosmont, west of Hereford, and in April at Pwll Melyn, near Usk. Northumberland's march south in 1408 ended in defeat and death at Bramham Moor, and though Owain survived for several years, his cause was broken, his wife and daughters in royal hands. He refused to take advantage of a pardon offered by Henry V in 1415 and spent his last years in caves and hideouts. Neither his date of death nor place of burial is known, though legend asserts that he was buried at Monington Court, the home of his son-in-law John Scudamore, in the Golden Valley. In 1916 an impressive statue to him was erected in the City Hall at Cardiff, the town he had burned.

DAVIES, R. R., *The Revolt of Owain Glyn Dwr* (1995).

Owain Glyn Dwr, statue in the City Hall, Cardiff. His shade was much in evidence in May 1999 at the opening of the Welsh Assembly, 594 years after he had held the previous Welsh Parliaments at Machynlleth and Harlech.

Mary Bohun, b. c.1368, da. of Humphrey Bohun, earl of Hereford, and Joan, da. of Richard, earl of Arundel; m. Henry Bolingbroke, earl of Derby (later Henry IV), c.1380; d. 4 July 1394; bur. Canterbury.

Mary, co-heiress to great estates, was married to Henry Bolingbroke when she was eleven or twelve. She claimed her inheritance in 1384, and her husband was recognized as earl of Hereford. Her first child, a son, was born in April 1382 but died in infancy; the next, the future Henry V, was born in September 1387. Mary died in childbirth in 1394 before her husband took the throne.

Joan of Navarre, queen of England, b. c.1370, da. of Charles, king of Navarre, and Joanna, da. of John II of France; m. (1) John IV, duke of Brittany; (2) Henry IV, 7 Feb. 1403; d. 9 July 1437; bur. Canterbury.

Henry IV's second wife was married first to John, duke of Brittany, who died in 1399, leaving her as regent to their young son; the union was intended to stave off French interference with the duchy. There were eight children by her first marriage, none by her second. She remained in England after her stepson had succeeded as Henry V in 1413, but in 1419 was accused of plotting his death by witchcraft, and for three years was kept in comfortable confinement. She was released on his deathbed and spent the rest of her life in honourable retirement.

Cardinal Henry Beaufort, b. c.1375, 2nd s. of John of Gaunt and Katharine Swynford; d. 11 Apr. 1447; bur. Winchester.

Beaufort was a half-brother of Henry IV, legitimized after his father's marriage to his mistress in 1396. He became one of the greatest of all churchmen, bishop of Lincoln 1398 (aged twenty-three), bishop of Winchester 1404, cardinal 1427. Beaufort served as Chancellor under three kings 1403–5, 1413–17, 1424–6, his own vast wealth enabling him to lend generously to the crown. His influence during the reign of Henry VI was mitigated by a long-running feud with his nephew, Humphrey, duke of Gloucester.

HARRISS, G. L., *Cardinal Beaufort: A Study of Lancastrian Ascendancy and Decline* (1988).

Henry V, king of England and lord of Ireland, b. 16 Sept. 1387, s. of Henry, earl of Hereford (later Henry IV), and Mary; acc. 20 Mar. 1413; m. Catherine, da. of Charles VI of France, 2 June 1420; issue: Henry; d. 31 Aug. 1422; bur. Westminster abbey.

Henry was twenty-five years of age when he succeeded his father. He had acquired considerable military experience campaigning against

Glyn Dwr and, at the age of sixteen, had been wounded at the battle of Shrewsbury. His relations with his father were not always easy, and the ailing king strenuously resisted the suggestion that he should abdicate.

Almost all of Henry V's short reign was taken up with war against France. First, though, he had to deal with disaffection at home. The false Richard II at large in Scotland offered little danger, but the earl of March, a great-great-grandson of Edward III, had a plausible claim to the throne. The plots were more alarming since they originated with Henry's close associates. Sir John Oldcastle had been a trusted lieutenant when the prince was campaigning against Glyn Dwr, but had become a convinced lollard, was sent to the Tower and escaped. The lollards were regarded as subversives and no one could be sure of their numbers, but a rising outside London early in 1414 was faced down and the hunt for Oldcastle continued. The 1415 plot to murder the king was more sinister since it involved Lord Scrope, a former Treasurer, and the earl of Cambridge, a grandson of Edward III, both knights of the Garter. They were executed at Southampton just before the king sailed for France on 11 August 1415.

Henry's claims in France had risen from a demand for the restoration of all former territories to an outright claim to the throne itself. His expedition took Harfleur on the Seine as a port and bastion, and marched on towards Calais. It was intercepted by a vastly superior French force, over which Henry gained an astonishing victory at Agincourt, near the spot where Edward III had gained a similar victory at Crécy. The king did everything that a commander should, encouraging his men, deploying them with skill, retaining control during the battle, and setting an example of superb courage in which his crown was split and his helmet dented by a French sword. The casualties on the French side were horrific. The following day, wrote the chronicler, when the English resumed their march to Calais, 'they passed that mound of pity and blood where had fallen the might of the French'.

Henry returned home in November 1415 to a hero's welcome. His triumph was underpinned in 1416 by an important naval victory gained off Harfleur by his brother, John, duke of Bedford. Henry's second expedition left in the summer of 1417, capturing Caen and overrunning Normandy. The following year, after a six-month siege, he took Rouen, and the French court began to sue for peace. At Troyes, in 1420, it was agreed that Henry should act as regent for Charles VI and would succeed as king of France on Charles's death; meanwhile the marriage with Catherine of Valois, Charles's daughter, would take place at once. In

December 1420 he entered Paris, and early in 1421 returned to England to introduce Catherine to her new country.

There remained the task of mopping up the territories which still adhered to the dauphin (the future Charles VII), who had been disinherited by the treaty of Troyes. A sharp defeat suffered by the English in March 1421 at Baugé, in which Henry's brother, the duke of Clarence, was killed, was a reminder that it would not be easy. Henry's last expedition could not take Orléans, but settled down to besiege Meaux, which fell in May 1422. It was Henry's last victory. By then it was clear that he was a very sick man, probably suffering from dysentery, and he died in August 1422. Since Charles VI died in October 1422, the new king of France and England was Henry and Catherine's one-year-old son, Henry VI.

In appearance, Henry was slender and tough, with a long face, accentuated by the pudding-basin hairstyle fashionable at his court. He had a natural authority which got things done, and was short and to the point in speech and writing. He was deeply, if conventionally, religious, and one of his last remarks was that he would go on crusade if spared; he was interested in reading and music, used English himself, and encouraged others to do so. In a lifetime of campaigning it was inevitable that he would be brutal, but his cruelty was not wanton: his sternness was in battle. One modern historian has called him 'the greatest man that ever ruled England', and over his tomb in Westminster abbey hangs the battered helmet he wore at Agincourt.
ALLMAND, C. T., *Henry V* (1992).

Richmond palace, Surrey

The earliest royal residence on this riverside site was the manor house at Sheen, used occasionally by Edward II but more regularly by Edward III, who died there (1377). The house was a favourite residence of Anne of Bohemia, wife of Richard II, and on her death in 1394 the distraught king ordered its demolition. This was incomplete, and Henry V rebuilt it during 1414–22. A huge fire broke out in 1497, which accelerated the process of grand rebuilding commenced by Henry VII; towers, courts, and

continued

Richmond palace, Surrey *continued*

generous glazing were completed by 1501, and the new palace was given Henry's former title of 'Richmond'. Henry VIII preferred Hampton Court, but Mary restored Sheen priory and Elizabeth gave her last public audience there in 1603. In the early Stuart period it became the principal country abode of the royal children, before crumbling during the Commonwealth.

Richmond Lodge, though, had survived, to be used in the eighteenth century by George II, and Kew House by Frederick, prince of Wales, and his wife Augusta, who later initiated the botanical gardens. After her death George III and Charlotte were able to move from the Lodge into Kew House, while the Dutch House (the present Kew palace) was taken over for their children until the family outgrew available space and moved to Windsor. Ambitious plans by George III to re-create Gothic glories at Kew were abandoned after his death, and building materials were reused in other residences. Charlotte died at the Dutch House in 1818, and Victoria presented the greater part of Kew Gardens to the nation, and subsequently the summerhouse, Queen's Cottage.

Catherine of Valois, queen of England, b. 27 Oct. 1401, da. of Charles VI of France and Isabella of Bavaria; m. (1) Henry V, 2 June 1420; (2) Owen Tudor, c.1428; issue: Edmund, Jasper, Owen, Jacina; d. 3 Jan. 1437; bur. Westminster abbey.

Catherine of Valois was the younger sister of Isabella who, as a child, had been married to Richard II. Marriage to prince Henry had been mooted by Henry IV and, on his death, the new king renewed the negotiation, but asked excessive terms. War followed, and the peace treaty in 1420 was buttressed by the marriage. Her son, the future Henry VI, was born in December 1421, but in little more than two years after the marriage Henry V died. Her subsequent affair and secret marriage to Owen Tudor, a gentleman of the household, produced more children. Protected by their half-brother, the family thrived, and Catherine's grandson took the throne in 1485 as Henry VII.

John, duke of Bedford, b. 20 June 1389, 3rd s. of Henry, earl of Hereford, and Mary Bohun; m. (1) Anne, da. of John, duke of Burgundy, June 1423;

(2) Jacquette, da. of Pierre, count of St Pol, 20 Apr. 1433; d. 15 Sept. 1435; bur. Notre-Dame, Rouen.

Bedford, younger brother of Henry V, was a reliable commander and administrator. During his father's reign he was in charge in the north, keeping an eye on the Scots. He served as lieutenant of the kingdom during his brother's absences abroad, and in 1416 won an important naval victory off Harfleur. On Henry's death in 1422, he became guardian to the infant Henry VI and took responsibility for ruling the conquered territories in France. In 1424 he defeated the supporters of Charles VII of France at Verneuil, killing the two Scottish commanders, Buchan and Douglas, but the intervention of Joan of Arc at Orléans in 1429 swung the balance and, even after her execution in 1430, Bedford's role was a rearguard action.

Humphrey, duke of Gloucester, b. 3 Oct. 1390, 4th s. of Henry, earl of Hereford, and Mary Bohun; m. (1) Jacqueline of Bavaria, Mar. 1423; (2) Eleanor, da. of Sir Reynold Cobham; no leg. issue; d. 23 Feb. 1447; bur. St Albans.

Gloucester was an important figure during the reign of his brother Henry V and his nephew Henry VI. He was wounded at Agincourt, fought bravely in Henry V's second campaign in France, and was named by Henry in his will as guardian of the realm. This led to jealousy with his elder brother, Bedford, and Gloucester had another long-standing feud with the Beauforts. The death of Bedford in 1435 left Gloucester as heir to the throne. In 1441, his second wife was accused of attempting the death of the king by witchcraft in order to gain the throne for her husband, and spent the rest of her life in custody. The king seems to have suspected Gloucester himself of treason, and in 1447 he was arrested. His death in prison within a week prompted suspicion of foul play. Gloucester was a patron of Lydgate and a benefactor of Oxford University, to which he left his library.

Owen Tudor, b. c.1400, s. of Meredudd Tudor and Margaret, da. of Dafydd Fychan; m. Catherine of Valois, wid. of Henry V, c.1428; issue: Edmund, Jasper, Owen, Margaret, Jacina; d. Feb. 1461; bur. Greyfriars, Hereford.

Owen Tudor was a gentleman of Catherine's household when he attracted her attention and made a secret marriage. After Catherine's death in 1437 he was shown some favour by Henry VI, and fought for the Lancastrians at Mortimer's Cross; captured in the battle, he was executed in Hereford market-place. His sons Edmund and Jasper were given greater recognition by their half-brother king Henry: Edmund was made earl of Richmond in 1452 and three years later was married to Margaret Beaufort, great-granddaughter of John of Gaunt; he died in 1456 but his posthumous son, Henry, acquired the throne in 1485 after his victory at Bosworth. Jasper Tudor, the second son, was created earl of Pembroke in 1452 and became the mainstay of the Lancastrian cause in Wales; he escaped from the defeat at Mortimer's Cross, and tried to organize resistance in Wales to Edward IV. He looked after his nephew Henry, and after Bosworth was created duke of Bedford, remaining an elder statesman of the new dynasty until his death in 1495.

Richard, duke of York, b. 22 Sept. 1411, s. of Richard, earl of Cambridge, and Anne, da. of Roger, earl of March; m. Cecily, da. of Ralph, earl of Westmorland, c.1429; issue: Edward, Edmund, George, Richard, Anne, Elizabeth, Margaret; d. 30 Dec. 1460; bur. Pontefract, rebur. Fotheringhay.

Richard was close to the crown. His father was a grandson of Edward III and was executed when Richard was three for conspiracy to murder Henry V. Richard succeeded to the dukedom of York in 1415 when his uncle was killed at Agincourt. He served in high office in France and in Ireland, and was Protector of the Realm when Henry VI became deranged 1454–5. He defeated and killed his rival Somerset at the battle of St Albans in 1455, and was once more in arms in 1459. On this occasion he claimed the throne but, in a compromise, was named as Henry VI's heir. A serious error of judgement led him to give battle at Wakefield in 1460 to forces loyal to Henry VI's queen, Margaret of Anjou. He was defeated and executed, and his head set up on Micklegate Bar at York, wearing a paper crown. Within three months his son, after a victory at Mortimer's Cross, seized the throne as Edward IV.

Henry VI, king of England and lord of Ireland, b. 6 Dec. 1421, s. of Henry V and Catherine; acc. 31 Aug. 1422; m. Margaret, da. of René, duke of Anjou, 23 Apr. 1445; issue: Edward; d. 21 May 1471; bur. Chertsey, rebur. Windsor.

Henry's reign was disastrous. His weakness and later insanity was accompanied by the loss of all English possessions in France, save Calais, and at home by a slide into civil convulsions and the 'Wars of the Roses'. Yet his minority passed without catastrophe. He was less than a year old when his father died on campaign in France. His mother remained in England and made a secret marriage to a Welsh gentleman, Owen Tudor, providing the young king with a half-sister and three half-brothers. Henry was crowned king of England at Westminster in 1429, and was taken to Paris in 1431 to be crowned king of France at Notre-Dame. There was little reason to believe that he would not become an effective ruler: he was tall and healthy, serious-minded, fluent in English and French, interested in reading, and delighted in hunting. His earliest personal acts as king were to found Eton in 1439 and King's College, Cambridge, in 1441. But there were shadows: his mother's father, Charles VI of France, had been subject to fits of ungovernable insanity; Henry was thought to be prudish, generous to a fault, over-sensitive in pardoning offenders, and, above all, totally uninterested in military matters. In 1445 he married Margaret of Anjou, aged fifteen. Henry soon became devoted to his wife, but the absence for eight years of any children encouraged restless ambition among possible contenders for the succession, who included the Beauforts and Richard, duke of York, a direct descendant of Edward III. Unsurprisingly, rivalry between Edmund Beaufort, duke of Somerset, and Richard of York began to shape court politics.

In 1450 Henry's reign began to fall to pieces. Somerset was badly beaten in France and lost most of Normandy. Suffolk, the king's chief minister, was impeached by the Commons, forced to flee abroad, and murdered. Kentish rebels under Jack Cade occupied London while the king and queen took refuge at Kenilworth. Meanwhile the French had begun the conquest of Gascony. Decline was followed by disintegration. In July 1453 the English were crushingly defeated by the French at Castillon and the loss of Gascony became inevitable. The following month, the king became insane, unable to converse or even to walk unaided. Under these circumstances, the birth of an heir in October 1453 seemed a miracle and a mockery. He regained awareness after a year, but recovery was far from complete, and though he was only in his early thirties, he was for the rest of his life the passive spectator of his own misfortunes. The leadership of the royalist party fell to the queen, who fought tenaciously for the rights of her small son.

Henry's derangement gave Richard of York his opportunity, and in March 1454 he became Protector, holding office until early 1455. When his rival, Somerset, was restored to power, York resorted to arms. Surprising the royalists at St Albans, he gained victory in a skirmish. Henry himself was taken prisoner, though treated with respect. With Somerset killed in the fight, the way was clear for York to resume the protectorate in November, holding it until early 1456. Fighting broke out again in 1459 when York, supported by the earls of Salisbury and

Warwick, was cornered at Ludlow and forced to flee abroad. Warwick returned in 1460, winning a crushing victory at Northampton, and once more capturing the king. However, when York returned to join them, he jeopardized the alliance by claiming the throne. Henry, deprived of the queen's advice, agreed to a compromise, whereby he would continue to reign but would be succeeded by York. This was scarcely satisfactory to York, who was ten years older than the king, and even less so to the queen, who refused to abandon her son's claim. When, with Scottish help, she invaded, York marched to meet her, but met his death at Wakefield. Continuing her advance, the queen brushed aside Warwick in the second battle of St Albans and liberated her husband. The Lancastrian triumph did not last. York's son claimed the throne as Edward IV, won an encouraging victory at Mortimer's Cross on the Welsh border, and followed it up by defeating the royalists in a bloody encounter at Towton, in Yorkshire. Henry and his queen fled to Scotland.

The next four years were spent in exile. While Margaret sought refuge in France with her father, Henry led a fugitive existence in Lancashire. Captured yet again in 1465, he spent five years in the Tower, his life spared by Edward IV since he was more of a liability than an asset to the Lancastrian cause. There was one last twist to his sad life. Edward quarrelled with his chief supporter, Warwick, and was forced into exile, and Warwick restored Henry to the throne in October 1470. In April 1471 Edward returned, and Warwick was killed at the battle of Barnet. The same day the queen and her son landed, but were beaten at Tewkesbury; Edward, the young prince of Wales, was killed, and the queen taken prisoner. Before the month was out, Henry had been murdered in the Tower.

Henry VI was one of the kindest, saddest, and most incompetent of English kings. He inherited two great thrones and lost them both. For two decades he was a chess king, protected by his redoubtable queen. When the Tudors came to power, they tried to have him recognized as a saint, but even in that he failed.

GRIFFITHS, R. A., *The Reign of King Henry VI* (1981).

Margaret of Anjou, queen of England, b. 23 Mar. 1430, da. of René, duke of Anjou, and Isabella, da. of Charles, duke of Lorraine; m. Henry VI, 23 Apr. 1445; d. 25 Aug. 1482; bur. Angers.

Disliked by many English as a meddlesome foreigner, Margaret of Anjou made a gallant attempt to preserve the throne for her hapless husband

and young son; by the time Edward was born in 1453, Henry had lapsed into insanity, and, though he made a partial recovery, she was thenceforth the main prop of the Lancastrian cause. She repudiated Henry's agreement in 1460 to recognize the duke of York as his heir and campaigned to restore him after Edward IV had taken the throne. After the defeat at Towton in 1461, she took refuge in Scotland, visiting France to raise troops and supplies. Her invasion in 1471 was dogged by bad timing, her ally Warwick was killed at Barnet, and her own troops defeated at Tewkesbury; her son was killed, her husband murdered, and she herself taken prisoner. From captivity in the Tower, she was rescued in 1475 by a ransom, and spent her last years in France. She was the founder of Queens' College, Cambridge.

Edward, **prince of Wales**, b. 13 Oct. 1453, s. of Henry VI and Margaret; m. Anne, da. of Richard Neville, earl of Warwick, 13 Dec. 1470; d. 4 May 1471; bur. Tewkesbury abbey.

Edward was an unlucky prince. The birth of an heir after eight years of married life was a joy to the Lancastrians, but his father had become insane and could not recognize him, and lost the throne in 1461. Edward's boyhood was spent with his mother in exile in Scotland or France, and he is said to have developed warlike, even bloodthirsty, tendencies. When he returned with her in 1471 to reclaim the throne, their army was cut to pieces at Tewkesbury. The young prince was killed, either in battle or immediately afterwards. He was seventeen.

Richard Neville, **earl of Warwick**, b. 22 Nov. 1428, s. of Richard, earl of Salisbury, and Alice, countess of Salisbury; m. Anne, countess of Warwick, 1434; issue: Isabella, Anne; d. 14 Apr. 1471; bur. Bisham abbey, Berks.

The career of Warwick 'the Kingmaker' was short and exciting. He was created earl in 1449 in right of his wife. He joined the party of Richard, duke of York, and in 1455 captured king Henry VI at St Albans. Forced in 1459 to flee to the continent, he returned in 1460 with his father to win the battle of Northampton and take the king prisoner again. His father was executed after the Yorkist defeat at Wakefield in 1460, but Warwick supported Edward IV and helped him gain the decisive victory at Towton in 1461. He became dissatisfied with his role in the new reign, rebelled, and drove out Edward in 1470, restoring Henry to the throne. In April 1471 he was defeated and killed by Edward at the battle of

Barnet. His vast estates and aristocratic connections made him
formidable, but his prowess as a warrior was exaggerated.

Edward IV, king of England and lord of Ireland, b. 28 Apr. 1442, s. of Richard,
duke of York, and Cecily, da. of Ralph, earl of Westmorland; acc. 4 Mar. 1461; m.
Elizabeth Woodville, da. of Richard, Lord Rivers, 1 May 1464; issue: Elizabeth, May,
Cecily, Edward, Margaret, Richard, Anne, George, Katherine, Bridget; d. 9 Apr. 1483;
bur. Windsor.

Edward was tall and well built, impressive in appearance, intelligent,
and cultivated, and a brave, capable, and successful soldier. But he was
also self-indulgent, drank heavily, became corpulent, and his early
death at the age of forty suggests unfulfilled promise.

The eldest son of Richard, duke of York, he was eighteen when his
father claimed the throne from Henry VI and was killed at Wakefield in
December 1460. Edward was then in the west country but resolved to
continue the struggle. He defeated the local Lancastrian supporters at
Mortimer's Cross in February 1461, and set out for London to join his
ally the earl of Warwick. There he was proclaimed king at the beginning
of March. He left within a week to give battle to the main Lancastrian
army and inflicted on it a shattering defeat at Towton, south of York. In a
matter of three months, he had transformed the Yorkist position from
black despair to brilliant triumph. Henry was captured in 1465 and
placed in honourable confinement in the Tower.

In 1464 Edward made his first political mistake, his marriage to a
widow, Elizabeth Woodville. It was clearly a love match, and the favours
showered upon the Woodville family alienated Edward's young brother,
George duke of Clarence, Edward's ally, Warwick 'the Kingmaker', and
Warwick's brother Montagu. By 1467, Warwick was in contact with the
Lancastrians. In the summer of 1469 there was a rising in Yorkshire led
by 'Robin of Redesdale', who may have been Warwick's cousin.
Clarence, who had just married Warwick's daughter, threw in his lot
with the rebels. A royalist force was defeated at Edgecote near Banbury,
and Edward fell into Warwick's hands, being sent to Warwick castle. A
number of his supporters, including the queen's father and brother,
were executed. But Edward regained his freedom of action and defeated
an army in Lincolnshire raised by men sympathetic to Warwick, at
Losecote Field in March 1470. Warwick and Clarence then fled to
France, where Louis XI negotiated a reconciliation with Margaret of
Anjou and the Lancastrians. An invasion in September 1470 declared in

favour of Henry VI. Edward, surprised and disconcerted by the defection of Warwick's brother, Montagu, took ship for the Low Countries, where his sister Margaret had married Charles of Burgundy in 1468. On 3 October 1470 Henry VI was taken from the Tower and hailed once more as king.

It was imperative for the Lancastrians to hold the throne long enough for the prince of Wales to take over from the hapless king Henry. This they failed to do, even though the force which Edward brought back in 1471 was far from imposing. Then Clarence abandoned his new-found friends, and many of the Lancastrians preferred to wait for Margaret of Anjou rather than help Warwick. Edward entered London unopposed, recaptured Henry, and turned to face Warwick at Barnet. In a heavy encounter, fought out in mist, Warwick and his brother Montagu were killed. The same day, queen Margaret landed at Weymouth: Edward marched west, intercepted her army at Tewkesbury, and destroyed it; the prince of Wales was killed, the queen captured. With the prince dead, there was no advantage in keeping king Henry alive, and he was murdered in the Tower within the month. The double victory established Edward securely for the rest of his life.

Edward's remaining years were more circumspect, though in 1472 he began planning a major invasion of France, claiming the throne, with Burgundy and Brittany in support, and in 1475 crossed the channel with a vast force. However, his allies soon disappointed him, and after a token show of force, he came to terms with the French king, accepting a yearly pension. Nothing more was said of his claim to the French throne. Slightly more glorious was a campaign against the Scots in 1482, conducted by his youngest brother, Gloucester, and resulting in the recovery of Berwick, which had been surrendered to the Scots by the Lancastrians. Increasingly, he relied upon Gloucester's assistance, causing resentment in Clarence. In 1477 Clarence was indicted for treason, condemned by Parliament, and murdered in February 1478 in the Tower.

Though Edward overloaded his frame with good living, his death was unexpected. He was buried with ceremony in the chapel at Windsor which he had built. It was fashionable at one time to call him the founder of the 'New Monarchy', developed further by the Tudors, but this concept and Edward's role have been challenged. The increased efficiency of government, the improvement in royal finances, and the reassertion of monarchical power were, to a considerable extent, by

contrast with his unfortunate predecessor, Henry VI, whose grasp on reality was so fitful that any successor would appear competent.
Ross, C. D., *Edward IV* (1974).

Elizabeth Woodville, queen of England, b. c.1437, da. of Sir Richard Woodville and Jacquette, wid. of John, duke of Bedford; m. (1) Sir John Grey; issue: Thomas, Richard; (2) Edward IV, 1 May 1464; d. 8 June 1492; bur. Windsor.

The foundations of the Woodvilles' rise was the marriage of Elizabeth's father to the widow of Bedford, uncle to king Henry VI. Elizabeth's first husband was killed at St Albans in 1461, fighting for the Lancastrians. She was reputed a great beauty, and Edward made a secret marriage to her in May 1464, acknowledged in October. The favours shown by the king to her family were an important factor in alienating Warwick and Clarence, and the Woodvilles remained unpopular. Her later years, after Henry VII's triumph at Bosworth, were spent in honourable retirement at Bermondsey abbey.

Edward V, uncrowned king of England, b. 2 Nov. 1470, s. of Edward IV and Elizabeth Woodville; acc. 9 Apr. 1483; d. Tower of London, 1483(?).

Edward was brought up for safety at Ludlow under his maternal uncle, earl Rivers. On the death of Edward IV in April 1483, the twelve-year-old proceeded to London, but at Stony Stratford the followers of his paternal uncle, Richard of Gloucester, took the boy into their keeping, while Rivers was arrested at Northampton. Edward was duly proclaimed king in London, and moved to the royal apartments in the Tower mid-May as part of the coronation preparations; he was joined there a month later by his younger brother Richard, when they were seen shooting and playing in the garden. Later, however, both boys (according to a visiting Italian) 'were withdrawn into the inner apartments of the Tower proper, and day by day began to be seen more rarely behind the bars and windows, till at length they ceased to appear altogether'.

Rumours and revulsion swept London, then Europe. The contested succession that ensued has been followed by continued controversy over the reliability of contemporary accounts (especially those by later Tudor propagandists anxious to blacken Richard III's name), the manner of the presumed death of the princes, and the degree of involvement of Richard, who had by then declared himself king. Sir Thomas More's account, inspiring Shakespeare and nineteenth-century artists, implicated Sir James Tyrell (his servant John Dighton smothering the boys at night), but this is little more than elaboration of several circulating tales. The incomplete skeletons of two juveniles unearthed in 1674 in the Tower grounds have been presumed to be those of the princes, but the 1933 exhumation in Westminster abbey merely confirmed them to be human in origin, of approximately the right ages.

Richard III, king of England and lord of Ireland, b. 2 Oct. 1452, 4th s. of Richard, duke of York, and Cecily Neville, da. of Ralph, earl of Westmorland; acc. 26 June 1483; m. Anne, da. of Richard Neville, earl of Warwick, 12 July 1472; issue: Edward; d. 22 Aug. 1485; bur. Greyfriars, Leicester.

Because of the presumed murder of the two princes in the Tower, Richard has been more savagely condemned and more staunchly defended than any other English king. Shakespeare portrayed him as a dastardly schemer, 'determined to prove a villain', while the Richard III Society maintains that he was without stain or blemish. Richard's life up to 1483 suggests a loyal and competent supporter of his brother, Edward IV, and the two years of his brief reign indicate that he was continuing the reassertion of royal authority begun by Edward IV.

Richard was nine years old when his father, claiming the throne of Henry VI, was killed at the disastrous battle of Wakefield. Richard and his brother George were sent to the court of Burgundy for safety, but were able to return when their eldest brother, Edward, was the victor at Mortimer's Cross and Towton, and took the throne as Edward IV. Richard was created duke of Gloucester and placed in the care of Warwick 'the Kingmaker', spending most of his time in Yorkshire. In 1469, when Edward IV fell out with Warwick, George, duke of Clarence, threw in his lot with Warwick, Richard with the king. Edward made him Constable of England but when, in 1470, the king was driven into exile, it looked as if Clarence had made the better choice. The following year, Edward returned, and victories at Barnet and Tewkesbury, in which Richard played a prominent part, secured the Yorkist dynasty.

Though Clarence was forgiven, Richard assumed the role of Edward's trusted lieutenant. In 1472, his marriage to Warwick's daughter and co-heir, Anne Neville, greatly increased his wealth and standing, and a son Edward was born in 1476. His immediate prospects were, however, overshadowed by the birth of a son to the king in 1470, and he was on increasingly bad terms with Clarence. He gained considerably from the disgrace and death of Clarence in 1478, though there is no evidence that he was directly implicated in the murder. In the early 1480s he was greatly concerned with the wars against the Scots, in which he held chief command, and which resulted in the permanent cession of Berwick-upon-Tweed to England.

One of the charges against Clarence had been the spreading of reports that Edward IV was illegitimate. The matter surfaced again when Edward died at the age of forty, leaving his twelve-year-old son as Edward V. Richard was on bad terms with the relatives of the widowed queen, Elizabeth Woodville, and a struggle for power took place. Though Edward IV had named Richard as regent or protector, Elizabeth's brother, earl Rivers, was the boy's governor. He was arrested at Northampton, while Richard's men took over the escort of the young king. Once in London, Richard's coup was carried out with speed and vigour: the coronation was cancelled, rumours were circulated that Edward and his two sons were all illegitimate, and on 26 June, in response to an arranged appeal, Richard took the crown, proceeding at once to a lavish coronation on 6 July.

A reign of little more than two years, much of it dominated by rebellion and the threat of invasion, can provide only pointers to long-term policies, but there are signs that Richard might have become an effective and forceful ruler. He made repeated progresses to gather support, established a Council of the North, set up the College of Heralds, and gave as generously as he could to the church and the universities. But his position remained precarious. Within three months of his coronation, there was an abortive and ill-coordinated rising in the south of England: Henry Tudor, with help from Brittany, threatened an invasion, which was prevented by storms. The duke of Buckingham, Richard's staunchest supporter during the coup, threw in his lot with the insurgents, was captured, and executed in Salisbury market-place. In 1484, to Richard's great grief, his only child, Edward, prince of Wales, died at the age of ten, and a year later Richard's wife, Anne, also died. In the summer of 1485, rumours that Richard was to marry his niece, Elizabeth of York, were sufficiently rife to necessitate an official denial.

In the summer of 1485, Richard moved to Nottingham, where he could survey developments and deploy troops quickly. News of Henry Tudor's landing near Milford Haven was received on 11 August, and Richard called in his supporters. The response was very patchy. Nevertheless, the army which the king took to Market Bosworth on 21 August was substantially larger than that which Henry Tudor had collected, though it included men whose loyalty to Richard was suspect.

RICARDVS · III · ANG · REX ·

Richard III. An enigmatic portrait of a complex man. Admirers see a face of spotless nobility, critics a scheming villain. But there is no surviving contemporary portrait and later copies show considerable variations in expression.

The earl of Northumberland, in charge of a large rearguard but discontented with the appointment of the earl of Lincoln, the king's nephew, to the presidency of the Council of the North, did not engage the following day. Sir William Stanley, whose nephew Lord Strange was a hostage in Richard's camp, changed sides at a critical moment. Richard died fighting in a desperate attempt to get at his rival and, according to legend, the crown he had worn so briefly was found in a thorn bush. His naked body, slung over a horse, was taken back to Leicester for unceremonious burial in the chapel of the Grey Friars. It is a comment on the extent to which Richard was mistrusted that a brave and experienced monarch should have been unable to rally a winning combination of supporters. Richard was small, wiry, and vigorous; portraits suggest a man of comely appearance, though tense. The stories of his monstrous birth, hunched back, long hair, and teeth—so deformed 'that dogs bark at me as I halt by them'—were spread subsequently by writers in the Tudor period, who had no reason to cherish losers.

Ross, C. D., *Richard III* (1981).

Anne Neville, queen of England, b. 11 June 1456, 2nd da. of Richard Neville, earl of Warwick, and Anne, da. of Richard de Beauchamp, earl of Warwick; m. (1) Edward, prince of Wales, 25 July 1470; (2) Richard, duke of Gloucester (later Richard III), 12 July 1472; d. 16 Mar. 1485; bur. Westminster abbey.

Anne Neville was as much a property as a person. Co-heiress to the vast estates of Warwick 'the Kingmaker', she and her sister Isabella were major matrimonial cards. In 1469 Isabella was married to George, duke of Clarence, brother of Edward IV, presumably to fix his allegiance to the Warwick cause. When Warwick was reconciled with the Lancastrians, his younger daughter Anne, then aged thirteen, was pledged to Edward, prince of Wales, son of Henry VI. In the spring of 1471, though, Anne lost both father and young husband at the battles of Barnet and Tewkesbury. She then married Edward IV's youngest brother, Richard, to Clarence's dismay; their only son, Edward, was born in 1476. When her husband seized the throne in 1483, Anne was crowned at Westminster on 6 July. Her son died the following year, and she herself died five months before her husband's death at Bosworth. Though Richard had at once begun looking for a new wife, there is no evidence to support Lancastrian rumours that he had poisoned Anne.

Edward, prince of Wales, b. 1476, only s. of Richard, duke of Gloucester, and Anne Neville; d. 9 Apr. 1484; bur. Sheriff Hutton, Yorks.

The only child of Richard III, he was created prince of Wales at York in September 1483, but died six months later at Middleham.

Lady Margaret Beaufort, b. 31 May 1443, only da. of John, duke of Somerset, and Margaret, da. of John Beauchamp of Bletsoe; m. (1) John, duke of Suffolk, 1450; (2) Edmund, earl of Richmond, 1455; issue: Henry; (3) Sir Henry Stafford, 2nd s. of Humphrey, duke of Buckingham, c.1464; (4) Thomas, Lord Stanley, later earl of Derby, 1482; d. 29 June 1509; bur. Westminster abbey.

Lady Margaret was mother of Henry VII, posthumous son of her second husband and born when she was thirteen. She was parted from her son in 1461 when he was four and, but for a brief visit, did not see him again until he had become king. Nevertheless, she worked tirelessly on his behalf, and after his accession was influential and honoured at his court. She was a remarkable benefactress of Cambridge and Oxford Universities, founded the colleges of Christ's and of St John's at Cambridge, and established the chair of divinity at Oxford, where the first women's college was named after her in 1879.

Tudors

The Tudor dynasty, from Henry VII to Elizabeth I, took its name from its Welsh ancestry, the Tewdwrs, kings of Deheubarth. This was rather misleading, however, since the important descent was from John of Gaunt, son of Edward III; Gaunt's children, the Beauforts, were illegitimate, but had subsequently been legitimized. The Welsh link was subordinate and arose when Henry V's widow, Catherine de Valois, married a minor courtier, Owen Tudor; their son Edmund married Margaret Beaufort, great-granddaughter of John of Gaunt, and was created earl of Richmond. His son, Henry of Richmond, claimed the throne at Bosworth in 1485. The red rose, symbol of the Lancaster dynasty and a Beaufort badge, was united with the Yorkist white rose by Henry VII's marriage to Elizabeth, daughter of Edward IV.

TUDOR AND STEWART
[showing the union of the
crowns under James VI & I]

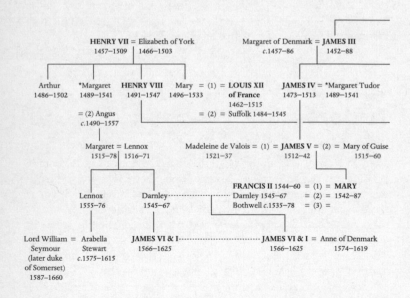

HENRY VII = Elizabeth of York
1457–1509   1466–1503

Margaret of Denmark = JAMES III
c.1457–86   1452–88

Arthur
1486–1502

*Margaret
1489–1541

HENRY VIII
1491–1547

Mary
1496–1533

= (1) = LOUIS XII
of France
1462–1515

JAMES IV
1473–1513

*Margaret Tudor
1489–1541

= (2) Angus
c.1490–1557

= (2) = Suffolk 1484–1545

Margaret = Lennox
1515–78   1516–71

Madeleine de Valois = (1) = JAMES V = (2) = Mary of Guise
1521–37   1512–42   1515–60

Lennox
1555–76

Darnley
1545–67

FRANCIS II 1544–60 = (1) = MARY
Darnley 1545–67   = (2) = 1542–87
Bothwell c.1535–78   = (3) =

Lord William = Arabella
Seymour   Stewart
(later duke   c.1575–1615
of Somerset)
1587–1660

JAMES VI & I
1566–1625

JAMES VI & I
1566–1625

Anne of Denmark
1574–1619

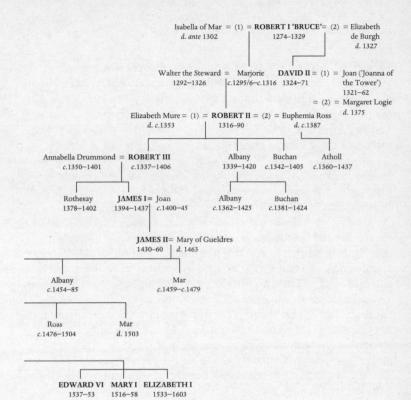

Henry VII, king of England, and lord of Ireland, b. 28 Jan. 1457, s. of Edmund Tudor, earl of Richmond, and Margaret Beaufort, da. of John, duke of Somerset; acc. 22 Aug. 1485; m. Elizabeth, da. of Edward IV, 18 Jan. 1486; issue: Arthur, Margaret, Henry, Elizabeth, Mary, Edmund, Catherine; d. 21 Apr. 1509; bur. Westminster abbey.

The first half of Henry's life held out little prospect of a crown. A grandson of Catherine of Valois by her second marriage to Owen Tudor, his father died three months before he was born. When Henry was four, the Lancastrian cause was shattered by defeats at Mortimer's Cross and Towton, and his grandfather, Owen Tudor, was beheaded in Hereford market-place. His uncle, Jasper Tudor, earl of Pembroke, was forced to flee. The death of Henry VI and his only son in 1471 made Henry the leading Lancastrian contender, but his years in exile in France were precarious, and he was in great danger of being handed over to Edward IV or Richard III.

His prospects brightened in 1483 when his enemies split. Richard's usurpation and the disappearance of his two nephews robbed him of much support. Henry opened up negotiations with Edward IV's widow and it was agreed that should he gain the throne, he would marry her eldest daughter, Elizabeth. Nevertheless, his first expedition in October 1483 was a disaster. His ally, Buckingham, was captured and executed at Salisbury; Henry's small fleet was dispersed by storms and he spent only one day ashore. His second invasion, with a small force supported by the French, was at Milford Haven in August 1485. He gathered a tolerable army on his march through Wales to Shrewsbury, but could not have won at Bosworth, where he fought bravely, had his adversary not been betrayed.

Henry found himself king of England at the age of twenty-eight, with very limited experience. His chief advisers were his formidable mother, Lady Margaret, his uncle Jasper (raised to the dukedom of Bedford), John Morton, archbishop of Canterbury from 1486, and Richard Fox, bishop of Winchester. His first task was to establish himself securely on the throne, bearing in mind that, of his four predecessors, two had been murdered, one had died in battle, and the fourth (Edward IV) had at one stage been ignominiously driven from his throne. Within less than a year he faced a rising by Lord Lovel and the Stafford brothers, but the rising barely got off the ground, and Henry pardoned all participants save Humphry Stafford. Early in 1487 a young man appeared, claiming to be Edward, earl of Warwick, though in fact he was Lambert Simnel, an impostor. Simnel met with support in Ireland and was crowned in Dublin as Edward VI. The invasion that followed was formidable and Henry was obliged to fight a major battle at Stoke, near Newark, before it was crushed. Even then, Simnel's life was spared. Plots continued. In the 1490s Perkin Warbeck posed as Richard IV, the son of Edward IV, and gained support from the kings of France and Scotland; his invasion in the south-west in 1497 soon petered out, and again, his life was spared until, in 1499, he began fresh treasons. In 1501 it was the turn of Edward, duke of Suffolk, nephew of Edward IV and Richard III, to claim the throne; he found little support abroad, was recaptured in 1506, and spent the rest of Henry's reign in the Tower. The leniency of Henry was remarkable and was not imitated by his son.

His foreign policy was cautious. Henry was that rare phenomenon, a brave and capable soldier who did not hanker after military glory; to some extent this was because he begrudged the expense, which would place him in thrall to Parliament. His boldest venture was an expedition to France in 1492 to help the Bretons, struggling to maintain their independence, but after laying siege to Boulogne for a few days with a large army, Henry came to terms and accepted compensation from Charles VIII sufficient to show a handsome profit. James IV of Scotland's support for Perkin Warbeck led to a brief war in 1496–7, but the first Scottish invasion lasted one day and penetrated only a few miles, while a second ravaged for a week those few buildings that could be found in the valley of the river Till. Again, Henry made a profit on the transaction. Once James had abandoned Perkin Warbeck, Henry negotiated in 1503 a marriage between his daughter Margaret and the Scottish king, which resulted, one hundred years later, in the union of the crowns. By the end of his reign, Henry had re-established England as a power to be reckoned with.

In domestic affairs, he was equally successful. He began the process of restoring English rule in Ireland, which had for some decades been a Yorkist bastion. His Welsh connections, though slight, enabled him to make some small concessions to the people of Wales, which were well received. His nobility was kept in order less by legislation against livery and maintenance than by taking bonds and recognizances as pledges of good conduct. Feudal rights were fully exploited and revenue boosted. His comparative frugality and personal attention to finance gained him a reputation as a miser, but allowed him to summon Parliaments infrequently. Henry's kingdom, which he had gained in such disarray, was passed on to his successor solvent and without opposition.

Henry VII. This terracotta bust by the Italian sculptor Torrigiano is probably the most lifelike representation of a British monarch of the time. It shows Henry late in life, about 1508.

If, by any tests that can be applied, Henry's record was outstanding, why was he not popular? He did not go in for florid gestures, like Henry VIII and Elizabeth, and his subjects' gratitude for firm, stable government was unlikely to last. He achieved no great victories over the French or the Scots. Attention to the detail of administration and finance was felt by many to be unkingly, revealing the soul of an accountant. Though he spent lavishly on ceremony, built a superb chapel at Westminster, and finished Henry VI's great chapel at King's College, Cambridge, he was thought mean and avaricious. Historians were greatly influenced by Bacon's *Life* which, though written 137 years after Bosworth, they often treated as a primary or contemporary source. Bacon struck off memorable phrases: Henry was 'sad, serious and full of thoughts... for his pleasures, there is no news of them.' But a careful reading shows that he balanced them with high praise: Henry was affable and comely, governed by none, a merciful prince and given to secret almsgiving, affectionate to his children, and dutiful towards the church; as a soldier, 'he did not know what a disaster meant', and as a ruler, he was 'a wonder to wise men'.

CHRIMES, S. B., *Henry VII* (1972).

Greenwich palace, London

Humphrey, duke of Gloucester, later regent to the infant Henry VI, acquired the estate in 1426 and built a country house called Bella Court. After belonging to Margaret of Anjou, who renamed it 'Plesaunce' following extensive alterations, the house came to Henry VII whose rebuilding led to it becoming one of the principal royal palaces in the vicinity of sixteenth-century London, aided by its position beside the Thames. Henry VIII and his daughters Mary and Elizabeth were born there; Henry had ample facilities for his many outdoor sports, and Elizabeth maintained Greenwich as a place of pleasure, her favourite residence outside London. James I gave the palace to his wife Anne of Denmark, who commenced the House of Delight (or Queen's House) linking gardens and park, to the designs of Inigo Jones; this was completed by 1635 for Henrietta Maria, but fell into decay during the civil war.

Charles II pulled down the derelict old palace, began a new block and relaid the gardens, but lost interest once Windsor had been renovated. Mary II, who with William III was building elsewhere, presented all the riverside area to the navy, and the new hospital for seamen was one of Wren's triumphs. After 1869 it became a naval college, and home to the National Maritime Museum. The Queen's House has recently been painstakingly restored, and the former Royal Naval College buildings taken over by Greenwich University.

Touching for the king's evil

A practice adopted from the French, used possibly by Edward 'the Confessor' but fairly consistently by monarchs from Henry II, with varying degrees of enthusiasm. Perhaps reflecting times when priesthood and kingship were conjoined, and when disease was attributed to demonic possession, the monarch ceremonially 'stroked' the neck and face of sick persons presented by the chief surgeon, to cure their scrofula (also called 'king's evil' or struma). This is essentially a tuberculous infection affecting lymph glands and bones, especially in children, but the term may earlier have been applied to other similarly located swellings. The office for the healing was drawn up in the time of Henry VII, based on the blessing for sore eyes and exorcism against evil spirits, though it was occasionally modified by later monarchs. Edward I had given money as alms, but Henry bestowed a small gold 'touch-piece', sometimes called an 'angel' from the device on the obverse; finances occasionally necessitated silver substitutes. The ceremony was accompanied by readings from the gospels (notably Mark 16) and ended with a formal washing of hands. The practice was discontinued by William III, revived by Anne, and finally abandoned by the Hanoverians.

Elizabeth of York, queen of England, b. 11 Feb. 1466, da. of Edward IV and Elizabeth Woodville; m. Henry VII, 18 Jan. 1486; d. 11 Feb. 1503; bur. Westminster abbey.

The marriage of Edward's eldest daughter was certain to be political. After the disappearance of her two brothers in 1483, she was the leading Yorkist, and after Richard III's wife Anne had died in March 1485 rumours circulated that he would marry his niece. However, the marriage to Henry of Richmond should he gain the throne had already been arranged secretly, and it took place as soon as he had won at Bosworth. In all respects it was highly successful. Their eldest son, Arthur, was born in September 1486; her relations with Henry were cordial and probably affectionate. A woman of great beauty, intelligent and cultivated, she was deeply grieved by the death of prince Arthur in April 1502, and died nine days after giving birth to a daughter, Catherine, in February 1503.

Perkin Warbeck, b. 1474; d. 23 Nov. 1499.

Warbeck was brought forward in 1491, claiming to be Edward IV's younger son, Richard, duke of York. He received much help from Henry VII's enemies, including the king of France, the Holy Roman emperor, and James IV of Scotland. He was, in reality, the son of John Osbeck of Tournai, and had been carefully coached. His main attempt in 1495 was a landing in Cornwall, where he was hailed as Richard IV. Failing to take either Exeter or Taunton, he surrendered on promise of his life at Beaulieu in Hampshire. When, in 1499, he hatched a plot to seize the Tower in which he was imprisoned, he was hanged. His conspiracy incriminated the rightful earl of Warwick, who was executed. Warbeck's widow, a daughter of the earl of Huntly, whom he had married while in Scotland, was kindly treated by Henry VII and went on to make three more marriages.

Lambert Simnel, b. c.1475; d. c.1535.

The son of an Oxford tradesman, Simnel was coached by Richard Simon, a priest, to impersonate Edward, earl of Warwick and nephew of Richard III. Taken up by opponents of Henry VII, he was brought to Dublin and there crowned as Edward VI. His supporters mounted a formidable invasion of England in 1487, but were defeated at Stoke. Simnel was allowed to live out his life as a scullion in the royal kitchens.

Arthur, prince of Wales, b. 19 Sept. 1486, elder s. of Henry VII and Elizabeth of York; m. Catherine, da. of Ferdinand of Aragon and Isabella of Castile, 14 Nov. 1501; d. 2 Apr. 1502; bur. Worcester.

The birth of prince Arthur, so soon after Henry VII's marriage to Elizabeth of York, seemed the culmination of his attempt to reconcile the two great factions of Lancaster and York. The long-awaited marriage to Catherine of Aragon took place at St Paul's in November 1501, and the young couple set up court at Ludlow, where the prince was in nominal charge of the Council of the Marches. However, he died of consumption less than five months after marriage, and was buried in a special chantry in Worcester cathedral. Catherine's marriage to his younger brother Henry took place in June 1509.

Henry VIII, king of England and Ireland, b. 28 June 1491, 2nd s. of Henry VII and Elizabeth of York; acc. 21 Apr. 1509; m. (1) Catherine, da. of Ferdinand of Aragon

and Isabella of Castile, 11 June 1509; issue: Henry, Mary; (2) Anne, da. of Sir Thomas
Boleyn, 25 Jan. 1533; issue: Elizabeth; (3) Jane, da. of Sir John Seymour, 30 May
1536; issue: Edward; (4) Anne, da. of John, duke of Cleves, 6 Jan. 1540; (5)
Catherine, da. of Edmund Howard, 28 July 1540; (6) Catherine, da. of Sir Thomas
Parr, 12 July 1543; d. 28 Jan. 1547; bur. Windsor.

The great portraits by Holbein and the complexity of his matrimonial
arrangements have made Henry VIII the best known of all English kings.
The death of his elder brother Arthur in 1502 set the pattern for most of
Henry's life, not only because it made him heir and (in 1503) prince of
Wales, but because the decision to marry his brother's widow had
momentous consequences. When Henry succeeded in 1509 there was
universal praise, and little regret for his father. The new king appeared
open, frank, engaging, well built, and athletic, excelling in music and in
jousting, and bursting with energy: 'the most handsome potentate I ever
set eyes on', wrote one foreign observer. His first action was to strike
down his father's financial advisers, Empson and Dudley—a popular
and facile gesture. His second was to go ahead with the much-postponed
wedding to Catherine of Aragon.

Even in the heady early years, there were shadows. His first son,
Henry, died after seven weeks in 1511. In 1514, rumour said that Henry
might divorce his wife on the grounds that she could not bear healthy
children, and the following year a diplomat reported that Catherine was
grown 'rather ugly'. Another glimpse of the future was the execution in
1513 of Suffolk, a Yorkist rival, whom his father had kept in the Tower,
and the execution in 1521 of the duke of Buckingham on very flimsy
grounds.

One of Henry's earliest ambitions was to humiliate the French. In
1512, in alliance with his father-in-law, Ferdinand, he launched an
invasion intended to reconquer Gascony. Ferdinand reneged on his
commitments and the campaign was a fiasco. The following year, Henry
took the field himself with an imposing army and won a skirmish in
northern France, dignified as the battle of the Spurs. The earl of Surrey,
left behind to guard the kingdom against France's ally, James IV of
Scotland, inflicted on them at Flodden a bloody defeat which left the
Scottish king dead among his nobility. The total absorption of Scotland
seemed a possibility and Henry began styling himself 'king of Scotland'.

The French campaigns brought to the fore Thomas Wolsey, bishop of
Lincoln in March 1514, archbishop of York in September 1514, cardinal
in 1515, and legate in 1518. The birth of a princess, Mary, in 1516

Henry VIII. Henry and his daughter Elizabeth took great pains with their portraits, intended to exude authority and power, and frequent copies were made. This portrait of Henry, late in life, seems to be a copy of a Holbein.

steadied the royal marriage, reviving hopes that the next child might be a boy. The campaigns had not brought Henry the throne of France, but one town, Tournai, surrendered to France after only five years. Deserted by his allies, Henry came to terms with the French and in 1518 agreed that princess Mary should marry the dauphin. The elaborate and expensive Field of the Cloth of Gold near Calais in 1520, when Henry and Francis I strove to outdo each other in conspicuous spending, was intended to consolidate the *rapprochement*. The reconciliation did not last, and by 1522 Henry was once more at war with France and Scotland, waged in desultory fashion until 1525.

By this time the marriage question had become more than rumour. In 1519 Elizabeth Blunt, one of the king's mistresses, gave birth to a healthy boy (the future duke of Richmond), confirming Henry's belief that either his wife was at fault or that their union had been cursed. Elizabeth Blunt was succeeded by Mary Boleyn. Divorce and remarriage became urgent, and a new candidate for royal consort emerged in Mary's younger sister, Anne Boleyn. Henry's argument was that marriage to a dead brother's wife was contrary to canon law; Catherine's retort was that her marriage to prince Arthur had never been consummated. The issue brought down Wolsey in 1529, after he had failed to persuade the pope to grant a divorce. He was replaced as Chancellor by Sir Thomas More, but effective power passed to Thomas Cromwell, who pushed through Parliament the legislation denying the authority of the pope, giving Cranmer, archbishop of Canterbury, the chance in 1533 to declare Henry's first marriage null and void. The new legislation was draconian. An early victim was More himself, who resigned in 1532 and was executed three years later for refusing to acknowledge Henry as head of the church. When Henry moved against the monasteries in 1538 and 1539, the abbots of Glastonbury, Colchester, Reading, and Woburn and the prior of Lenton were hanged. At the same time, a vigorous persecution of protestants was maintained, particularly after the Act of Six Articles in 1539 marked a return to catholic orthodoxy. Henry was, at least, impartial in his religious terror.

Meanwhile, he remained preoccupied with matrimony and the succession. Anne Boleyn, heavily pregnant, was crowned queen of England on 1 June 1533, but the birth of a daughter, Elizabeth, was a disappointment, and by 1536 Henry had begun to weary of Anne. When his eye lighted upon Jane Seymour, Anne's fate was sealed, and she was beheaded on charges designed to discredit her, including incest with her brother, Lord Rochford. The king was betrothed to Jane the following day, and married within the fortnight; this third marriage produced, in prince Edward, the desired male heir, but the birth cost the life of his mother. The fourth marriage, to Anne of Cleves in 1540, was never consummated, and was declared invalid after six months. Henry's fifth wife was Catherine Howard, whose youth and vivacity entranced the king until he discovered that she had been unchaste before marriage and probably afterwards: she went to the block in February 1542. Despite advancing bulk, Henry's unlucky experiences had not wholly deterred him, and in July 1543 he embarked on his last marriage, to Catherine Parr, which saw him through to the end.

The work of reasserting royal authority continued under Henry, particularly in the 1530s when Cromwell was in charge. The rising of the Pilgrimage of Grace in the northern counties on behalf of the old religion shook the throne and frightened Henry; his revenge was characteristically brutal, but it resulted in the foundation of the Council of the North to bring that remote region under more effective control. Wales was more closely integrated with England by acts of 1536 and 1543. In Ireland, direct rule was still confined to the Pale, around Dublin, but a determined effort to extend the authority of the king's lieutenant began in 1520 when the earl of Surrey, son of the victor of Flodden, was sent over with a large army. The effort was too expensive and Henry fell back on the old expedient of relying upon the earls of Kildare. When the tenth earl rebelled in 1534, Henry took savage revenge, executing him in the Tower, despite a safe conduct, along with five of his uncles.

After 1540, when Cromwell was executed, there is a sense of drift. The most prominent counsellor was Norfolk, a conservative in religion, but he was no Wolsey or Cromwell. Debasement of the coinage, which began in the 1540s, contributed greatly to a steep rise in prices. In 1542 war began with France's ally, Scotland, where Henry pushed the marriage of his son, Edward, to the infant queen Mary. When the Scots demurred, he responded with the 'rough wooing', sending expeditions to burn and destroy the south-eastern towns. In 1543 he added to his problems by agreeing with Charles V to attack the French. Henry hoisted himself on horseback for one last attempt at military glory and succeeded in capturing Boulogne. Approaching bankruptcy forced a peace in 1544 whereby Boulogne was to be handed back in eight years.

Personally and politically there is little to admire in Henry. His treatment of his wives has been much condemned, but at least he was convinced of the guilt of Anne Boleyn and Catherine Howard. In some respects, the treatment of his ministers was worse: Wolsey destroyed, More and Cromwell executed, Norfolk condemned to beheading and saved only by Henry's own death, with one day to spare. He hounded the Kildares and Poles as though they were vermin to be exterminated. Henry had no pity, save for himself in abundance.

The traditional view of his reign saw a great strengthening of the crown, the papacy routed, clergy cowed, nobility brought to heel, administration reformed, the wealth of the monasteries acquired. But the reservations are severe. If Henry's great object was to secure the succession, he could hardly have done worse: his six marriages produced one sickly boy, and two princesses whose inheritance had been jeopardized by repeated bastardization and reinstatement. The gains from the dissolution were squandered and went largely to the gentry, and roaring inflation undermined the monarchy's finances, causing great problems for successors. His religious policy produced not unity but deep and enduring divisions, while his use of Parliament as a weapon against the papacy built it into an institution capable of overthrowing the monarchy itself a hundred years later. His foreign policy was highly personal, markedly eccentric, and counter-productive. Of the political acumen of his father, there is little trace.

SCARISBRICK, J., *Henry VIII* (1968).

Hampton Court, London

Created by Thomas Wolsey on the site of a manor-house leased from the Knights Hospitallers (1514) as a country residence, but surrendered to Henry VIII in hope of retaining royal favour, Hampton Court was taken over by Henry on Wolsey's downfall in 1529. A new great hall was constructed, Cloister Green Court, tennis courts and bowling alleys added, the chapel embellished, and kitchens remodelled. Anne Boleyn and subsequent queens resided and Edward VI was born there. The Hampton Court Conference was called by James I (1604) to examine current religious divisions, but authorization of a new translation of the Bible was the only real achievement.

Many of the Tudor royal apartments were demolished by Wren in response to William and Mary's order to 'beautify and add some new buildings to that fabric, their Majesties taking great delight in it', and his state apartments and private rooms were embellished by the painter Verrio and French smith Tijou.

continued

Hampton Court, London *continued*

William preferred this riverside palace to London because of his asthma, but a riding accident there led to his death two weeks later (1702). Charles II had already begun to lay out the gardens in formal French style, and Anne later added a maze to William's chestnut avenue and Mary's orangery. George II was the last monarch to reside at the palace. Public access was gradually allowed, and the apartments became divided into 'grace-and-favour' residences. A fire originating in one of these in 1986 destroyed much of the south wing of Fountain Court, including the King's Audience Chamber and art works.

Whitehall palace, London

Initially the London residence of the archbishops of York, hence named York Place, it was seized (like Hampton Court) by Henry VIII from Cardinal Wolsey in 1529. Henry began rebuilding with a new embankment on the riverside, and adding tiltyard, tennis court, cockpit, and bowling alley on acquired fields to the west (later St James's Park); there he married Anne Boleyn and Jane Seymour, and died. Elizabeth I received the duke of Alençon as suitor there in 1581 in temporary canvas pavilions since the huge sprawl of buildings had no permanent banqueting hall; James I's first attempt burnt down in 1619, but its replacement designed by Inigo Jones is the only part of the palace surviving today. Charles I built up an impressive art collection, but this was dispersed after his execution in front of the Banqueting Hall (1649).

The court returned after the Restoration, and Charles II lavished money on its interiors, housed his mistresses extravagantly, built a chemical laboratory, and took his tennis more seriously than Henry VIII. James II fled from Whitehall via the Privy Stair in 1688, but although Mary was delighted with the apartments, William III found the riverside site unfavourable to

continued

Whitehall palace, London *continued*

his asthma, so Kensington palace and Hampton Court were developed instead. A major fire in 1698, reputedly arising from a Dutch laundrywoman's carelessness, proved disastrous: 'nothing but the walls & ruines left' noted Evelyn tersely. Plans for rebuilding were shelved, and government offices gradually took over the site.

Catherine of Aragon, queen of England and Ireland, b. 15 Dec. 1485, da. of Ferdinand of Aragon and Isabella of Castile; m. (1) Arthur, prince of Wales, 14 Nov. 1501; (2) Henry VIII, 11 June 1509; issue: Henry, Mary; d. 7 Jan. 1536; bur. Peterborough cathedral.

Catherine was unfortunate. She arrived in England at the age of sixteen to marry prince Arthur; her husband was fifteen, and a head shorter. Within five months Arthur had died at Ludlow. Fresh negotiations were begun for a marriage to Arthur's brother Henry, then a boy of eleven: the difference in ages was to become important. However, for several years the marriage was postponed, leaving Catherine lonely and short of money. In 1509, seven weeks after his accession, Henry concluded the marriage.

A short period of happiness followed, but between 1510 and 1514 Catherine had four still births or infant deaths; princess Mary, her only surviving child, was born in 1516. By 1520 Henry had taken as mistress Mary Boleyn, and observers commented that Catherine had grown stout and plain. Not until 1526 did Henry break the news that his conscience would not allow him to live with her, since she had been his brother's wife. By this time, Henry's affections had moved on to Mary Boleyn's sister, Anne.

Catherine made a tenacious but hopeless struggle against any divorce or annulment, and refused to enter a nunnery. She appeared in person before the legatine court in 1529 to deny its jurisdiction and to insist that her first marriage had never been consummated. After July 1531 the king left her, and she never saw him again. She took what solace she could find in her religion, her daughter Mary, and the support of her nephew, the emperor. She moved to Kimbolton in 1534, where she died in 1536 at the age of fifty. Her last action was to write to Henry to assure him of her forgiveness and love: it was misplaced.

Anne Boleyn, queen of England and Ireland, b. c.1501, da. of Sir Thomas Boleyn (later earl of Wiltshire), and Elizabeth, da. of Thomas, duke of Norfolk; m. Henry VIII, 25 Jan. 1533; issue: Elizabeth; d. 19 May 1536; bur. Tower of London.

Though the Boleyns were resented as upstarts, they were, in fact, well connected. Anne's grandfather was the duke of Norfolk, the victor of Flodden, and her aunt Anne was a younger daughter of Edward IV; her father was a courtier and diplomat, and her sister Mary had become mistress of Henry VIII by 1520, when Anne was finishing her education at the French court. She made her debut at Henry's court in 1522 at a time when the queen was growing plump, and when Henry was beginning to worry that he had committed a mortal sin by marrying his brother's widow. Anne Boleyn was cool, sophisticated, and well groomed, slim and graceful, with good eyes and dark hair. She was not prepared to be a mistress, but the divorce, first mooted in 1526, did not take place until 1533. Towards the end of 1532, Anne and Henry became lovers, in December she found she was pregnant, and in January they were privately married. The divorce—more strictly an annulment—was not granted by Cranmer until May, and at her coronation in June, Anne was heavily pregnant.

The last three years of her life can have offered little enjoyment. In September the birth of a daughter, Elizabeth, was a disappointment. The following September, Anne had a miscarriage, and in January 1536 another. Dangerously for Anne, the death of Catherine of Aragon in January 1536 opened up the possibility of a third marriage for Henry, free from dispute, and with a new bride. By February, rumour identified the probable candidate as Jane Seymour.

The catastrophe that overwhelmed Anne in May 1536 was swift, master-minded by Thomas Cromwell. On 30 April Mark Smeaton, a young musician, was arrested and accused of adultery with the queen; under threat of torture he admitted it. Anne herself was arrested on 2 May and taken to the Tower. The indictment against her included adultery with her brother George and other men, and plotting to kill the king by witchcraft and poison. She denied the charges resolutely but to no avail. Her brother and the others were executed on 17 May, all save Smeaton denying their guilt. Anne was beheaded in the Tower on 19 May, dying with dignity. Chapuys, the emperor's ambassador and Anne's religious and diplomatic opponent, conceded of 'the concubine' that 'no one ever showed more courage and greater readiness to meet death than she did'.

IVES, E. W., *Anne Boleyn* (1986).

Jane Seymour, queen of England and Ireland, b. c.1509, da. of Sir John Seymour and Margaret Wentworth, da. of Sir Henry Wentworth of Suffolk; m. Henry VIII, 30 May 1536; d. 24 Oct. 1537; bur. Windsor.

Described by the emperor's ambassador, Chapuys, as 'of middle stature and no great beauty', though intelligent and gentle, Jane was lady-in-waiting to both Catherine of Aragon and Anne Boleyn, before attracting Henry's attention. She quietly resisted Henry's dishonourable proposals, but his infatuation precipitated the legal proceedings against Anne which culminated in her execution. They were married privately shortly afterwards. Though delicate, Jane was safely delivered of a son (the future Edward VI) on 12 October 1537, but died twelve days later, to Henry's genuine grief. Her brother Edward, created duke of Somerset, acted as Protector in the early years of Edward VI's reign.

Anne of Cleves, queen of England and Ireland, b. 22 Feb. 1519, da. of John, duke of Cleves, and Mary, da. of William, duke of Juliers; m. Henry VIII, 6 Jan. 1540; d. 16 July 1557; bur. Westminster abbey.

If Henry VIII's first two marriages were tragedies, the fourth was farce. Since he had a male heir by Jane Seymour, the motive was primarily diplomatic. Enquiries about Anne elicited the warning that his ambassador had heard 'no great praise neither of her personage nor beauty', but his minister Thomas Cromwell pushed the match which would help to unite the protestant princes of Germany in the face of a possible catholic crusade. Holbein's portrait appeared encouraging, and when she landed at Rochester, Henry rushed to meet her 'to nourish love'. He was bitterly disappointed and declared that he would not go through with the marriage were it not for offending her brother. Anne's opinion of her bloated husband is not recorded. A closer inspection merely confirmed his misgivings, which he related to Cromwell in some detail: he had, he confided, 'done all he could to move nature', but to no avail. Henry's attention turned to a more nubile eighteen-year-old, Catherine Howard and, in July 1540, Convocation obligingly declared the marriage null and void. The same month, Henry married for the fifth time; Anne settled for a very large pension and chose to remain in England in the odd position of the king's 'sister'. She may have felt that she had had a lucky escape.

Catherine Howard, queen of England and Ireland, b. c.1520, da. of Edmund Howard and Joyce, da. of Sir Richard Culpeper; m. Henry VIII, 28 July 1540; d. 13 Feb. 1542; bur. Tower of London.

Henry's fifth queen was the niece of Thomas, duke of Norfolk, a useful pawn in court. She was small, pretty, vivacious, and flighty, and it was therefore only a matter of time that, appointed maid-of-honour to Anne of Cleves, she should catch the king's eye. The marriage took place in July as soon as Anne's marriage had been declared invalid. 'The King is so amorous of her that he cannot treat her well enough', wrote one observer, 'and caresses her more than he did the others.' The idyll lasted until November 1541 when an extremely reluctant archbishop of Canterbury presented Henry with evidence that Catherine had had lovers, before and after marriage. Within five weeks confessions had been extracted, and two of her lovers, Francis Dereham and Thomas Culpeper, were executed as traitors. Though Henry had assured Catherine of mercy, he wriggled out of his pledge by using a parliamentary attainder. She was beheaded in the Tower, dying with composure near the spot where Anne Boleyn had been killed.

Catherine Parr, queen of England and Ireland, b. c.1512, da. of Sir Thomas Parr and Maud, da. of Sir Thomas Green; m. (1) Sir Edward Burgh, c.1529; (2) John, Lord Latimer, 1533; (3) Henry VIII, 12 July 1543; (4) Thomas Seymour, 3 Mar. 1547; d. 7 Sept. 1548; bur. Sudeley castle.

Catherine Parr's matrimonial history was nearly as complex as that of her third husband, the king. Her first marriage, made when she was seventeen, lasted some four years. She next became the third wife of Lord Latimer, who died in March 1543 at a time when Henry VIII was casting around for a sixth wife. Catherine had already decided to marry Thomas Seymour, brother of the king's third wife, Jane Seymour, but the match was forbidden 'by a high power'. This was the king, whom she married in July. 'She was quieter than any of the young wives the king had had,' wrote one commentator, 'and knew more of the world.' She behaved discreetly, bowed respectfully to his intellectual superiority, and flattered his monstrous ego. On his death in January 1547 she made a secret marriage almost at once to her old admirer, Seymour, and settled down at Sudeley, but died of puerperal fever after the birth of a baby daughter, who did not long survive her mother. Her fourth and last husband overreached himself and was executed six months later.

Mary Tudor, queen of France and duchess of Suffolk, b. Mar. 1496, 3rd da. of Henry VII and Elizabeth of York; m. (1) Louis XII of France, 9 Oct. 1514; (2) Charles Brandon, duke of Suffolk, 13 May 1515; issue: Henry, Frances, Eleanor; d. Westhope, Suffolk, 25 June 1533; bur. Bury St Edmunds.

Younger sister of the future Henry VIII and of queen Margaret of Scotland, Mary had inherited her mother's delicate fair beauty, which added a further dimension to the diplomatic marriages that would inevitably be proposed. She was contracted first to prince Charles of Austria and Castile, grandson of emperor Maximilian, in 1508, but despite some mutual affection, the marriage was never finalized because of political realignments; she was then married, at eighteen, to the far older Louis XII of France. Widowed after three months, Mary took advantage of brother Henry's promise that she might freely choose her next husband, and very promptly, while still in France, married his lifelong intimate, Charles Brandon, duke of Suffolk. Henry's wrath was eventually placated by gifts of her French jewels and gold, and the Suffolks were always in debt until the arrears of her dowry were paid off and Henry eased their repayments to him. Affectionate relations between brother and sister were regained—his flagship *Mary Rose* had been named in her honour—though later strained by Mary's support of Catherine of Aragon in the divorce crisis. For a while second lady in both England and France, her son was created earl of Lincoln (d. 1527), and her daughter Frances became the mother of Lady Jane Grey, whose claim to the throne in 1553 was brief.

Edward Seymour, duke of Somerset b. c.1500, s. of Sir John Seymour of Wiltshire and Margaret Wentworth; m. (1) Katherine, da. of Sir William Fillol, c.1527; issue: John, Edward; (2) Anne, da. of Sir Edward Stanhope, c.1533; issue: Edward, Edward, Henry, Edward, Anne, Margaret, Jane, Mary, Catherine, Elizabeth; d. 22 Jan. 1552; bur. Tower of London.

Of gentry stock, Seymour made modest progress until, in 1536, his sister Jane became the third wife of Henry VIII. A week later he was created viscount, advanced to earl (of Hertford) the following year, and as soon as he became Protector to his nephew Edward VI, in 1547, declared himself duke of Somerset. He had some military success against the Scots in 1547, but riots in Cornwall against his protestant religious policy, coupled with the Norfolk rising, brought about his downfall in 1549. He was pardoned in 1550, but executed in 1551, when power passed to his rival, Northumberland.

Edward VI, king of England and Ireland, b. 12 Oct. 1537, s. of Henry VIII and Jane Seymour; acc. 28 Jan. 1547; d. 6 July 1553; bur. Westminster abbey.

Edward's short reign was dominated by the struggle to act as adviser to the young king. His uncle, Edward Seymour, was appointed Protector and hastily made himself duke of Somerset, but when he fell from power in October 1549 his place was taken by the duke of Northumberland. Both men favoured a move from catholic practice towards protestantism. A new Book of Common Prayer was issued in the spring of 1549; a second in 1552 moved further towards the reformers. There is little doubt that Edward was in sympathy with these moves. His tutors had been reformers, he had threatened his elder sister Mary if she did not conform to the new religion, and his part in the Lady Jane Grey plot was an attempt to slam the door on catholicism.

Edward is one of the few monarchs who have left diaries. His is terse and factual, suggesting a cool, dispassionate intelligence—'a cold-hearted prig', according to one modern historian. He observed the execution of two of his uncles with detached unconcern. Negotiations for his marriage to Mary, queen of Scots, were received without enthusiasm by her subjects, who feared for their independence, and the 'rough wooing' which Somerset conducted against them merely confirmed their obduracy. Edward died, unmarried, at the age of fifteen from tuberculosis.

LOACH, J., *Edward VI* (1999).

Lady Jane Grey, b. Oct. 1537, da. of Henry, duke of Suffolk, and Frances, da. of Charles, duke of Suffolk; m. Lord Guildford Dudley, 21 May 1553; d. 12 Feb. 1554; bur. Tower of London.

As the granddaughter of Mary Tudor, younger sister of Henry VIII, Lady Jane had a good claim to the throne if Mary and Elizabeth were put aside, as they had been at times during his reign. When Edward VI's illness became apparent, the duke of Northumberland used her in an attempt to ward off the accession of Mary, a devout catholic, whose reign would mean his political ruin. She was married to his son, Lord Guildford Dudley, and on his deathbed Edward was persuaded to name her as his heir. She was declared queen by the council but her support dwindled rapidly and after nine days Northumberland gave up. She and her husband were executed after spending the last six months of their lives in the Tower.

Mary I, queen of England and Ireland, b. 18 Feb. 1516, da. of Henry VIII and Catherine of Aragon; acc. 6 July 1553; m. Philip (later king of Spain), 25 July 1554; d. 17 Nov. 1558; bur. Westminster abbey.

Mary's birth in 1516, after her mother had suffered several miscarriages and still births, was a source of great joy to her parents. There was little chance of her reaching the throne, since England had never had a queen regnant. She was, however, a valuable diplomatic pawn and, from her infancy, schemes of matrimony were entertained. The shadows which ultimately overwhelmed her did not become apparent until she was about ten, when rumours of a divorce between her parents began to spread. When the royal divorce was accompanied by the breach with Rome, it was inevitable that Mary should side with her mother and with the papacy. After Henry had married Anne Boleyn in 1533, Parliament declared Mary illegitimate and removed her from the order of succession; her execution was discussed, and in 1535 she contemplated flight to the continent. After Anne's execution in 1536, Mary's prospects improved, and Anne's daughter Elizabeth was declared illegitimate in turn. Mary, on the advice of her friends, made her submission to Henry and was received once more at court, though the birth of Jane Seymour's son, Edward, made the throne seem further off than ever.

In 1544, by which time her father had embarked upon his sixth marriage, Mary was restored to her place in the succession, but the accession of her brother in 1547 brought further trials. She was totally out of sympathy with the move towards protestantism, refused to give up the mass, and looked to the emperor Charles for protection. In 1551 she had an audience with her brother who ordered her 'as a subject to obey'. On the king's death in July 1553, the Council proclaimed Lady Jane Grey as queen, but Mary received strong support when she fled to Framlingham. Within a few days the coup collapsed, and in August she returned to London to begin her reign at the age of thirty-seven.

The two great questions facing her were the restoration of the catholic religion and her own marriage. The title 'Supreme Head of the Church' was abandoned, the breach with Rome healed, and Reginald Pole welcomed back in November 1554 as papal legate and made archbishop of Canterbury in 1556. Mary's marriage was urgent if she was to have any chance of producing a catholic successor. It was natural enough for her to look to the son of the emperor, Philip, who was eleven years her junior, but had become a widower in 1545. A Spanish marriage was far from popular with many of her subjects, who feared domination, and Wyatt's rising in February 1554 put the queen in some danger for a time. She and Philip were married at Winchester in July 1554. Mary was a short, plump woman, with reddish hair, her bloom gone, and Philip's courtiers were not impressed: 'If she dressed in our fashions', wrote one, 'she would not look so old and flabby. To speak frankly, it will take a great God to drink this cup.'

Philip was recognized as king of England, but was never crowned. His bride was enchanted with him and pined greatly at his protracted absences. The Spaniards gained their principal objective when the English declared war on France in the summer of 1557; within six months the English lost Calais, which they had held for more than two hundred years. Mary comforted herself with the belief that she was with child and, as late as the summer of 1558, was making plans for her delivery. In the autumn she accepted that she was deluded, that her days were numbered, and that Elizabeth would succeed her. She died peacefully at St James's.

An earlier marriage or a longer reign might have enabled Mary to achieve more of her objectives. Though she restored the catholic religion, she was unable to persuade the gentry to give up the gains they had made at the expense of the monasteries, and her own attempts to re-found religious houses were limited. The loss of Calais discredited the regime. The fierce persecution of obdurate protestants, undertaken against the views of her more moderate advisers, provided the reformed church with its glorious company of martyrs, and gave her the epithet 'Bloody Mary'.

LOADES, D. M., *Mary Tudor: A Life* (1992).

Philip of Spain, b. 21 May 1527, s. of Charles V of Spain and Isabella of Portugal; m. (1) Maria Manuella of Portugal, 13 Jan. 1543; issue: Carlos; (2) Mary Tudor, 25 July 1554; (3) Elizabeth of Valois, 31 Jan. 1560; issue: Isabella, Catalina; (4) Anne of Austria, 14 Nov. 1570; issue: Ferdinand, Carlos, Diego, Philip, Maria; d. 13 Sept. 1598.

Philip's marriage to Mary Tudor was but an episode in his long life, his motive being primarily to secure England's help in his war against France. He was cold by nature, did not speak English, and his bride was eleven years his senior. Though he was declared king by proclamation in July 1554, he spent only fifteen months in England, disregarding Mary's pitiful letters begging him to return during her last year, when she believed herself pregnant. In December 1558 he wrote politely: 'I felt a reasonable regret for her death', before showing some interest in a new marriage to her half-sister, Elizabeth, who prudently declined the honour. Subsequently he became her determined enemy, supporting assassination attempts and despatching the Armada in 1588.

Elizabeth I, queen of England and Ireland, b. 7 Sept. 1533, da. of Henry VIII and Anne Boleyn; acc. 17 Nov. 1558; d. 24 Mar. 1603; bur. Westminster abbey.

If one of the most striking characteristics of Elizabeth was circumspection, it may well be traced to the vicissitudes of her early life, when it was less a question whether she would ever become queen than whether she would survive at all. She was a little girl of two-and-a half when her mother was executed; six weeks later, Parliament, at her father's behest, declared her illegitimate. In October 1537 the birth of Jane Seymour's son, Edward, appeared to rule out her succession to the throne. Nevertheless, she received a good classical education, and in 1544 was reinstated in the order of succession after Edward and her half-sister Mary. The accession of Edward in 1547 should have made life easier for her, since they were on good, though not close, terms, and shared a protestant outlook. But Elizabeth allowed herself to become involved with Thomas Seymour, ambitious brother of the duke of Somerset, though she refused his offer of marriage in 1547. When Seymour was executed for treason in the spring of 1549, Elizabeth was questioned at length before being placed in comfortable confinement at Hatfield.

Mary's accession brought her into obvious peril. Elizabeth was then nineteen, and the Venetian ambassador wrote of her: 'her figure and face are very handsome, and such an air of dignified majesty pervades all her actions that no one can fail to suppose she is a queen... her manners are very modest and affable.' She complied with Mary's wish that she should attend mass, making it clear that she did so without enthusiasm. In February 1554 Sir Thomas Wyatt led a dangerous rising against Mary's proposed Spanish marriage. For two months, Elizabeth was confined to the Tower, while Wyatt and his supporters were racked to produce evidence to incriminate her; the emperor's envoy urged her immediate execution, but no evidence was forthcoming and once more she was sent into retirement. An unexpected ally emerged in her new brother-in-law, Philip of Spain, who found her more alluring than his middle-aged wife, and regarded her as an insurance should Mary suffer an early death.

In the event, Elizabeth's accession was peaceful and unopposed. Philip, not affecting immoderate grief, at once suggested marriage, which Elizabeth politely declined. Her coronation in January 1559 showed the religious problems she faced. The bishop of Carlisle was brought in to crown her, the gospel was read in Latin and English, and, though the mass was performed, the queen withdrew at the elevation of the host. Parliament's renewal of the Supreme Governorship of the Church and the refusal of the bishops to take the oath of supremacy, however, put her on course to a breach with Rome. Philip advised restraint on the papacy, arguing that Elizabeth might still submit, and there were a few encouraging signs. The new queen disliked clerical marriage, preferred the old vestments and, in November 1559, zealous protestants were horrified when candles and a crucifix reappeared in the chapel royal. But no further concessions were made, and in 1570 she was finally excommunicated by Pius V.

The question of Elizabeth's own marriage was at once raised. Within three months of accession, Parliament begged her to consider the matter, only to be told that she would live and die a virgin. At that stage, most people thought her reply an evasion or maidenly modesty rather than a determined policy, but the choice of husband would involve great difficulty. Despite the attraction she felt for Robert, earl of Leicester, marriage to a subject would mean a loss of dignity; Leicester was already married, and when his wife was found dead in mysterious circumstances, the scandal made marriage to the queen impossible. Marrying a foreign husband would probably mean taking sides in the European conflicts from which she had just extricated herself in 1559, and a catholic husband would probably reopen the religious question. Elizabeth had some lucky escapes. The archduke Charles was reported to be singularly unprepossessing and, perhaps remembering the fiasco of Anne of Cleves, Elizabeth refused to trust to portraits. The earl of Arran was, for a time, a front runner, but subsequently went mad, while Erik of Sweden, who pressed his suit warmly in the early 1560s, became a homicidal maniac and was deposed. As late as 1580 the queen was still engaged in heavy flirtation, sending her night-cap to the duke of Alençon, *pour encourager*.

Marriage, religion, the succession, and foreign policy were inextricably mixed. Elizabeth's first objective was to recover Calais, but the peace of Cateau-Cambrésis which she signed in April 1569 promised only that the French would return it in eight years, which nobody believed. Her general policy was disengagement, since war was

Elizabeth I. In this portrait, the heavily bejewelled queen is painted against scenes of the defeat and shipwreck of the Spanish Armada in 1588. The artist was probably George Gower.

expensive and her throne was far from secure, but disengagement itself carried risks, and could leave her isolated in the face of a Spanish/ French/Scottish catholic coalition. Scotland was ruled by Mary of Guise on behalf of her daughter-in-law, Mary Stuart, who succeeded as queen of France in July 1559. When the Scottish lords rebelled to set up a presbyterian form of government, Elizabeth, with great hesitation, gave them assistance. The result was to take Scotland out of the French sphere of influence, and though Mary returned to Scotland in 1561, after the death of her husband, she abandoned her use of the title of 'queen of England', hoping to be accepted as Elizabeth's successor.

Elizabeth's next intervention, in France, was a disaster. She took advantage of the religious dissensions to send an army to assist the Huguenots and to seize Le Havre, which she could then exchange for Calais. The French united against the English, her forces were decimated by plague and obliged to surrender. The settlement in Scotland unravelled rapidly. Mary lost control of the situation and in 1568 fled to England, and for nearly twenty years Elizabeth pondered what to do with this most unwelcome guest. Once the papacy had declared Elizabeth a heretic and usurper, Mary became the centre of a series of plots: the rising of the Northern earls (1569), Ridolfi plot (1571), Throckmorton (1584), Parry (1585), Babington (1586). Persuaded at last that her own life would never be safe while Mary lived, Elizabeth gave the order for her execution in 1587.

By this time, Elizabeth was in the midst of the most violent storms. Dutch discontent with the rule of Philip II in the 1560s led to the revolt of the 'sea-beggars' in 1572, who appealed for help to French Huguenots and English protestants. Elizabeth was reluctant to support rebels and concerned lest intervention should drag her into an expensive and dangerous war, but in 1585 the Dutch seemed on the verge of ruin and Burghley, her chief adviser, urged that the policy of permitting volunteers to help the Dutch was no longer adequate. Violence escalated but with both sides hoping to avoid outright war. In 1585 Philip seized English ships and crews in Spanish ports, whereupon Elizabeth retorted by setting Drake free to prey upon Spanish commerce. Planning for a great invasion of England began before the execution of Mary, queen of Scots, but her death in February 1587 sent a shudder through the crowned heads of Europe and armed Elizabeth's adversaries with moral fervour. Philip's financial difficulties caused the invasion fleet to be scaled down, and though the Armada remained formidable, it was no longer invincible. In the event, the victory was overwhelming. The Spaniards lost at least fifty ships and some 15,000 men, while the English lost no vessels and fewer than one hundred men in action, though, as usual, deaths from disease were appalling. The queen's heroic speech to her troops at Tilbury was the start of her transformation into a living legend, 'the great lioness'.

The last fifteen years of her reign were less dramatic, though the war with Spain continued. Two more Spanish invasion fleets, in 1596 and

1597, were dispersed by gales. After Leicester's death in 1588, his place as favourite-in-chief was taken by his stepson, Essex, handsome and headstrong. Sent to deal with another Irish rising in 1599 by Tyrone, Essex came to terms with him, which Elizabeth condemned as 'perilous and contemptible'. His loss of favour prompted Essex to a half-baked rising in 1601, for which he paid with his life. The queen faded quietly thereafter, still performing, capable of rising to the occasion, but old and tired.

In character Elizabeth was a mixture of her father and grandfather, Henry VII. She had Henry VIII's imperious and tempestuous nature, his inordinate vanity, his love of finery, his gift for self-advertisement, but not his savagery. She played her public role to perfection, at court, on progresses, and to Parliament, grand but condescending. She reserved for her last meeting with Parliament one of her finest orations: 'and though you have had, and may have, many princes more mighty and wise sitting in this seat, yet you never had, nor shall have, any that will be more careful and loving.' Her policies, though, were those of Henry VII—unwillingness to fight if it could be avoided, and frugality to the point of meanness, lest she be drawn into dependence upon parliaments. She brought vacillation to a fine art, keeping suitors dangling, playing ministers off against one another, prevaricating over the succession, postponing decisions until the eleventh hour. Modern historians have been critical of her, but the fair comparison is with the two previous reigns and the two subsequent, and from that she emerges as shrewd and capable, not least in her choice of advisers.

JOHNSON, P., *Elizabeth I: A Study in Power and Intellect* (1974).

Nonsuch palace, Surrey

In 1538 Henry VIII bought the manor and estate of Cuddington and commenced construction of a showplace, demolishing both manor house and village. Basically a Gothic building with heavy Classical ornamentation, the square Inner Court was raised over the former parish church's burial yard, with the Outer Court sited on its northern side; walls, towers, a separate banqueting house, gardens, deerpark, and sumptuous decoration throughout

continued

Nonsuch palace, Surrey *continued*

entailed huge expenditure. Mary Tudor, having no use for it, contemplated demolition, but sold it in 1556 to the earl of Arundel, who completed the gardens and began to build up the library. The property passed to his son-in-law, John, Lord Lumley, but he surrendered it to the Crown in 1592 in settlement of a long-standing debt; Elizabeth so loved Nonsuch (cf. *non pareil*, without equal) that this was its 'golden age'.

In 1603 palace and park were granted by James I to his wife, Anne of Denmark, and similarly bestowed by Charles I upon Henrietta Maria (1625), to whom it was restored in 1660 after the Restoration. Following her death (1669) Charles II granted it to his mistress, the duchess of Cleveland, but demolition was commenced in 1682. Full-scale excavations in the early 1960s finally confirmed the site of the palace, and revealed fragments of the lavish decoration.

Stuarts

Whatever its achievements in Scotland, the Stuart (this spelling became more common in the course of the sixteenth century, under French influence) dynasty did not transplant well in England. Louis XIV called them an unlucky family, but most of their ill-fortune was of their own making. They brought with them exalted concepts of kingship which took little account of the changed circumstances of their new country, and particularly of the much greater importance of the English parliament. Their problems were compounded by their association with Mary, queen of Scots, as a catholic martyr, reinforced from 1625 onwards when Charles I married Henrietta Maria, a catholic princess. Charles II's marriage to another catholic, Catherine of Braganza, and James II's personal conversion in 1670 and second marriage to Mary of Modena in 1673 split the dynasty from its natural supporters among the Anglican gentry. Nor could they redeem themselves by prowess in war.

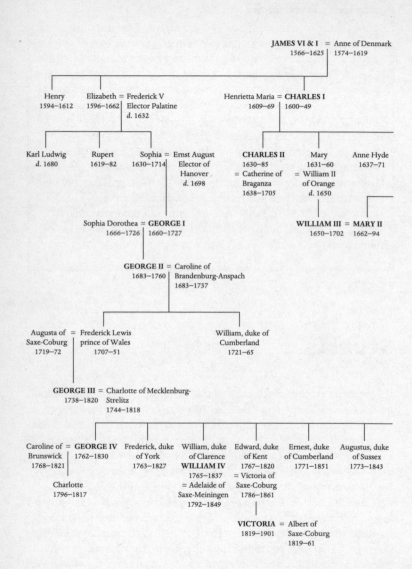

STUART AND HANOVERIAN
[showing the disputed succession
after 1688]

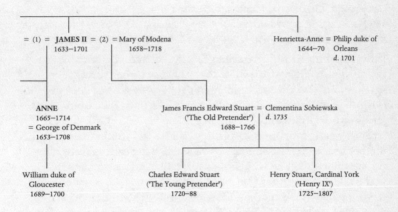

= (1) = **JAMES II** = (2) = Mary of Modena
1633–1701   1658–1718

Henrietta-Anne = Philip duke of
1644–70   Orleans
               d. 1701

ANNE
1665–1714
= George of Denmark
1653–1708

James Francis Edward Stuart = Clementina Sobiewska
('The Old Pretender')   *d.* 1735
1688–1766

William duke of
Gloucester
1689–1700

Charles Edward Stuart
('The Young Pretender')
1720–88

Henry Stuart, Cardinal York
('Henry IX')
1725–1807

Adolphus duke
of Cambridge
1774–1850

James I's campaigns were ineffective, Charles I's disastrous, Charles II's humiliating, and James II's ludicrous. It was left to Cromwell to demonstrate what strength England possessed when ruled competently. Not until William and Anne did the Stuarts find rulers of judgement and capacity. Their behaviour in exile from 1688 to the death of Henry IX in 1807 confirms it as a dynasty whose grasp of reality was fitful.

James I, king of England, James VI of Scotland, b. 19 June 1566, s. of Henry, Lord Darnley, and Mary, queen of Scots; acc. Scotland 24 July 1567; England 24 Mar. 1603; m. Anne, da. of Frederick II of Denmark, 20 Aug. 1589; issue: Henry, Elizabeth, Margaret, Charles, Robert, Mary, Sophia; d. 27 Mar. 1625; bur. Westminster abbey.

James spent his first thirty-seven years in Scotland, the remaining twenty-two in England. His claim to the English throne was that both his parents were descendants of Margaret Tudor, elder sister of Henry VIII. Nevertheless, there were other claimants and, until the last moment, James could not be certain of his accession.

James's early years were difficult. While he was still in the womb, his mother's secretary, David Rizzio, was stabbed to death in front of her; rumour hinted that he was James's real father. James was less than a year old when his father was murdered at Kirk o'Field, probably with the complicity of his mother. Losing control of the situation after her precipitate marriage to Bothwell, Mary was forced to abdicate in favour of James in July 1567 and escaped to captivity in England in May 1568, never seeing her son again. During his childhood there were four regents: the first, Moray, was shot; Lennox died in a brawl; Mar was believed poisoned, and Morton was executed in 1581. In 1582 James was kidnapped by Lord Gowrie and held captive for ten months. In 1587 his mother was executed at Fotheringhay. James's first ambition was therefore to survive, the second to restore some authority to the Scottish monarchy, the third to harvest his English succession.

Even the first ambition was not easy. James had a rough passage back from Denmark in 1590 with his new bride, and discovered that more than three hundred North Berwick witches had been at work; he turned the episode to advantage in a small treatise on *Daemonologie*. Equally terrifying was the earl of Bothwell, nephew of Mary's third husband, who besieged the king in Holyrood House in 1591 and at Falkland Palace in 1592. In 1600, according to the king's own testimony, which many doubted, he was lured by the Gowrie brothers to Perth, locked in a turret and told to prepare to die. It must have been with some relief that James

James VI and I. The anxious expressions in many portraits of James VI and I may reflect the hazardous life he had led, exposed to dangers and plots. 'He tormented himself', wrote Sir John Oglander, 'with fear of some sudden mischief', and his doublets were padded against dagger thrusts. Painted in c.1606, soon after the gunpowder plot.

travelled south in 1603, where his new subjects attempted to blow him up two years later.

The restoration of royal authority in Scotland was achieved slowly. After Bothwell had been driven into exile in 1594, James gained a measure of control over the nobility. More opposition to the crown came from the kirk, whose extreme claims to domination James could never accept; they encourage the ignorant to cry down their betters, he wrote in *Basilikon Doron*. General assemblies in 1597 were warned to confine themselves to ecclesiastical matters, and in 1600 James succeeded in reintroducing bishops into the church.

At first James was uncertain how to attain his third objective, the throne of England. He toyed with the idea of papal support and was interested in Spanish proposals to free and restore his mother. But that could hardly be done without restoring her to effective power, which James did not relish. In 1586 he opted for reliance upon Elizabeth, accepting a pension of £4,000; consequently, when his mother was executed in 1587 his protests to Elizabeth were decent but muted. In Elizabeth's later years, James safeguarded his interests by opening up in 1601 a correspondence with her chief minister, Sir Robert Cecil.

In his new kingdom, James faced considerable difficulties. Unlike Scotland, the country was at war with Spain, draining its resources and endangering its control of Ireland. Though England was incomparably wealthier than Scotland, decades of inflation had bitten into the royal finances, and the crown itself was impoverished. James had to provide for a queen not inclined towards economy and for a growing family with lavish tastes. He faced in England a Parliament quite different in character and power from that of Scotland. He was from a country which had been at war with England within living memory and which few English respected. There were persistent complaints at the number of indigent but hopeful Scots who followed him south. James's theoretical view of monarchy was lofty but, though he had brooded long on the duties of kingship, he had little natural dignity, drinking too much, caressing his young male favourites in public, and alternating between primness and coarse bawdy. The pen-portrait by Sir Anthony Weldon has often been dismissed as malicious, but in 1584 Fontenay, a Frenchman working for James's mother, offered a similar study: he granted James learning, memory, and intelligence, but disapproved of his reliance on favourites, adding that his manners were crude, that he lacked application, and had a very high opinion of himself.

The war with Spain was easily wound up. Both combatants were exhausted, and made peace in 1604. Not until the end of his reign, when he was urged to rescue his son-in-law the Elector Palatine and the protestant cause, did foreign affairs return to centre stage. At home, one of his earliest initiatives was to seek religious consensus in the Hampton Court Conference between the bishops and their puritan critics. Though not a total fiasco, the Conference produced few areas of agreement, leaving many puritans dissatisfied. The policy closest to James's heart was a governmental union between his two kingdoms, but he handled the matter badly. The English Parliament dragged its feet and the declaration of Great Britain had, in the end, to be made by royal proclamation. Repeated attempts to reform the finances made little progress in the face of the court's own extravagance. Salisbury's proposal for the Great Contract in 1610 collapsed with mistrust on both sides, and Cranfield's attempt to impose retrenchment clashed with court interest and brought about his downfall in 1624.

James's private life was dominated by his love of hunting, and though he complained bitterly of the burden of kingship, he was no slave to duty. He was not on close terms with his wife, who enjoyed dancing and music. His son Henry died in 1612, his daughter Elizabeth left for the Palatinate in 1613, and Charles, his second son, was taciturn and reserved. James's favourites filled the gap, and rewards for the lucky few were speedy. Robert Carr, a fellow Scot, had the good fortune to break his arm at a tournament in 1607, when onlookers noted that the king's concern was greater than required by common solicitude. He was made viscount Rochester in 1611 and earl of Somerest in 1613, before crashing from favour through a murder in 1615. His career contrasted with James's treatment of Ralegh, imprisoned in the Tower for fourteen years, before execution in 1618. The rise of Carr's sucessor, George Villiers, was even more spectacular: viscount Villiers 1616, earl of Buckingham 1617, marquess 1618, duke 1623. James doted on him: 'I love the earl of Buckingham more than anyone else', he told his surprised Council in 1617.

During his later years, James's health slowly declined, and government of the country fell to a strange triumvirate of James, Charles, and Buckingham. The last two had been on bad terms until 1618 when they were reconciled. In 1623 Buckingham and 'Baby Charles' decided on a madcap dash to Spain to secure Charles' marriage to the Infanta, and when that collapsed ignominiously, resolved on an equally madcap war with Spain.

Like most monarchs, James has been subjected to 'revisionist' treatment, which has emphasized his attempts to deal with problems that Elizabeth had refused to touch. There is some truth in this, but his success rate was not high and often he was himself the chief stumbling block. A union of England and Scotland was sensible, but James showed little understanding of the apprehensions of his English subjects. The

Great Contract might have put royal finances on a better footing, but the chief obstacle was James's own extravagance: 'the royal cistern has a leak', observed one member of Parliament. The sale of baronetcies, then of peerages, helped to discredit honours and titles and undermine respect for rank. Bishop Williams, in the funeral oration, referred to James as 'the British Solomon'; Henry IV of France had dismissed him as 'the wisest fool in Christendom'.

WILLSON, D. H., *King James VI and I* (1956).

Divine right of kings

In ancient times most kings, like the pharaohs, claimed to be gods, or at least descended from them, and the coronation ceremony was intended primarily to demonstrate divine approval. The doctrine was spelled out more fully in the sixteenth century, when estates and parliaments were beginning to challenge royal authority. In Britain, the most explicit exposition was by James VI of Scotland in two treatises, *The Trew Laws of Free Monarchies* and *Basilikon Doron*. He maintained the same view when he moved to England as James I in 1603, telling Parliament in 1610 that 'kings exercise a manner of resemblance of divine power on earth, accountable to none but God only'. Parliament disagreed. In the later seventeenth century, the doctrine was attacked as slavish, and theories of a contract between ruler and ruled gained favour. After the Glorious Revolution of 1688, the doctrine found few defenders.

Anne of Denmark, queen of Scotland and of England, b. 12 Dec. 1574, da. of Frederick II and Sophia, da. of Ulric, duke of Mecklenburg; m. James VI of Scotland, 20 Aug. 1589; d. 2 Mar. 1619; bur. Westminster abbey.

Sister of Christian IV of Denmark, Anne was fifteen when married and eight years younger than her husband. When his bride was held up in Denmark by gales and the malevolence of Danish witches, James gallantly went to fetch her and spent six months in the country. His bride was blonde, with a good complexion and a graceful manner. Despite James's interest in young men, the marriage produced seven children, the last born in 1606. In England, the queen delighted in masques and pageantry, commissioned Inigo Jones to begin the Queen's House at Greenwich, and ran up enormous debts. Later she followed her own pattern of life at Somerset House (renamed Denmark House), visited only occasionally by the king. She had an interest in catholicism and the papacy entertained hopes of her conversion, but she died a protestant.

Arabella Stuart, b. c.1575, da. of Charles, earl of Lennox, and Elizabeth, da. of Sir William Cavendish; m. William Seymour (later earl of Hertford and duke of Somerset), 22 June 1610; d. 27 Sep. 1615; bur. Westminster abbey.

Descended through her grandmother from Henry VII of England and through her grandfather from James II of Scotland, Arabella Stuart was the cousin of James I and VI, and very close to the throne. When she made a secret marriage in 1610 to William Seymour, twelve years her junior, who had English royal blood through his grandmother, Lady Catherine Grey, James I was alarmed. She was sent to the Tower where she died five years later, having become deranged.

Henry Frederick, prince of Wales, b. 19 Feb. 1594, s. of James VI of Scotland and Anne of Denmark; d. 6 Nov. 1612; bur. Westminster abbey.

Nine years old when his father succeeded Elizabeth, Henry was brought to England by his mother. He grew up athletic and intelligent, deploring his father's treatment of Ralegh. His death at the age of eighteen, probably from typhoid, left his less gifted brother Charles as heir to the throne.

Elizabeth, queen of Bohemia, b. 19 Aug. 1596, da. of James VI of Scotland and Anne of Denmark; m. Frederick V, Elector Palatine, 14 Feb. 1613; issue: Henry Frederick, Charles Ludwig, Elizabeth, Rupert, Maurice, Louise, Ludwig, Edward, Henrietta, Philip, Charlotte, Sophia, Gustavus Adolphus; d. 13 Feb. 1662; bur. Westminster abbey.

Elizabeth's marriage to the young Elector Palatine was praised by most Englishmen as support for the protestant interest in Europe. In 1618, when her husband accepted the throne of Bohemia in defiance of the Habsburgs, he was driven out and lost the Palatinate as well. Known as 'the Winter Queen' for her brief stay in Prague, Elizabeth spent most of her life in exile, much of it in penury. In her youth she was the recipient of Sir Henry Wotton's poem, 'Ye meaner beauties of the night'. Her third son, Rupert, fought in the English civil wars for his uncle, Charles I, and her daughter Sophia married the elector of Hanover and was mother to George I.

Charles I, king of England and Scotland, b. 19 Nov. 1600, 2nd s. of James VI of Scotland and Anne of Denmark; acc. 27 Mar. 1625; m. Henrietta Maria, da. of Henry IV of France, 1 May 1625; issue: Charles, Mary, James, Elizabeth, Anne, Catherine, Henry, Henrietta-Anne; d. 30 Jan. 1649; bur. Windsor.

Charles became heir to the throne in 1612 when his elder brother Henry died of typhoid. He was very small, reserved, unimpressive in appearance, and with a residual stammer. He was at first on bad terms with his father's favourite Buckingham, but from 1618 they became inseparable. In 1619, when Charles's sister Elizabeth was driven out of her new kingdom of Bohemia, James hoped that a marriage between Charles and the Spanish infanta would induce Spain to demand her reinstatement. Negotiations were protracted and in 1623 Charles rushed off to Spain with Buckingham, thinly disguised, to urge his suit. The result was a fiasco. The Spaniards insisted on impossible concessions to the English catholics, and, in disgust, Charles married the French princess, Henrietta Maria. Not to be outdone in zeal by the Spaniards, the French also insisted on concessions, and since there was no chance that Parliament would agree to them, Charles promised them in a secret clause.

James's death in the spring of 1625 found Charles and Buckingham demanding war with Spain. This was initially popular. Charles's first enterprise was an attack upon Cadiz (evoking memories of Elizabethan glories), but it proved an unmitigated disaster. Having demonstrated their incapacity to wage war, Charles and Buckingham proceeded to quarrel with France as well. This time France was to receive a deadly blow with an expedition to assist the Huguenots at La Rochelle against Louis XIII. To ensure success, Buckingham himself took command. The outcome was bitter and humiliating failure, with heavy losses.

These disasters had a profound effect upon Charles's political position, playing into the hands of Buckingham's opponents. In the Parliament of 1628 Buckingham was denounced as 'the grievance of grievances', and a Petition of Right carried, attacking forced loans, arbitrary arrests, and billeting. Charles complained that members were eager for a protestant war but unwilling to vote the resources; many members thought that the king was not competent to wage war or control expenditure.

Charles I. Charles lived in a dream world. Here Lely, following Van Dyck, changes a very short stuttering man into an image of dignified majesty. Compare with Cromwell on p. 291.

A combination of factors gave Charles a new start. In August 1628 Buckingham was stabbed to death at the Greyhound Inn, Portsmouth, while preparing for another expedition. Relations between Charles and the queen improved dramatically, and in May 1630 an heir to the throne, Charles, was born. Peace with France was made in 1629, with Spain in 1630. Charles dismissed his third Parliament in anger in 1629, after rowdy scenes in which the Speaker was held down in his chair, and began the experiment of his personal rule without Parliaments.

The early 1630s were probably the happiest years of the king's life. He conducted his court on regular and sober lines: etiquette was rigid, ceremony dignified, with some danger that Charles was shielded from reality. He was able to indulge his passion for painting, music, and the masque. He had a powerful vision of an orderly, decent, and obedient kingdom, reinforced by masques in which he often took a leading and heroic role. There were three hidden hazards. After the 1629 Parliament had been dissolved, several members were put in prison, some for as long as twelve years; any future Parliament would demand redress. The financial expedients, such as forced loans, distraint of knighthood, and ship money, to which Charles resorted in the absence of parliamentary grants, caused considerable resentment among the gentry. Lastly, rule without Parliament could continue only as long as Charles could avoid war.

The collapse of personal rule was brought about not by foreign war, but by events in Scotland and Ireland. In the former, he shared his father's dislike of calvinism and worked to introduce greater reverence in the kirk. His visit to Edinburgh in 1633 for his coronation was not a total success, and there was criticism that he had used the Anglican service book. This did not prevent him from ordering in 1637 that a revised Anglican service should be used throughout Scotland. It was received with riots and protests, and Charles decided that his opponents must be crushed. Since he had no money for an army, the northern levies were ordered to assemble, a scratch force with little training and less zeal. With characteristic duplicity, he instructed Hamilton, his commander in the north; to 'flatter them [the Scots] with what hopes you please ... until I be ready to suppress them'. In 1639 the king took direct command but his men would not fight, and he was forced to agree to a truce. Meanwhile, he returned to Whitehall, where he watched another masque in which he descended from a golden throne to restore peace, concord, and harmony. It was the last masque he ever commissioned. Real life broke in. The Short Parliament, summoned in the spring of 1640, had little inclination to provide money to suppress the Scots, with whom they had much sympathy. Charles dissolved them after three weeks. When in the summer of 1640 Charles advanced once more to teach the Scots a lesson, they brushed aside his makeshift force, captured Newcastle, and dictated terms at Ripon. They were to receive £850 a day while they occupied the northern counties. Charles had lost control of the situation, a new Parliament would have to be summoned, and the Scottish army was its guarantee that it, too, would not be dissolved in dudgeon.

The Long Parliament, when it met in November 1640, wasted no time in dismantling the apparatus of personal rule, impeaching Strafford, and imprisoning archbishop Laud, releasing victims of wrongful imprisonment, declaring ship money illegal, and insisting that it could not be dissolved without its own consent. The outbreak of catholic rebellion in Ireland, accompanied by the massacre of protestants, raised the stakes yet again. An army was needed to restore English control, but neither side would trust the other to command it. Parliament claimed the right to name the senior officers; Charles in the summer of 1642 moved to York to assemble his own army.

Charles fought the civil war which followed with bravery and determination. His handling of the Lostwithiel campaign, as late as 1644, was expert. Nevertheless, he made fundamental mistakes. First, he should not have abandoned London, leaving the seat of government to his opponents; he never returned, save as a prisoner. Secondly, given a chance after Edgehill to retake his capital, he hesitated and allowed his enemies to rally. Thirdly, he overestimated the value of catholic Irish help, and underestimated the damage it would do to his reputation in the eyes of his protestant English subjects.

After the surrender of the last royal army in March 1646, Charles hoped to regain control by diplomacy, splitting his adversaries. His greatest success was to strike a deal with the Scots whereby, in exchange for accepting presbyterianism for a trial period, they would send an army to restore him. In the second civil war of 1648, the Scottish forces were crushed by Cromwell at Preston. Charles's Parliamentary opponents decided that he was incorrigible and put him on trial as 'a tyrant, traitor, murderer, and public enemy to the good people of this nation'. At his trial and execution, Charles behaved courageously, dying, he maintained, for the monarchy and the rule of law. Neither claim will really stand up. At his execution outside the Banqueting House in Whitehall, he explained that he had been brought there because he would not give way 'to the power of the sword'. But he himself had drawn the sword against the Scots, only to find it rusty. His martyrdom may have led to the Restoration in 1660 and, to that extent, he saved the monarchy. But without his actions, it would never have been in danger.

CARLTON, C., *Charles I: The Personal Monarch* (1983).

Henrietta Maria, queen of England and Scotland, b. 26 Nov. 1609, da. of Henry IV of France and Marie de Médicis; m. Charles I, 1 May 1625; d. 21 Aug. 1669; bur. St-Denis, Paris.

Small, dark, vivacious, with protruding teeth, Henrietta Maria was fifteen years old when she was married by proxy to Charles I. The early years of the marriage were stormy, with frequent quarrels about the queen's catholic attendants. Relations with her husband improved after Buckingham's death in 1628, and the early 1630s were years of contentment, the queen preoccupied with family and court life. As civil war approached, she gave strong support to her husband, spending February 1642 to February 1643 on the continent raising men and supplies. Rejoining the king at Oxford in 1643 she left for France a year later and received the news of Charles's execution in 1649 while at the Louvre. She returned to England after the Restoration of her son, Charles II, but went back to France in 1665. Her political influence was considered high during her lifetime but has probably been exaggerated.

Rupert, prince, b. 17 Dec. 1619, s. of Frederick V, Elector Palatine, and Elizabeth, da. of James VI of Scotland; d. 29 Nov. 1682; bur. Westminster abbey.

Nephew of Charles I, Rupert was born in Prague, where his parents briefly held the Bohemian throne. He arrived in England in 1642 and quickly made his name as a brilliant cavalry commander. However, he was badly beaten at Marston Moor in 1644 and the following year was denounced by the king when he was forced to surrender Bristol. After the Restoration he was a prominent figure at the court of his cousin, Charles II, and held naval command in the second and third Anglo-Dutch wars.

Commonwealth and Protectorate

The execution of Charles I was not part of a long-term plan, but it was followed by the abolition of the monarchy and of the House of Lords. A formal act on 19 May 1649 declared that England was a Commonwealth. The executive was a Council of State of forty-one members. In practice, power was disputed between the Rump

continued

> **Commonwealth and Protectorate** *continued*
>
> Parliament and the army. Cromwell dismissed the Rump in April
> 1653 and in December, under the Instrument of Government,
> was appointed Lord Protector. A new constitution, the Humble
> Petition and Advice, in 1657 brought back a second chamber and
> provided for a Privy Council, though Cromwell refused the crown.
> Cromwell's son, Richard, was appointed Lord Protector in 1658
> but lost power the following year. The return to the traditional
> monarchy followed at the Restoration in 1660.

Cromwell, Oliver, b. 25 Apr. 1599, s. of Robert Cromwell and Elizabeth
Steward; m. Elizabeth Bourchier, 22 Aug. 1620; issue: Robert, Oliver, Richard, Henry,
Bridget, Elizabeth, Mary, Frances; d. 3 Sept. 1658; bur. Westminster abbey, exhumed
1661.

For five weeks in 1657, while Cromwell hesitated whether to accept the
crown, it looked as if he would become Oliver I, king of England. He had
long had many of the prerogatives of a monarch, using the royal palaces
and creating peers, and more real power than most monarchs had ever
wielded. He declined, and apologized politely: 'I must acknowledge
publicly I have been unreasonably troublesome.'

Cromwell grew up in Huntingdon, a small, quiet town, a man of
modest property. He spent one year at Cambridge, choosing a new
college, Sidney Sussex, with a puritan tradition. In 1628 he represented
his native borough in Parliament, without making any particular mark.
In the early 1630s he experienced a profound religious conversion,
acknowledging his sins and hoping for redemption; henceforward his
thoughts and speech were couched in deeply religious terms. In the
Short and Long Parliaments, summoned in 1640, he sat for the borough
of Cambridge. A contemporary description noted a plain, blunt, sturdy
man, reddish in the face and speaking loudly, with 'a speck or two of
blood upon his neck-band'.

Once fighting broke out in 1642, Cromwell's rise was rapid. He left
Westminster for Cambridge in the summer, seized the county magazine
and prevented college plate reaching the king at York. At Edgehill, he
fought as a cavalry officer and was promoted colonel. His regiment, he
claimed proudly, was composed of 'honest, sober christians ... honest
goodly men', who knew what they were fighting for. His success at

Marston Moor in 1644 gave him national standing and he was charged with training the New Model Army, which won the decisive victory at Naseby in 1645. The first civil war concluded, he took a prominent part in 1647 in the army debates at Putney, resisting the arguments of the extreme democrats and levellers. From political theory, he was summoned back into action by the outbreak of the second civil war in 1648 when a Scottish army under Hamilton marched south to rescue the king. Cromwell intercepted it at Preston and won a shattering victory. The king's appeal once more to force persuaded Cromwell to approve his execution as a man of blood, and he signed third on the death warrant of 1649.

During the next two years Cromwell was the hammer of Parliament, in Ireland until 1650, where he defended his ferocity at Drogheda and Wexford with the hope that it would 'prevent the effusion of blood for the future', and then in Scotland, where the young prince Charles hoped to rally the royalists. In September 1650, again badly outnumbered, he destroyed Leslie's army outside Dunbar. The royalists managed a recovery and in 1651 Charles led an army south towards their old recruiting regions of Wales and the west country. In his last battle at Worcester—'the crowning mercy'—Cromwell destroyed his opponents as a fighting force.

The parliamentary army was now the arbiter of England and Cromwell stood head and shoulders above the rest. No other man could claim his prowess on the battlefield and his long experience in Parliament. But reaching a settlement within the Commonwealth framework proved burdensome. Cromwell believed that, after the overthrow of traditional institutions, a strong executive was necessary to prevent a slide into anarchy; his Parliaments were as jealous of their authority as their predecessors had been. An independent in religion, he manœuvred uneasily between presbyterians who would curtail religious toleration and sectarians who denied the need for any national church. Though he genuinely wished to restore a civilian government, the army was necessary as long as royalist plots continued. From 1652 war with the Dutch, largely over commercial rivalry, made it impossible to reduce army or navy, and when that was wound up, war with the Spaniards followed.

Cromwell's breach with the Rump Parliament (the remnant of the Long Parliament) came in 1653, when he dissolved it in anger: 'you have sat long enough unless you had done more good—in the name of God, go.' His next experiment was close to his heart: a nominated assembly of

140 godly and righteous men, 'Barebones Parliament'. Cromwell welcomed it in July 1653 with tears of joy. They soon dried up. The members set about reform with uncommon zeal, demanding the abolition of tithes and the destruction of any national church system. Cromwell saw any hope of reconciling the gentry to the new order disappearing and, after only five months, a majority of the members surrendered their authority back into his hands. The next constitution, the Instrument of Government, accepted the reality of Cromwell's power and moved a step closer to monarchy. Cromwell was made Lord Protector, given the palace of Whitehall, and was to be addressed as 'Your Highness'. He would be assisted by a Council and Parliament, but the latter was not to challenge the constitution itself. Scotland and Ireland were incorporated into the new arrangements, sending members to the Westminster Parliament.

The new Parliament did not meet until September 1654, when it immediately began to unpick the constitution, insisting on its own supremacy. Cromwell warned it that it must accept at least the 'fundamentals' and one hundred members refused. The rest began an interesting debate on how fundamental were fundamentals. When they voted to reduce the army and place it under their direct control,

Oliver Cromwell. 'Paint me warts and all' Cromwell is said to have told Peter Lely. In this miniature, Samuel Cooper takes him at his word.

Cromwell dismissed them: 'it is not for the common or public good for you to continue here longer.' To fill the gap, Cromwell turned to the rule of the major-generals, with the countries divided into twelve regions. Penruddock's rising in Wiltshire in March 1655 gave some excuse for the imposition of military rule, but it was deeply unpopular. In 1656 Cromwell called a second Parliament, but though the elections had been carefully supervised, a hundred members had to be excluded as disaffected. The remainder denounced the major-generals and refused supplies to support them. The situation changed with an assassination plot against the Lord Protector, and a majority of the House begged him to take the title 'king' as a safeguard.

Though he refused, the new constitution under the Humble Petition and Advice strengthened the executive. The Protector was empowered to nominate his successor, and a second chamber was introduced to slow down radical reform—the old House of Lords, risen from the ashes of 1649. Cromwell greeted the new Parliament in January 1658 as heralding harmony and legality, all divisions healed: 'if there be any higher work which mortals can attain unto in this world, I acknowledge my ignorance of it.' The Commons responded by picking a quarrel with the House of Lords, calling it disparagingly 'the other House', and Cromwell was forced to dissolve them. It was his last Parliament. The summer was comparatively peaceful. 'His power and greatness', wrote Clarendon, seemed 'to be better established than ever it had been', but Cromwell's health was giving out. On 20 August 1658 George Fox, the quaker, saw him riding at the head of his guards at Hampton Court: 'he looked like a dead man.' He died in the great storm of 3 September, the anniversary of his two victories at Dunbar and Worcester.

Cromwell remained all his life a family man, on loving terms with his wife, and he was greatly distressed in August 1658 by the death of his daughter Bettie. He was frugal, dressed plainly, and had little love for finery; his relaxations were hunting and hawking, smoking, and music. 'He lived', it was written, 'in the condition of a prince, with the moderation of a private man.'

It was inevitable that Cromwell should be attacked and defended in extreme terms. Devoted cavaliers joined forces with disappointed republicans to denounce him as a tyrant and a hypocrite. His admirers thought his reluctance to accept power was genuine, praised his efforts to restore civilian rule, and approved his defence of religious toleration for all but papists and prelatists. The disagreement has rolled on ever since. But few would deny him one attribute, competence, and his rule is a yardstick by which his predecessor and successor, Charles I and Charles II, look painfully inadequate. Cromwell's power was the astonishment of Europe and he was courted by kings and cardinals. Blake made the British navy a force to be reckoned with, and an expedition in 1655 captured Jamaica; in alliance with the French, Cromwellian troops won an important battle of the Dunes in June 1658. Edward Hyde, earl of Clarendon, for so long his adversary, gave grudging admiration. Though a wicked man, he was 'not a man of blood'; 'wickedness as great as his could never have accomplished those trophies without the assistance of a great spirit, an admirable circumspection and sagacity, and a most magnanimous resolution...as he grew into place and authority, his parts seemed to be renewed, as if he had concealed faculties till he had occasion to use them.' In December 1660 the new royalist Parliament ordered that the body of Cromwell be dug up and dragged to Tyburn. Samuel Pepys, a newly zealous royalist, wrote that 'it did trouble me, that a man of so great courage as he was should have that dishonour'.

COWARD, B., *Cromwell* (1991).

Cromwell, Richard, b. 4 Oct. 1626, 3rd but 1st surv. s. of Oliver Cromwell and Elizabeth Bourchier; m. Dorothy, da. of Richard Major of Hursley, Hants, 1 May 1649; issue: Oliver, Elizabeth, Anne, Letitia; d. 12 July 1712; bur. Hursley, Hants.

Richard served in the Parliaments of 1654 and 1656, and in 1657 was appointed to the Council of State and the Protectorate House of Lords. On his father's death in September 1658, he took over as Lord Protector. His manner was conciliatory and dignified, but effective power remained with the army, which he did not control. When the army resolved to recall the Long Parliament, Cromwell was forced out and beset by debt. He left England just before the Restoration and did not return until 1680. The rest of his life he passed in safe obscurity in Cheshunt, Hertfordshire.

Charles II, king of England and Scotland, b. 29 Mar. 1630, s. of Charles I and Henrietta Maria; acc. 30 Jan. 1649; rest. 29 May 1660; m. Catherine of Braganza, da. of John, king of Portugal, 21 May 1662; d. 6 Feb. 1685; bur. Westminster abbey.

Charles's features reflected his Italian ancestry on his mother's side, and he grew up tall, swarthy, and saturnine; 'Odd's Fish,' he told the painter Lely cheerfully, 'I am an ugly fellow.' His early years were happy, but when he was twelve civil war broke out in England. He was with his father at Edgehill and then at Oxford. When the king's cause collapsed, he rejoined his mother in France in July 1646. He was in Holland when he received news of his father's execution in January 1649. He was then approached by envoys from Scotland, where he had been proclaimed king, offering to support him in exchange for acceptance of the covenant and a presbyterian church order. He left for Scotland in the summer of 1650.

His position there became precarious after Cromwell had defeated the royalist army at Dunbar in September, but he was able to hold his coronation at Scone in January 1651. He then resolved on a desperate march into England, which, despite Charles's bravery, ended in disaster at Worcester, and was followed by his escape to France. The next seven years saw Cromwell in charge in England and afforded few opportunities to the royalists. But after Cromwell's death in 1658, his son Richard lost control of the situation, and power passed to Monck, military commander in Scotland. After he marched south in January 1660 events moved at an astonishing speed. From Breda in April, Charles issued a declaration promising religious toleration and a free Parliament, and on 8 May was proclaimed king in Westminster Hall. His return at the end of a month was a triumph.

Charles was then thirty. From his adventures and misfortunes he had learned wariness; there had been little to do in exile, and Charles had acquired a liking for entertainment and no great habit of application. Much of his time had been devoted to seductions and he was already father of a number of illegitimate children. His primary objective was not to go on his travels again, and he had been welcomed home mainly because he seemed to offer reconciliation and stability. Charles was much less vindictive than many ardent royalists wished, and the famous Act of Oblivion and Indemnity produced the jibe that it was oblivion for his friends and indemnity to his opponents. Nevertheless, the executions of Vane and Argyll show that Charles could also be unforgiving.

There is no clear pattern to Charles's reign, partly because he had no master plan and was content to respond to events. High on the list of decisions to be made was matrimony, and the choice fell upon Catherine of Braganza, a Portuguese princess. Charles treated his bride with courtesy and affection, but his liaisons with Lady Castlemaine, Nell Gwyn, and others continued, and no children were born of the marriage.

The euphoria that greeted Charles's return did not last. In 1665, Charles entered into an unnecessary war against the Dutch. It was unlucky that it coincided with two national disasters, the plague of 1665 and the Great Fire of London in 1666. The war itself produced little glory except a naval victory off Lowestoft at the beginning. The naval battle off the Downs in June 1666 was, at most, a draw, while the brilliant Dutch attack upon the English fleet at harbour in the Medway a year later was one of the greatest humiliations ever suffered by the country, the *Royal James* burned, the *Royal Charles* towed away to Holland. Pepys, in April 1667, wrote that most people he met agreed 'that we shall fall into a commonwealth in a few years whether we will or no...nor are things managed so well nowadays as it was heretofore'. Charles's response was to sacrifice his chief minister, Clarendon, who went into exile, and to change tack. He had already had difficulties with Parliament over his attempts to grant toleration to his catholic subjects, and he resented parliamentary scrutiny of his finances. In 1668 he put out feelers for a *rapprochement* with Louis XIV of France. Dutch power was to be destroyed in a co-ordinated attack, and in a secret treaty he offered, in exchange for a subsidy and, if necessary, an army of enforcement, to declare himself a catholic.

The Treaty of Dover (1670) has been admired by those who argue that Charles outwitted Louis with worthless promises. It is not a noble defence, nor does it meet the main objection. Charles's policy involved assisting France at a moment when many observers were alarmed at the rapid growth of French power. It placed the king in thrall to Louis. It involved Charles in a categorical lie to Parliament, and when, in 1674, he assured the two Houses that there was no secret treaty, it was observed that his hands shook. To help keep him straight, Louis kindly provided him with a new mistress, Louise de Kéroualle, created duchess of Portsmouth in 1673.

The dangers of Charles's policy were accentuated by the conversion of his brother, James, to catholicism in 1668. It was impossible to keep the matter secret. In 1672 Charles duly declared war on the Dutch. With his catholic advisers and James urging him to announce his conversion, he decided on a Declaration of Indulgence, offering toleration to protestant and catholic dissenters. But his government was almost bankrupt and Parliament demanded the Declaration's withdrawal, insisting that religious policy should be made by statute. Charles gave way, and Parliament, in a counter-attack, passed the Test Act, which prohibited catholics from public office. James was obliged to resign all his posts, including that of Lord High Admiral, which posed the question how a man who could not be trusted to serve the crown could become king.

Meanwhile, though Louis made great inroads into Dutch territory, the performance of his English allies was lacklustre. A sharp naval engagement in June 1672 off Southwold was a draw. The sea campaign going badly, Charles resolved on an invasion; the commander of the troops, Schomberg (borrowed from the French) dismissed them as 'a drunken rabble'. The Dutch refused to wait to be annihilated and inflicted a stinging defeat on Rupert's fleet off the Texel. With Parliament refusing to subsidize incompetence, the war had to be hastily wound up in 1674, leaving Charles to make his apologies to Louis.

Charles enjoyed a short respite before the next great storm. Revenue was beginning to rise as trade increased. The king was able to begin refashioning Windsor, rode winners at Newmarket, dabbled in scientific enquiry, sailed his yacht, and took a new mistress in Hortense Mancini, duchess of Mazarin. In 1677, as a counter-balance to suspicions of catholicism, he married his niece Mary to William of Orange, calvinist stadtholder of the Dutch Republic, urging on his nephew with broad jests. In August 1678, out of the blue, came the first allegations of a popish plot to assassinate the king. From the first, Charles had grave doubts about Titus Oates and scoffed at his assertion that the queen was proposing to poison him in revenge for his many infidelities. Before Christmas his chief minister, Danby, had been impeached, and the secretary to James executed as a traitor. In 1679 Parliament, urged on by Shaftesbury, brought in a bill to exclude James from the succession. Charles dissolved it. Summoned again in 1680, it refused supplies until James had been excluded. But the opposition suffered from three serious drawbacks. It was split whether the succession should go to William and Mary or to Monmouth, Charles's illegitimate son; its strength was in Parliament, which could be dismissed if the king could raise money; many people drew back from the prospect of another civil war. In March 1681, after he had negotiated another subsidy from Louis, Charles called a Parliament for Oxford and dismissed it after a week.

After 1681 Charles was in control. The Whig opposition was in disarray and Shaftesbury fled to Holland. A vigorous counter-attack filled the benches with loyal JPs and dozens of parliamentary boroughs had their charters remodelled to improve the chance of obtaining a friendly Parliament. Nonconformists were harried as never before, many of them dying in prison. The improvement in revenue allowed the creation of a substantial army. But although the apparatus of absolutist government was erected, Charles did little with it, content that he had secured the succession for his brother, James.

Charles's death in the spring of 1685 at the age of fifty-four was unexpected. A catholic priest was smuggled into the bedchamber and the king signified his acceptance. Polite to the end, he apologized for being 'an unconscionable time dying'. The link with Nell Gwyn gave him a popular reputation as 'the merry monarch', but he was good-humoured and courteous rather than light-hearted. Many observers testified to a basic coolness, a defensive detachment: 'he lived with his ministers', wrote Halifax, 'as he did with his mistresses: he used them, but he was not in love with them ... but if a hard thing was done to another man, he did not eat his supper the worse for it.'

HUTTON, R., *Charles II* (1989).

Regalia

The institution of an hereditary coronation regalia, serving as symbols of kingship, is attributed to the eleventh-century abbots of Westminster. Regarded as 'monuments of superstition and idolatry' by the Commonwealth authorities, much of it was sold or melted down for coinage in 1649, so new regalia was required for the coronation of Charles II in 1661.

The crown is the chief symbol: the remade St Edward's Crown regained its central role in the coronation ceremony in 1911, but the current Imperial State Crown (worn also on parliamentary occasions) is a replica of Victoria's lighter crown of 1838. The other main symbol is the sceptre, depicted on the coinage of Edward 'the Confessor' in 1057; the King's Sceptre, signifying temporal power, has from 1910 contained the Cullinan I diamond, while the Rod of Equity and Mercy, representing the spiritual role, bears a dove. Though shown on Edward's first seal (1055), the orb was not introduced into the regalia until the fifteenth century. Charles II's new 'Ball and Crosse of Gold' was damaged during Captain Blood's failed attempt to steal the Crown Jewels in 1671. The Swords of Temporal and Spiritual Justice were introduced in the early seventeenth century, but the present Sword of State dates from 1678; the broken point of the Sword of Mercy ('Curtana') symbolizes the tempering of royal justice by

continued

Regalia *continued*

clemency, while the Sword of Offering with which the new monarch is invested was added by George IV (1821). The present anointing spoon is twelfth-century, though the hollow golden eagle ampulla which holds the consecrated oil is Restoration. The Sovereign's Ring has been a constant feature since the tenth century, the present one being made for William IV (1831). Armillas (bracelets) have been used intermittently, but new ones were made for Elizabeth II in 1953, presented by the United Kingdom and seven Commonwealth governments. The first recorded use of spurs was in 1189 (for Richard I), the present St George's Spurs being fundamentally unchanged since 1661.

The English regalia is housed in the Jewel House of the Tower of London, on show to paying visitors since the 1660s. The 'Honours of Scotland' were feared lost following the Union in 1707, but were discovered in Edinburgh castle by Sir Walter Scott (1818), where they are now displayed with the Stone of Scone. They include a sceptre given to James IV (1494), a sword from pope Julius II (1507), and a crown made for James V in 1540.

Catherine of Braganza, queen of England and Scotland, b. 15 Nov. 1638, da. of John, king of Portugal, and Louisa, da. of the duke of Medina Sidonia; m. Charles II, 21 May 1662; d. 31 Dec. 1705; bur. Belem, Portugal.

The Portuguese, anxious for an alliance with England which would help to protect the newly won independence from Spain, offered substantial inducements for a marriage: Tangiers, Bombay, and a large dowry. The princess was small, brought up in some seclusion, and did not command languages. Charles reported cautiously that there was nothing in her face to disgust; in 1662, Pepys thought her 'not very charming', but a year later, seeing her riding with the king, decided she was 'mighty pretty'. She learned at an early stage to accept Charles's infidelities. The most important aspect of the marriage was her childlessness, leaving Charles's younger brother, James, as heir. Charles refused suggestions that he should divorce her, and stood by her during the Popish plot, when she was the victim of wild accusations that she intended to poison him. She remained in England after his death until 1692, spending the rest of her life in her native land.

Sophia, electress of Hanover, b. 13 Oct. 1630, da. of Frederick, Elector Palatine, and Elizabeth, da. of James I of England; m. Ernst August, later elector of Hanover, 30 Sept. 1658; issue: Georg Ludwig, Friedrich August, Maximilian, Sophia, Karl, Christian, Ernst; d. 8 June 1714; bur. Herrenhausen.

Granddaughter of James I, Sophia would have been queen of England if she had lived two months longer. The death in 1700 of princess Anne's only surviving child, the duke of Gloucester, led to the Act of Settlement, which gave the succession to the Hanoverian line. She was an intelligent and cultivated woman, and her niece Liselotte, married to Philippe, duke of Orléans, wrote 'you are the one person in all the world worthy of being a great queen'. She did not have the chance, and her son, Georg Ludwig, succeeded to the throne of Great Britain as George I.

James II, king of England and Ireland, James VII of Scotland, b. 14 Oct. 1633, 2nd s. of Charles I and Henrietta Maria; acc. 6 Feb. 1685; deemed to have abdic. 11 Dec. 1688; m. (1) Anne, da. of Edward Hyde (later earl of Clarendon), 3 Sept. 1660; issue: Mary, Anne; (2) Mary, da. of Alfonso IV of Modena, 30 Sept. 1673; issue: James, Louisa; d. 6 Sept. 1701; bur. St Edmund's, church of the English Benedictines, Paris.

James's conduct during his short reign was so inept that premature senility has been suggested. He inherited a stable throne, a healthy revenue, a large army, and a loyal Parliament, and within three years was in exile. A recent and sympathetic biographer has described James as 'utterly humourless, lacking the intellect to rise above the minutiae of government ... so egocentric that he was incapable of understanding the views of others'.

James was fifteen when his father was executed. He had escaped from England in 1648 disguised as a girl. In the 1650s he fought with gallantry in the army of Louis XIV and, after the *rapprochement* between Cromwell and Mazarin, transferred to the Spanish army. In 1658 he was at the battle of the Dunes, fighting against Cromwell's Englishmen. He accompanied his brother to England at the Restoration. In 1660 his marriage to Anne Hyde, the eight-months-pregnant daughter of Lord Clarendon, the king's chief minister, was thought a *mésalliance*.

Appointed Lord High Admiral in 1661, he was in command at the great victory over the Dutch off Lowestoft in 1665, and again in command during the third Dutch war, though sharing the honours off Southwold in 1672 with de Ruyter. James's difficulties then began. In

1668 he made a private conversion to catholicism, and when Parliament in 1673 passed the Test Act, forbidding catholics to hold public office, he was forced to resign. Henceforward the promotion of his religion was his main objective. By this time it seemed probable that Charles II would not have children by Catherine of Braganza and that James would succeed his brother on the throne. Alarmed protestants brought forward Monmouth, Charles's illegitimate son, as an alternative, and in the Exclusion crisis of 1679–81 Charles fought to preserve James's inheritance. James was sent to a safe distance to govern Scotland on behalf of his brother, where he used strong measures against the covenanters.

Surprisingly, James's accession in 1685 was undisputed. His first remarks were sensible. He had been accused, he told the Privy Council, of favouring arbitrary rule, but his intention was to preserve the constitution in church and state. Parliament voted him generous revenues, Louis sent him a new subsidy, and the coronation went off well. When Monmouth attempted an invasion in June 1685, it was crushed without difficulty, and James had him beheaded. Soon there was a change of tone. When Parliament in the autumn protested against filling the army with catholic officers in defiance of the Test Act James replied loftily 'I did not expect such an address from the House of Commons'; Parliament was prorogued and did not meet again in his reign. His drive to promote catholicism gathered pace. The great bastions of government—the law, the church, Parliament, the Privy Council, the army, the navy, the universities, and the bench of magistrates—all felt James's hand. In 1686, he dismissed six judges who had queried his dispensing power. In 1687, he issued a new Declaration of Indulgence giving toleration to dissenters, despite the fact that his brother's Declaration had been declared illegal by Parliament. Catholics were appointed to supreme command in Ireland and Scotland, and a catholic placed in charge of the channel fleet. A new commission of the peace in October 1686 dismissed 248 justices of the peace and appointed 460 new ones, two-thirds of them catholic. An ecclesiastical commission was set up to supervise the Church of England. Charles's campaign to remodel the parliamentary boroughs was revived and the Lords Lieutenant were dismissed if they refused to support the religious changes. Sunderland, the chief minister, announced his conversion to catholicism, and four catholics were brought into the Privy Council. The Vice-Chancellor of the university of Cambridge was dismissed, and the Fellows of Magdalen, Oxford, turned out of their college.

When James reissued the Declaration in 1688 his preamble observed, rather unnecessarily, that 'we cannot but heartily wish that all the people of our dominions were members of the Catholic Church'. Many of his co-religionists, including pope Innocent XI, were dismayed at his headlong campaign, fearing it would misfire. It did. The birth of a son to James in June 1688 raised the stakes by appearing to rule out the policy of waiting for the king to be succeeded by his protestant daughter, Mary. When James prosecuted seven bishops for refusing to endorse his Declaration, they were acquitted at Westminster amid cheers, and the message sent to William of Orange to intervene on behalf of English liberty.

When William landed at Torbay in November 1688, James's nerve broke. He was an experienced soldier with a large army and was in little personal danger, since William would hardly execute his own father-in-law. Nevertheless, James brooded on the fate of his father and of Richard II. He advanced to Salisbury where he was incapacitated by nose-bleeds. His support melted away. When William advanced towards London, James sent his wife and infant son to France and prepared to follow them. On 11 December he attempted to flee but bungled it. William, only too anxious to see him go, left the door open, and on 22 December James tried again, this time with success. Louis XIV received him kindly, placing St-Germain at his disposal; his courtiers, less charitably, remarked that 'when one listens to him, one understands why he is here'.

His attempt to recover Ireland ended on 1 July 1690 at the battle of the Boyne. James fled once more, explaining, 'I do now propose to shift for myself'. His folly may have put back the cause of catholic toleration by a hundred years.

MILLER, J., *James II* (1978).

Anne Hyde, b. 12 Mar. 1637, da. of Edward Hyde (later earl of Clarendon) and Frances, da. of Sir Thomas Aylesbury; m. James, duke of York (later James II), 3 Sept. 1660; issue: Mary, Anne; d. 31 Mar. 1671; bur. Westminster abbey.

Both of Anne Hyde's daughters became queen of England. Anne was a maid-of-honour to Mary, wife of William II of Orange and sister to Charles II and James II. James made an engagement of marriage with her in 1659 and married her in England soon after the Restoration, when she was eight months pregnant. Four sons and two daughters died as infants. The duke continued to have mistresses but Anne's influence over him was said to be considerable. She converted to catholicism shortly before she died from cancer at the age of thirty-four. Pepys thought her plain, and she grew plump, but was said to enter a room like queen Elizabeth.

Mary of Modena, queen of England and Scotland, b. 5 Oct. 1658, da. of Alfonso IV of Modena and Laura, da. of Girolamo Martinozzi, cousin of cardinal Mazarin; m. James, duke of York (later James II), 30 Sept. 1673; issue: James, Louisa; d. 7 May 1718; bur. Chaillot, France.

Mary became the second wife of James, duke of York in 1673, by which time it seemed probable that Charles II would have no legitimate children. Her hope had been to enter a convent, but she was persuaded to marry James as a sacrifice for her religion. She was described as tall, dark, good-looking, and with attractive eyes. Four daughters and a son did not survive, but in June 1688 she gave birth to her son James, who lived to become 'the Old Pretender'. The rumour that her pregnancy had not been genuine was no more than a desperate political ploy. She fled to France in December 1688 with her young son and was shortly followed by the king. The rest of her life was spent in exile, mainly at St-Germain-en-laye.

James Scott, duke of Monmouth, b. 9 Apr. 1649, s. of Charles II and Lucy Walter; m. Anne, countess of Buccleuch, da. of Francis, earl of Buccleuch, and Margaret, da. of John, earl of Rothes, 20 Apr. 1663; issue: Charles, John; d. 15 July 1685; bur. Tower of London.

Charles II was eighteen and in exile when his liaison with Lucy Walter produced his first illegitimate son. The boy was reckoned remarkably handsome, and other fathers have been suggested. He was brought to London in 1662 and became a great favourite with the king, who gave him the dukedom of Monmouth in February 1663. Monmouth was present at the naval victory off Lowestoft in 1665 and fought as an army officer in the second and third Dutch wars. The conversion of James, duke of York, to catholicism brought Monmouth into play as a possible protestant successor to Charles II. In 1679 he was given command of the forces sent to suppress the covenanters in Scotland, which he did at Bothwell Bridge, but he lost favour with Charles. Accused of complicity in the Rye House plot (1683), he was sent into exile. Returning after James's accession to lead an invasion, his army was crushed at Sedgemoor in 1685. James refused to pardon him and he was executed in the Tower.

William III, king of England, Ireland, and Scotland, b. 4 Nov. 1650, s. of Wilhelm II, prince of Orange, and Mary, da. of Charles I and Henrietta Maria; acc. 13 Feb. 1689; m. Mary, da. of James, duke of York (later James II), 4 Nov. 1677; d. 8 Mar. 1702; bur. Westminster abbey.

William, known as 'William of Orange' from his small principality near Avignon in France, was the nephew of Charles II and James II. His father died of smallpox a week before William was born, and his mother died of the same disease when he was ten. The influence of the House of Orange in the Dutch Republic was in decline, but his prospects improved in 1660 when his uncle was restored to the throne of England. In 1670 he made his first visit to England, visiting Parliament and receiving honorary degrees from the two universities. Charles was personally gracious but did not confide to his nephew that he had just signed a secret agreement with Louis XIV to launch a co-ordinated attack on the Dutch. Two years later England and the Netherlands were at war, but this worked to William's advantage. Louis's shattering onslaught smashed the oligarchical regime of De Witt, who was murdered, and William was brought forward to save his country as Captain and Admiral-General.

In 1675 William survived an attack of smallpox and the following year was wounded in the arm while fighting the French. His supporters urged him to marry to safeguard the interests of the Orange family, and in 1677 he arrived in England to negotiate a marriage with Mary, eldest daughter of James, duke of York. By 1677 it was clear that Charles's marriage would probably not produce children. Four of James's sons had already died as infants, and a fifth, by his second wife, was about to last one month. Unless Charles decided to put forward his illegitimate son, the duke of Monmouth, Mary would succeed to the throne. Her father, James, objected strongly to the marriage, but the king consented in order to strengthen his protestant credentials. The bride, aged fifteen, wept copiously, and the court observed, with concern, a groom who was very short, asthmatic, hunched, taciturn, and ill-at-ease. Louis XIV, well understanding the diplomatic implications, wrote reproachfully to his co-religionist James that 'you have given your daughter to my mortal enemy'.

The conclusion of the war between Louis and the Dutch in 1678 gave William a brief respite. His marriage settled into one of deep affection, though no children were born; his relations with Elizabeth Villiers, which caused Mary anguish, were, in view of his health, more probably for show than pleasure. William's great relaxation was hunting. He had no great interest in books or music, but spent lavishly on gardens and furniture, particularly at Honselaersdijck and at Het Loo, started in 1685.

The interests of William and Mary were directly involved in the Exclusion crisis of 1679–81, during which the Whig opposition tried to remove James from the succession, which would make Mary next in line for the throne. William remained cautious. The opposition collapsed and James succeeded in 1685 without protest or limitations. When Monmouth launched an invasion later that year, he paid for it with his life.

James's behaviour as king proved that the Whigs had been right to insist that he could not be trusted with power. When, in June 1688, James's son was born, William received a message from 'the immortal seven' begging his help. The risks in responding to the appeal were great. Many Englishmen would resent interference from a country with which they had been at war three times during William's lifetime. James had a large army and a powerful fleet; the expedition might fail, as Monmouth's had. Louis XIV might take the opportunity to launch another attack upon the Dutch as soon as William set sail. What in the end persuaded him to move was his conviction that Louis was bent on universal power and could be prevented only by a coalition which included the English and the Dutch. Despite a storm when he set out, the expedition was totally successful. James's position collapsed ignominiously and he fled to France. William made it clear that he was not willing to serve as Mary's consort, and Parliament offered them the throne in February 1689 as joint rulers, with 'the sole and full exercise of the regal power' to be with him.

The remainder of William's life was devoted to securing his position and attempting to frustrate Louis's plans. First was the task of obtaining submission to the new regime within the British Isles. The Scottish Parliament insisted on a presbyterian church establishment, which William was prepared to agree to, and a Jacobite rising under Viscount Dundee was defeated after Killiecrankie in July 1689. The subjugation of the Highlands led in 1692 to the massacre of Glencoe, and though William was not directly involved, his opponents accused him of butchery. The reconquest of Ireland took longer and was close run. James had taken possession of most of Ireland in 1689 and held a Parliament at Dublin in May. Londonderry held out for the protestant cause and was relieved in July, but another year passed before William in person won the decisive victory of the Boyne.

The thirteen years William spent in England as king were far from agreeable and on several occasion he threatened to return to the Netherlands. The war against Louis dragged on until 1697 with few victories to offset serious defeats at Steenkirke in 1692 and Neerwinden in 1693. After three years of peace it became clear that a further instalment of the long struggle against French supremacy was about to start, though William did not live to see it. Mary's death from smallpox in 1694 was a great grief to him, and campaigning had taken its toll of his health. His new subjects complained bitterly of his Dutch friends, and Parliament resumed its old struggle against the influence of the crown. After the crisis of 1679–81, it was anxious to weaken the royal prerogative, granting William customs for four years only in 1689 in order to ensure frequent Parliaments, and bolting the door in 1694 with a Triennial Act that necessitated a Parliament at least every three years. Further limitations were imposed by the Act of Settlement in 1701, made necessary by the death of Anne's only surviving child, the duke of Gloucester.

William survived an assassination plot in 1696, which produced public expressions of concern for his welfare. In 1699 Parliament ordered his Dutch Blue Guards out of the country; when William asked, as an act of kindness, for them to remain, he was told, peremptorily, that he should entrust his safety to his English subjects. In February 1702 his horse stumbled at Hampton Court over a mole-hill and the king broke his collar-bone; his lungs congested, and within a fortnight he was dead.

Attention moved at once to the new queen, who declared that her heart was 'entirely English'. William's funeral at midnight was so low-keyed that bishop Burnet thought it 'scarce decent'; though the Privy Council ordered a monument, no one troubled to erect it. It was left to Defoe in 1705 to launch a blistering attack upon English ingratitude. William, he pointed out, had undertaken an invasion, at the risk of his life, to save them from what they believed to be popish despotism. In return, he had been treated with suspicion and dislike that 'ate into his very soul, tired it with serving an unthankful nation, and absolutely broke his heart'.

BAXTER, S., *William III* (1966).

Kensington palace, London

Originally a Jacobean house in Kensington village, then a private residence of the Finch family known as Nottingham House, it was purchased by William III from the 2nd earl of Nottingham in 1689, since it better suited William's asthma than Whitehall and was nearer London than Hampton Court. Wren was instructed to enlarge it, and it became a favourite if modest home, both William and Mary dying there. The orangery was added by Anne, who also died there. William Kent then transformed the King's Staircase and interior aspects for George I, and the Round Pond and Serpentine in the gardens were completed by his successor. Both George II and his wife Caroline loved the place, but George III preferred Buckingham House, and the palace fell into disrepair. Subsequent alterations (heavily distorting Wren's original designs) enabled other members of the royal family to have suites in Kensington palace, hence the births there of Victoria to the duchess of Kent (1819) and Mary (future wife of George V) to the duchess of Teck (1867). It is still used as a royal residence. The state apartments were restored and opened to the public in 1899, and include a permanent exhibition of court dress; the palace gardens had become increasingly accessible to the public from the time of George II, and now include the Albert Memorial.

Mary II, queen of England, Ireland, and Scotland, b. 30 Apr. 1662, da. of James, duke of York (later James II), and Anne Hyde, da. of Edward, earl of Clarendon; acc. 13 Feb. 1689; m. William of Orange (later William III), 4 Nov. 1677; d. 28 Dec. 1694; bur. Westminster abbey.

Mary was brought up as a protestant and remained so after her parents converted to catholicism. She was above average height, graceful, with dark hair and a good complexion. Pepys saw her as a girl of seven dancing so finely 'almost to ravish me'. The marriage to her cousin William was proposed by Charles II to improve his standing with his protestant subjects, though disliked by her father, an ardent catholic. Mary, aged fifteen, was unenthusiastic, 'weeping all afternoon and the following day'. William was short, unimpressive, and reserved. Liselotte, niece to the electress Sophia, reported that at the public ceremony, the groom 'went to bed in woollen drawers': when Charles suggested removing them, William replied stolidly that 'he was accustomed to wearing his woollens and had no intention of changing now'.

After this inauspicious start, the marriage prospered, though William kept a mistress and was rumoured to have an interest in young men. Unless James's second marriage produced a healthy boy, Mary would inherit the throne of England on his death. When James's son was born in June 1688, Mary's sister Anne persuaded her that the pregnancy had been false and a substitute baby smuggled in with the warming-pan. Mary gave whole-hearted support to William's expedition against her father in November 1688 and joined him in England in February 1689.

The settlement of the succession was complex. Mary's preference was that William should become regent for her father, but that was impracticable. William refused to act only as consort to his wife and they were declared joint rulers. To safeguard William's position should Mary die before him, princess Anne agreed to postpone her right to succeed, which led to bad feeling. In practice, Mary left affairs of state to her husband, though governing formally during his absences. Her letters to William show great affection and concern for his safety. In December 1694 she caught smallpox and died at the age of thirty-two. Her burial service was impressive and immortalized by Henry Purcell's great funeral music.

Anne, queen of England, Scotland, and Ireland, and (from 1707) of Great Britain, b. 6 Feb. 1665, da. of James, duke of York (later James II), and Anne Hyde, da. of Edward, earl of Clarendon; acc. 8 Mar. 1702; m. George, s. of Frederick III of Denmark, 28 July 1683; issue: Mary, Anne Sophia, William, Mary, George; d. 1 Aug. 1714; bur. Westminster abbey.

For the first half of her life there was little reason to think that Anne might become queen. When she was born, her uncle Charles II had already demonstrated his capacity to produce children out of wedlock and might, in due course, produce them within it. Her father, James, heir to the throne, was thirty-two and likely to have more sons. Her elder sister, Mary, and any children she might have would take precedence. The revolution of 1688 changed all that.

The two princesses were brought up as protestants under the supervision of Henry Compton, bishop of London. Anne's mother died when she was six. Her father's conversion to catholicism and second marriage to a woman Anne regarded as 'a very great bigot' put distance between them. In compensation she had close friendships with Sarah Jennings, later duchess of Marlborough, and with Frances Apsley, whom she addressed in effusive letters as 'Semandra', signing herself 'Ziphares'. In 1683 she married prince George of Denmark, with whom she was very happy, though only one of their children survived infancy. When James succeeded to the throne in 1685 he made some slight efforts to convert her, which she resisted strongly. She was among the first to doubt the genuineness of the queen's pregnancy, writing of the new baby in June 1688 that 'it may be that it is our brother, but God only knows'.

When William of Orange, Mary's husband, invaded in November 1688, the defections of Anne and prince George were heavy blows to James. In the settlement of 1689, William insisted on joint rule with Mary, and to preserve his position in case the queen predeceased him, Anne agreed to postpone her own right of succession. This created an awkward situation, and Anne's position in the 1690s was irksome. She clung for comfort to John and Sarah Churchill, calling them 'Mr and Mrs Freeman', and signing herself 'Mrs Morley'. William she referred to as 'Caliban' or 'the Dutch monster', and looked forward to the 'sunshine day' when she would succeed him. In 1692 she refused to dismiss Sarah, quarrelled bitterly with the queen, and did not see her again before her death from smallpox in 1694. Formal relations with William improved after Mary's death, but Anne's health began to deteriorate. She suffered from gout and had severe eye trouble, while her husband became corpulent and asthmatic. Plagued by multiple miscarriages, she suffered another blow in 1700 when her only surviving child, William, duke of Gloucester, died at the age of ten, which necessitated declaring the Hanoverian line successors, as the nearest protestant relatives.

The famous speech on her accession that 'I know my heart to be entirely English' was therefore a political manifesto and an opportunity to pay off family scores. But in succeeding William she also succeeded to his policy of resisting French aggrandizement, and war was declared within two months. It dominated the rest of her reign. She was very short of governmental experience and relied heavily at first upon the Churchills. Her main principles were to preserve the Church of England and to avoid becoming prisoner of either Whigs or Tories. But retaining independence of action did not prove easy. The high point of her reign was the extraordinary victory won by Churchill, now duke of Marlborough, at Blenheim in 1704. It was followed in 1707 by the Act of Union with Scotland, designed to avoid a disastrous rift between the two countries in the middle of a great war. By this time Anne's friendship with Sarah was showing signs of strain in the face of her incessant demands for honours and places for her friends. In August 1708 Sarah and the queen had a blazing row in the state coach *en route* to a thanksgiving service at St Pauls to celebrate Marlborough's triumph at Oudenarde. In October 1708 the prince of Denmark died, to Anne's great grief. The long friendship finished in rancour and recrimination. To Marlborough the queen wrote in October 1709: 'I believe nobody was ever so used by a friend as I have been since my coming to the Crown. I desire nothing but that she would leave off teasing and tormenting me.' This was a prelude to the political upset which followed in 1710, placing Harley and the Tories in power for the rest of her reign, and setting in train the negotiations which wound up the war with France.

In 1707 Sir John Clerk commented on the contrast between the triumphant queen and the shattered woman who hobbled round her palaces on crutches: 'Her Majesty was labouring under a fit of the gout, and in extreme pain and agony ... Her face, which was red and spotted, was rendered something frightful by her negligent dress, and the foot affected was tied up with a poultice and some nasty bandages ... Nature seems inverted when a poor infirm woman becomes one of the rulers of the world.'

Anne had serious illnesses in 1711 and 1713, and her last years were increasingly dominated by the succession question. There can be little doubt that she had some sympathy for the Stuarts. As early as 1691 she had written a letter of 'duty and submission' to her father, and in 1701 had thought it 'monstrous' that William had fobidden her to dress her lodgings in mourning for James's death. But though the Jacobites retained great hopes, nothing materialized, and she told her physician in 1713 that the Pretender was 'a poor creature'. She seems to have aimed at a balancing act, holding aloof from both sides. Her relations with the family in Hanover were correct but cold. When the electress suggested in 1714 that a member of her family should take up residence in England, the queen replied that it would be 'contrary to my royal authority' and that nothing could be more disagreeable. How much she understood when, on her deathbed, she handed the stick of office to Lord Shrewsbury, thus confirming the Hanoverian succession, must be doubtful.

Anne's popularity was great, and her reign looked back on as glorious and golden. Sarah erected at Blenheim a magnificent statue of her by Rysbrack, majestic and imposing, but her private opinion of Anne was rather at variance: 'she certainly, as is said on the inscription, meant well and was no fool; but nobody can maintain that she was wise, nor entertaining in conversation. She was in everything what I described her: ignorant in everything but what the parsons had taught her as a child.' 'Her drawing rooms', wrote Lord Chesterfield, 'were more respectable than agreable, and had more the air of sollemn places of worship, than the gayety of a court.'

GREGG, E., *Queen Anne* (1980).

Queen Anne's Bounty

On the queen's birthday in 1704 the government introduced in the House of Commons plans for the Crown to surrender its traditional income from tenths of benefices and first fruits (a tax, usually of the first year's income, paid to a feudal or ecclesiastical superior) to the Church of England, for the relief of poorer clergy. These moneys had been appropriated from the papacy after the Reformation, to become a source of royal revenue; during the Commonwealth they had been used to support preachers and schoolmasters, but Charles II put them to non-ecclesiastical ends such as maintenance of his bastards. Bishop Burnet had already suggested to William III that this bounty should be directed towards the more needy, and Anne's move was immediately popular and beneficial since some livings were worth barely £10 a year.

George, prince of Denmark, b. 2 Apr. 1653, s. of Frederick III of Denmark and Sophia Amelia, da. of George, duke of Brunswick-Lüneburg; m. princess (later queen) Anne, 28 July 1683; d. 28 Oct. 1708; bur. Westminster abbey.

Prince George was reputed to be stolid and uninteresting, but his marriage to Anne was a great success in everything but the production of healthy children. At the English court he was nicknamed 'Est-il possible?' from his habitual ejaculation. In 1688 he and the princess joined William of Orange, but they were not on good terms with him for much of his reign. Anne failed to secure for her consort the title of king, but he was appointed Generalissimo and Lord High Admiral. He became fat, suffered greatly from asthma, and, to the queen's great grief, died in October 1708. In a formal letter, Anne wrote that she had lost 'an inestimable treasure'.

James Francis Edward Stuart, b. 10 June 1688, s. of James II and Mary of Modena; m. Maria Clementina, da. of James Sobiewski, 28 May 1719; issue: Charles Edward, Henry; d. 1 Jan. 1766, bur. St Peter's, Rome.

James Stuart, 'the Old Pretender', is one of the submerged characters of British history. He was 'the warming-pan baby' of 1688, whose birth precipitated James II's downfall, and was taken by his mother to France in December. He remained all his life a devoted catholic, refusing to change his religion for political advantage. On the death of his father in September 1701, he was declared king as James III and VIII, and recognized by Louis XIV. His main attempt to recapture the throne came in the winter of 1715 when he spent six weeks in Scotland. Cold and disconsolate, the impression he created was not heartening; 'our men asked if he could speak', wrote one Jacobite. His marriage to a granddaughter of John Sobiewski was not successful and his wife left him after five years. He was a spectator of the gallant effort by his son Charles in 1745–6, and fell subsequently into a pious melancholy. The poet Thomas Gray saw him in Rome in 1740 and was disparaging: 'a thin, ill-made man, extremely tall and awkward, of a most unpromising countenance, a good deal resembling King James the Second, and has extremely the air and look of an idiot, particularly when he laughs or prays. The first he does not often, the latter continually.'

William, duke of Gloucester, b. 24 July 1689, s. of princess (later queen) Anne and George, prince of Denmark; d. 30 July 1700; bur. Westminster abbey.

William, the only one of Anne's children to survive infancy, was a cheerful little boy and a great admirer of his uncle, William III. His death in 1700 resulted in recourse to the Hanoverian line.

Charles Edward Stuart, b. 31 Dec. 1720, s. of James Stuart ('the Old Pretender') and Clementina, da. of James Sobiewski; m. Louise, da. of Gustav Adolf of Stolberg-Gedern and Elizabeth, da. of Maximilian de Hornes, 28 Mar. 1772; d. 31 Jan. 1788; bur. Frascati, Italy.

In 'Bonnie Prince Charlie', 'the Young Pretender', the Jacobite cause at last found a man who had some qualities of leadership. Unfortunately for him, his enterprise in 1745 came thirty years too late. The Hanoverians had been allowed to establish themselves in England, the critical arena, where the response to the Jacobite appeal was derisory.

James Francis Edward Stuart. The 'Old Pretender' spent all his life in exile, save for six unpleasant weeks in Scotland in the winter of 1715–16, when he caught a heavy cold.

Fair-haired, blue-eyed, and slim, Charles was twenty-four when he landed with seven followers on Eriskay on 2 August 1745. Highland support enabled him to take Perth and Edinburgh, and to defeat Cope's scratch army at Prestonpans on 21 September. Charles crossed the English border near Carlisle on 8 November with an army of some four thousand men. They reached Derby without gaining many English recruits and on 5 December, at a council of war, resolved to retreat. Only Charles argued for the advance to continue. Both sides were right. A further advance was extremely hazardous, yet it probably represented the only chance of success remaining. The retreat ended at Culloden in April 1746, when Charles's disposition of his men was not good, and his troops were slaughtered. After a daring escape, with the help of Flora Macdonald, he made his way back to France by September 1746.

The rest of his life in exile was a sad anti-climax. He took to drink and became sleepy and corpulent. In 1766 he succeeded his father, taking the title Charles III, but was recognized by few courts. His marriage in 1772 was a disaster and his wife left him for the poet, Alfieri. Horace Mann reported in 1773 that he was 'seldom quite sober'. His funeral service was conducted by his brother, Cardinal York, who succeeded him as the titular Henry IX.

Henry Stuart, Cardinal York, b. 6 Mar. 1725, s. of James Stuart ('the Old Pretender') and Clementina, da. of James Sobiewski; d. 13 July 1807; bur. St Peter's, Rome.

The younger brother of 'Bonnie Prince Charlie', Cardinal York was regarded by Jacobites as the rightful Henry IX, succeeding his brother on 31 January 1788. His creation as cardinal in 1747 did little to help the Jacobite cause in England. During the French Revolution he fell on hard times and was given a pension by George III. He left the English crown jewels, taken away by James II, to the prince regent who, in return, paid for a handsome monument by Canova in St Peter's.

Hanoverians

The dynastic connection between Britain and Hanover, which lasted from 1714 until 1837, was purely fortuitous. Elizabeth, daughter of James I, had married the Elector Palatine in 1613: their daughter, Sophia, married Ernst August of Hanover in 1658. The English, having repudiated James II and his son in 1688, were in a predicament when Mary, William, and Anne failed to produce a surviving child. The death of Anne's son, William, in 1700 led to the Act of Settlement, which

CHARLES EDOUARD D'ANGLETERRE PRINCE DE GALLES

Charles Edward Stuart. Copy of a pastel drawing of Bonnie Prince Charlie done in France in 1748, soon after Charles's return from the heroic Scottish adventure. Many copies and engravings were made for Jacobite sympathisers.

placed the succession with Sophia, as the nearest protestant relative. The connection was far from popular. The Hanoverians had a ruler whom they rarely saw and were in danger of being dragged into British wars; the British complained that they often had to give up colonial conquests at the end of a war to recover Hanover. George I suggested that the link should be broken, but his son did not act on the advice; in

George III's reign, the connection became of less importance, since he never visited his German dominions. The royal family was often referred to as the House of Brunswick, after the original duchy. Under the operation of the Salic law, which forbade the succession of women, the link ended in 1837 when Victoria became queen of England, and her uncle, Ernest Augustus, duke of Cumberland, became king of Hanover.

George I, elector of Hanover and king of Great Britain and Ireland, b. 28 May 1660, s. of Ernst August (later elector of Hanover), and Sophia, da. of Frederick, Elector Palatine; acc. 1 Aug. 1714; m. Sophia Dorothea, da. of Georg Wilhelm, duke of Lüneburg-Celle, 21 Nov. 1682; issue: Georg August, Sophia Dorothea; d. 11 June 1727; bur. Leineschloss church, Hanover, rebur. Herrenhausen.

Georg Ludwig had been elector of Hanover for sixteen years when he succeeded Anne on the throne of Britain in 1714. His family were the nearest protestant descendants of James I, through his grandmother, Elizabeth, queen of Bohemia. He had paid one visit to England in 1680/1 when a marriage to princess Anne was under consideration, but nothing came of it. His subsequent marriage to his cousin proved unfortunate. Sophia Dorothea had a passionate affair with Count Königsmarck. In 1694 the count was ambushed at Hanover and never seen again; rumour said that his body was buried under the palace floors. Sophia Dorothea was divorced and Jacobites took the opportunity to hint that George's children were not his own.

From 1701 the English succession beckoned. George's main interest was in the consolidation and extension of Hanover, and he hoped that English naval power would help him gain Bremen and Verden at the expense of Sweden. He joined England in the Grand Alliance against Louis XIV and was disgusted when the Tories, after their election victory in 1710, made a separate peace with France. There were also rumours that the Tory leaders, Harley and St John, were conspiring to bring back the Stuarts. George urged Anne to allow a member of the Hanoverian family to reside in England, but met with a sharp rebuff. Nevertheless, his succession in 1714 was effected without immediate opposition.

George was fifty-four when he arrived at Greenwich in September 1714. He was an experienced soldier, a knowledgeable diplomat, and a tried ruler. In character he was stolid and uncommunicative, handicapped by a modest command of English, and set in his ways. He travelled little and seemed to have limited interest in his new realm. His original policy, like that of his predecessors Anne and William, was to employ advisers irrespective of party, but the flirtation of some Tories with the Jacobite court ruled out some, and others were reluctant to serve. He finished up with a Whig ministry and was increasingly identified with that party. This prompted the Tories to complain that he surrounded himself with Germans, and to make fun of his middle-aged mistress, created duchess of Kendal in 1719.

George succeeded in his first objective, and the British navy helped to extract Bremen and Verden from Sweden in 1719. In Britain, his task was to consolidate the new dynasty, giving it time to take root. He faced a serious Jacobite rebellion in 1715, but it was ill-coordinated and the French, at peace after more than twenty years of gruelling warfare, were unwilling to send assistance. In 1720, the monarchy was scorched by the South Sea bubble, in which the king, his mistress, and his half-sister (later countess of Darlington) had invested heavily, but public anger was diverted to the directors of the Company. More damaging was a furious and embarrassing quarrel with his son, the future George II, which coincided with a rift between the Whig ministers, Stanhope and Sunderland, and Walpole and Townshend. In 1717 the king commanded the prince to leave St James's palace, took control of the education of his children, and not until April 1720 was a strained reconciliation achieved.

From 1721, with Walpole in power, George I had more time to relax. He was interested in science, fond of music, laid out Kensington Gardens, made improvements to Hampton Court, visited nearby country houses, played cards, and hunted. He had little desire to seek popularity and preferred quiet evenings to court entertainments and receptions. He made five lengthy visits to Hanover, and on the sixth was struck down by a heart attack near Osnabrück, eighty miles from his palace of Herrenhausen at Hanover. Few contemporaries were impressed by George I. Lady Mary Wortley Montagu called him 'an honest blockhead ... our customs and laws were all mysteries to him, which he neither tried to understand, or was capable of understanding'. Lord Chesterfield thought him 'an honest, dull German gentleman, as unfit as unwilling to act the part of a king ... lazy and inactive, even in his pleasures, which were therefore lowly sensual ... England was too big for him'.

HATTON, R., *George I* (1978).

Sophia Dorothea, b. 3 Feb. 1666, da. of Georg Wilhelm, duke of Lüneburg-Celle, and Eléonore Desmiers d'Olbreuse; m. Georg Ludwig (later George I), 22 Nov. 1682; d. 3 Nov. 1726; bur. Celle.

The marriage of Sophia Dorothea to her cousin ended in disaster. In the 1690s, she became involved in a passionate affair with Count Königsmarck. In 1694 he was waylaid at the palace and never seen again; she was divorced and spent the rest of her days at Ahlden in Celle, without access to her children. Her confinement was strict but comfortable, with servants and visitors. George II was reputed to be devoted to the memory of a mother he never saw after the age of eleven. The florid love-letters between Sophia and Königsmarck have been published.

George II, king of Great Britain and Ireland, b. 30 Oct. 1683, s. of Georg Ludwig (later George I) and Sophia Dorothea; acc. 11 June 1727; m. Caroline, da. of Johann Friedrich, margrave of Brandenburg-Anspach, 22 Aug. 1705; issue: Frederick, Anne, Amelia, Caroline, George, William, Mary, Louisa; d. 25 Oct. 1760; bur. Westminster abbey.

George II spent his first thirty years in Hanover, where the most important event of his boyhood was his parents' divorce when he was eleven; he never saw his mother again. In 1705 he married Caroline of Anspach, an imposing and handsome woman, to whom, despite the existence of mistresses, he was devoted. He won a considerable reputation in 1708 when fighting at Oudenarde under the command of Marlborough.

The impression he made in England when he arrived in September 1714 with his father was agreeable. He was small but sturdy, spoke English well, though with a heavy accent, and was far more sociable than his father. His wife was a great asset, particularly since there was no queen. The prince's court was more lively than that of his father, he was less dependent upon German friends, and flattering in his admiration of things English. There was rivalry between the two courts, which erupted in 1717 into a furious public quarrel. The initial cause was a dispute with the duke of Newcastle at the christening of the prince's son, but the king's reaction suggests simmering resentment. If the prince behaved foolishly, the king was absurdly heavy, ordering his son out of the palace, and taking custody of his children. Not until 1720 was there even a formal reconciliation, and onlookers remarked that the king and prince remained tense and aloof.

News of his accession in June 1727 was brought to him at Richmond by Sir Robert Walpole, his father's chief minister. Although George II at once named Sir Spencer Compton as minister, Walpole was reinstated within a few days, with Caroline using her influence on his behalf. Walpole remained in office for the next fifteen years, giving stability to the first half of George's reign. A brilliant account of the king's domestic life, spent largely at St James's palace, Kensington palace, and Hampton Court, is given in Lord Hervey's *Memoirs*, though the sparkle is plentifully spiced with malice. The king's temper was extremely uncertain. He enjoyed a routine of hunting and cards, diversified by summer visits to Hanover; the princess royal explained to Hervey that when her father was at 'his most peevish and snappish', it was not because of an affair of state but because 'some housemaid set a chair where it does not use to stand'. In December 1728, without enthusiasm, the king sent for his son, Frederick, from Hanover. Very soon the prince and the rest of the royal family were on terms of unmitigated hatred. Curiously enough, this saved the prince from most of the king's irritability, since his father would not speak to him or of him. In 1737, when the prince drove his wife in labour from Hampton Court so that she would not give birth under his father's roof, there was a violent quarrel which replayed many of the scenes from 1717–20. The prince was ordered out of St James's palace, and set up at Leicester House, where he began organizing an opposition to Walpole that contributed a good deal to his overthrow in 1742.

In November 1737 queen Caroline died of an undisclosed rupture. That the king was greatly upset is not in doubt, but he comforted himself by bringing over from Hanover his current mistress, Mme Walmoden, created countess of Yarmouth in 1740. Walpole's retirement in 1742 triggered off several years of political confusion, which agitated the king greatly. He had long admired Lord Carteret, who spoke German well and was familiar with European diplomacy. Carteret took office as secretary of state, advocating a more forward policy in Europe. Britain intervened in the War of the Austrian Succession, which had started when Frederick 'the Great', George's nephew, had seized Silesia from Maria Theresa of Austria. In 1743, George took personal command of an army put into the field to assist her, winning an important victory over the French at Dettingen, and demonstrating great courage. But Carteret, who had been present at the battle, was soon on bad terms with the remnants of Walpole's team, the Pelham brothers and Lord Hardwicke, and in 1744, to the king's disgust, he was forced to resign. The king, as was his wont, alternately sulked and stormed at his ministers: 'I am weary of you all', he told Lord Harrington. From politics he was given a brief respite in the autumn of 1745 by the Jacobite invasion, which caught George on his regular Hanover visit. He made a leisurely return, professing no doubt about the outcome, and calling his youngest son, William, duke of Cumberland, from Flanders to deal with the rebels. Once the Scots had retired to their own country, political battle could be resumed, and his ministers made a collective resignation in February 1746 to force his hand. George tried to float a Carteret ministry, with the support of Lord Bath, but it was stillborn. He was forced to make the best terms he could with the returning ministers, confirming Henry Pelham as chief minister and submitting, gloomily, to finding an office for young William Pitt, who had given mortal offence by his shrill attacks upon Hanover.

The disaster was a blessing in disguise. George learned to get on well with Pelham and in 1751, in a gesture of reconciliation, Carteret was brought back in a dignified senior post. The same year, the prince of Wales died at the age of forty-four, leaving his twelve-year-old son as the heir apparent. When Pelham died unexpectedly in 1754 the king remarked, with some prescience, 'Now I shall have no more peace'. The duke of Newcastle took over his brother's ministry, but was forced to resign in 1756 after the Seven Years War had opened disastrously with the loss of Braddock's army in America (July 1755) and the capture of Minorca by the French (June 1756). The king was outraged at the failure of Admiral Byng to relieve Minorca, and refused the appeal for mercy made by his court martial. Newcastle's administration was followed by a Pitt–Devonshire ministry, which the king disliked, but in 1757 the Pitt–Newcastle coalition gave George a stable coalition for the rest of his reign. The new government got off to a bad start, with the failure of expeditions against Louisbourg and Rochefort. Worst of all, from the king's point of view, was news that his son, the duke of Cumberland, in command of a force assisting Frederick 'the Great' in Germany, had signed an armistice with the French at Kloster-Zevern on humiliating terms. George reacted in fury, repudiated the agreement, and recalled his son. When Cumberland in October 1757 reached Kensington palace he found the old king playing cards: 'here is my son', George greeted him, 'who has ruined me and disgraced himself.' Cumberland resigned all his military posts and never served again. From this nadir, the balance of the war tipped until George's reign ended in triumph, with heady victories at Minden, Quebec, Quiberon Bay, and in 1760 at

Wandewash, which secured British supremacy in India. By this time the king was almost blind and increasingly deaf, but he remained in touch with events. He died at Kensington palace of a massive heart attack early one morning.

George's eccentricities obscured his virtues. His judgement was basically sound, but bad temper and bluster made it seem erratic. Though he aimed at royal dignity, it was marred by pomposity and self-satisfaction; his courage was undoubted, but he talked about it too often. His ungraciousness was proverbial, but he was lacking in malice, and honest to a fault. 'He might offend', wrote Lord Chesterfield, 'but he never deceived'.

CHEVENIX TRENCH, C., *George II* (1973).

St James's palace, London

Built by Henry VIII on the site of the Augustinian Hospital of St James, later a leper hospital for young women and briefly owned by Eton College, the red-brick palace was constructed around four courtyards. Mary I died there, her heart and bowels being buried in the Chapel Royal; Elizabeth, then later the princes Henry and Charles, also held court there. Charles II renovated the palace after its intervening use as a barracks, and laid out the park which was opened to the public. The 'warming-pan baby', later known as 'the Old Pretender', was born in St James's in 1688, and Anne, who was also born there, spent much time in this palace since Whitehall had been destroyed by fire, adding the Banqueting and Throne Rooms.

It regained its place as centre of society under George II while still prince of Wales, and princess Augusta was delivered there in 1737 rather than under her grandparents' roof at Hampton Court. George III's subsequent move to Buckingham House meant that St James's was used increasingly only for official receptions, royal marriages, and christenings; as headquarters of ceremonial, foreign ambassadors are still accredited to the court of St James even though received at Buckingham palace. York House and Clarence House within the precincts remain royal residences, however, and the Children of the Chapel Royal maintain the choral traditions of their predecessors.

Caroline of Brandenburg-Anspach, queen of Great Britain and Ireland, b. 1 Mar. 1683, da. of Johann Friedrich, margrave of Brandenburg-Anspach, and Eleanora, da. of Johann Georg, duke of Saxe-Eisenach; m. Georg August (later George II), 2 Sept. 1705; d. 20 Nov. 1737; bur. Westminster abbey.

Caroline was blonde and blue-eyed, handsome in her youth, and remaining imposing, though she became very stout. Her tact covered much of her husband's brusqueness, and she exercised considerable influence over him, largely by deferring to his opinions, even to the extent of tolerating his mistresses. She had an interest in theological matters, which her husband did not share, and a taste for reading which led him to complain that she was more like a schoolmistress than a queen. The best account of her is in Lord Hervey's *Memoirs*, and there is a statue of her at Queen's College, Oxford, of which she was a benefactress.

Frederick Lewis, prince of Wales, b. 6 Jan. 1707, s. of Georg August (later George II) and Caroline; m. Augusta, da. of Friedrich of Saxe-Gotha, 26 Apr. 1736; issue: Augusta, George, Edward, Elizabeth, William, Henry, Louisa, Frederick, Caroline; d. 20 Mar. 1751; bur. Westminster abbey.

Frederick was twenty-one before he was brought over from Hanover and created prince of Wales. Relations with his father were already strained by the prince's desire to marry Wilhelmina, daughter of Frederick William I of Brandenburg-Prussia, whom George II disliked intensely. A second cause for animosity soon appeared. The allowance his father gave him was not generous, and Frederick gambled heavily and ran up debts; in February 1737 he appealed without success to Parliament. Six months later, an open breach with the king followed, when the prince drove his wife, princess Augusta, in labour from Hampton Court to St James's palace, presumably to prevent queen Caroline being present at the birth. He was ordered to leave the palace and took up residence in Leicester House, where he began organizing a political interest. In 1742 he refused to come to any agreement that would save Walpole, and in the late 1740s was negotiating with the Tories for a patriot monarchy that would extirpate party distinctions. His unexpected death from an abscess at the age of forty-four dashed these hopes and, as his enemies jeered, left the ghosts of promised peers stalking the land. The prince seems to have been insincere, and a hunter for popularity, yet nothing explains the hatred which his family felt towards him. His father called him 'Griff' (a half-caste) and wondered whether he was a *wechselbalg* (changeling); his mother, who refused to see him on her deathbed,

Queen Caroline, consort of George II. Rysbrack's magnificent bust of Queen Caroline (one of a pair with her husband), catches her impressive appearance.

'wished the ground would open this moment and sink the monster to the lowest hope of hell'.

Augusta, princess of Wales, b. 30 Nov. 1719, da. of Friedrich, duke of Saxe-Gotha, and Magdalen of Anhalt-Zerbst; m. Frederick, prince of Wales, 26 Apr. 1736; d. 8 Feb. 1772; bur. Westminster abbey.

Princess Augusta was sixteen when she came to England and knew no English; Lord Hervey described her as tall, pleasant, but a little awkward. She was at once plunged into the turmoil of court politics when, the following year, her husband removed her from Hampton Court when she was in labour, to the fury of George II. As a result, they were turned out of St James's palace and made their home at Leicester House. Eight more children in the next twelve years suggests that she found her husband less disagreeable than most others did. Frederick's early death in 1751 left her son, George, as heir to the throne. As princess dowager, she would have attracted little attention had she not been used as a weapon to attack Lord Bute, her son's Groom of the Stole and chief minister, with whom, in countless squibs and ballads, she was accused of improper relations. Such allegations seem most improbable, nor was she the baneful influence on her son which gave her the pivotal role in Horace Walpole's demonology. She shared with Bute a love of plants, and was responsible for the development of Kew Gardens.

William Augustus, duke of Cumberland, b. 15 Apr. 1721, 2nd surviving s. of George, prince of Wales (later George II), and Caroline; d. 31 Oct. 1765; bur. Westminster abbey.

The favourite son of George II, Cumberland followed a military career. He distinguished himself at Dettingen in 1743 and was in command at Fontenoy in 1744, when he fought a drawn battle against Saxe. From Flanders he was recalled to put down the Jacobite rebellion, conducting a competent campaign which ended at Culloden. The repression which followed gave him the nickname of 'the Butcher', though his admirers in England called him 'Sweet William' and he became a national hero. He returned to his duties in Flanders and was defeated by Saxe in 1747 at Lauffeld.

The death of his elder brother Frederick in 1751 enhanced his prominence, since he was an obvious guardian to the young prince George should the king die. Princess Augusta, Frederick's widow, regarded Cumberland with suspicion, fearing a military coup. He was again employed in the Seven Years War, but in 1757 was forced to sign an armistice at Kloster-Zevern; when George II repudiated it and recalled Cumberland in disgrace, he resigned all his military commands. In the new reign, his role was political and in July 1765 he was godfather to the Rockingham ministry. He had become grossly fat, and died aged forty-four after several strokes.

George III, king of Great Britain and Ireland, b. 24 May 1738, s. of Frederick, prince of Wales, and Augusta; acc. 25 Oct. 1760; m. Charlotte, da. of Karl Ludwig, duke of Mecklenburg-Strelitz, 8 Sept. 1761; issue: George, Frederick, William, Charlotte, Edward, Augusta, Elizabeth, Ernest, Augustus, Adolphus, Mary, Sophia, Octavius, Alfred, Amelia; d. 29 Jan. 1820; bur. Windsor.

George III was twelve when his father died in 1751, and was brought up by his mother, princess Augusta, and her adviser, Lord Bute. They formed an isolated group, at odds with the political establishment, and with a tendency towards self-congratulation and censoriousness: 'he has rather too much attention to the sins of his neighbour', wrote one of the prince's governors. At his accession, the duchess of Northumberland thought him tall and robust, with fair hair and blue eyes, dignified and pleasant, and Horace Walpole echoed the description, writing: 'his countenance florid and good natured, his manner graceful and obliging.' He had important advantages: Jacobite pretensions were no longer a threat, and he was the first Hanoverian monarch to be born in Britain, to which he referred in his first public speech. From his father he took over the ambition to be a 'patriot' king, ruling without party prejudice, which made it easier for the Tories, in opposition since 1714, to come back into royal favour. By contrast, two of his earliest decisions created problems. He was bitterly opposed to the Seven Years War and determined to wind it up; this would cause trouble with Pitt, the great war minister. Secondly, he insisted on bringing forward his tutor, Lord Bute, for whose judgement he had vast, but misplaced, admiration. First, it was necessary to find a queen. After a considerable search, George and Bute settled on princess Charlotte, aged seventeen. The marriage was a great success, and George's pious wish that it should be fruitful was abundantly granted with fifteen children.

A peace treaty with France was negotiated, but domestic peace proved more difficult. Pitt took himself into opposition in 1761, and was joined in 1762 by Newcastle. Worse, Bute, the victim of mountainous abuse as a Scot in newspapers, ballads, and cartoons, decided in 1763 that he

William Augustus, duke of Cumberland. Badly wounded in the leg at Dettingen when he was 22, Cumberland put on weight rapidly. This portrait by Reynolds shows him aged 37.

could not carry on. In the *North Briton*, John Wilkes took up his pen to argue that the liberties of the subject were in danger. For another six years, the king rang ministerial changes without much success in the attempt to find a stable and effective government.

The seeds of even greater conflict were sown in 1764 when Grenville, a minister whom the king disliked intensely, tried to raise money in America by means of a Stamp Act. Though the measure was repealed by Lord Rockingham in 1766, good relations with the colonies did not return, and there was further escalation in 1767 when Charles Townshend introduced port duties in America. In 1770 the king found in Lord North a minister who was both congenial and competent, but fighting broke out at Lexington in April 1775. In the American Declaration of Independence, George was denounced as a tyrant unfit to be the king of a free people, but, in practice, he was merely supporting ministerial and parliamentary policy. The recognition of American independence was conceded by George with great reluctance and he drafted an abdication speech, which was never delivered. From the resignation of North to the advent of Pitt the younger, there were a series of political crises which agitated the king greatly. They coincided with distress in his family life. The king's eldest son, George, was now old enough to be extremely troublesome. In 1781, the king was obliged to buy back love-letters which the prince had written to his mistress, 'Perdita' Robinson. The prince's political mentor was Charles Fox, whom the king hated. In 1783, when Fox tried to obtain an increased allowance for the prince, already heavily in debt, the king responded with 'indignation and astonishment'. In 1785, the prince made a secret marriage to Maria Fitzherbert, a catholic, thereby forfeiting his right to the throne. These accumulated disasters may have contributed to the king's first period of insanity, which lasted for three months over the winter of 1788/9. His behaviour was at times extremely violent, his conversation indecent, and his doctors resorted to a strait-jacket. The king's illness triggered a political crisis since the prince, if given full powers as regent, would certainly use them to turn out Pitt and bring in Fox. In the event, George's recovery ushered in another twelve years for Pitt as first minister.

George's way of life was now very settled. His early indolence had given way to meticulousness, and his preference was for regularity and routine. He had no great interest in travel, disliking romantic and mountainous scenery. He stayed away from London as much as he could, preferring Windsor, where he hunted, rode, and supervised his farms. His tastes were simple to the point of frugality, and though he enjoyed the theatre and concerts, most evenings were devoted to quiet games of cards. Court life was sober and predictable, diversified by family seaside holidays at Weymouth. His illness kindled much personal sympathy, and the outbreak of the French Revolution saw his transformation into an image of British stability and common sense.

There was a recurrence of political instability from 1801 until 1807, originating in the king's refusal to agree to catholic emancipation, which led to Pitt's resignation. A second attack of insanity in 1804 threw a shadow over the future, and though the king recovered quickly, he aged fast. In 1810 began his final period of madness. At first there were hopes of another recovery, but gradually he lapsed into a twilight world, unable to distinguish past and present, and conversing with long-dead ministers. His son was appointed prince regent in 1811, and the custody of the king was given to queen Charlotte, and after her death in 1818 to the duke of York. George spent his last years at Windsor, blind and increasingly deaf, comforted by his old and battered harpsichord. Of events in the world outside, he knew nothing.

BROOKE, J., *George III* (1972).

Royal Marriages Act

This was passed in 1772 (12 Geo III, *c*.11), and forbids the marriage of a member of the royal family under the age of twenty-five, without the formal consent of the sovereign; any unsanctioned union would be declared null and void. It had been prompted by the secret nuptials of Henry, duke of Cumberland (younger brother of George III), and the bill was bitterly opposed at the time by both Charles Fox and Chatham as 'wanton and tyrannical'. As soon as it was law, another brother (William) revealed his marriage. It caused problems for the future George IV in 1785 when he secretly married Mrs Fitzherbert, and affected princess Margaret who eventually chose not to marry the divorced Peter Townsend (1955). The act remains in force.

Charlotte Sophia of Mecklenburg-Strelitz, queen of Great Britain and Ireland, b. 19 May 1744, da. of Karl Ludwig, duke of Mecklenburg-Strelitz, and Elizabeth of Saxe-Hildburghausen; m. George III, 8 Sept. 1761; d. 17 Nov. 1818; bur. Windsor.

Charlotte was chosen by the young George III after a protracted hunt through almanacks for German princesses. The marriage was very successful, king and queen sharing domestic and private tastes, and much occupied with their fifteen children. The queen took little interest in politics: 'my taste', she wrote, 'is for a few select friends.' George's derangement in 1788/9 was a terrible blow; his incessant talking exhausted her and his violence terrified her. Its return in 1804 was almost more than she could bear. It was sad, wrote Lord Hobart, 'to see a family that had lived so well together completely broken up'. From 1810 the queen had formal custody of her husband, who had become permanently insane, while her son, George, acted as prince regent.

George IV, king of United Kingdom of Great Britain and Ireland, b. 12 Aug. 1762, s. of George III and Charlotte; acc. as regent, 5 Feb. 1811; as king, 29 Jan. 1820; m. Caroline, da. of Karl Wilhelm of Brunswick-Wolfenbüttel, 8 Apr. 1795; issue: Charlotte; d. 26 June 1830; bur. Windsor.

George IV was a handsome and intelligent youth, who began his lifelong pursuit of pleasure at an early age. He reacted strongly against the soberness of his parents, finding their court dull and oppressive; by the time he was eighteen his father was complaining that his 'love of dissipation has been trumpeted in the public papers'. He was drawn to the fast set, drinking heavily, gambling, pursuing women, and associating with Charles Fox and the parliamentary opposition. In the summer of 1781, the prince had to confess that he was being blackmailed by the actress 'Perdita' Robinson, who was threatening to sell his love-letters, and the king had to lay out £5,000 to clear 'this shameful transaction'. The prince immediately switched his attentions to Mme Hardenburg, so 'divinely pretty' that he thought his brain would split; the king, sensibly, told Hardenburg to take his wife abroad. To his brother Frederick, the prince complained that 'the king is excessively cross and ill-tempered, and uncommonly grumpy'. In 1783, an attempt by Fox to obtain a larger allowance for the prince nearly brought down the coalition ministry, the king responding with fury. In 1784, he fell madly in love with Maria Fitzherbert, a catholic widow, and when she refused him, inflicted a slight graze on himself in what passed for a romantic attempt at suicide. The following year, they went through a secret marriage conducted by a Fleet parson. Under the terms of the Act of Settlement this would rule him out of the succession, unless under the Royal Marriages Act it was deemed invalid. To compound his difficulties, he spent lavishly on Carlton House and began to develop Brighton Pavilion. In 1787, when applying once more for an enhanced allowance, he authorized Fox to deny the marriage, thus creating an awkward scene with Mrs Fitzherbert; when Fox assured the Commons that the rumours were false, his friends had to explain to him that the prince had lied. The following year, the king's derangement raised the question of a regency for the prince. Since it was presumed that he would use his power to turn out Pitt and bring in Fox, the ministers prevaricated until the king recovered.

By 1794 the prince's debts were impossible and he resolved to embark upon matrimony. Mrs Fitzherbert was temporarily put to one side, and the prince married his cousin, Caroline of Brunswick. In two respects the marriage was successful: Parliament increased his allowance to that of a married man, and the sole nuptial encounter delivered a daughter, Charlotte, nine months later. In all other respects it was a disaster. The prince took an instant dislike to his bride, complaining of her 'personal nastiness', and refused to live with her. Princess Caroline went abroad with a strange entourage and, in 1806, a parliamentary enquiry found that if she had not committed adultery she had certainly been indiscreet.

The permanent incapacity of the king from 1810 led to the prince becoming regent in February 1811. He had long since lost sympathy for the Whigs and did not turn the Tories out of office. By this time he was growing extremely fat, drank to excess, and was dependent upon laudanum. In November 1811, when he was reported extremely ill and strangely agitated, one observer wrote 'what will become of us if as well as our king our regent goes mad'. He recovered, but his popularity was at a low ebb, since wartime taxation was heavy and distress widespread. He continued to build at Brighton, spent lavishly on his mistresses, and asked the cabinet for £500,000 to pay off his debts. Lord Liverpool, prime minister after the assassination of Spencer Perceval, replied that it was the 'decided and unanimous opinion' of the ministers not to pay them.

The prince's pleasure at succeeding to the throne in 1820 was marred by the reappearance of his estranged wife, Caroline, demanding her rights. The king retorted by insisting that the government introduce a divorce bill, which Liverpool found he could not carry. George IV's coronation, though lavish, was spoiled by queen Caroline's attempt to force an entry, though her death a month later afforded her husband some relief. His private life continued to be as demanding as corpulence would permit, with a succession of mistresses—Lady Jersey supplanted by Lady Hertford, who in turn gave way to Lady Conyngham. He made visits to Ireland, Hanover, and Scotland in the early years of his reign, assuring the crowd at Dublin that 'his heart had always been Irish', but he became increasingly embarrassed at his girth and spent his later years in virtual seclusion at Windsor. His attention to political matters was fitful and ineffective, and the influence of the crown deteriorated rapidly. He tried to resist the promotion of Canning to the foreign secretaryship in 1822, but was forced to give way. In 1827, when Liverpool suffered a stroke, George could not decide on a successor and put the matter to the cabinet; it was left to Peel and Wellington to

George IV. Henry Bone's portrait on enamel was painted when the prince was in his early forties. He retained his youthful good looks until overtaken by obesity.

explain that he was throwing away a vital royal prerogative. In 1828, he declared that his conscience could never consent to catholic emancipation but thought better of it.

Greville wrote of George IV that he was 'a spoiled, selfish, odious beast', and *The Times*, in an obituary, declared that 'there never was an individual less regretted by his fellow creatures than this deceased king'. There is little to be said in mitigation. He could, when he chose, be a pleasant and amusing companion, with an easy, if florid, manner. His interest in architecture left not only Brighton Pavilion but the grand reconstructions of Windsor castle and Buckingham palace, and the development of the Regent's Park area of London. He had some interest in music, a knowledge of painting, and a gift for mimicry.

SMITH, E. A., *George IV* (1999).

Brighton Pavilion, Sussex

The future George IV first visited Brighton in 1783, before leasing a farmhouse there for his own use. This was enlarged into a Marine Pavilion by the architect Henry Holland, who repeated the farmhouse and connected the two buildings with a domed rotunda. The estate was finally purchased in 1800, and by 1803 the interiors had been converted into *chinoiserie*. The prince was so taken with William Porden's dome for the new adjacent royal stables that Humphry Repton submitted drawings for an Indian Pavilion. The conversion was finally carried out (1815–22) by John Nash, who retained the building's general shape but threw over it a bizarre froth of cupolas, columns, and scalloped arches, at enormous expense. The interiors were extravagantly oriental and inventive, the Music Room being the most splendid, and the Great Kitchen a showplace of practicality.

George IV's visits to Brighton eventually dwindled, but the Pavilion was used by both William IV and Victoria until she moved much of the furniture away and settled instead on Osborne House. The Town Commissioners purchased it from the Crown in 1850 and used it as assembly rooms. In 1956 much of the original furniture was returned, enabling a restoration closer to its original style, and it now houses a permanent Regency exhibition which includes Mrs Fitzherbert's wedding ring from 1785.

Caroline of Brunswick, queen of the United Kingdom of Great Britain and Ireland, b. 17 May 1768, da. of Karl Wilhelm, duke of Brunswick-Wolfenbüttel, and Augusta, da. of Frederick, prince of Wales; m. George, prince of Wales (later George IV), 8 Apr. 1795; d. 7 Aug. 1821; bur. Brunswick.

Caroline's marriage to the prince of Wales was designed to release him from his great burden of debt and to secure the succession to the throne. Their first meeting on 5 April 1795 produced mutual disenchantment,

Brighton Palace. Probably the most exotic building in Britain, starting life as a farmhouse. George, prince regent had it transformed by John Nash into an Indian palace between 1815 and 1822. Sydney Smith commented that it looked as thought St Paul's had gone down the south coast and littered.

and the groom was reported to have been extremely drunk on the wedding night. Immediately after the birth of their only child in 1796, the prince left his wife. In 1806 rumours of her conduct were so bad that Parliament ordered a 'delicate investigation', which cleared her of adultery but found her behaviour unbecoming. For some years she travelled on the continent with a handsome favourite, Bartolomeo Bergami, and his family, and a further enquiry was initiated in 1818.

Queen Caroline of Brunswick. Painted in characteristically flamboyant costume in 1804 when she was thirty-six. The princess holds a modelling tool to indicate her own attempts at sculpture, and the bust gazing down is that of her father, the duke of Brunswick.

She returned to England in 1820, to claim her position as queen. George IV insisted on a divorce bill being introduced but, though the evidence of witnesses was damning, the government decided that it could not carry the measure. The king's unpopularity was so great that many people were willing to regard the queen as the 'poor, forlorn woman' she claimed to be. She overplayed her hand when she appeared at the coronation in 1821, demanding admittance to the abbey, and died shortly after. Lady Bessborough, who saw her at a ball in 1815, described her as 'a short, very fat, elderly woman, with an extremely red face', wearing a white frock cut 'disgustingly low'.

Charlotte, princess, b. 7 Jan. 1796, da. of George, prince of Wales (later George IV), and Caroline; m. Leopold of Saxe-Coburg (later king of the Belgians), 2 May 1816; d. 6 Nov. 1817; bur. Windsor.

The only child of George IV, Charlotte was heir presumptive. In the bitter dispute between her parents, she tended to side with her mother. In 1813 she was betrothed to William, prince of Orange, but stipulated that she should be under no obligation to leave England. This led to the collapse of the arrangement, to her father's fury. In 1816, she married Leopold, but died giving birth to a stillborn son, the fault of her accoucheur, Sir Richard Croft, who shot himself.

Frederick, duke of York, b. 16 Aug. 1763, 2nd s. of George III and Charlotte; m. Friederike, da. of Friedrich Wilhelm II of Prussia, 29 Sept. 1791; d. 5 Jan. 1827; bur. Windsor.

Frederick's appointment to the lucrative sinecure of the bishopric of Osnabrück at the age of six months did not prevent him from following a military career, finishing as Field Marshal. He was unsuccessful as a commander in the field against the French in the 1790s, but was a capable and energetic Commander-in-Chief from 1798. In 1809 he was obliged to resign when it was revealed that his mistress, Mary Anne Clarke, had been selling commissions in the army, but he resumed his post in 1811 and held it until his death. From 1820 he was heir to the throne but died before his elder brother George. His later years were spent at Oaklands, Surrey, in a badly run house, tormented by debt, helping his wife to look after their vast menagerie of dogs, monkeys, and parrots. He was unlucky to be remembered chiefly in a nursery rhyme.

William IV, king of United Kingdom of Great Britain and Ireland, b. 21 Aug.
1765, 3rd s. of George III and Charlotte; acc. 26 June 1830; m. Adelaide, da. of
Georg, duke of Saxe-Meiningen, 11 July 1818; issue: Charlotte, Elizabeth; d. 20 June
1837; bur. Windsor.

Until he succeeded his brother George in 1830, William, duke of
Clarence, was known mainly for his eccentricity. He pursued a naval
career and all his life had the forthright speech of a sailor. When he
joined the navy as a midshipman at the age of thirteen, his father wrote
that 'no marks of distinction' should be accorded him. This was scarcely
practicable, since few midshipmen were Knights of the Garter (1782).
His first independent command was the *Pegasus* in 1786, when his
reputation was as a strict disciplinarian. By the age of twenty-four, he
was a rear-admiral, becoming Admiral of the Fleet in 1811. He retired
from active service in 1790 and set up house with Mrs Jordan, an Irish
comic actress with five illegitimate children to her credit. The duke
helped her to add ten more, known as the FitzClarences. Their way of
life demanded that she should continue her profession, and the
newspapers speculated who was keeping whom.

The duke did not re-emerge into the public gaze until 1817, when the
death of princess Charlotte, and the continued failure of the duke of
York to produce children, moved him up in the succession. In 1818 he
married, but both his daughters died in infancy. The death of the duke
of York in 1827 made him heir presumptive, and Canning suggested
that he should become Lord High Admiral to give him some
governmental experience. This was a spectacular error of judgement.
He quarrelled violently with colleagues, made frenzied speeches, and,
according to Greville, showed such remorseless activity that it suggested
'incipient madness'. He was forced to resign the following year.
Nevertheless, when he succeeded in 1830, he was thought to be an
improvement on his predecessor. His marriage was respectable and
even affectionate, he had little reserve and enjoyed company; indeed,
his obvious delight at his brother's funeral was thought by many to be
unbecoming, since he chatted to all his friends 'incessantly and loudly'.

There was little that William IV could do in his brief reign to prevent
the influence of the crown from declining further. He inherited a
difficult position, since catholic emancipation in 1829, by splitting the
Tory party, held out the possibility of the Whigs taking office pledged to
parliamentary reform. The Reform Act of 1832 dealt the monarchy a
blow by vastly extending the power of public opinion and reducing the

electoral influence of the crown, and the way it was carried—by a threat to swamp the House of Lords through the wholesale creation of new Whig peers—showed how that institution could be intimidated in the future. But in the protracted crisis over reform, the king played a bad hand with some skill, attempting to occupy the role of a constitutional chairman. He agreed to grant Grey's request for a dissolution in 1831, though the previous election had been only six months before, and, with great reluctance, gave a pledge to create enough peers if necessary to carry the bill. In 1831, while granting the dissolution, he told Grey that though he would personally have refused, 'as a sovereign it was his duty to set those feelings and prejudices aside'. It is a distinction that his father, George III, would never have made.

Towards the end of his life, a major preoccupation was to thwart his sister-in-law, the duchess of Kent, who would become regent if her daughter Victoria succeeded while under age. In August 1836, at a birthday banquet with both ladies present, in another of his voluble speeches, he declared that his ambition was to survive another nine months, to save the country from a regent who was 'incompetent to act with propriety'. He got his wish with a month to spare.

ZIEGLER, P., *William IV* (1971).

Adelaide of Saxe-Meiningen, queen of United Kingdom of Great Britain and Ireland, b. 13 Aug. 1792, da. of Georg, duke of Saxe-Meiningen, and Luise of Saxe-Hildburghausen; m. William, duke of Clarence (later William IV), 11 July 1818; d. 2 Dec. 1849; bur. Windsor.

The death of princess Charlotte in 1817 led to the 'rush to the altar', when three of George III's unmarried sons embarked on matrimony. The duke of Clarence divested himself of Mrs Jordan, his mistress for many years, and married princess Adelaide, twenty-seven years his junior. Their two daughters died as infants but the marriage succeeded. She incurred some unpopularity as queen, when falsely accused of political interference, but her widowhood after 1837 was spent in quiet retirement and good works.

Ernest Augustus, duke of Cumberland (later king of Hanover), b. 5 June 1771, 5th s. of George III and Charlotte; acc. in Hanover, 20 June 1837; m. Friederike, da. of Karl, duke of Mecklenburg-Strelitz, 29 May 1815; issue: George; d. 18 Nov. 1851; bur. Hanover.

Sent to Göttingen in 1786, Ernest was destined for a career in the

Hanoverian army. He served with distinction as a cavalry officer against the French, losing an eye and being wounded in the arm. He subsequently became a Field Marshal in the British army. In 1810, he was discovered badly wounded in bed, having apparently been attacked by his valet, who then killed himself, though Cumberland's enemies hinted that the duke had been the aggressor. During the reign of his brother, George IV, he became prominent as a Tory politician, resisting parliamentary reform and catholic emancipation. The operation of the Salic law brought him to the throne of Hanover in 1837, when his niece Victoria became queen of England. He ruled firmly, cancelling the liberal constitution granted by his brother William IV, but his German subjects welcomed a resident monarch, and he survived the year of revolutions in 1848 without difficulty.

Victoria, queen of United Kingdom of Great Britain and Ireland, from 1876 empress of India, b. 24 May 1819, da. of Edward, duke of Kent, and Mary Louise Victoria, da. of Francis, duke of Saxe-Coburg-Saalfeld; acc. 20 June 1837; m. Albert, 2nd s. of Ernst, duke of Saxe-Coburg, 10 Feb. 1840; issue: Victoria, Edward, Alice, Alfred, Helena, Louise, Arthur, Leopold, Beatrice; d. 22 Jan. 1901; bur. Windsor.

The death of princess Charlotte in 1817 persuaded the duke of Kent and two of his brothers that it was their duty to marry at once, and all three produced offspring in 1819. The path to the throne of Kent's only daughter Alexandrina Victoria (known at first as 'Drina') was cleared when her cousins, the two daughters of the duke of Clarence, died as infants. The duke of Kent, his duty done, died at Sidmouth seven months after Victoria's birth, leaving her to be brought up in Kensington palace in a German household, traces of which remained in her speech. During William IV's reign her mother was anxious that she should not be contaminated by the FitzClarences, the children of the king's long liaison with Mrs Jordan, and the princess grew up somewhat isolated, comforted by her 132 dolls. She did not attend the coronation in 1831, and in March 1837 wrote to her uncle Leopold, 'we have been for these last three months immured within our old palace and I longed sadly for some gaiety'.

Her father's place was filled, to some extent, by her uncle Leopold, who kept up a stream of good, if patronizing, advice in his letters— 'persons in high situations must particularly guard themselves against selfishness and vanity', he wrote on her fourteenth birthday. A more entertaining mentor appeared after her accession in Lord Melbourne, her Whig prime minister, for whom she developed a warm affection.

Her partisanship in favour of the Whigs led to some unpleasant, if passing, unpopularity, and she mishandled the Bedchamber crisis on 1839, propping up a weak Whig government for two further years.

In April 1836 Victoria's half-sister Feodore (princess Hohenloe) had written of a proposed visit by their cousins from Saxe-Coburg, Ernest and Albert: 'Ernest is my favourite, although Albert is much

Queen Victoria. Photographed in 1887 at the time of the Golden Jubilee when she was nearly seventy. We may suspect that a few lines have been smoothed away.

handsomer.' The visit had been arranged by uncle Leopold and it served its purpose. Victoria found them 'most delightful...Albert is extremely handsome...he has the most pleasing and delightful exterior and appearance you can possibly see'. The accession and coronation drove matrimony out of her mind for a while, but a second visit by Albert in 1839 rekindled her enthusiasm—'Albert's *beauty* is *most striking*', she told Leopold, and within two days her mind was 'quite made up...he seems *perfection*'.

The marriage was a great success, though Victoria was 'furious' to find herself pregnant within six weeks, and Albert complained that he had no real authority in the palace but was 'only the husband'. Victoria's repeated pregnancies made her rely more and more on Albert, while he gained in confidence as his command of English improved. Indeed, within a few years, the position was reversed and he was in danger, not of insipid indolence, but of breakdown from overwork. As the family increased, their joint interests built up. A visit to the Isle of Wight in 1844 led them to buy Osborne House, and they began rebuilding it. They visited Scotland for the first time in 1842, purchased Balmoral estate in 1852, and had the castle ready for occupation in 1855. At home, their pleasure in music was a great bond: Victoria sang sweetly, Albert played the organ and composed.

In December 1861 Albert died at the age of forty-two and the second half of Victoria's life began. Plans were laid for the Albert Memorial (opened in 1863), for the Frogmore mausoleum at Windsor, and for countless busts, statues, and tributes to the departed. For several years, she could not bring herself to perform public duties and unsympathetic comments appeared in the press. Family life, however, could not stand still. 'Vicky', her eldest daughter, married to the crown prince of Prussia, already had two children, the first the future kaiser Wilhelm II, and there were thirty-eight more grandchildren to come—'such swarms of children', wrote the queen, unsentimentally. In July 1862 her second daughter, Alice, married the grand duke of Hesse-Darmstadt; Vicky commented that the ceremony was 'more like a funeral'. Victoria's eldest son 'Bertie' (the future Edward VII), who had caused his parents great anxiety, was provided with a bride from Denmark, Alexandra. The queen trusted that she would prove the prince's 'SALVATION' and that he would become 'a steady husband'. There was no harm in hoping. As the children and then the grandchildren married off, Victoria became the matriarch of Europe, and her life became a giddy succession of birthdays, illnesses, assassination plots, engagements, deaths, and yet more births.

Gradually weaned back to public duties, the queen found herself without the prince consort's guiding hand, and was totally unwilling to trust the prince of Wales with any responsibility. She had long since got over her sympathy for the Whigs, helped partly by the confidence she felt in Peel and the strong disapproval her husband had felt for Palmerston. Later on, advancing years, her dislike of Gladstone, and her admiration for Disraeli moved her towards the Conservatives. Though she was never a negligible force, her direct influence must not be exaggerated. She could win skirmishes, make life disagreeable, and resist change, but she could scarcely determine the great issues of political life. Her threat to abdicate rather than become 'the queen of a democratic monarchy' could not stop progress towards democracy in the Reform Acts of 1867 and 1884. Her disapprobation of Palmerston did not prevent him from becoming prime minister in 1855 at the age of seventy-one and dying in office ten years later, while her even greater contempt for Gladstone did not stop him being prime minister four times during her reign, the last time at the age of eighty-four. It was increasingly difficult for even the most dedicated monarch to keep up with the expansion and complexity of public business, and although Victoria did her best, her eyesight deteriorated.

By the end of her life Victoria had become a national institution. Her reign had also seen a vast increase in British possessions overseas, and she became a symbol of empire in a way that none of her predecessors had been. The Indian Mutiny of 1857, which had shaken British rule, led to the crown assuming formal sovereignty, and in 1876 Victoria took the title of 'queen empress'. Canada became a dominion in 1867, Australia on 1 January 1901, three weeks before her death. These developments were reflected in her golden jubilee of 1887 and the diamond jubilee of 1897. At the first, the Indian cavalry attracted much admiration, the service of thanksgiving at Westminster abbey included music by prince Albert, and the Queen wrote that '*all* was the most perfect success'. At the second, Victoria was too frail for a long ceremony, and a short service was held outside St Paul's, the queen in her carriage: 'no one ever, I believe', she wrote complacently, 'has ever met with such an ovation.' She died peacefully at Osborne, during the Boer War, aged eighty-one, having ruled for sixty-three years—the longest reign in British history. She was buried alongside Albert in the mausoleum she had built at Frogmore, near Windsor, for the two of them.

WEINTRAUB, S., *Victoria: Biography of a Queen* (1987).

Balmoral castle, Aberdeenshire

A stone castle had been erected by 1390 on this former hunting seat for Robert II, the lands being held by the Gordons but passing in 1662 to the Farquharsons of Inverary. A Jacobethan house built in 1834–9 was so successful a holiday home for queen Victoria that after four years' leasing, she bought the estate in 1852. The house was rebuilt in 1855 as a large, white granite, castellated mansion in Scots baronial style, with modifications by prince Albert and demolition of the remains of the old castle. Victoria retreated to Balmoral for prolonged periods after Albert's death, but the atmosphere was no longer carefree and the house could be bitterly cold. Edward VII and George V were less keen, but George VI loved the estate, and it remains the private holiday home of the royal family.

Albert, **prince consort**, b. 26 Aug. 1819, 2nd s. of Ernst, duke of Saxe-Coburg, and Luise, da. of August, duke of Saxe-Coburg-Alterburg; created prince consort, 25 June 1857; m. Victoria, 10 Feb. 1840; d. 14 Dec. 1861; bur. Windsor.

The prince consort had more influence on the character of the British monarchy than most ruling monarchs have had. The first cousin of queen Victoria, his parents were divorced when he was a small boy and he never saw his mother again. He was summoned over to England in 1836 on a visit of approval which went well, and a second visit, after Victoria's accession, clinched the matter: 'it was with some emotion that I beheld Albert', wrote the young queen, 'who is *beautiful*'. Albert, homesick and seasick, arrived in 1840 for the marriage. He was handsome, well-educated, cultivated (with a gift for music), had a serious attitude towards life, and spoke English well, though with a heavy German accent which he never lost.

Albert was never securely popular. At first there were jeers that he was a penniless German on the make at the expense of the British taxpayer; the gentry found him too intellectual, and the politicians thought him meddlesome. As late as January 1854, just before the Crimean War, there were rumours that he had been arrested as a Russian agent, and crowds gathered to see him brought to the Tower of London. At first the queen was adamant that she would retain all power,

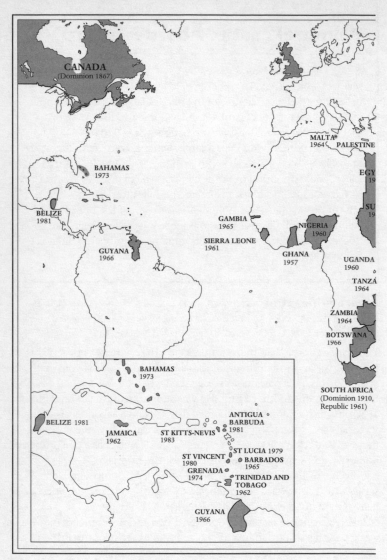

Retreat from Empire, showing dates of independence

CYPRUS 1960
1948
JORDAN
1946
QATAR
BAHRAIN 1971
PT
56
UNITED ARAB
EMIRATES 1971
DAN
56
OMAN
1971
DEM. REP OF
YEMEN 1967
ADEN 1967
BR. SOMALILAND
1960
KENYA 1963
SEYCHELLES
1976
NIA
TANGANYIKA 1961
ZANZIBAR
1963
MALAWI
1964
ZIMBABWE
1979

PAKISTAN
1947
E. PAKISTAN
1947
BANGLADESH
1971
INDIA
1947
BURMA 1948
HONG KONG
1997
SRI LANKA
1948
MALDIVES
1965
SINGAPORE
1965
BRUNEI
1984
MALAYSIA
1963
PAPUA NEW
GUINEA
1975

MAURITIUS
1968

AUSTRALIA
(Dominion 1901)

KIRIBATI
1979
NAURU
1968
TUVALU
1978
SOLOMON IS.
1978
VANUATU
1980
FIJI
1970
TONGA
1970
NEW ZEALAND
(Dominion
1907)

but as a succession of children arrived (to her considerable dismay), Albert came to share the routine of government. Under the influence of Melbourne, Victoria had been an avowed partisan of the Whigs; Albert's advice to cultivate a more neutral position was unquestionably wise. Of greater importance was the air of respectability he brought to the monarchy after two reigns of extraordinary eccentricity. The image was of an ideal family, sharing the delights of Balmoral, playing on the beach at Osborne. He was helped by two innovations. The growth of a railway network enabled the queen and her consort to show themselves as never before. The advent of daguerreotype and photography made their appearance more and more familiar, often gazing at each other with mutual respect. Nor was it all show. Presiding over the Society for the Improvement of the Working Classes, the prince reminded his listeners of 'that class of the community which has the most of toil and the least of the enjoyments of the world'. The Great Exhibition was his brain-child, and he worked hard to make it the enormous success it became. As early as 1852 the queen wrote that he had become 'a *terrible* man of business and so preoccupied'. He paid a heavy price, ageing rapidly and complaining of fatigue, the prince of hearts of 1840 transformed by 1857, when the queen made him consort, into a heavy-jowled and balding man. He died of typhoid at Windsor in 1861 at the age of forty-two. His last act, 'so weak I can scarcely hold the pen', was to soften the severity of Palmerston's protest to the American government over the *Trent* case, helping to avoid what would have been a foolish and disastrous war.

WEINTRAUB, S., *Albert, the Uncrowned King* (1997).

Osborne House, Isle of Wight

As her young family increased, Victoria was desperate for 'a place of one's own, quiet and retired' away from court ceremonial. Rejecting Brighton but recollecting visits to the Isle of Wight in her youth, she rented Osborne House, near Cowes, for a trial year before purchasing house and estate from Lady Blachford in 1845. This building was relatively small, so Albert promptly designed a Neapolitan-style villa, with help from the master-builder Thomas

continued

Osborne House, Isle of Wight *continued*

Cubitt; many trees were planted on the former farmland, gardens were laid out and installed with a 'Swiss Cottage' for practical education of the children, and the whole family relished their private beach.

After Albert's death Victoria spent much time secluded at Osborne. Ceremonial hardened and the place began to resemble a mausoleum, although the 'Durbar Room' was built in 1891 to allow for the occasional large function. She died there in 1901. Edward VII disliked the house, and gave most of the estate to the nation; the gardens and state apartments were opened to the public, and one wing became a convalescent home. In 1954 Elizabeth II opened the private suites, where furniture and furnishings have been maintained as they were a century earlier.

Edward VII, king of United Kingdom of Great Britain and Ireland, emperor of India, b. 9 Nov. 1841, eldest s. of Victoria and Albert of Saxe-Coburg; acc. 22 Jan. 1901; m. Alexandra, da. of Christian IX of Denmark, 10 Mar. 1863; issue: Albert, George, Louise, Victoria, Maud, John; d. 6 May 1910; bur. Windsor.

Victoria's fervent wish when her first son was born was that he should prove the image of his father 'in *every*, *every* respect', and he was named Albert Edward. She was sorely disappointed. 'Bertie', she decided, had 'a small, empty brain' and knock-knees, while the prince consort wrote 'I never in my life met with such a thorough and cunning lazybones'. As a youth he was small and unimpressive, his chin weak, his temper uncertain, his powers of concentration limited, and he had an unpleasant habit of bullying companions and servants. It was difficult to know what to do with him. A few weeks in the army closed off that career since he could not remember the commands. He was sent to both Oxford and Cambridge without acquiring any capacity for reading. His main interests were clothes, food, pleasure, and talking, though he could, when he wished, make himself agreeable, and he was fluent in French and German.

In 1861 a short stay in Ireland brought an escapade with a nubile actress. This produced suggestions that Bertie should be married as soon as possible and there was the usual hunt for possible brides, one 'shockingly dressed', another 'too delicate', and a third 'not clever or

Edward VII and Queen Alexandra. 'Am I not a funny-looking old man?', Edward VII asked his grandchildren when dressed for his coronation. Here the king and queen are photographed before the state opening of Parliament in 1905.

pretty'. The doubtful prize went to princess Alexandra, 'outrageously beautiful'. 'I do not envy his future wife', wrote his elder sister bluntly. It was explained to Alexandra that 'our poor innocent boy' had been led into a scrape, but she kindly overlooked it. Many other scrapes followed, which she also learned to overlook. Soon it was apparent, even to the queen, that marriage would not be Bertie's 'salvation': Alix, she wrote indulgently, 'is very fond of Bertie, but not blind'.

Edward had to wait until he was nearly sixty before he succeeded to the throne. He passed the time as best he could, subpoenaed once in a divorce case, witness in an embarrassing case of cheating at baccarat. A serious attack of typhoid in 1871 gave him a fleeting popularity, and he resumed the round of holidays, visits, theatres, regattas, clubs, country-house parties, and enormous weekend shoots on his estate at Sandringham. He was given little share in government since the queen regarded him as totally irresponsible.

The success of his short reign would have astounded his parents. He began with a gesture of independence, even of defiance, announcing that he would not rule as Albert I, as planned, but as Edward VII. It was once common to attribute to him profound political influence, but that is doubtful. He was conventionally conservative, regarding Lloyd George's budget proposals as socialism run mad, but his attention to public affairs was fitful. The developing entente with France and Russia had more to do with Germany's naval programme than with Edward's visits to Paris and to Reval. He died in the middle of the crisis over the Parliament Act, resisting Asquith's attempt to flood the House of Lords with Liberal peers. His main achievement was to raise the profile of the monarchy. He could scarcely fail to be more entertaining than his aged, widowed predecessor, and his own assets came into play; Alexandra proved a splendid foil to her husband's bonhomie. He enjoyed making public appearances, looked good in uniform, could remember names, and make pleasant little speeches. The solemnity of the High Victorian period had long since vanished: court society, which had almost disappeared, recovered, and the general public regarded his infidelities with amusement or even admiration. He was fortunate to die before the Great War brought his world crashing, and was lucky in his pleasures—he won the Derby in 1896, both the Derby and the Grand National in 1900, and the Derby again in 1909. On his deathbed in 1910, his son George was able to tell him that his horse had won the 4.15 at Kempton Park.

HIBBERT, C., *Edward VII* (1976).

Sandringham House, Norfolk

The Sandringham estate (then of some 700 acres) was purchased in 1861 from Charles Spencer Cowper from revenue accumulated by the Duchy of Cornwall during the future Edward VII's minority, for his use as a private residence. It became the country home of Edward and his bride, Alexandra, but soon proved too small for their many guests at weekend parties and shoots. Rebuilding was commenced in brick, in modified Elizabethan style; a ballroom was added in 1883, and further additions made in the local carrstone after a fire in 1891. York Cottage, built in the grounds, was the East Anglian home of George V for over thirty years until the death of Alexandra (1925), and birthplace of the future George VI. The duke of Clarence, queen Alexandra, George V, and George VI all died at Sandringham, and the burial ground attached to the estate church contains the graves of the princes Alexander (infant son of Edward VII) and John (fifth son of George V). The house is the present royal family's preferred Christmas residence.

Alexandra of Denmark, queen of United Kingdom of Great Britain and Ireland, empress of India, b. 7 Dec. 1844, da. of Christian IX of Denmark and Louise, da. of Wilhelm, Landgrave of Hesse-Cassell; m. Edward, prince of Wales (later Edward VII), 10 Mar. 1863; d. 20 Nov. 1925; bur. Windsor.

Married at eighteen to the future Edward VII, Alexandra was tall, slim, and elegant. At first her strong Danish sympathies created difficulties with her mother-in-law, queen Victoria, who took the Prussian side in the war of 1864. Alexandra was not particularly intellectual, and was from an early age greatly handicapped by severe deafness. She was on affectionate terms with her husband and did not appear to resent the attentions he paid to other women. She enjoyed travel and entertaining, but increasingly devoted herself to charitable work, especially after Edward's death in 1910. She lived on at Sandringham in retirement, vague, impunctual, and somewhat isolated.

Albert Victor Christian Edward, duke of Clarence, b. 8 Jan. 1864, eldest s. of Edward, prince of Wales (later Edward VII), and Alexandra; d. 14 Jan. 1892; bur. Windsor.

Queen Victoria insisted that her senior grandson should be called Albert, though he was known in the family as 'Eddy'. His behaviour was so odd that it suggests some defect from birth. At thirteen he was sent to the naval college at Dartmouth, but could not cope with the course: his tutor reported him 'abnormally dormant . . . sits listless and vacant . . . this feebleness and lack of power to grasp almost anything'. Trinity College, Cambridge, was suggested, though another tutor warned that the prince scarcely knew how to read; the University responded in 1888 by awarding him an honorary degree. He next tried the army, where his instructors at Aldershot were '*astounded* at his utter ignorance'. As late as 1891 his father wrote that 'the difficulty of rousing him is very great', but he had an interest in clothes and pursued women with some vigour. As usual, his family decided that marriage was the remedy and, at length, princess Mary of Teck was fixed upon. The prince of Wales's secretary wrote that Eddy should be 'told he *must* do it', but he died at Sandringham of pneumonia six weeks before the wedding. His brother George inherited his place in the line of succession and also his fiancée.

Windsors

The very powerful anti-German feeling during the Great War persuaded George V and his advisers that a change of family name might be prudent to distance it from the hated enemy. There was some difficulty in ascertaining what the original name of the Hanoverian line had been. It was usually assumed to have been Guelph, from a ninth-century Bavarian count, but Brunswick had also been used, while prince Albert had been a Wettin of the Saxe-Coburg line. The Royal College of Heralds was uncertain and suggested it might have been Wipper, scarcely an improvement on Guelph. Various alternatives were considered: 'FitzRoy' suggested bastardy, 'D'Este' was obviously foreign, and 'Stuart' reminded people of the fate of Charles I. Lord Stamfordham, the king's private secretary, then suggested Windsor, which was ideal, easily pronounceable, both solid and romantic. The change was promulgated on 17 July 1917. At the same time, the Teck family became marquesses of Cambridge, and the Battenbergs became Mountbattens, marquesses of Milford Haven. In 1960 Elizabeth II decreed that her more distant descendants would be known in future as Mountbatten-Windsors.

George V, king of United Kingdom of Great Britain and Ireland, emperor of India, b. 3 June 1865, 2nd s. of Edward, prince of Wales (later Edward VII), and Alexandra acc. 6 May 1910; m. (Victoria) Mary, da. of Francis, duke of Teck, 6 July 1893; issue: Edward, Albert, Mary, Henry, George, John; d. 20 Jan. 1936; bur. Windsor.

Prince George pursued a naval career from the age of twelve, serving in the *Britannia* at Dartmouth. Small but sturdy, he found it at times a rough school. He was given his first command of a torpedo boat in 1889, but the death of his elder brother, the duke of Clarence, in 1892 changed his whole life. Not only was he created duke of York and became second in line to the throne, but the following year he married his brother's fiancée, Mary of Teck.

His first years of marriage were quiet. George did not share his parents' taste for high life and travel, but enjoyed a domestic existence with his wife and growing family, mainly at York Cottage, Sandringham. His outdoor delight was shooting, his indoor stamp-collecting. His naval training made him punctual to the point of obsession, and he relished good order and discipline. An observer wrote that his life was essentially that of a squire. He could not avoid public engagements altogether, but they were few until his father succeeded, when he was sent on overseas trips, to Australia (1901), India (1905), and Canada (1908).

On his accession in 1910 he faced an immediate political crisis arising out of Lloyd George's budget, which the House of Lords had rejected. The Parliament Bill, designed to curb the Lords' power, could be passed only by the threat to create enough Liberal peers to swamp the Tory opposition. Asquith asked the new king for a pledge, which one of his secretaries advised him to give, while the other advised him to refuse. He gave it, and subsequently regretted that he had done so. Once again, a royal prerogative had been exploited for party advantage. The crisis then moved to Ireland, since the nationalists, on whom Asquith relied, demanded Home Rule. In July 1914 the king brought both sides together at the Buckingham House conference, but no agreement could be reached. From this crisis, George was rescued by an even bigger one, the outbreak of the Great War.

The king was greatly involved, visiting hospitals and the trenches, and setting an example by practising austerity at home. But the war came closer than that. It stimulated fierce anti-German feeling, which reminded many people that the royal family itself was essentially German, kaiser Wilhelm being the king's first cousin. Lord Louis Battenberg was forced to resign as First Sea Lord, and Lord Haldane, who had once said that Germany was 'his spiritual home', had to leave the woolsack. George's response in 1917 was to change the family's name, and hit upon Windsor; the Battenbergs became Mountbattens, the Tecks became marquesses of Cambridge. Monarchy was to be more closely identified with the nation itself.

From 1918 George V emerged into a changed world. Society in the old sense had almost collapsed, and many of the gentry were hard hit by penal levels of taxation. The younger generation seemed to its elders bent on a frantic pursuit of pleasure, with the prince of Wales leading the dance. The king and queen appeared at times visitors from a lost world, George in a cocked hat with white plumes, Mary in a strange turban or toque hat. The great empires of Germany, Russia, and Austria had gone; by 1921 Southern Ireland was independent in all but name; women voted for the first time at the general election of 1918, and in increased numbers in 1929. In 1923 the first Labour government took office and, whatever his private views, the king did his best to smooth its arrival; MacDonald wrote that the king was 'human and friendly', Clynes that he was 'genial, kindly and considerate'. His action in 1931 in suggesting that MacDonald should stay on as a coalition prime minister was much criticized, especially by the Labour opposition, but the crisis was real, and the king's action was overwhelmingly endorsed at the general election.

Slowly, George won widespread popularity. His home life was irreproachable, his devotion to duty unchallenged; his plain tastes and dislike of modernism in art and music were shared by many of his subjects. During the winter of 1928/9, a severe attack of bronchitis brought him close to death, and his recovery was slow. His Christmas broadcast (1932), written by Rudyard Kipling, and containing an appeal to the empire, was a great success. The silver jubilee celebrations in 1935 were widespread and gave the king much pleasure. George died, as he would have wished, at Sandringham, apologizing on his last day to the privy counsellors seeking a signature authorizing an emergency Council of State: 'I am sorry to keep you waiting like this. I am unable to concentrate.' John Betjeman, poet of melancholy and champion of Victorian values, wrote one of his best poems in tribute.

ROSE, K., *George V* (1983).

(Victoria) Mary of Teck, queen of United Kingdom of Great Britain and Ireland, empress of India b. 26 May 1867, da. of Francis, duke of Teck, and Mary, da. of Adolphus, duke of Cambridge; m. George, duke of York (later George V), 6 July 1893; d. 24 Mar. 1953; bur. Windsor.

Thanks in part to the development of photography and the cinema, Mary became one of the best-known queens, instantly recognizable. Though she was a great-granddaughter of George III, her family was relatively impoverished, and she was thought to have done very well when she was chosen in 1891 to marry and redeem the duke of Clarence, eldest son of the prince of Wales. On Clarence's death from pneumonia, she married his younger brother George, to whom she became devoted. Though shy, she was composed and dignified, inspiring respect rather than affection, and carrying herself so well that she appeared taller than she was. Like her husband, she preferred a quiet domestic life, mainly at York Cottage at Sandringham, a large cottage but a small royal residence. She read widely, was informed about painting and tapestry, and collected antiques and *objets d'art*, sometimes ruthlessly. Her life was punctuated by sadness. Her youngest son, John, suffered from epilepsy and died at thirteen in 1919; her first son abdicated in 1936; her fourth son, George, duke of Kent, was killed in an air-crash in 1942 while on active service, and she lived to witness the death of her second son, George VI, in 1952. To the end, she remained tactful and self-effacing.

Edward VIII, uncrowned king of United Kingdom of Great Britain and Northern Ireland, emperor of India, b. 23 June 1894, eldest s. of George, duke of York (later George V), and Mary; acc. 20 Jan. 1936; abdic. 11 Dec. 1936; m. Wallis Simpson, 3 June 1937; d. 28 May 1972; bur. Windsor.

At the age of thirteen, Edward (known in the family by his last name David) was sent to naval college, and at eighteen to Magdalen College, Oxford. Commissioned at the outbreak of the Great War, he spent much time in France and, though efforts were made to keep him out of danger, saw much carnage and suffering. Small but vigorous, good-looking with a hint of vulnerability, he was widely popular. To many, he seemed the perfect prince of Wales, and after the war he made successful visits to Canada, New Zealand, Australia, India, and the United States.

Difficulties emerged as he grew older. Relations with his father, who could be heavy, were often tense. The king preferred a quiet domestic life, diversified by outdoor sports, while the prince seemed to get most pleasure from night-clubs, dancing, and dining out. There was no indication that he was contemplating matrimony, but he had a number of affairs, the most long-standing with Mrs Dudley Ward. At the same time, he found official duties irksome and often allowed his boredom to show. He also dabbled in politics, expressing kindly if vague sympathy for the plight of the unemployed, which some took as criticism of the government. That George V believed that his son would not last a year on the throne is far from conclusive, since fathers are often dismissive of their sons, and monarchs almost always of their heirs. But many others worried about his behaviour. 'I see nothing but disaster ahead', wrote Godfrey Thomas, his private secretary in 1929, and John Aird, after witnessing eccentric behaviour during a meal, wondered if the prince was going mad. Lloyd George commented on a visit to Caernarfon that 'the prince made a bad impression, evidently disliking the ceremonies he attended, and being unpunctual and ungracious in his appearances'. There was a notable tendency in the prince towards self-pity, and increasingly he isolated himself at Fort Belvedere in Windsor Great Park with a few select friends.

One reason for the prince's lack of interest in public affairs was that since 1934 he had taken up Wallis Simpson, a twice-married, once-divorced American, to the exclusion of his other women friends. His determination at his accession to marry her brought about his downfall, though it was reinforced by his casual conduct as sovereign. Alex Hardinge, another private secretary, thought that he despised the routine and regularity of his father and 'appeared to be entirely ignorant of the powers of a constitutional monarch'. His instability was not helped by heavy drinking.

The final crisis was provoked when Mrs Simpson obtained a decree nisi against her second husband on 27 October 1936 and would be free to remarry in six months. The cabinet resolved that she was quite unacceptable as a queen, and the leaders of the opposition concurred. A morganatic marriage was also ruled out, and the king abdicated, delivering a moving farewell broadcast. His younger brother George became king and, in turn, created Edward duke of Windsor.

The ex-king had another thirty-five years of life. He and Mrs Simpson married the following year. During the Second World War he served as governor of the Bahamas, and afterwards lived in some style in a large house in the Bois de Boulogne, outside Paris. Relations with the rest of his family were soured by a long-running grievance that his brother would not allow the duchess the rank of 'Her Royal Highness'. The duke's own version of events was published in 1951 as *A King's Story*. ZIEGLER, P., *King Edward VIII* (1990).

Wallis Simpson, duchess of Windsor, b. 19 June 1896, da. of Teackle Wallis Warfield and Alice Montague; m. (1) Earl Winfield Spencer, 8 Nov. 1916; (2) Ernest Simpson, 2 July 1928; (3) Edward, duke of Windsor (formerly Edward VIII), 3 June 1937; no issue by any marriage; d. 24 Apr. 1986; bur. Windsor.

Born in Pennsylvania, USA, Wallis Warfield's first marriage to an aviator was dissolved in December 1927. She then married Ernest Simpson, a wealthy English businessman with an American mother. She met the prince of Wales in 1931, and by 1934 had moved aside Lady Furness to take over as his mistress. The nature of her appeal to him has been much debated. She was well groomed and confident, with a good figure, but her features were hard and her behaviour brash. There was certainly an element of domination in her attitude towards the prince, who became king in January 1936 and abdicated in December when the government refused to approve the marriage. After the war, during which she accompanied her husband to the Bahamas where he was governor, they settled in France. She was never accepted by the royal family, and, after the duke's death in 1972, led an increasingly lonely life in declining health. Her memoirs, *The Heart Has its Reasons*, were published in 1956.

George VI, king of United Kingdom of Great Britain and Northern Ireland, emperor of India, b. 14 Dec. 1895, 2nd s. of George, duke of York (later George V), and Mary; acc. 11 Dec. 1936; m. Elizabeth Bowes-Lyon, da. of Claude, earl of Strathmore, 26 Apr. 1923; issue, Elizabeth, Margaret; d. 6 Feb. 1952; bur. Windsor.

Christened Albert George and known in the family as 'Bertie', he was faced throughout his life with difficulties. He was not particularly gifted and, as a boy, was overshadowed by his more extrovert elder brother. At the age of eight he developed a stammer which made public speaking an ordeal. At Royal Naval College, Dartmouth, he passed out 61st out of 67 cadets, an improvement on his previous position. Though he grew up a well-built and handsome man, his problems encouraged shyness and

occasional outbursts of rage; in addition, he was dogged by gastric
trouble. The outbreak of the Great War in 1914 found him a midshipman
on the cruiser HMS *Collingwood*, but he had six months ashore after
appendicitis. He remained unwell through much of 1915, but rejoined
his ship in time to see action at the battle of Jutland in May 1916; three
months later, he was again ill and had to be invalided out of the navy. He
then transferred via the Royal Naval Air Service to the Royal Air Force,
where he learned to fly. He followed it with a rather undemanding year
at Trinity College, Cambridge, where he read Bagehot on the
constitution, who may have given him a false impression of the decay of
the royal prerogative. Created duke of York in 1920, he gained much
pleasure from sport, played cricket and golf well, became an excellent
shot, and won the RAF tennis doubles in 1920 with his friend Louis Greig.

Two developments then changed his life. In 1920 he met Elizabeth
Bowes-Lyon and, after some setbacks, married her in 1923. She added
enormously to his self-confidence as well as easing his relationships
within the family. Secondly, in 1925, the therapist Lionel Logue heard
the duke stumbling through a speech at the Empire Exhibition and
offered his services. Within a month, the duke was writing of the great
improvement he was making and, while he never gained total fluency,
his ordeal was much reduced. His enjoyment of public life increased,
and he was particularly relaxed at the camps he founded in 1921 to
bring together boys from different social backgrounds.

When the prince of Wales decided to marry, his choice fell upon
Wallis Simpson, an American divorcee he had met in 1931. The matter
became public ten months after he had succeeded as Edward VIII, and
when the government made it clear that she was quite unacceptable as
queen, he abdicated. To his consternation, the duke found himself king,
taking the title George VI to emphasize continuity and stability. Many
people, not least the new king, thought that the crisis might have
irretrievably damaged the monarchy. He was conscious that he had little
experience of government or the easy charm that his brother could
produce when he felt like it. Nevertheless, he was carried forward on a
wave of goodwill and respect, and his coronation, of which he wrote an
amusing account, went off well.

In one sense he was fortunate that the royal crisis was soon
overshadowed by a much greater one, the outbreak of the Second World
War. The role which the new royal family played gave them immense
popularity, especially the decision to remain during the blitz in
Buckingham palace, which was hit nine times. The friendly relations

which he had established with Roosevelt on an American visit just before the war started were of substantial benefit and, though on Chamberlain's resignation in 1940 the king would have preferred Halifax, he was soon on cordial terms with Churchill.

The post-war years were sombre, with a slow recovery and the start of the process of decolonization. Despite dismay at the more radical parts of the Labour programme, George VI got on well with Clement Attlee, another shy man. In the family, the most important events were the marriage of his elder daughter Elizabeth to Philip Mountbatten in November 1947, and the birth of prince Charles the following year. By this time, the king's health was very poor. In November 1948 a proposed tour of Australia had to be cancelled and it was feared that he might need a leg amputated. In September 1951, his left lung was removed, and he died at Sandringham in February 1952 of a blood-clot, after a good day's shooting. On taking over in 1936 he had told Baldwin that he hoped to live long enough 'to make amends for what had happened'. When the news came through, Attlee, not much given to shows of emotion, spoke of him with tears in his eyes, and Churchill wrote on the cabinet's wreath the words 'For Valour'.

JUDD, D., *King George VI* (1982).

Elizabeth Bowes-Lyon, queen of United Kingdom of Great Britain and Northern Ireland, empress of India, b. 4 Aug. 1900, da. of Claude Bowes-Lyon, earl of Strathmore, and Nina, da. of Revd. Charles Cavendish-Bentinck; m. Albert, duke of York (later George VI), 26 Apr. 1923; d. 30 Mar. 2002; bur. Windsor.

The family of Elizabeth Bowes-Lyon (known from 1952 as the Queen Mother) was ancient and well connected but not particularly wealthy. They had suffered as Jacobites in the early eighteenth century, though the seventh and eighth earls redeemed the position by marrying Durham coal-heiresses. Born at St Paul's Waldenbury in Hertfordshire, Elizabeth described her childhood in a large family as extremely happy— 'a marvellous sense of security'. She always seemed more at ease with herself than many other members of the royal family. Good-looking and greatly admired, she hesitated before accepting the duke of York's offer of marriage in 1923; thereafter she was extremely protective towards her husband, who was shy and whose health was uncertain. The abdication of her brother-in-law Edward VIII in 1936 made her husband king as George VI, and she became a remarkably popular queen, with a warm personality and a gift for putting people at their ease. The early death of her husband in 1952 plunged her into a long widowhood, during which she performed the role of queen mother with tact and skill. Fond of outdoor pursuits, she fished, shot, and was a keen supporter of horse-racing. Her London residence was Clarence House, her Scottish home the castle of Mey in Caithness-shire. Her one-hundredth birthday in August 2000 was the occasion for a genuine show of national affection.

Elizabeth II, queen of United Kingdom and Northern Ireland, b. 21 Apr. 1926, da. of Albert George, duke of York (later George VI), and Elizabeth; acc. 6 Feb. 1952; m. Philip, s. of prince Andrew of Greece, 20 Nov. 1947; issue: Charles, Anne, Andrew, Edward.

Elizabeth's childhood was affectionate and secure, with only a slight possibility at first that she might become queen, since her uncle (the prince of Wales) might well marry and have children, or her parents might have a son. Neither event happened, and in 1936 when Edward VIII abdicated, she became heir presumptive to her father, George VI. She was educated privately, with nurses and governesses playing a prominent part in her life. Her schooling was therefore comfortable, sheltered, and pleasant, if limited; with only a younger sister, there was little sense of competition and no great variety of experience. She learned to ride and grew up with a fondness for dogs.

Things changed at the outbreak of war in 1939. Most of her time was spent at Windsor castle; she was introduced gently into political and constitutional duties, making her first broadcast at fourteen and appointed a Counsellor of State at eighteen. In 1944 she launched a battleship HMS *Vanguard*. The following year she joined the ATS, was commissioned, and qualified as a driver; as always, palace spokesmen insisted that she would be treated like everyone else, but she was driven to Aldershot for the training, returning to the castle each evening. The first phase in her life ended in 1947 when, at the age of twenty-one, she married Philip, like her father a naval officer, whom she had known and admired for several years. A year later, her son Charles was born.

She was given little time to develop her own family life before she was called to the throne in 1952 by the early death of her father. The mood and atmosphere of the country was still post-war. Economic recovery was slow, there was still rationing, and decolonization had already started with the independence of India, Pakistan, and Burma. The press wrote fatuously about a 'New Elizabethan Age', but there was little evidence for it. After the euphoria of welcoming a young and attractive queen, and the excitement of her coronation, watched by millions clustering round small black-and-white television sets, the mood began to change, and voices were heard in criticism. Though there could be no doubt of the new queen's devotion to duty, she did not seem to enjoy it much. Lord Altrincham in 1957 complained that she sounded like 'a priggish schoolgirl, captain of the hockey team', and was promptly threatened with horsewhipping. Thoughtful people were prepared to admit that the royal family seemed remote, while the public was less respectful and more critical than its forebears. Debate began on the extent to which 'the curtain' should be raised on royal activities, and modernizers and traditionalists began to draw up battle lines. Meanwhile, the queen settled down to visiting countries of the empire, only to discover that this involved her in further controversy that she was allowing herself to be the lead in 'the Commonwealth charade'.

There were few significant political or constitutional issues, though the royal prerogative was involved in the choice of prime ministers in 1956 and again in 1963, and relations within the Commonwealth have often been delicate. Her greatest problems were within the royal family, and were accentuated by the growth of an avid, intrusive, and censorious press. The days of 1936, when a 'gentleman's agreement' of newspaper proprietors could keep their readers in ignorance for months of the king's infatuation with Mrs Simpson, were replaced by fierce competition for royal scoops or leaks. In 1955, when princess Margaret was undecided whether to marry a divorcee, Group Captain Townsend, newspapers polled their readers to offer advice. Two years later, rumours that prince Philip was involved with another woman prompted the palace to issue an official denial of any rift with the queen, which merely fed the monster. Henceforward, piquant stories followed at regular intervals. Lord Harewood, the queen's cousin, was sued for divorce in 1967; princess Margaret announced a separation from her husband Lord Snowdon in 1976; the marriage of prince Charles to Lady Diana Spencer, a television spectacular in 1981, was clearly in trouble by the early 1990s; the marriages of princess Anne and prince Andrew also ended in divorce. In 1992 the queen referred openly and ruefully to her '*annus horribilis*', which had included much criticism of the cost of the royal family, a difficult visit to Australia where republicanism was gaining ground, two royal divorces, details of the breakdown of the prince of Wales's marriage, and a disastrous fire at Windsor castle. 'Not a year on which I shall look back with undiluted pleasure', summarized the Queen.

Queen Elizabeth II. A radiant queen attends a royal performance at the Odeon, Leicester Square, in October 1955 of Hitchcock's film *To Catch a Thief*.

The Palace was uncertain how to respond to a prurient and raucous press. One reply was a documentary film, *Royal Family*, shown in 1969, and regarded at the time as a daring initiative. An exercise in studied informality, it was well received, but the new press was not long to be satisfied with the revelation that the duke of Edinburgh could fry sausages. The running was taken up by paparazzi, who pursued the royal family without mercy from behind hedges and hired rooms, aiming particularly at the younger royals, preferably female and preferably lightly clad. Prince Charles's response was a series of speeches on contemporary issues, especially environmental, but even these were not wholly successful. While they illuminated the issues and the prince's opinions were often popular, those criticized tended to answer back, and an increasingly sophisticated public wondered what qualifications the prince had for setting up as mentor to the nation.

A very different approach landed the royal family in the unmitigated disaster of *It's a Royal Knock-out!*, shown on television in 1987, and including princess Anne and the new duchess of York in prominent parts. It was intended to demonstrate that the royal family had the common touch and could be good sports, and was reported to have been put on despite the queen's misgivings. The catastrophe was compounded the following day when prince Edward, who had master-minded it, lost his temper at the press conference and stalked out. Even more extraordinary were the television interviews in which the prince and princess of Wales, their marriage in ruins, took the screen in a bizarre competition of candour about infidelity.

From these populist gestures, the queen held aloof and emerged unscathed. It is unlikely that her way of life will change much in the twenty-first century: the pattern of garden parties at Buckingham palace in the summer, autumn among the heather at Balmoral, and Christmas at Windsor or Sandringham has been established over the years. There are, from time to time, rumours that she may abdicate, but they are invariably followed by strong denials, and prince Charles seems likely to be one of the oldest monarchs to inherit the throne. Her reign has seen slow but substantial recovery from the Second World War, and her subjects are infinitely more prosperous than those she ruled over in 1952. The importance of the Commonwealth has receded, the issue of devolution has come to the surface, and Britain's attitude towards the European Community remains deeply divisive.

PIMLOTT, B., *The Queen* (1996).

Buckingham palace, London

The original Buckingham House was built on the site of the 1670s Arlington House by William Winde (1702–5) for John Sheffield, 1st duke of Buckingham. It was sold by his son to the Crown in 1762, for the young queen Charlotte's use, to bring up her increasing family in more privacy than at St James's palace, and it became known as the 'Queen's House'. George III commenced enlargements and modernization, but the main transformation was undertaken by Nash (1825–30) for George IV, incorporating the house into a new palace at considerable expense, and completed by Edward Blore who added the new east front (1847–50). Victoria was the first sovereign to live there.

Buckingham palace is more than the official residence of Elizabeth II and London home of the royal family, since it serves as the administrative centre of the monarchy, where foreign heads of state are received and entertained, and investitures held. The state rooms on the first floor were opened to the public in the summer of 1993 to help pay for the rebuilding of Windsor castle after the fire of the previous year. A fragment of the Royal Collection is displayed in the Picture Gallery, and the Royal Mews house the historic State coaches. The private gardens of nearly forty acres are essentially an English park, and now include a lake instead of a canal, sweeping lawns (used for garden parties), and a wide variety of plants and trees.

Philip, **duke of Edinburgh**, b. 10 June 1921, s. of prince Andrew of Greece and princess Alice of Battenberg; m. princess Elizabeth (later Elizabeth II), 20 Nov. 1947.

A great-great-grandson of queen Victoria, and grandson of prince Louis of Battenberg, who had a distinguished career in the British navy before 1914, Prince Philip went to Gordonstoun and entered the navy in 1938. He was mentioned in despatches at Cape Matapan in 1941 and through his cousin, Lord Louis Mountbatten, joined the royal circle. Before his marriage in 1947 he was created duke of Edinburgh. His role as consort is difficult, but his patronage of the duke of Edinburgh's award scheme for young people has given him an autonomous area of interest. His naval upbringing taught him to speak his mind, and his forthright comments have often been a joy to journalists.

Charles, prince of Wales, b. 14 Nov. 1948, s. of princess Elizabeth (later Elizabeth II), and Philip; m. Diana, da. of Edward, Earl Spencer, 29 July 1981; issue: William, Henry (Harry).

Prince Charles attended preparatory school at Cheam and then his father's old school at Gordonstoun in Morayshire. He spent a term at Geelong in Australia before going to Trinity College, Cambridge, where he read history, and to Aberystwyth, where he studied Welsh. He played the cello, acted, rode, shot, fished, and played polo. In 1969 he was invested prince of Wales at Caernarfon, having been created prince in 1958. Next, he entered the navy and gave a splendid performance as action man, flying jets, piloting helicopters, training in submarines, and commanding a mine-sweeper. Few heirs to the throne have demonstrated greater versatility. He was not greatly rewarded for his enterprise. The press chose increasingly to represent him as a harmless eccentric, with rather cranky views on the environment, architecture, and complementary medicine, and a propensity to talk to flowers. In 1981 his marriage to twenty-year-old Lady Diana Spencer seemed, as the newspapers put it, to be the stuff of fairy stories: the bride was beautiful, the ceremony magnificent, and two sons appeared obediently in 1982 and 1984.

It soon became apparent that there were marital difficulties. The couple separated in 1992 and were divorced in 1996. Sympathy for the princess brought the prince considerable unpopularity, and there were suggestions that he should step aside from the succession in favour of his son, William. Lady Diana's death in a car crash in 1997 raised speculation that the prince might remarry, and there are indications that he might.

Diana, princess of Wales, b. 1 July 1961, da. of Edward, Earl Spencer, and Frances, da. of Edward, Lord Fermoy; m. Charles, prince of Wales, 29 July 1981; divorced 15 July 1996; d. 31 Aug. 1997; bur. Althorp, Northamptonshire.

The most controversial member of the royal family in the twentieth century, Lady Diana Spencer was educated at Riddlesworth Hall, Norfolk, and then at West Heath school, near Sevenoaks in Kent. Despite the family's wealth and standing, her childhood was mixed; when she was eight, her parents had an acrimonious divorce, and relations with her stepmother were strained. After leaving school she shared a flat in London with other girls, and helped in a kindergarten. She married the prince of Wales when she was twenty, in a dazzling ceremony at St Paul's Cathedral watched on television by tens of millions.

The marriage was soon in trouble—according to the princess when she realized that her husband's friendship with Camilla Parker Bowles was far from over. She found the royal family aloof, and her unhappiness expressed itself first in bulimia, then in a number of affairs. An attractive and highly photogenic woman, she was pursued without mercy by paparazzi, who caused her great distress, though when she appealed to the press commission its chairman declared unsympathetically that she had 'invaded her own privacy'. In 1992 a biography, *Diana, Her True Story*, revealed the depth of her despair and, in a pirated tape, she called her marriage 'torture'. An unexpected development was the increasing interest she took in charities and good causes, where she revealed a remarkable, though well-publicized, capacity for comforting and cheering people in distress. In the last year of her life she was conducting an effective campaign against the indiscriminate use of land-mines, which had claimed many victims, particularly children. After an escalation of bitterness between the princess and her husband, queen Elizabeth suggested a speedy divorce. The negotiations were protracted and the settlement expensive. Diana then began a friendship with Dodi, son of Mohamed Al-Fayed, the owner of Harrods, which ended when both were killed in a brutal car-crash in the early hours in the centre of Paris. She was buried on an island in the lake at Althorp, her childhood home.

William, prince, b. 21 June 1982, s. of Charles, prince of Wales and Diana.

Second in succession to the throne, William was sent to Wetherby pre-preparatory school in Notting Hill in January 1987, and then to Ludgrove in Berkshire, an expensive boarding school with extensive grounds, where (in 1991) he suffered a fractured skull when accidently struck by a friend with a golf club. He transferred to Eton in 1995 and then attended the university of St Andrews. The very public split between his parents produced suggestions that his father should step aside and allow William to inherit the crown, but such an event is most unlikely.

Acknowledgement of Sources

Further Reading

Adamson, J., *The Princely Courts of Europe, 1500–1750* (1999).

Anderson, M. O., *Kings and Kingship in Early Scotland* (1973).

Asch, R. G. and Birke, A. M. (eds), *Princes, Patronage and the Nobility: The court at the beginning of the Modern Age, c. 1450–1650* (1991).

Bassett, S. (ed), *The Origins of Anglo-Saxon Kingdoms* (1989).

Beattie, J. M., *The English Court in the Reign of George I* (1967).

Bogdanor, V., *The Monarchy and the Constitution* (1995).

Brooke, C., *The Saxon and Norman Kings* (1967).

Byrne, F. J., *The Rise of the Uí Néill and the High Kingship of Ireland* (1969).

Cannon, J. A. (ed), *The Oxford Companion to British History* (1997).

—— and Griffiths, R., *The Oxford Illustrated History of the Monarchy* (2nd edn. 1992).

Clanchy, M. T., *England and its Rulers, 1066–1272* (2nd edn. 1998).

Davies, W., *Wales in the Early Middle Ages* (1982).

Dornier, A. (ed), *Mercian Studies* (1977).

Duncan, A. A. M., *Scotland: The Making of the Kingdom* (1975).

Fleming, R., *Kings and Lords in Conquest England* (1991).

Frere, S., *Britannia* (3rd edn. 1991).

Gillingham, J., *The Angevin Empire* (1984).

Higham, N. J., *An English Empire: Bede and the Early Anglo-Saxon Kings* (1995).

Hooke, D., *The Anglo-Saxon Landscape: The Kingdom of the Hwicce* (1985).

Loades, D., *The Tudor Court* (1986).

Morris, M., *The British Monarchy and the French Revolution* (1998).

Nicholson, R., *Scotland: The Later Middle Ages* (1974).

Prochaska, R. K., *Royal Bounty: The Rise of a Welfare Monarchy* (1995).

Purdue, A. W. and Golby, J., *The Monarchy and the British People: 1760 to the Present* (1988).

Rose, T., *The Coronation Ceremony and the Crown Jewels* (1992).

Sawyer, P. H., *Early Medieval Kingship* (1977).

Smyth, A. P., *Scandinavian Kings in the British Isles, 850–880* (1977).

—— *Scandinavian York and Dublin* (1979).

—— *Warlords and Holy Men: Scotland AD 80 to 1000* (1984).

Starkey, D., *The English Court from the Wars of the Roses to the Civil War* (1987).

Yorke, B., *Kings and Kingdoms in Early Anglo-Saxon England* (1990).

Glossary

atheling member of a noble family; prince, lord, baron

bretwalda Old English title given to some kings said to have held overlordship

burh fortified town; town with municipal organization

cantref Welsh term for a county division, equivalent to cantred or hundred

Danelaw area in which customary law was influenced by Danish practice.

ealdorman high-ranking noble (later, earl)

fyrd local militia in which all Anglo-Saxon freemen had to serve when called upon

high-king Irish title of a ruler claiming overlordship of other province kings

hundred division of an English county

jarl Scandinavian chief or noble, equivalent to earl

landgrave title of certain German princes

margrave German nobleman, equivalent to English marquess

merk the old Scots mark or 13s. 4d. Scots, reckoned as 13d. sterling

mise arbitration or adjudication

mormaer northern Celtic title for a high steward of a province

procurator manager of affairs, or authorized to act for another

reeve supervising official in shire, hundred, or manor

sceatt(as) small silver, occasionally gold, coin(s), of different value in different kingdoms

tailzie Scots form of tail or entail

thane Scottish baron or clan leader

thegn Anglo-Saxon landholder, obliged to serve the king in battle

tocher dowry

tuath Irish tribe or people

wergeld blood-price payable by a killer and his kin to his victim's kinsmen

Index